現代建築家による

GAIA
ガイア
〝地球〟建築

企画　マリアロザリア　タリアフェッリ
翻訳　乙須　敏紀

目次
CONTENTS

地球と建築、その根源的関係　4

第1部　建築　10

リヴォ・ハウス　12　ペソ・フォン・エルリッヒスハウゼン建築設計事務所
輪の家　18　武井　誠＆鍋島　千恵／TNA一級建築士事務所
ラスティック・キャニオンの住宅　26　グリフィン・エンライト建築設計事務所
ガンダリオの住宅　32　カルロス・クインタンス・エイラス
ラス・エンシーナスの住宅　38　ヴィセンス＋ラモス
タマリュの住宅　42　ジョルディ・ガルセス
ジェニングス邸　48　ワークルーム・デザイン
ブチュプレオの住宅　54　アルヴァロ・ラミレス＆クラリサ・エルトン
マターヤ邸　60　ベルツバーグ建築設計事務所
OSハウス　66　ノラスター
乱気流の家　72　スティーブン・ホール建築設計事務所
ブラウン・デュブイ邸　76　ヴェルナー・シュミット建築設計事務所
リギ・シャイデックの住宅　82　アンドレアス・フェーリマン―ガブリエル・ヘフラー
ラ・レセルバの住宅　86　セバスチャン・イラリャズバル
レンガウのロッジ　92　ジョン・ジェニングス／ドライ・デザイン
ストーン・ハウス　100　三分一　博志　建築設計事務所
ヒュッテの家　106　スタジオNL-D
トーレス邸　112　ルイス・デ・ガリード
カンタロプスの住宅　118　ニコラ・トレマコルディ／NM建築設計事務所
ハウス9×9　124　タイタス・ベルンハルト建築設計事務所
ピクセル・ハウス　128　スレード・アーキテクチュア＆マス・スタディーズ
リアス・アルタスの住宅　132　J・トーレス＆R・リャマサーレス／A-Cero
ワイルドキャット・リッジの住宅　136　ヴォーサンガー建築設計事務所
サルゾー近郊の住宅　140　エリック・グースナール
ミ・デリリオの住宅　144　ルイス・フローレス・アベジャン
フリンダース・ビーチの住宅　148　サイモン・スワニー建築設計事務所
葡萄畑の住宅　152　ジョン・ウォードル建築設計事務所
ポルケラ・デ・ロス・インファンテスのロフト　156　ヘス・カスティージョ・オリ

第2部　インテリア　164

ポルタス・ノヴァスの住宅　166　ヴィクトール・カニャス
サバデルの改築住居　168　M2建築設計事務所
ブッチェルダの住宅　172　カルレス・ジェルピ・アロヨ
サン・ヴィチェンテの住宅　174　マルセール・デル・トルト
アストリッドの別荘　176　ウィンガーズ・アーキテクトコントロール
アル・マーレ　178　マーティン・ゴメス建築設計事務所
ベリマ通りの住宅　180　ウォーハ・デザイン
アベル邸　182　1100アーキテクト
ブエノスアイレスの住宅　184　パブロ・サンチェス・エリア建築設計事務所
オストゥーニの住宅　186　スタジオ・トランジット

ヴィラドマの住宅	188	ベナサール・ノゲラ／アルバート・アウバッハ
クーヴィオ・ヴァレーゼのロフト	192	シモーネ・ミケーリ建築設計事務所
カルデテスの住宅	196	ジョルジュ・スビータ
ミナス通りのロフト	198	ウンルガール
アイオルフィ邸	200	パガーニ・ディ・マウロ建築設計事務所
ムジェーヴの住宅	202	カルロ・ランパッツィ
Pペントハウス	204	クラウディオ・シルヴェストリン建築設計事務所
ポダール邸	208	所有者
ポジターノの別荘	210	ラッツァリーニ・ピカリング建築設計事務所
ビアジョッティ邸	212	所有者
フロリダの住宅	214	プレストン・T・フィリップス建築設計事務所
カンビの集合住宅	216	パガーニ・ディ・マウロ建築設計事務所
アルゼンチンの海浜住宅	218	マネイロ・ヴァスケス建築設計事務所
ラック邸ロフト	220	ラック・ビンスト／クレパン・ビンスト建築設計事務所
イズリントンの住宅	222	クラウディオ・シルヴェストリン建築設計事務所
ラ・アデュアナの住宅	224	マーティン・ゴメス建築設計事務所
マドリードからの天然スレート	226	ペドロ・ボニーラ
カルデス・デ・モンブイの住宅	230	アントニー・グラウ・ギルバー／エウセビ・グティエレス
ソレダード邸	232	パブロ・サンチェス・エリア建築設計事務所
プロジェクト・ヨー	234	フィリップ・スタルク／ヨー
サン・ジュセッペの住宅	236	グイド・アントネッロ／クリスティアナ・ヴァンニーニ
ヴェミグナーノの別荘	238	グイド・アントネッロ／クリスティアナ・ヴァンニーニ
モンテ・タウロの住宅	240	レゴレッタ＋レゴレッタ
パルマの集合住宅	244	パガーニ・ディ・マウロ建築設計事務所
迷宮の家	246	オスカー・トゥスケッツ・ブランカ
ロンドンの住宅	248	ウェルドン・ウォルシュ
ゴルドの別荘	250	リラ・コンラッド／LKDコンセプト
ラス・エンシーナスの住宅	252	A-Cero
ソーラー・ボックス	254	ドリエンドル建築設計事務所
アンドリュー・テート邸	256	テート＆ヒンドル建築設計事務所
デュ・プレシ邸	258	マルシオ・コーガン建築設計事務所
ブライトン・ガーデン	262	アン・ファーズ
コルドヴァのパティオ祭り	264	所有者
砂漠の庭	266	テイラー・カリティ・レスリーン
龍門庭	268	枡野　俊明
ポルトラ・ヴァレーの住宅	272	ピーターソン建築設計事務所
エリー・サーブ邸	276	ウラジミール・シュロヴィッチ・ランドスケープ・アーキテクチュア
サンタクルーズのプール	278	ファン・ロカ・パジェホ
サン・ベルナールの住宅	280	ビオタイッヒ／J.Nジャルダン・ナチュレルス
ゴリオンのプール	282	ビオタイッヒ／J.Nジャルダン・ナチュレルス

作品・建築家一覧　284

「…自然の風景と対立するのではなく、それと一体になって建てたいという願望、そしてそれとともに働く必要」
オービー・G・ボウマン

"… a desire to build and a need to work with rather than against the natural landscape"
(Obie G. Bowman)

地球と建築、その根源的関係

われわれ人類が生存している地球という惑星、そしてその惑星が提供してくれるさまざまな素材、それらと建築との根源的関係を真正面に見据えた作品群が本書の内容である。そのすべてが自然の持つ簡潔さを尊敬し、そこから発想を生み出している。

地球が与えてくれる素材を最大限に活用したいという復活した欲求、そしてそれらの素材に囲まれて生活しているあらゆる生命体の生息環境と一体化しなければならないという強い意識、建築家とインテリアデザイナーは、一見背反するかに見える両者を建築の中に見事に統一している。あるものは方法論的に、あるものは技巧的に。そうして生まれた住居は、周囲の環境と可能な限り一体化しようとし、この地球という惑星の根源からその設計思想を汲み出したかのようである。これらの住居は地球に融け込み、環境に対する負荷を最小限にとどめながら、地理的条件、気候、エネルギー、土着の文化との関係などから派生するさまざまな問題を解決している。

考え抜かれ、決然と提起された計画に建築が応えていくその方法──それは「持続可能な建築」という概念と似ていなくもない──は、すべてを自然素材から構成しているという揺るぎない確信と、感性に訴える比類なき優雅さを示すことによって、建築家たちの起源に対する瞑想的かつ論理的な熟考を具現化している。これらの住居は地球と同じ香りを放ち、地球と同じ荒々しさを感じさせながら、移ろい行く時の

The relation between the earth – as a natural element and the planet on which we live – and architecture is illustrated in this volume where the respect for nature's simplicity inspired each of the cases here presented.
With a renewed desire to make use of the materials the earth can offer and a strong sense of identification with the habitat that surrounds them, these architects and interior designers offer solutions – some more technical, others artisanal – that ensure that their projects are as well-integrated into their surroundings as possible, with designs that seem to retro-nourish themselves from the planet: they adapt to it and resolve, with as little environmental impact as possible, the challenges in topography, climate, energy and culture planted before them.
This way, architecture is responding with efficient and conclusive proposals that, similar to the concepts of sustainable architecture, symbolize a meditative and logical contemplation of origins by displaying more confidence in materials that are 100% earthen and of great sensorial elegance: they can be smelled, are rugged to the touch and adapt different physiognomies and colors with the passage of time.
In this fashion, the *Architecture* section displays a set of planned and executed instances which have maintained maximum respect for nature, sometimes

中でさまざまな地相、色相と呼応している。

　第1部建築では、建築家がいかに発想し、具体化していったかを、素描からディテールまでさまざまな段階で紹介する。建築家は自然に対する最大限の尊敬を失わず、時にその住居は完全なまでに自然と融合し、建築という行為それ自体がその痕跡を消滅させている。またある時は、外的自然要素——草原、樹木、峡谷の眺望など——が住居の不可欠な構成要素となり、自然の本源的な営みが、住む人の情感を豊かに呼び覚ましている。

　本書では、これまで以上に室内に目を向けた。ある住居では、岩盤は母なる石となり、文字通り家庭を支える礎石となって室内に現出し、プロジェクトの必要性と地形の決定的要因との間の絶妙な均衡が図られている。また古い建物を改築した住居は、地球環境を守るという観点から、その破壊は改築よりももっと費用がかさむということを証明している。

　一方もう1つの関心事である持続可能な建築という視点からは、プールに溜めた水の熱伝達力の利用、壁構造における熱絶縁空間の使用、あるいは独特の空調システム、さらには夏季の冷房負荷削減のための礫石のスロープによる通風効果など、建築家たちが住居のエネルギー効率を上げるために考え抜いたさまざまな方策を見ることができる。

　地形と同様に気候も、乾燥、あるいは強風といった困難は、逆にその解決策を見出すなかで、建築家に大いなる閃きを与える要因となる。

achieving that their labors disappear into the neighboring landscape completely. On occasion, this implicates external natural elements – a meadow, a tree, a valley view – into becoming a part of the home's interior, so that nature lives *in situ* in an extraordinarily emotional way.

This section concentrates on interiors where mother stone has literally become a part of the home, fruit of an excellent balance between the necessities of the project and the determining factors of the terrain. In addition, the renovation of ancient buildings demonstrates that, from the environmental point of view, demolition is always costlier than recycling. Sustainable construction, another point of interest, is measured in conjunction with a home's energy efficiency, such as the convective power of the water found in a pool, the use of thermal isolation chambers in wall paneling, the air-conditioning system used or the creation of slopes of pulverized rock to facilitate cross ventilation in the summer.

Much like terrain, the climate also presents itself as a factor of inspiration in those cases where arid or windy conditions become a challenge for the architect come time for planning the best construction solution.

Much like the amalgam of materials presented here – natural stone, limestone, siltstone, slate, marble, terracotta, adobe, *rammed earth*, straw or untreated brick – a

建築家たちはまた、自然石、石灰岩、シルト岩、粘板岩、大理石、テラコッタ、日干し煉瓦、版築(土を叩き締めて造る建築材料)、藁、無焼成煉瓦など多様な素材を自在に組み合わせ、さまざまな種類の羽目板、耐力壁、擁壁、あるいはインテリアではタイル張り壁、バスルーム、天板などを実験、適用することによって、建築の可能性を広げている。

第2部インテリアでは特に、さまざまな石またはその派生品が、独創的な形で、構造材として、あるいは不可欠な構成要素として用いられている建築群を探索する。ミニマリズムからネオ・バロックまで、洗練されたものから質朴なものまで、現在のさまざまな建築様式が持つ可能性が、石の持つ根源的な特性——強さ、記憶を呼び覚ます触感、装飾性——を顕示しながら、多彩な住宅のなかに示されている。建築家とインテリアデザイナーは、この自然の宝物である石を自由な発想で巧妙に住居のなかに取り込んでいる。

本書「現代建築家による〝地球〟建築」は、地球という惑星の根源から霊感を受け、その本質を知悉し、それと一体化することを目標として建築された住居を巡る、手で触れるといっても良いほどの臨場感溢れる写真でつづる旅である。創造的で、美しく、根源的でありながら最も現代的なさまざまな素材、そして地球と人類の関係を内省させるさまざまな建築的適用、それらはすべて1篇の詩となり、本書を手にするすべての人に、大いなる霊感を与えるであろう。

variety of possibilities are demonstrated through the exploration and application of different types of paneling, load bearing walls, retaining walls, or when it comes to interiors, tile covered walls, bathrooms and counter-tops.

The *Interiors* section is laid out as a trip through the varied creative uses of stone and its mineral derivatives for different applications and supports. The availability of a variety of relevant styles – from minimalism to the neo-baroque, the industrial to the rustic – applied to different types of homes, serves to highlight the intrinsic properties of the materials themselves: strength, refreshing to the touch and esthetically decorative. Making this a natural treasure at the disposal of architects and interior designers, suggesting technical solutions all throughout this publication.

By definition, *Earth* is conceived as a visual and almost textural journey which aims to bring us closer to the type of architecture where planner and designer alike understand nature as a source of inspiration and an end unto itself, thus framing the final construction. This is an aspiration not lacking in poetry at the planning stage, alluding in equal parts to creative, artisanal and earthen elements, and which seeks out its own place in the modern realm.

第1部 建築

自然環境を自分自身の一部として観想すること。これから紹介するプロジェクトは、住居を完璧に周囲の景観と統合することを建築の使命と考える建築家たちの作品である。住居は気候や地形に逆らわず、それに巧妙に適応している。建築家たちは、住居の内外を問わず、鉱物資源の新たな適用を提起している。これらの住居は、これまでは住居を取り巻く景観と考えられてきた場所に入りこみ、生活空間でありながら、それ自体が景観となっている。人は自然環境から切り離された家に住むのではなく、家に住むことによって自然の真っ只中に棲む。そのことによって、自然を全身で感じ、生命の源泉を汲み、本当の美しさに気づく。

To view the natural environment as part of one's self. The projects shown here give praise to the architectural task of fully integrating the home with its surroundings, illustrating ingenious responses to the demands of climate and terrain.
They propose alternative uses of mineral materials in exteriors and other rooms. These are living spaces which have been intrinsically conceived for the landscape which surrounds them, made to be lived in as much as they were made to be lived outside of; contributing life, an esthetic sense and a textured environment to their owners.

リヴォ・ハウス
森に潜む

ペソ・フォン・エルリッヒスハウゼン建築設計事務所
撮影：クリストバル・パルマ

PEZO VON ELLRICHSHAUSEN ARCHITECTS
PHOTO: © Cristobal Palma

RIVO HOUSE
Intangible among trees

クティペイ、バルビディア ― チリ ― 2003

世界中を覆っている喧騒から逃れたいと、所有者である新婚の夫婦は、サンティアゴから1000km離れた深い原生林の中に彼らの避難所を建てることを決意した。しかし当初の空想的な衝動が具体化するにつれ、孤独感に襲われるのではないかと2人は心配し始めた。2人の気持ちを理解した建築家が提案したプランは、住居はかなり高さのある簡潔なモノリスとし、広い開口部をできるだけ多く取るというものであった。四方に開かれた窓からは、それぞれに異なった雄大な景色が眺望でき、昼間は、ほとんどどこからか日光が家の中に射し込む。

The desire to get away from worldly noise drove this married couple to create their own refuge among a dense mass of autochthonous trees 620 miles from Santiago. Once their initial romantic urge was complete, the owners wound up feeing afraid of being lonely. The architect understood how they felt and suggested a plan that consisted of a compact, monolithic volume of considerable height, and with wide openings that offers spectacular views with sunlight almost the whole day through.

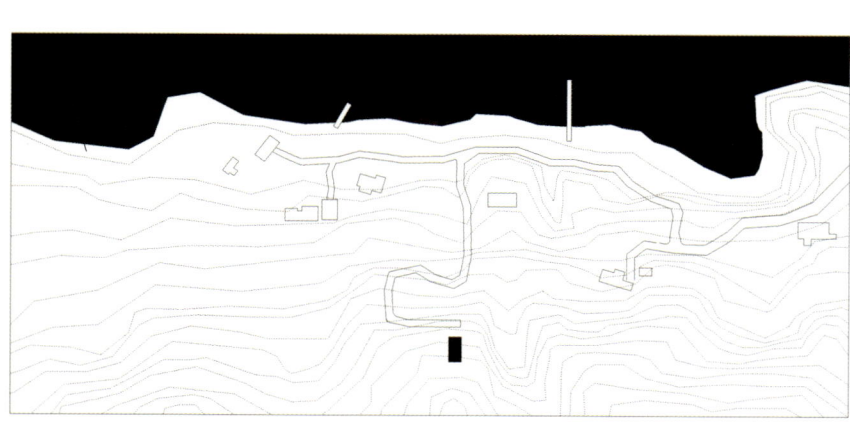
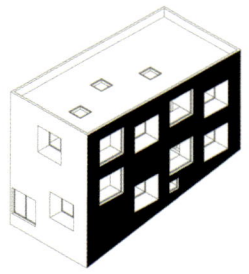
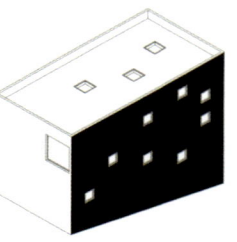

中央開放空間が住居の中心部を貫くことによって、自然エネルギーが積極的に導入されている。1階では北向きに開かれたバルコニーが、自然を住居内部に招き入れている。それは周囲の地形に対して、いつでも侵入しておいでと言っているようだ。

The southern facade represents the conceptual opposite of the northern facade: an invitation to light and transparency; difinitively isolating the plot of land from the trees along the path and inviting one to look towards Gandario Beach.

輪の家
透明感

武井 誠 & 鍋島 千恵／TNA一級建築士事務所
撮影：阿野 太一

RING HOUSE
Transparency

MAKOTO TAKEI & CHIE NABESHIMA /TNA
PHOTO: © Daici Ano

軽井沢、長野県 ― 日本 ― 2006

　東京から1時間で来ることができ、道路からほんの2、3mしか離れてない林間の平地に、この透明な事務所兼住宅は立っている。立地はオーナーであるアーティストの希望にぴったりの場所であった。オーナーの意向は、道路の脇に幻想的に浮かび上がるような建物というものであった。3層構造で、半分土に埋もれている格好になっている1階部分は応接間、約4m上の2階部分はリビングルーム、そして3階は寝室とバスルームになっている。周りを囲む樹々と建物との間の完璧な交感、見落とされがちであるが、それこそがまさにこの建築の持つ本質である。

An hour from Tokyo, this modern and translucent-looking office/home rises from a flat plot of land only a scant few meters from the road. This situation was befitting for the artist's intentions, who wanted the home to literally emerge from the side of the road. The space is divided into three floors; a half-buried lower floor for guests, a 13 foot tall first floor where the living room is, and a top floor with bedrooms and bathrooms. A perfect communion between the wooded surroundings and the constructed edifice is a gift to behold that one can almost pass a hand through.

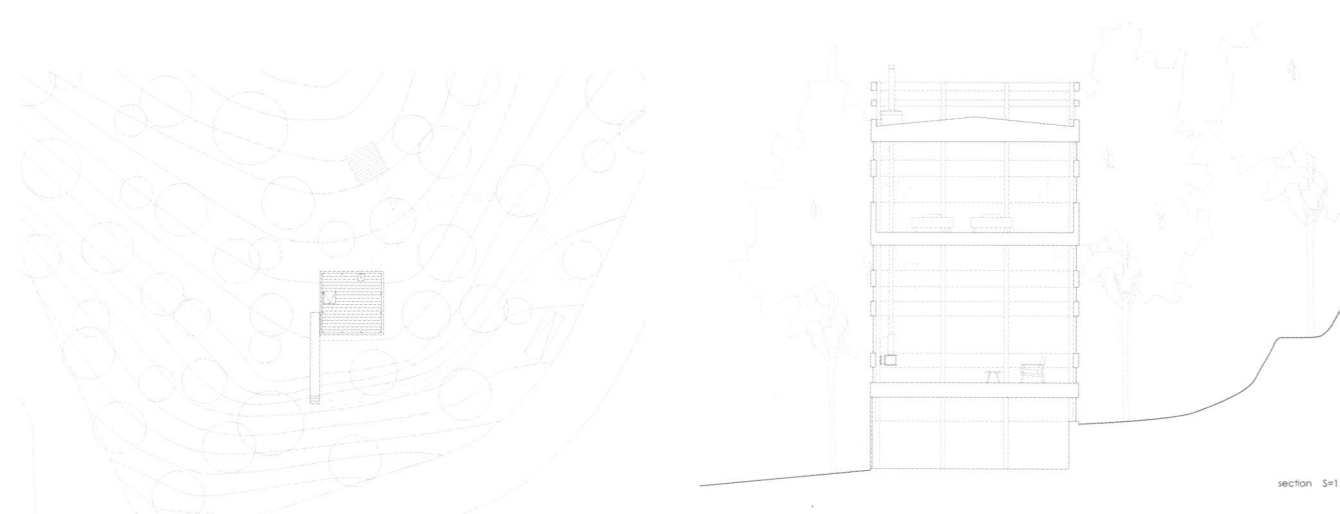

section S=1

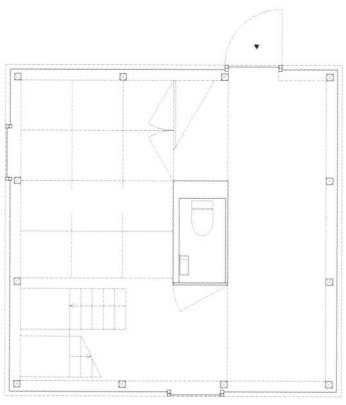
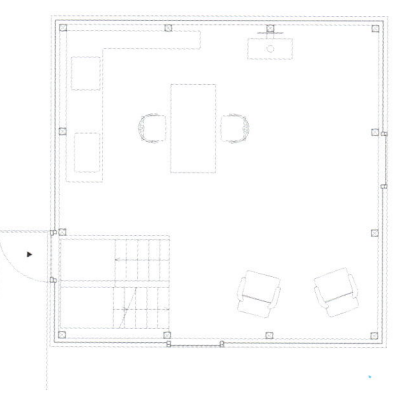
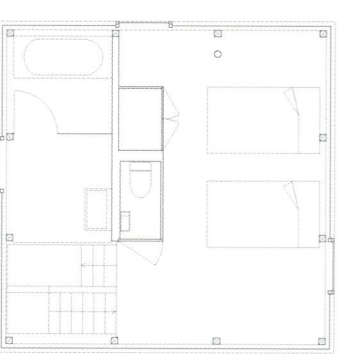

22 建 築
Architecture

透明構造のため、幾重にも家を囲む樹々の連なりを360度楽しむことができる。すぐ近くに山小屋風の別荘があり、豊かな自然林のなかに佇んでいるにもかかわらず、建物の線が喚起する感覚は非常に優美で、現代的である。

The structure's transparency allows for a 360-degree appreciation of the splendorous mass of trees outside. Despite the proximity of a neighboring cabaña and the eminently natural surroundings, the modern lines transmit an exceptional sensibility.

早朝、まだ明けそめたばかりで霧が谷を這う頃に、かつてル・コルビュジエが言った「風景を切り取る」という建築的主張が一番よく感じられるだろう。現代的美意識を放棄せずに、いかに自然を享受するかという問いに対する明確な答えがここにある。

The architectural insistence on framing the landscape – as Le Corbusier once said – may be seen when the light is faint and a mist invades the valley. A clear example of how to enjoy nature without renouncing modern esthetics.

ラスティック・キャニオンの住宅
取り込まれた景観

グリフィン・エンライト建築設計事務所
撮影：アート・グレイ

GRIFFIN ENRIGHT ARCHITECTS
PHOTO: © Art Gray

RUSTIC CANYON RESIDENCE
Nature inside

パシフィック・パリセーズ ― アメリカ ― 2001

周囲を取り巻く自然に融け込むような、あるいは自然の浸透を許すかのような建物は、かつての大牧場の家屋を改築したもの。広いリビングルームの剥き出しの軸組構造と、折板型の屋根は、住宅の背後に位置する丘陵との連続性を意図したものである。書斎の前で威容を誇る樹齢300年のシカモアは、新しくなったこの住宅の中枢神経となり、書斎に、キッチンに、リビングルームに、そして寝室に、大地の息吹を注ぎ込んでいる。

This edifice, permeable to the nature surrounding it, is the fruit of a ranch-home remodeling. The new structural skeleton frames a grand living room under a wavy roof, evoking the adjacent hill sitting behind the house. In front of the library, a 300 year old Sycamore becomes the nerve center in this new arrangement; its majestic appearance – seen from the library, the kitchen, the living room and the bedroom – converts the landscape into an interior element of the home.

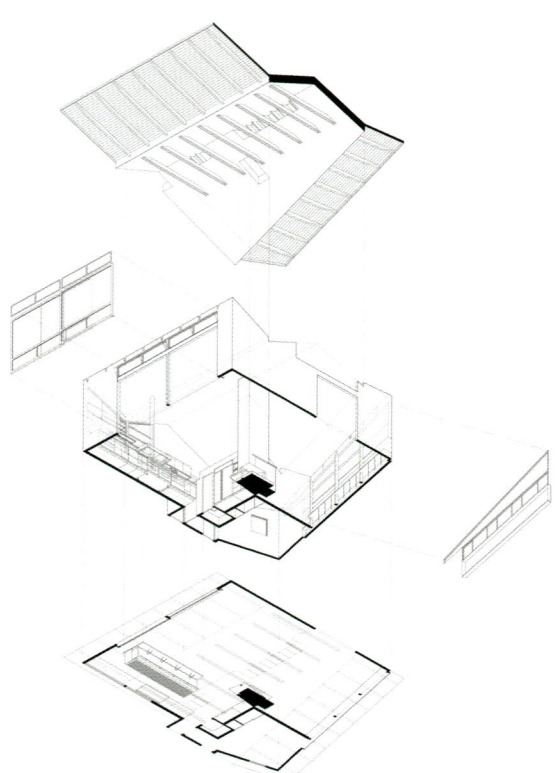

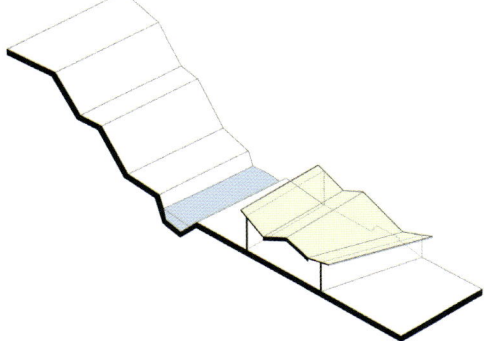

住居のもう1つの特徴は採光である。リビングルームの天井には縦方向に天窓が開けられ、広い部屋に十分な自然光を注いでいる。自然の持つ深い質感は、ファサード一面に広がるガラス窓を通して体感へと変わる。

Illumination is one of the more relevant aspects of this house. In the living room, the ceiling opens lengthwise in search of natural light. The deeply textured exterior landscape factors into the experience by way of the crystallized facade.

ガンダリオの住宅
開かれていて、閉じられている

カルロス・クインタンス・エイラス
撮影：アンジェル・バルタナス

CARLOS QUINTÁNS EIRAS
PHOTO: © Ángel Baltanás

HOUSE IN GANDARiO
Opened and closed

ベルゴンドースペイン ― 2005

　ガリシア文化の伝統的景観を継承しながら、北側ファサードの構造的基礎としての役割を果たしている石の壁が、この住宅の主人公である。栗の樹の小さな群生の傍に屹立した石壁の閉鎖性が、南に向って大きく開放された全面ガラス張りのファサードや構造の不浸透性、海の感動的眺望と絶妙の対照を創りだしている。閉ざされた3立面は外皮である天然スレートで覆われていて、その淡色の中性的色合いは、下部の組石のヴォリュームと質感を視覚的に強調している。しかし雨が降ると一転して、艶やかに濡れたその緑色と灰色が光彩を放つ。

The stone wall, descendant of the cultural Galician landscape and acting here as the structural base of the northern façade, is the protagonist of this home.
The enclosure effected by the rear façade, which is next to a small forest of chestnut trees, contrasts with the generous glass façade that faces south and with the impermeability of the structure and its impressive views of the water. The three enclosed sides of this edifice make use of slate on their exterior walls. In doing so, they've sought out a neutral esthetic that strengthens the stone visually, so that when it rains, its greens and grays may be highlighted.

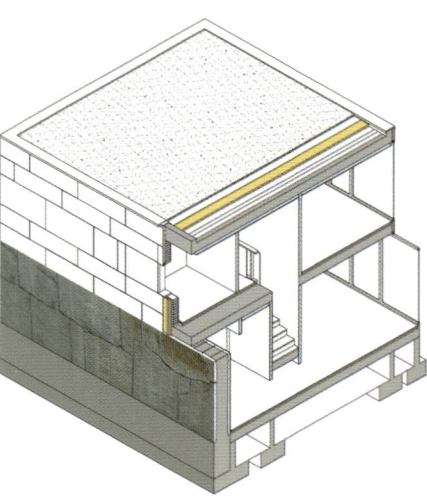

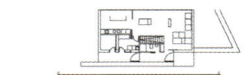

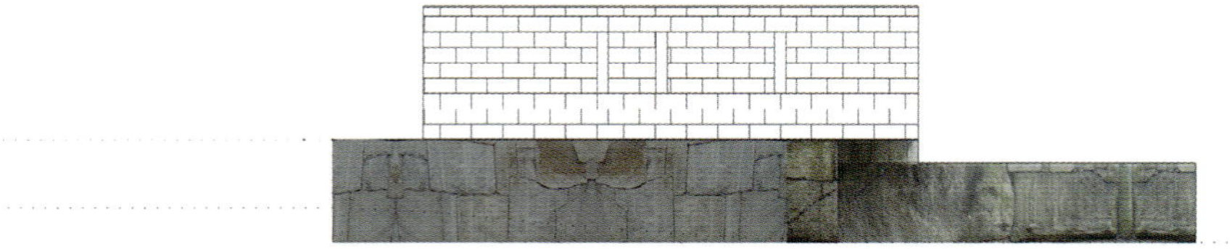

ALZADO PRINCIPAL CC

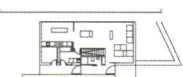

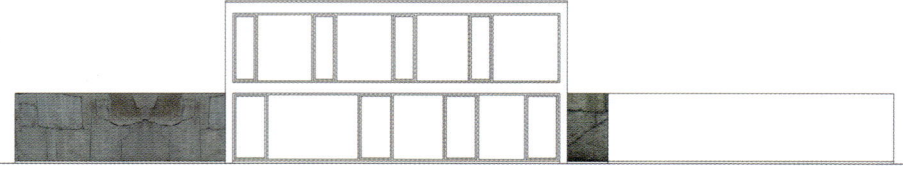

ALZADO PRINCIPAL DD

南面ファサードの概念は、北面ファサードの概念と正反対である。それは一言でいうならば、光と透明感への誘い。住宅の内部空間は、小道に沿って続く栗の群生から決然と切り離され、訪れる人をガンダリオ・ビーチの眺望へと誘う。

The southern facade represents the conceptual opposite of the northern facade: an invitation to light and transparency; definitively isolating the plot of land from the trees along the path and inviting one to look towards Gandario Beach.

ラス・エンシーナスの住宅

晶洞

ヴィセンス＋ラモス
撮影：エウゲニ・ポンス

VICENS + RAMOS
PHOTO: © Eugeni Pons

LAS ENCINAS RESIDENCE
The artificial geode

マドリード ― スペイン ― 2003

　スペインの首都マドリードの郊外に忽然と姿を見せるこの巨大な石の塊は、「晶洞」と呼ばれている。晶洞とは岩石中にできた空洞で、地下水に融解した鉱物が結晶となって発見される場所。結晶の入っている地層を想起させるため、壁面を花崗岩の石板で被った。その堅固で荒々しいヴォリュームの下1階部分には、それと対照的な大きなガラス張りの開口部が開かれている。それは自然の晶洞のなかで秘かにきらめく水晶のように美しい。

Located in a residential neighborhood of Spain's capital city, the edifice was generally conceived as a geode, a rocky cavity in which minerals are crystallized through dissolution by subterranean waters. The desire to evoke mineral strata forced the architects to opt for an exemplary wall paneling of granite base. The solid and robust character these display contrasts well with the large glass openings on the first floor, an analogy for the crystalline pieces layered throughout the natural geodes.

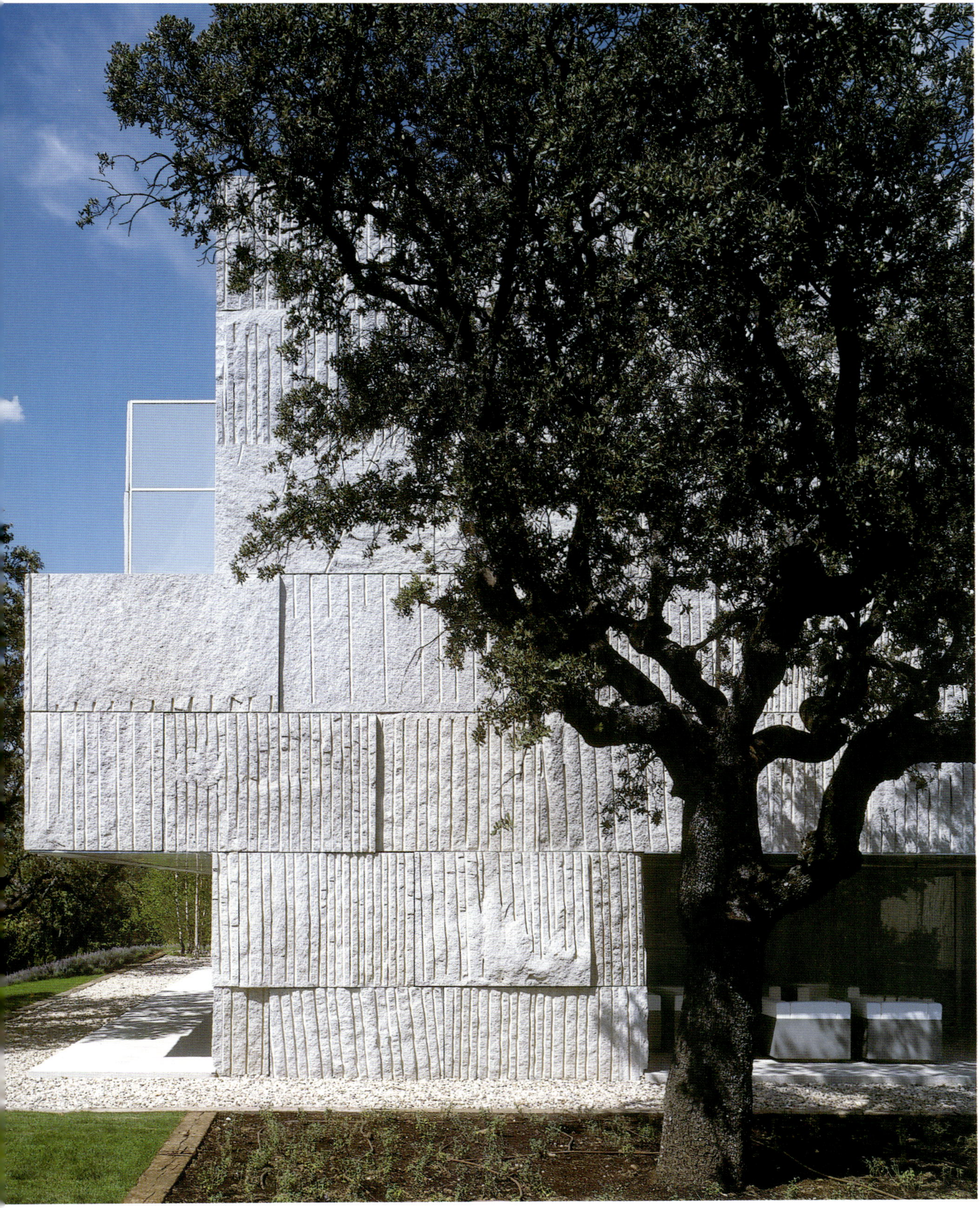

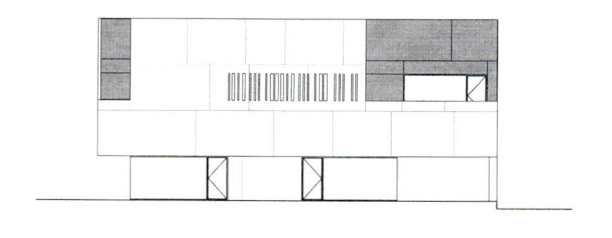

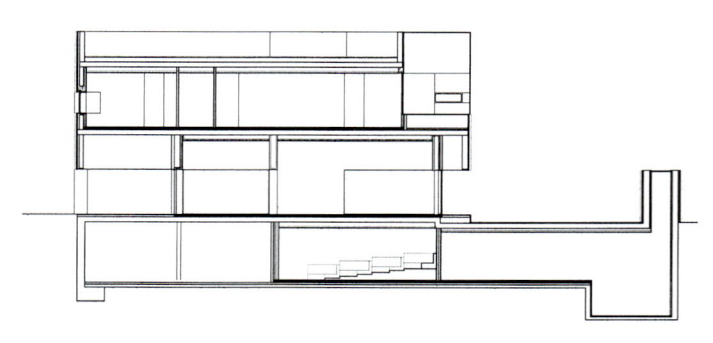

40 建 築
Architecture

中央ユニットが圧倒的な量塊感を誇示しているため、建物は地階部分の隠れたガラス開口部と、2階の花崗岩の板石と交互に現れる広い窓を通して、静かに呼吸しているように見える。

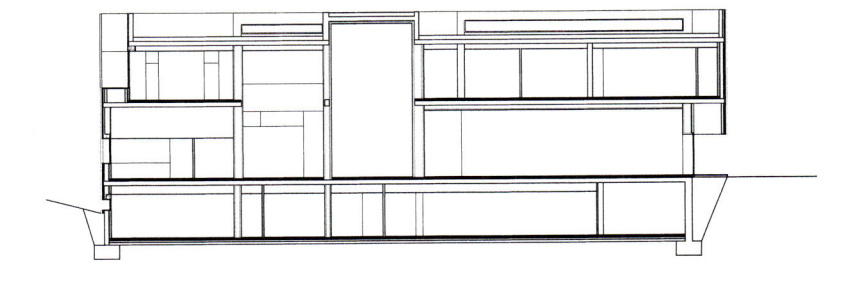

Thanks to the monumental expressionism of the central unit, this edifice seems to breathe through its glass enshrouded lower floor and the ample windows that alternate with blocks of granite on the first floor.

タマリュの住宅
断崖と一体化して

ジョルディ・ガルセス
撮影：ジョルディ・ミラレス

JORDI GARCÉS
PHOTO: © Jordi Miralles

HOUSE IN TAMARIU
On the cliff

タマリュースペイン ― 2006

　斬新でありながら、断崖の絶景を壊さない、そのような住宅を考究した建築家が出した結論は、断崖に住宅を建てることそれ自体の利点を最大限に生かすということであった。コスタ・ブラバの海岸線のなかでも聳え立つ岩壁がひときわ目立つ特権的場所に位置しているため、岩の開削は最小限にとどめられた。構造は2本の角柱を一部重ね合わせて横に寝かせ、パティオのテラスが海に面している構造とした。テラスフロアには、滑落防止のため石目に逆らってカットしたトラヴァーチン大理石を敷き詰め、あえて手すりは設けていない。そのためパティオに立つ訪問者は、地中海の雄大さをダイレクトに体感することができる。

With a mind to innovate, but without breaking up the impressive coastal landscape, the architect sought to fully exploit the virtues of building on the cliff itself. It was proposed that very little rock would actually be cut on this privileged little corner of the Costa Brava, so the edifice was structured in two over-lapping prisms with a patio-terrace facing the sea. The patio, dressed with a Travertine marble-tiled floor cut against the grain, is free-standing, like a special guest standing before the immensity of the Mediterranean.

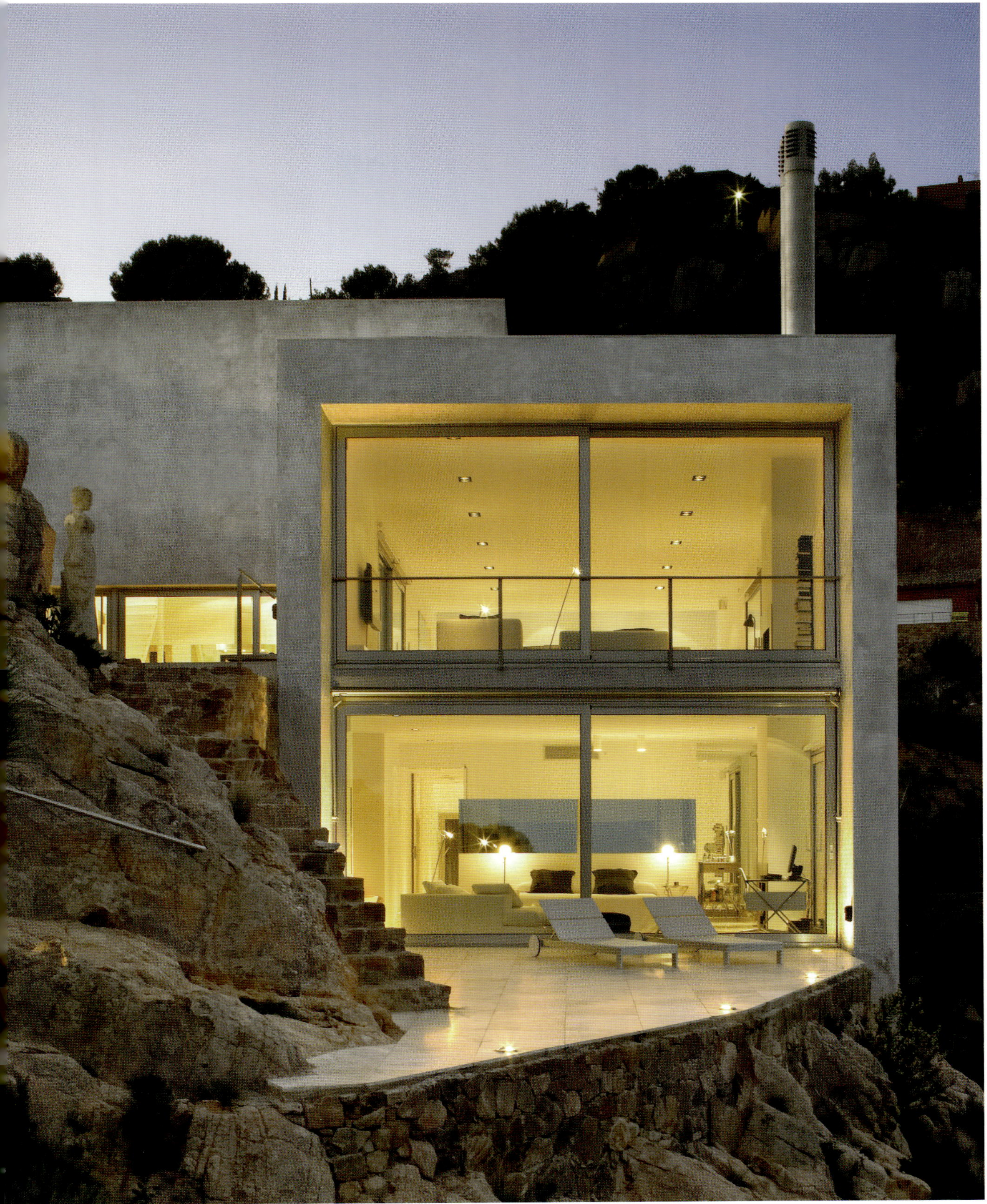

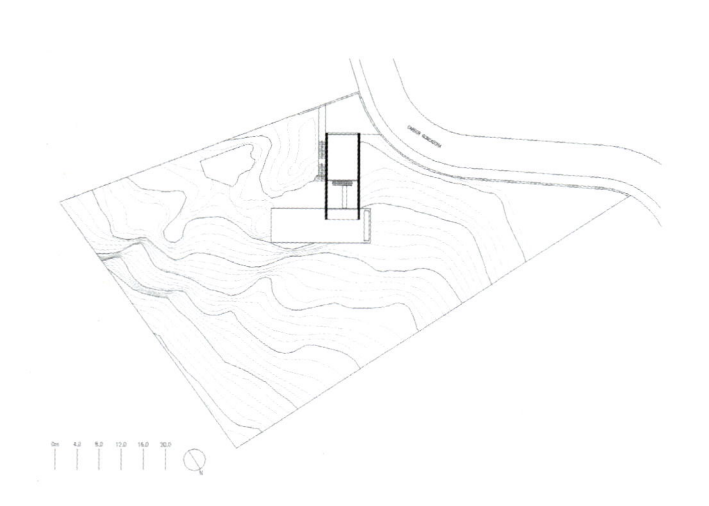

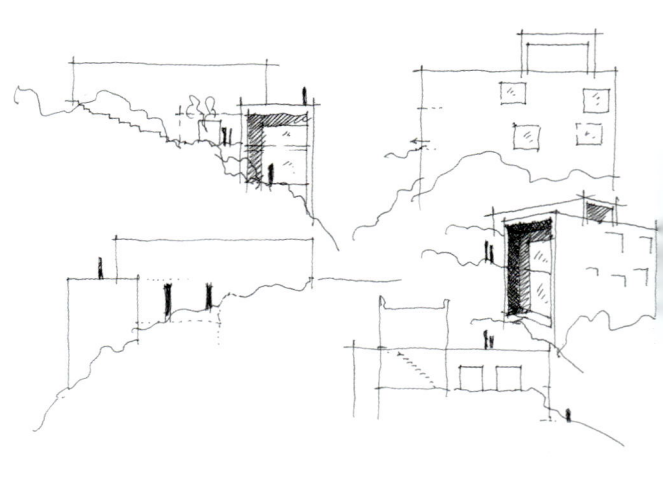

44 建 築
Architecture

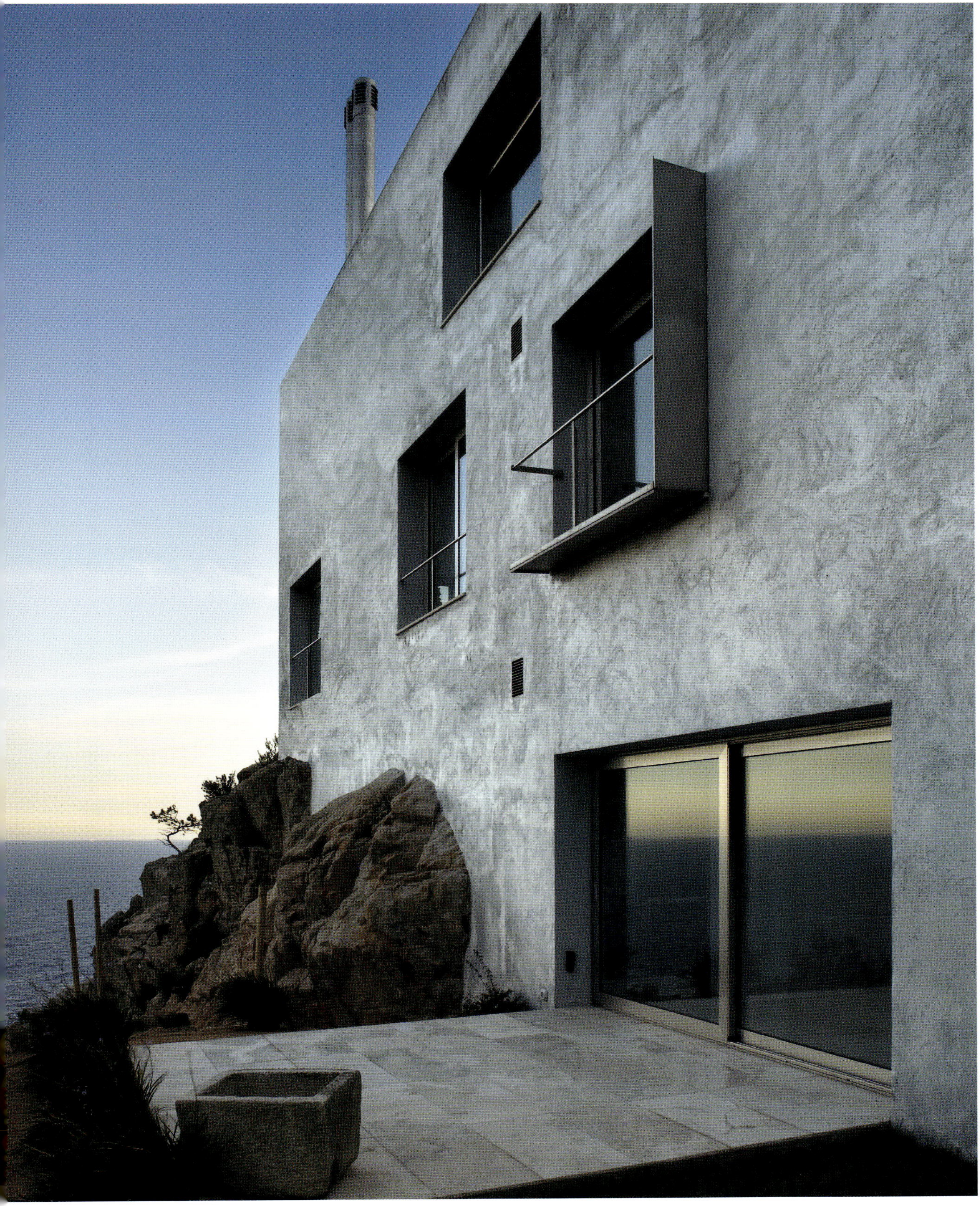

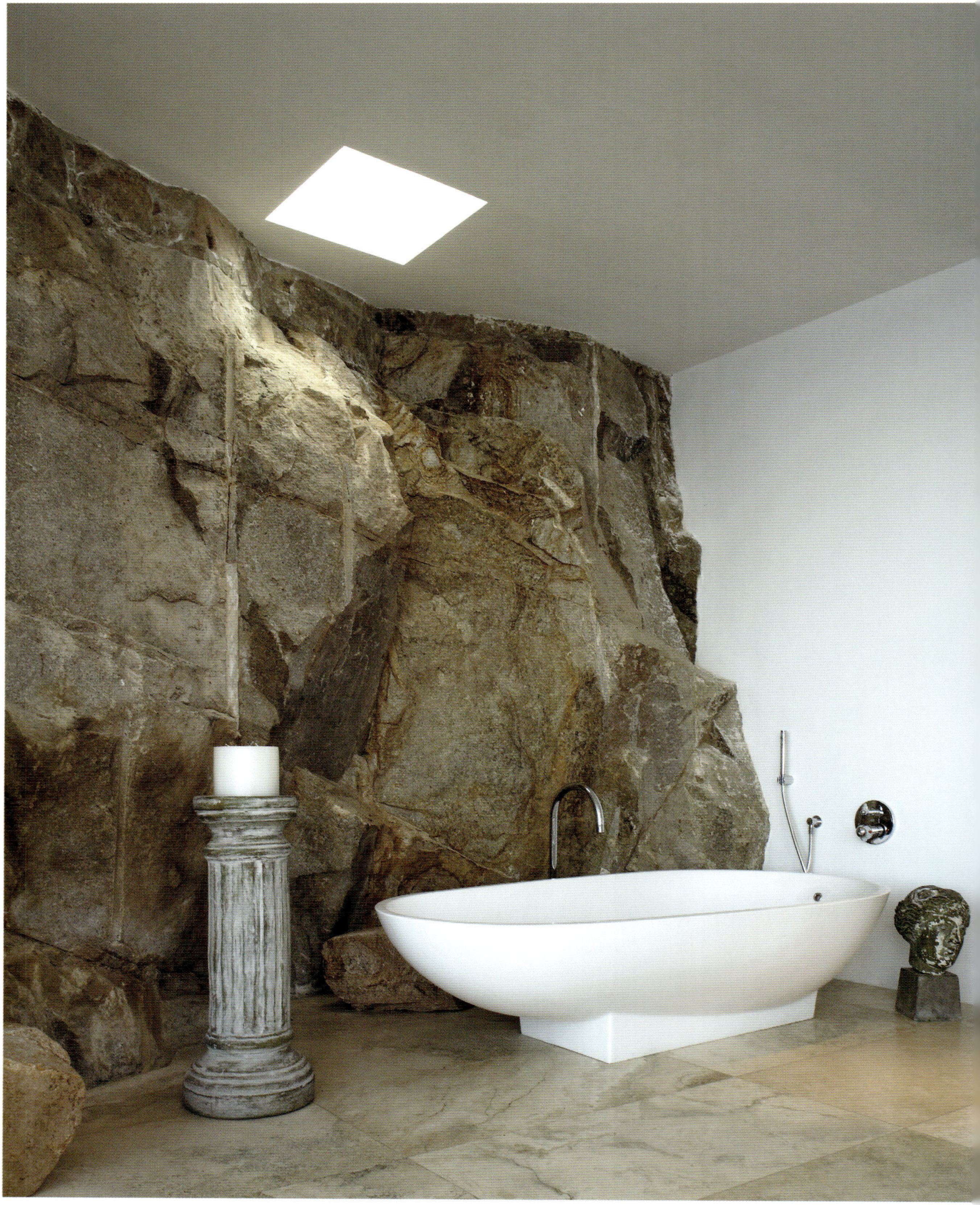

いくつかの部屋では、自然の岩がそのまま内壁になり、外部から見た景観が部屋の内部に取り込まれている。バスルームと寝室では、岩の精髄に手で触れ、体を寄せることもできる。

The use of natural rock as a wall can create a spectacular image in some rooms. From the bathroom and bedroom these mineral essences can be richly experienced.

ジェニングス邸
風を回避する

ワークルーム・デザイン
撮影：トレバー・マイン／マイン・フォト

WORKROOM DESIGN
PHOTO: © Trevor Mein / Mein Photo

JENNINGS RESIDENCE
Rebuffing the wind

ホプキンス岬、ワーナンブール ― オーストラリア ― 2002

　インド洋の波打ち際からわずかに50mほどしか離れていない、常に強風にさいなまれる場所にこの住居は建っている。雄大な景観を我が物としながら風の虐待を避けるという難題に対して出された結論は、海に突き出した岩盤そのものを基礎として、円弧状の平たい建物をそれに定着させるというものであった。住居は適度な高さまで岩盤のなかに埋められた。海に面した主要立面の全面ガラス張りのファサードは、海の眺望を満喫させるだけでなく、自然を尊敬しながら生活することの大切さを日々強く自覚させる。

This residence is located 160 feet away from the Indian Ocean in an area traditionally punished by strong winds. With the idea of avoiding its abuse, it was gambled that the edifice be anchored, in a curved and flattened fashion, into the jutting rock itself. A good portion of its interiors are partially buried beneath the rock. The completely glass covered façade on the main elevation enhances the view of the sea and the spirit of living with a respect for nature.

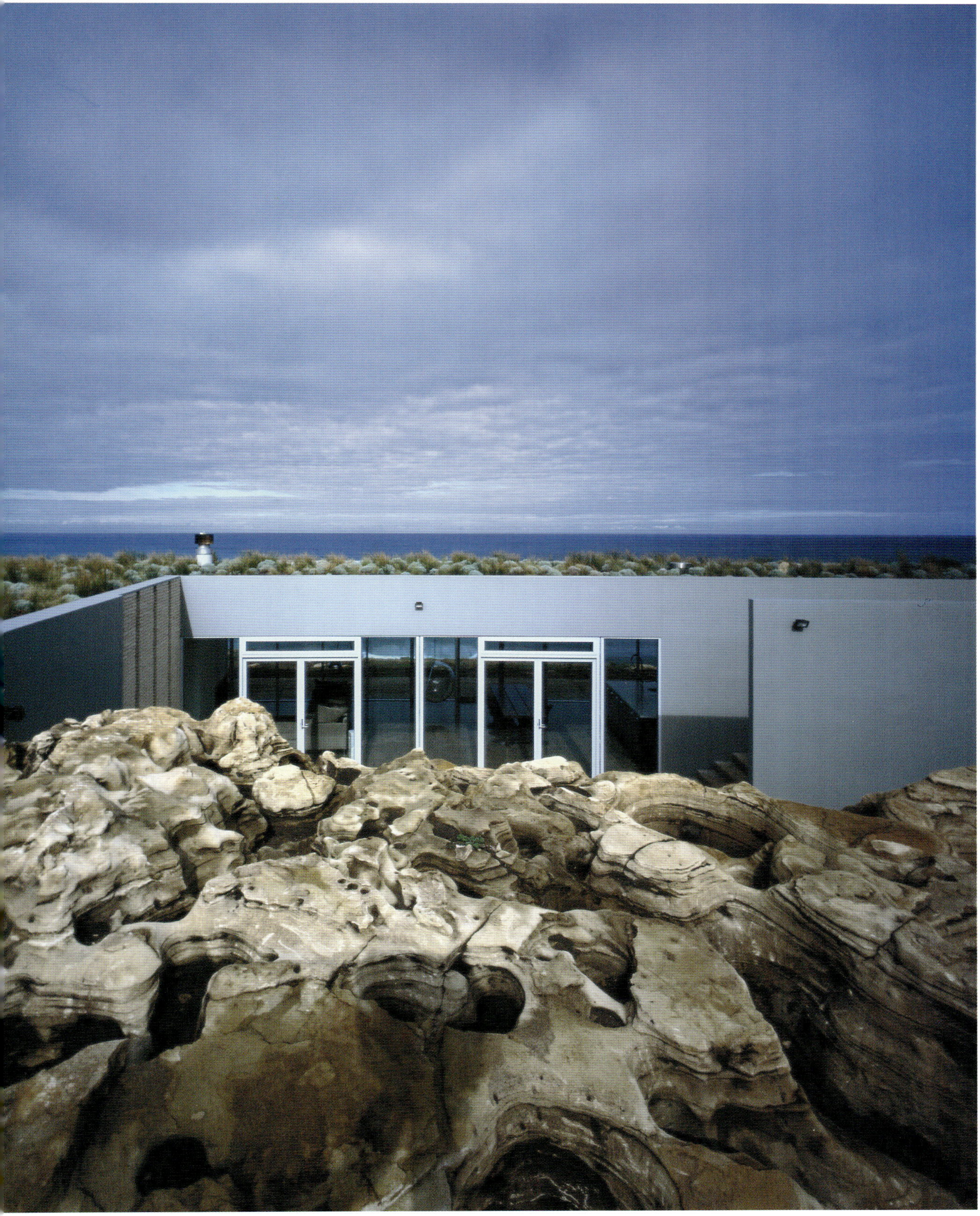

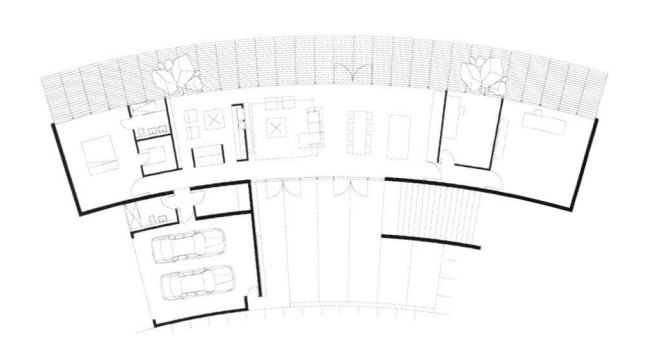

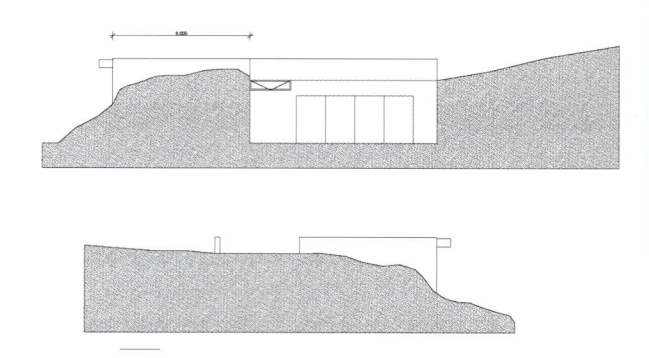

50 建 築
Architecture

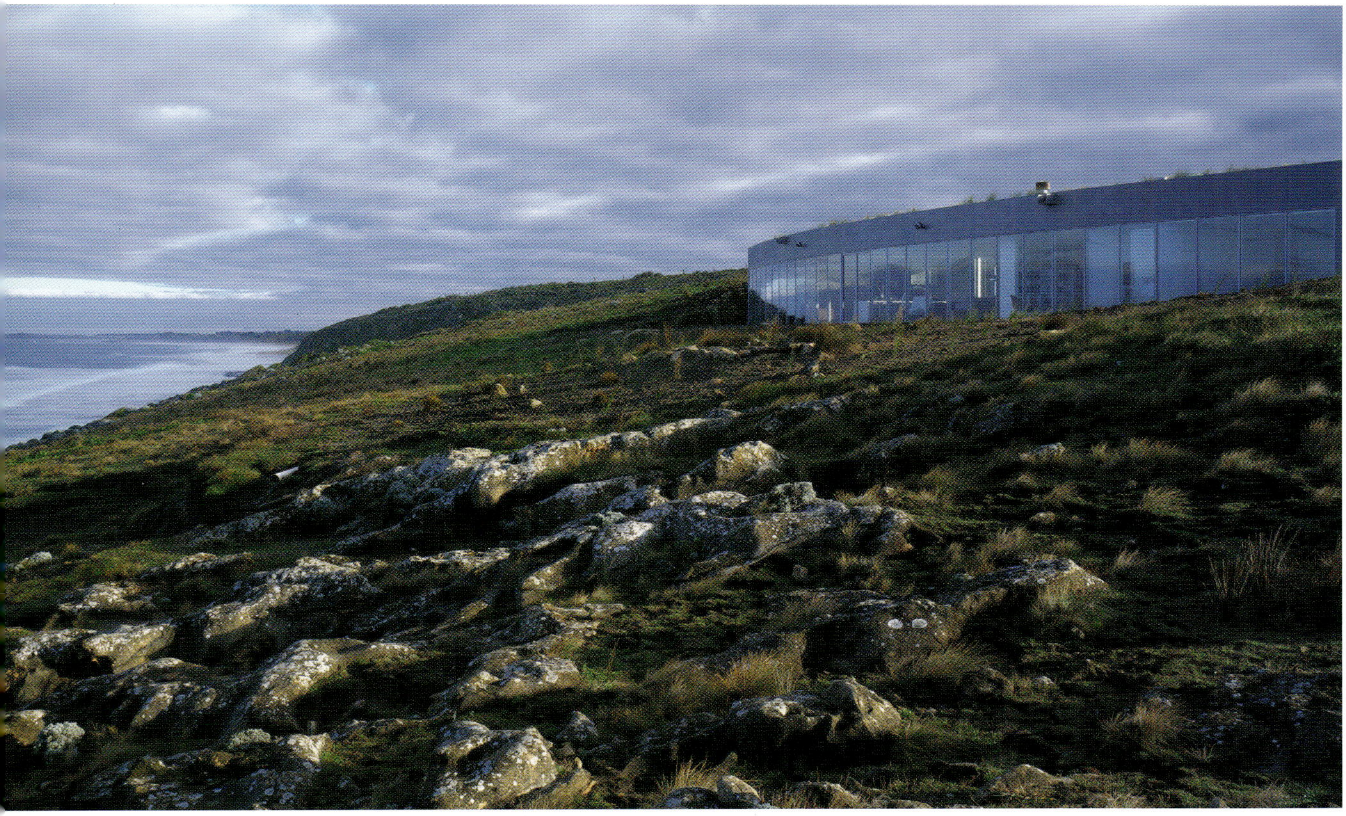

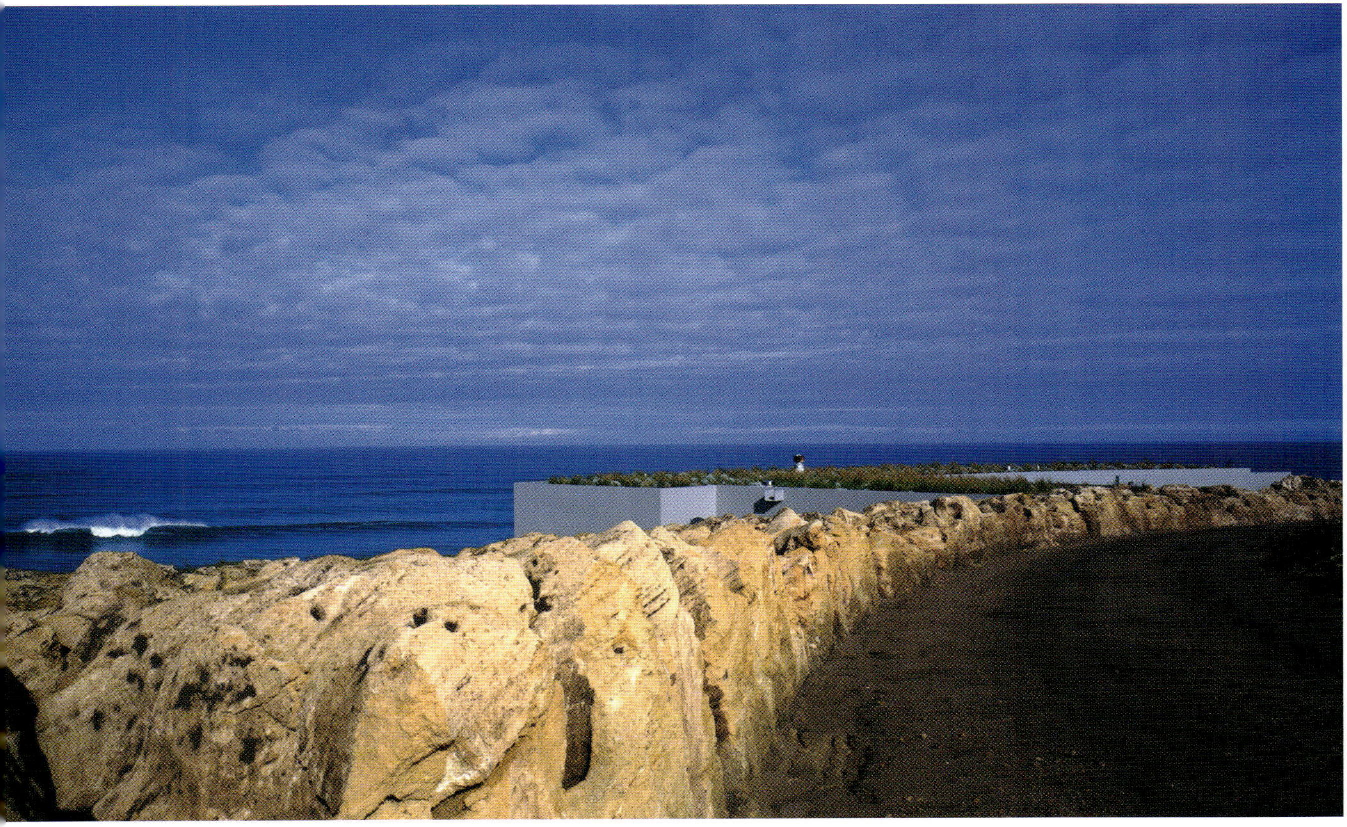

オーストラリア海岸線のこのあたりの地層は風と波に浸食されやすく、海側を除く3立面のファサードには、この立地ならではの特別なお客様が顔を見せる。主入り口が岩盤の露頭と同じ高さに見える。

The geologic strata in this part of the Australian coast, easily eroded by wind and water, makes a special guest appearance on three of the facades. Main entry is found at the same level as the rocky outcropping.

ビクトリア州西海岸のワーナンブールは、旅行者が好んで訪れる場所である。雄大なインド洋の眺めは、見る人を虜にする。空気力学的なデザインによって、ガレージを除く大半の部屋を海側に向けたのは、そのためでもある。

On the west coast of Victoria, Warrnambool is a favorite tourist destination. The sea is experienced with excitement, which is why the aerodynamic design of this home places the majority of the rooms, except the garage, facing the water.

ブチュプレオの住宅
家の中の海

アルヴァロ・ラミレス & クラリサ・エルトン
撮影：アルヴァロ・ラミレス & クラリサ・エルトン

HOME IN BUCHUPUREO
Sea inside

ÁLVARO RAMIREZ & CLARISA ELTON
PHOTO: © Álvaro Ramirez & Clarisa Elton

ブチュプレオ、第7州 ― チリ ― 2006

　首都サンティアゴから遠く離れたチリ中南部に、この小さな別荘はある。オーナーの望みは、ここで過ごす全時間を周囲の自然に対する尊敬と対話に費やしたいというものであった。その意を受けて、軸組みには松材を使い、屋根は天然スレート葺きとしたが、何よりもよくその精神を示しているのが、地盤に対する建物の配置である。
　住宅は急峻な崖に突き出した格好で建っているが、それを支えているのが垂木を組んだ懸崖造りの支柱である。その構造により自然環境に対する住宅の侵襲は最小限にとどめられ、雨の日には水は自然のままに住宅の下を流れ落ちる。松材と天然スレートは、この地で古くから用いられている建築材料である。

This small cabana is located in a remote point of the central-southern Chilean coast. The objective was to dialogue and respect the surroundings at all times, thanks to the materials used – pine wood and slate for the roof – and to the arrangement of the land itself.
The house rests along an abrupt incline by way of pylons that minimize the home's impact on the ground, and at the same time allows rain-water to flow freely beneath it. The wood and slate are two elements with strong roots in the architecture of this area.

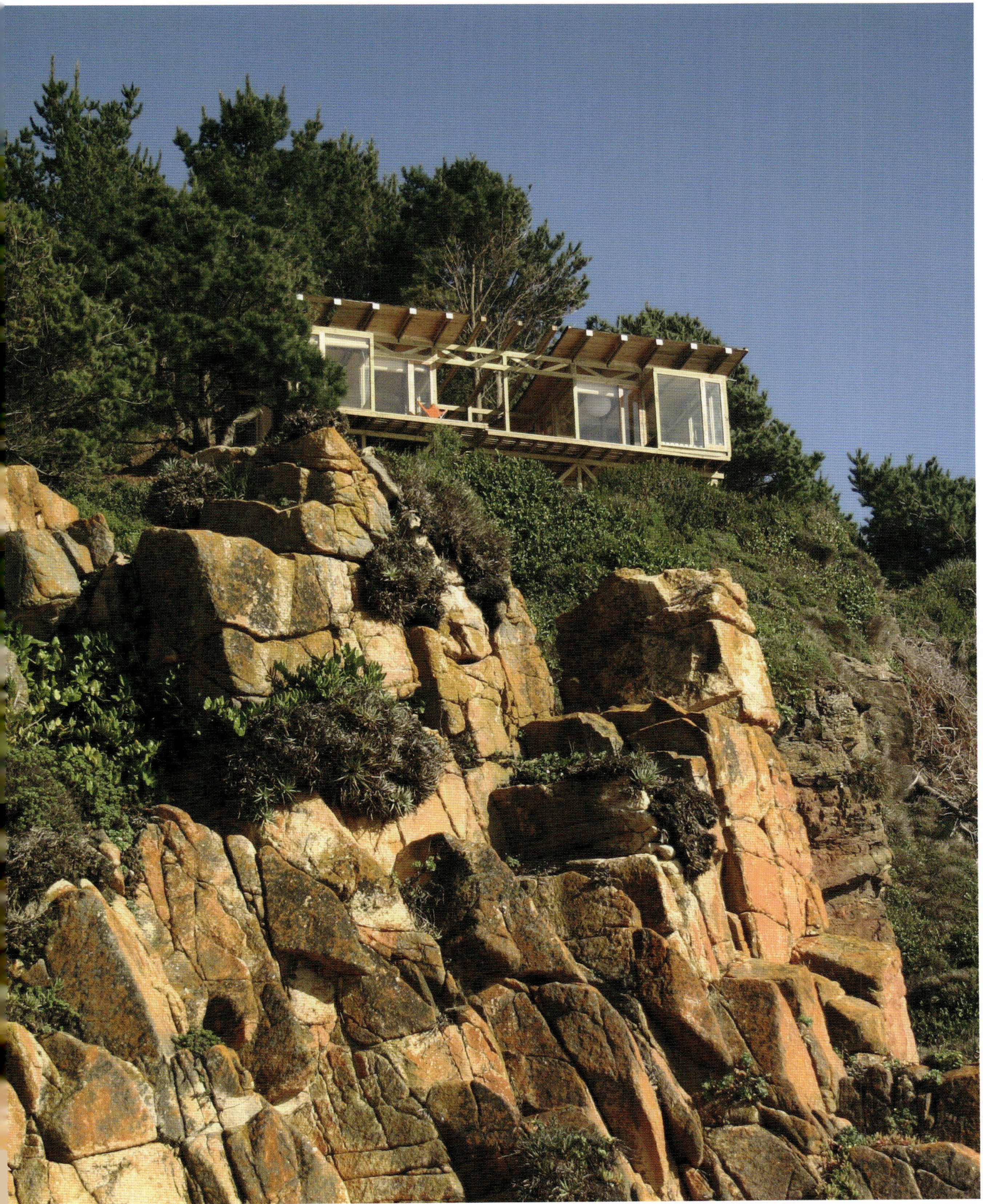

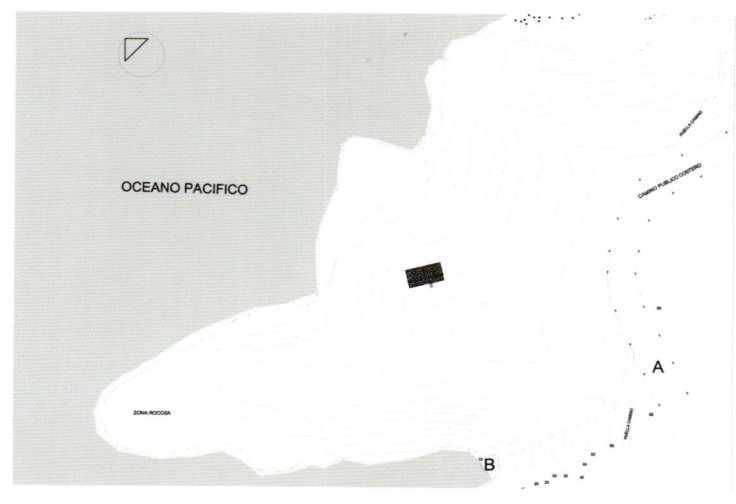

OCEANO PACIFICO

ZONA ROCOSA

A

B

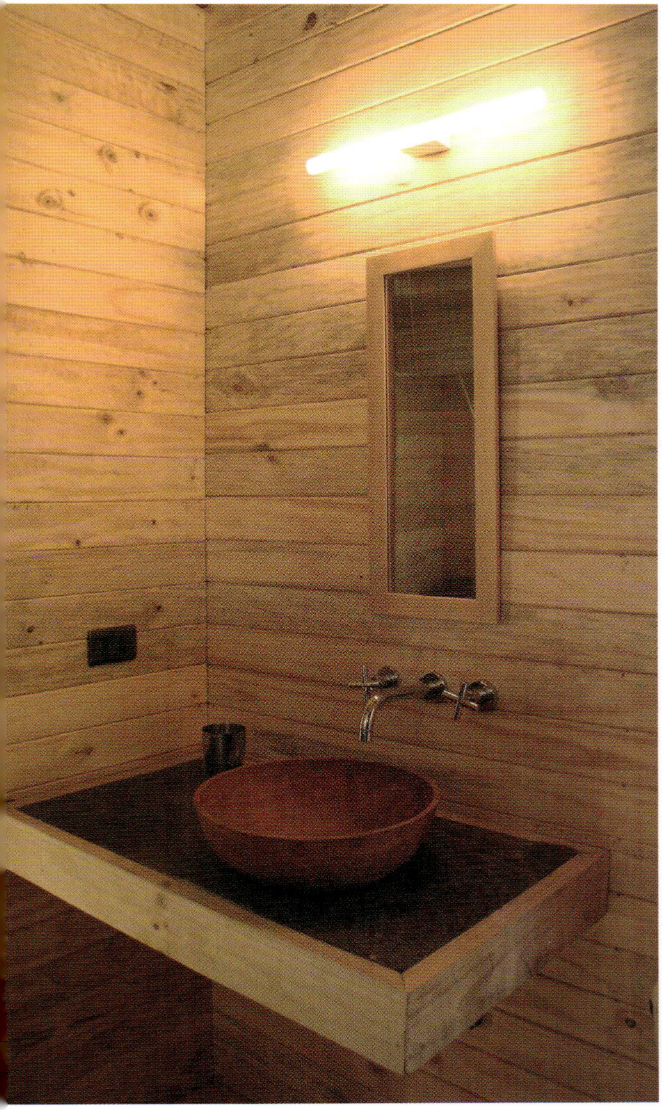

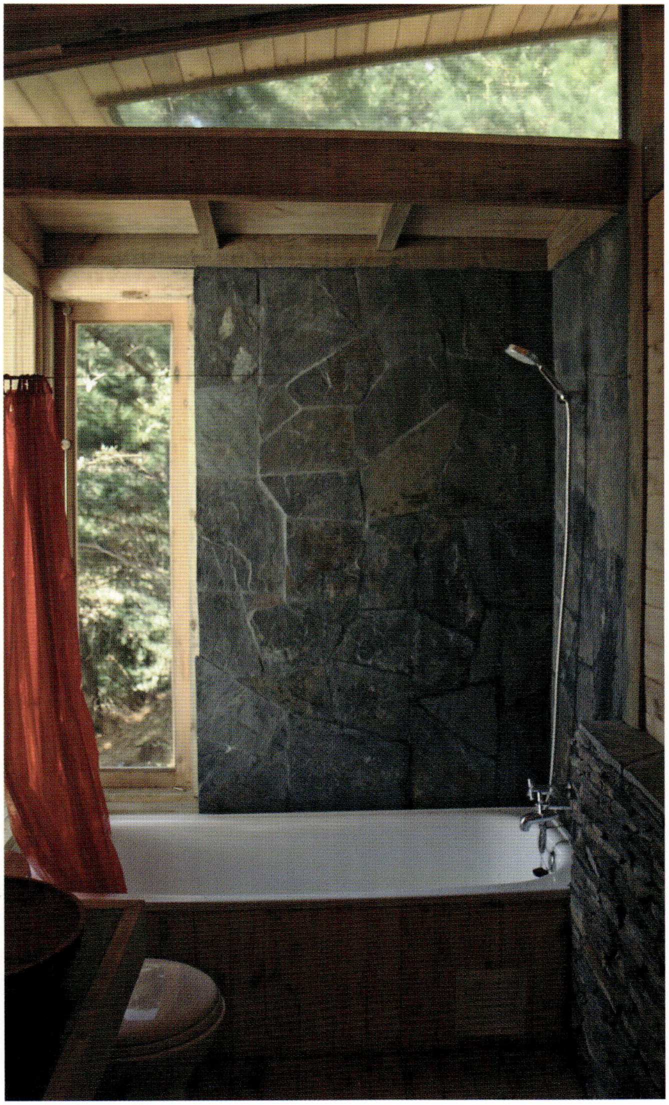

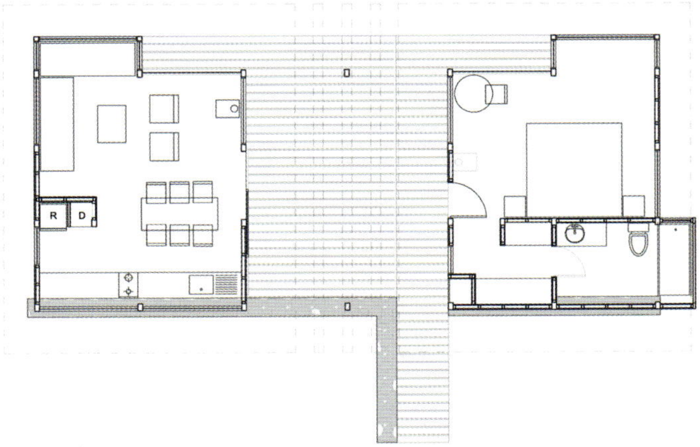
R
D

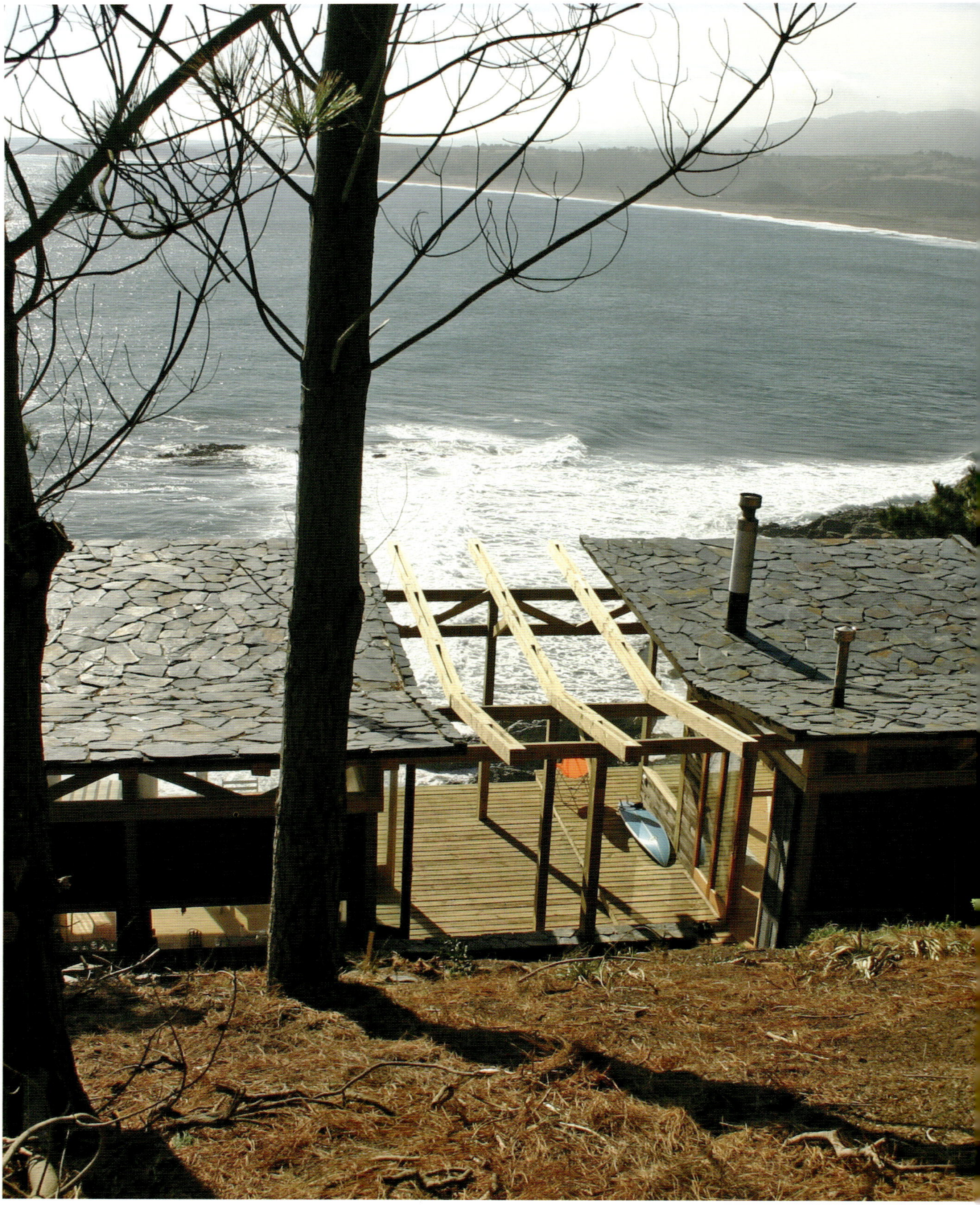

屋根のないポーチが天然スレート屋根を真ん中で分けながら、住宅の2つの区画を結合している。一方が居間で、もう一方が寝室である。どちらからも家の内部に居ながら、太平洋の広がりを全身で受け止めることができる。

An open porch divides the slate roof right through its center, connecting two parts of the house: the foyers and the bedroom. Every room enjoys a panoramic view of the Pacific Ocean.

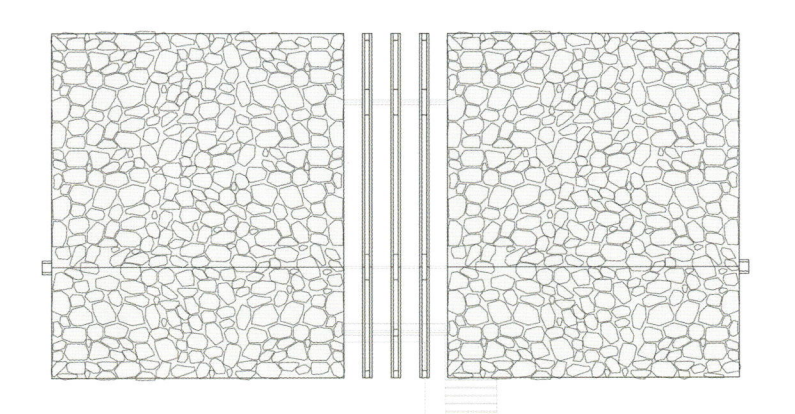

マターヤ邸
地形を克服して

ベルツバーグ建築設計事務所
撮影：ティム・ストリート - ポーター

BELZBERG ARCHITECTS
PHOTO: © Tim Street-Porter

MATAJA RESIDENCE
Overcoming topography

サンタモニカ・マウンテンズ、ベンチュラ郡 — アメリカ — 2002

　環境への負荷が少ない建造物にしか建築許可が下りないカリフォルニア州ベンチュラ郡に、この住居はある。この一家族用住宅は、多くの巨石と離れ岩の間に展開されている。建築家は巨大な花崗岩の露頭に着目し、それを風除けに使うことにした。またこの地区は有名なハイキングコースとなっていることから、建物はできるだけ偽装して地形に隠れるようにする必要があった。特徴的なバタフライ屋根は日光を最大限浴びるためであると同時に、雨水の経路を設け、庭の植生のための水を貯留するためでもある。

Located in Ventura County, where local laws only allow projects with a low environmental impact to be built, this one-family home was raised between large rocks and boulders. The architects have taken note of the rocky granite outcroppings and used it as a windscreen. They also managed to camouflage the edifice out of respect for the numerous hiking trails in the area. Its "Butterfly" roof, installed so as to maximize exposure to the sun, also re-routes and stores rain water for the nearby gardens.

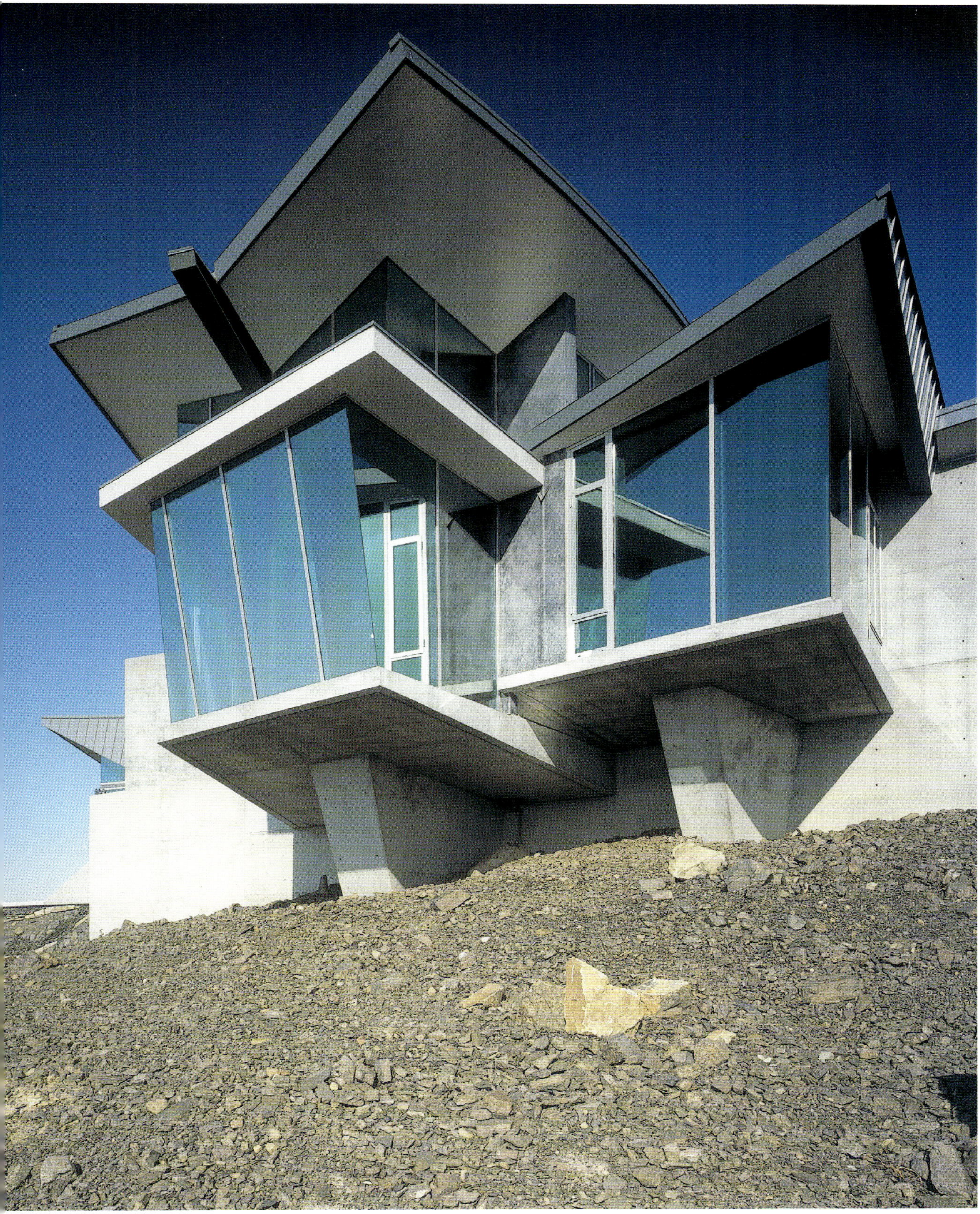

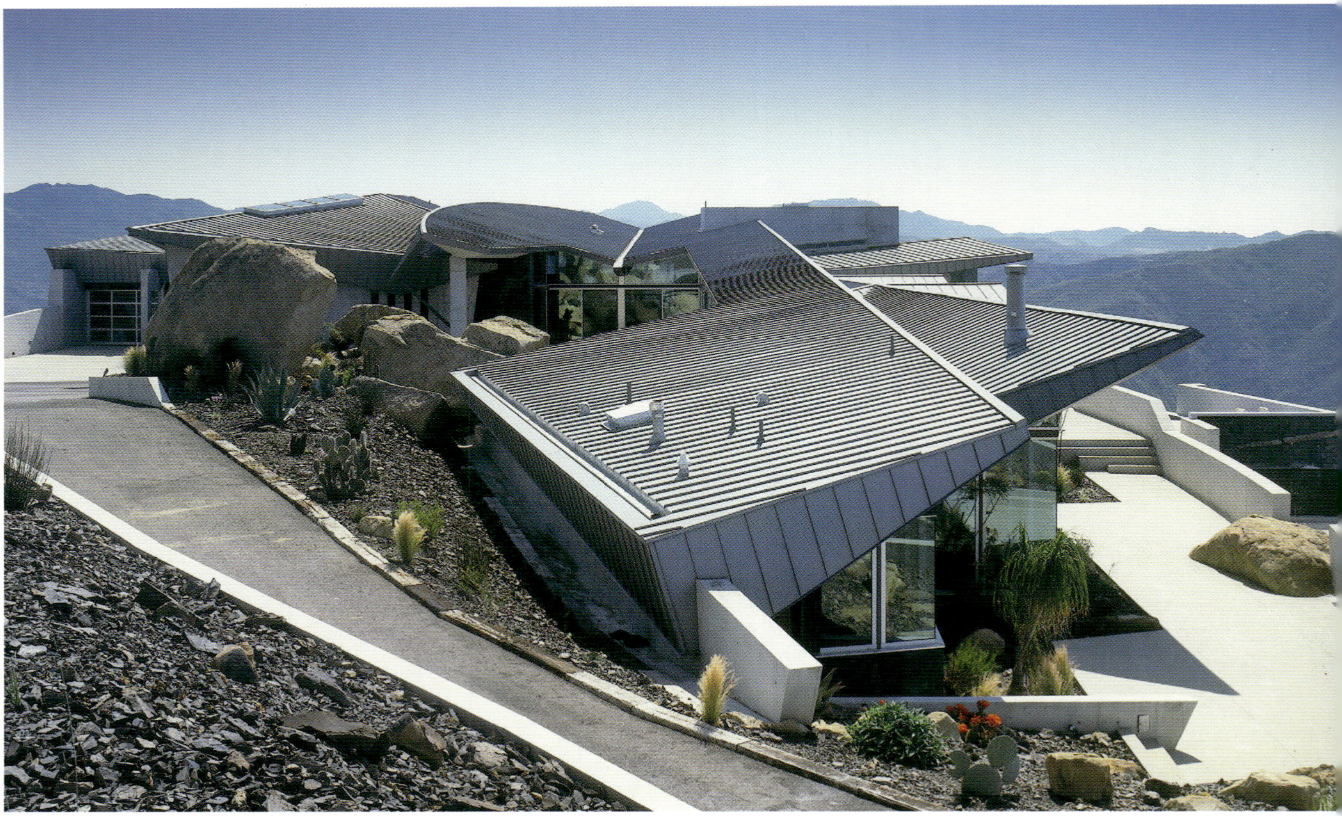

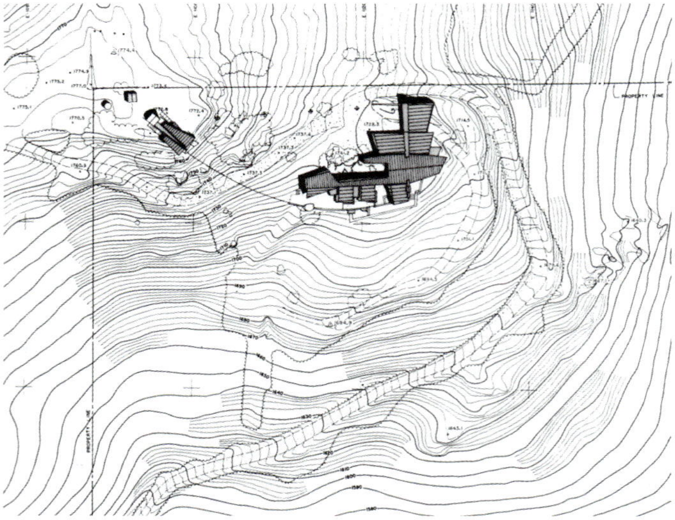

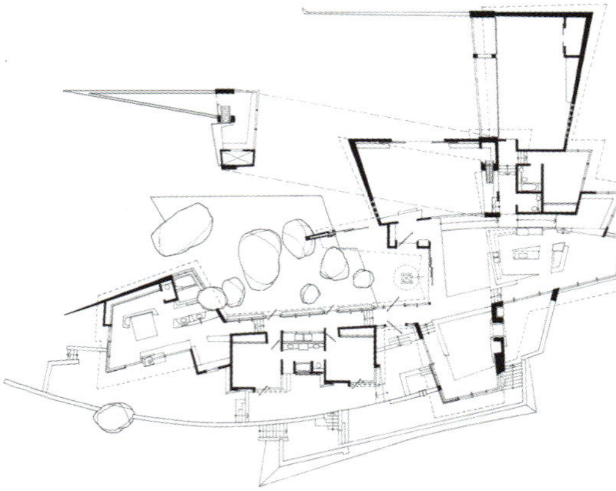

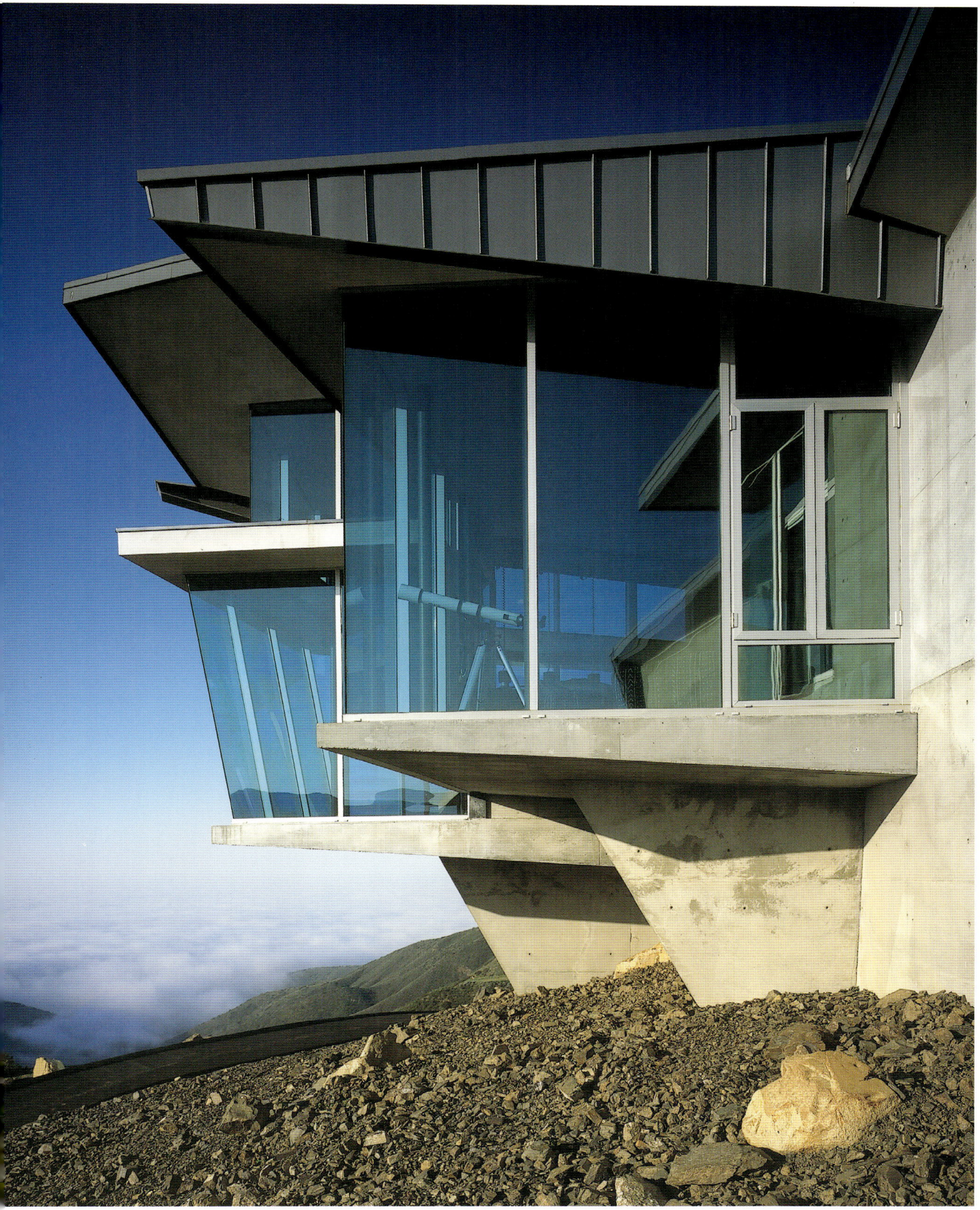

実際、かつてサンタモニカ・マウンテンズに定住していたアメリカ原住民のチュマッシュ族は、このようにして水を確保していた。コンクリート打放しの外壁が、岩の多い乾燥した地形と呼応している。

Surely, the rituals characteristic of the Santa Monica Mountains were practiced in this area once inhabited by Chumash Indians. The esthetic of the exterior cement walls serves to complement the dry and rocky surrounding terrain.

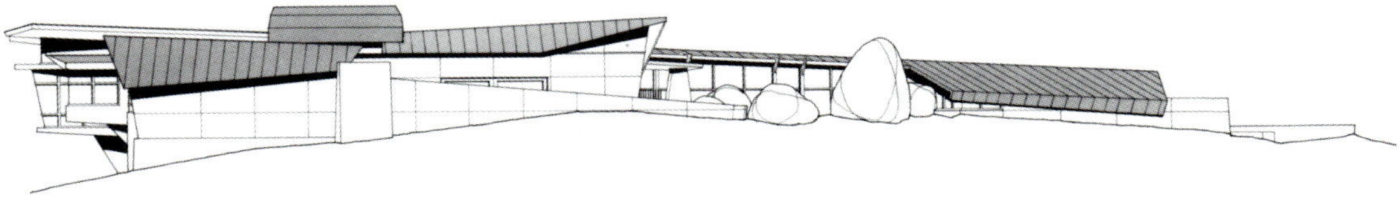

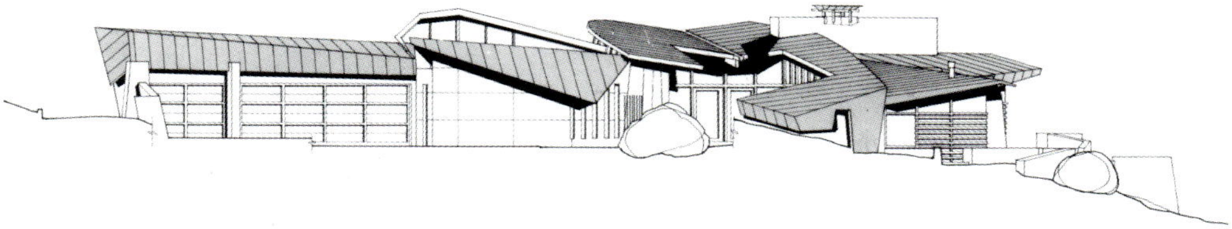

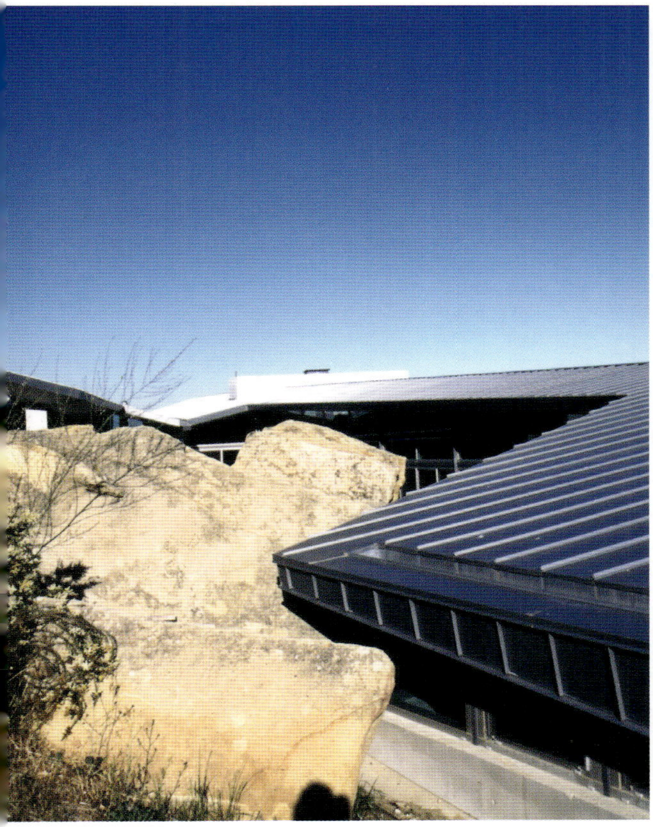

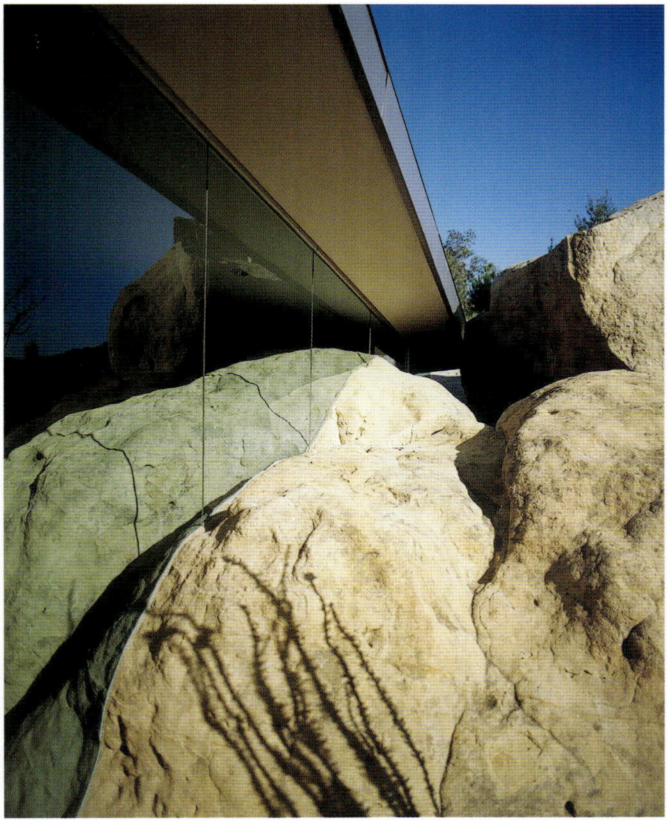

OSハウス
海に隠されて

OS HOUSE
Hidden by the sea

ノラスター
撮影：ホセ・エビア

NOLASTER
PHOTO: © José Hevia

ロレド ― スペイン ― 2005

　大西洋の波が砕ける高さ30mの断崖絶壁に向ってなだらかに下る、カンタブリア海岸沿いの斜面にこの住宅はある。この地方特有の北西から吹く強い海風に対して楯となるような建物を建て、その楯に守られた穏やかな庭を造るというのが設計概念であった。風の衝撃は、大半を屋根で受け止めることとした。雄大な景色をできるだけ邪魔しないように、住宅は文字通り地面に嵌めこまれ、屋根とファサードは周囲の景観とダイレクトに調和しながら溶け込んでいる。

En la costa cantábrica, en una parcela en pendiente hacia un acantilado de 30 metros donde rompe el mar, el arquitecto se ha propuesto crear un jardín protegido del viento marino –violento y del Noroeste– cuya cubierta, ecológica y transitable, es la fachada más expuesta de la vivienda. La voluntad de interferir lo menos posible en el paisaje ha llevado a pegar literalmente la casa al terreno y establecer modalidades de cubierta y fachada que se relacionen de forma directa y armónica con el entorno.

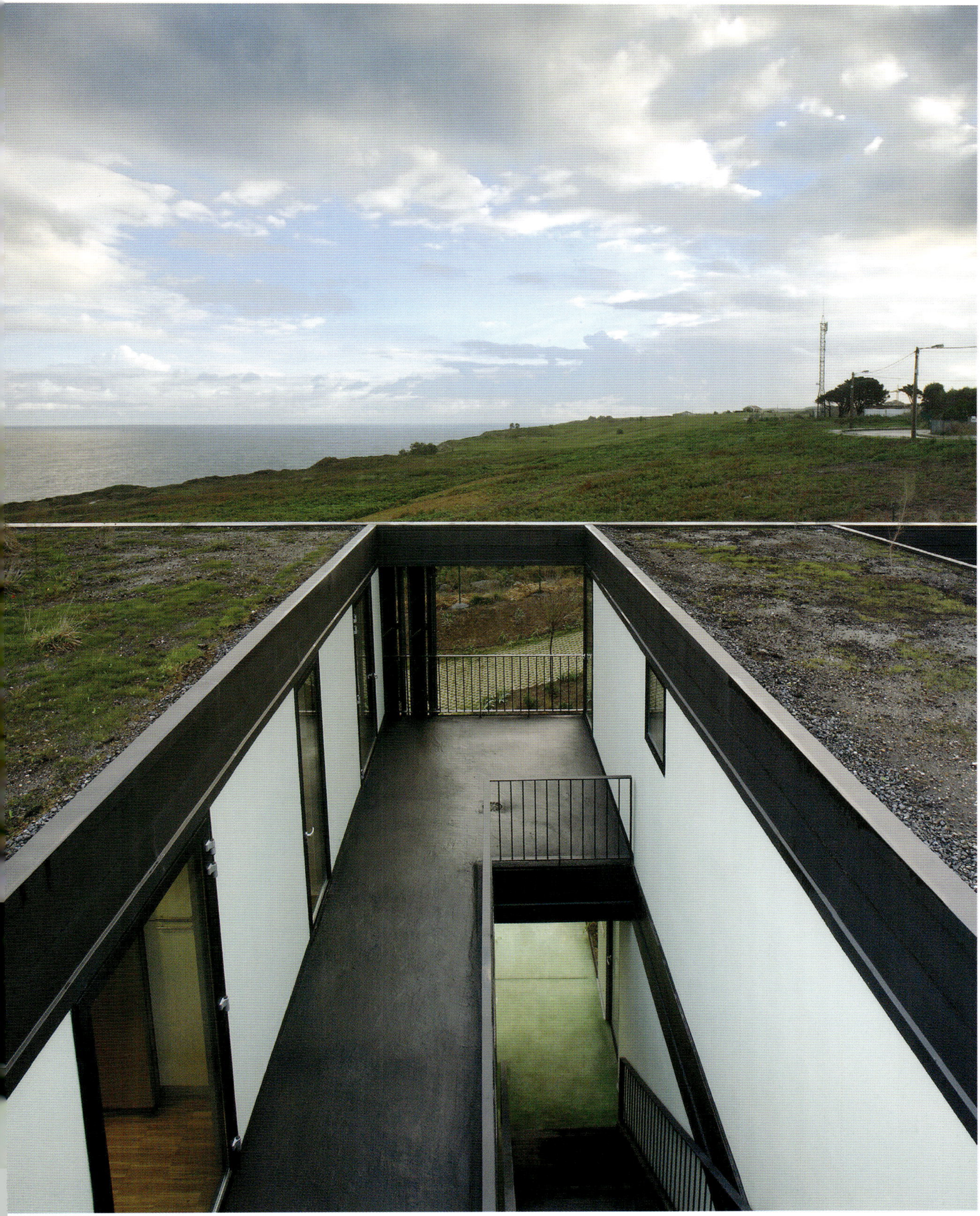

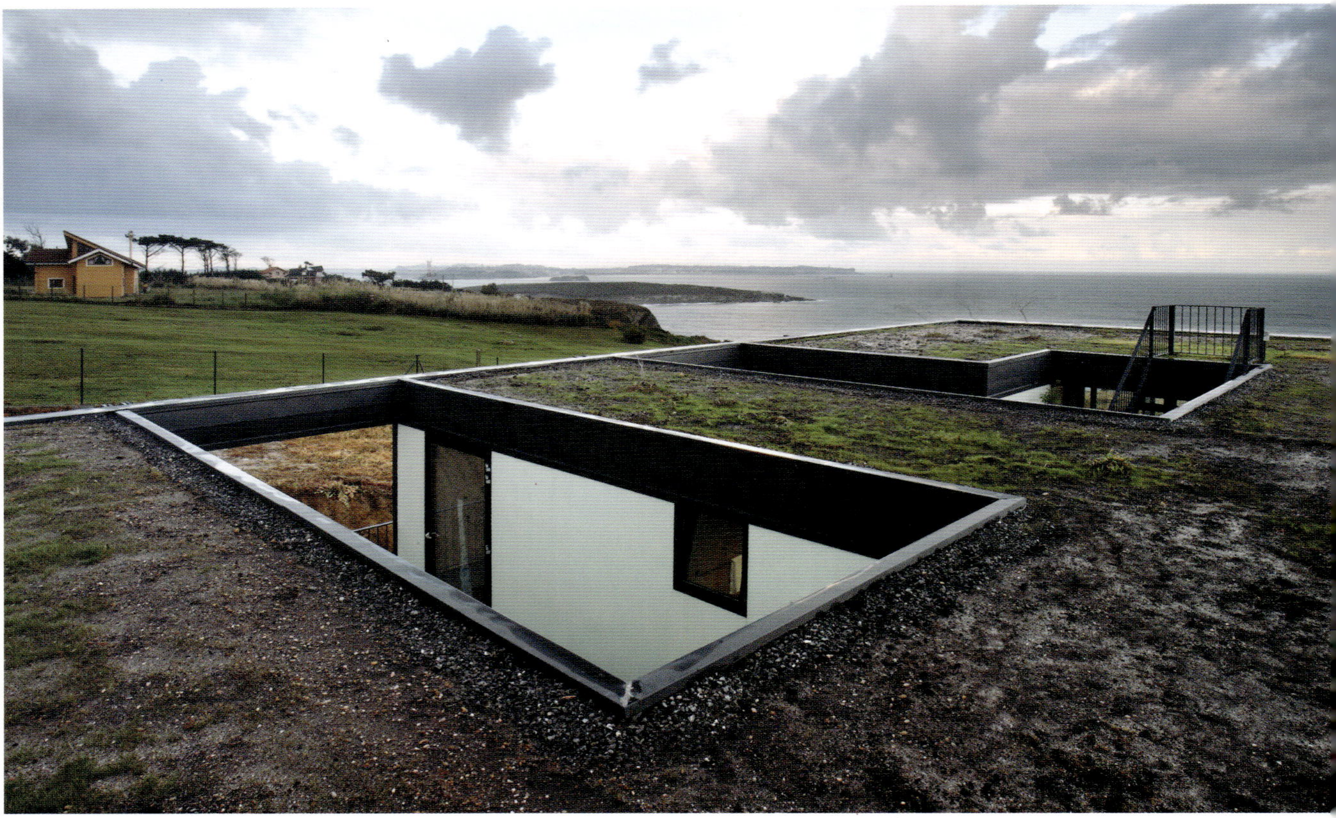
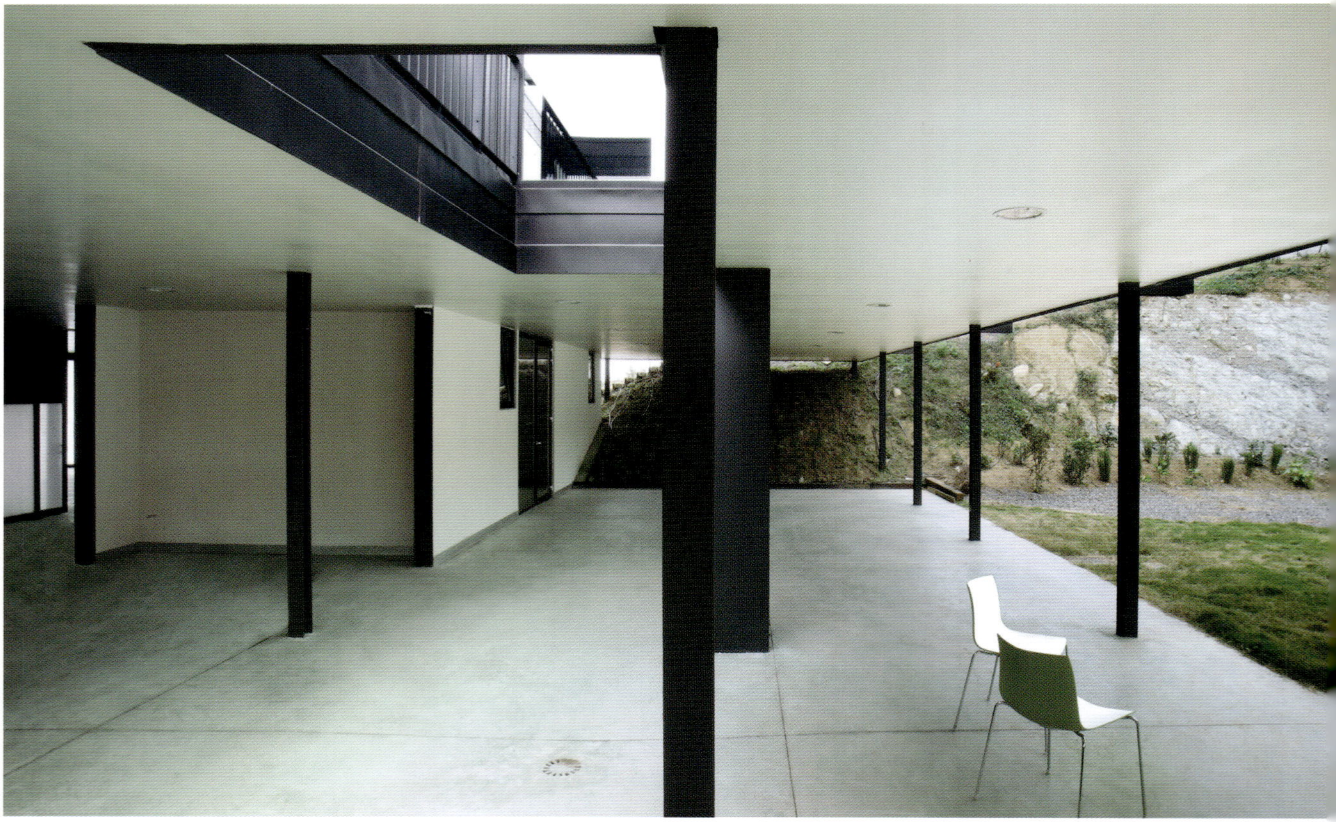

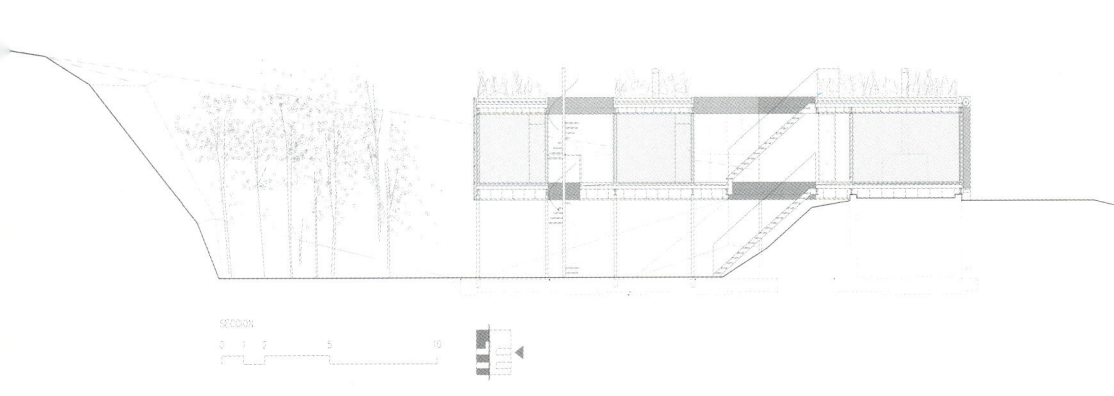

69 建 築
Architecture

屋根は、どんなエレメント（煙突、手すりなど）であれ、斜面の上の道路に立つ人の視線の高さを超えないようにした。この住宅は、南向きの斜面に建って海から顔を背けている、近隣の大半の住宅とは正反対の立場にある。

Not one rooftop element (chimneys, railings, etc.) rises above the horizon line of a person standing at street level; as opposed to most homes, which are built on the southern slope and facing away from the sea.

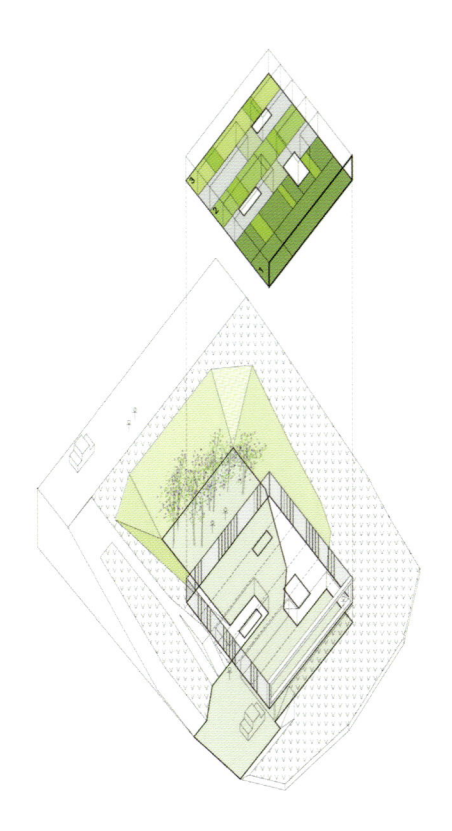

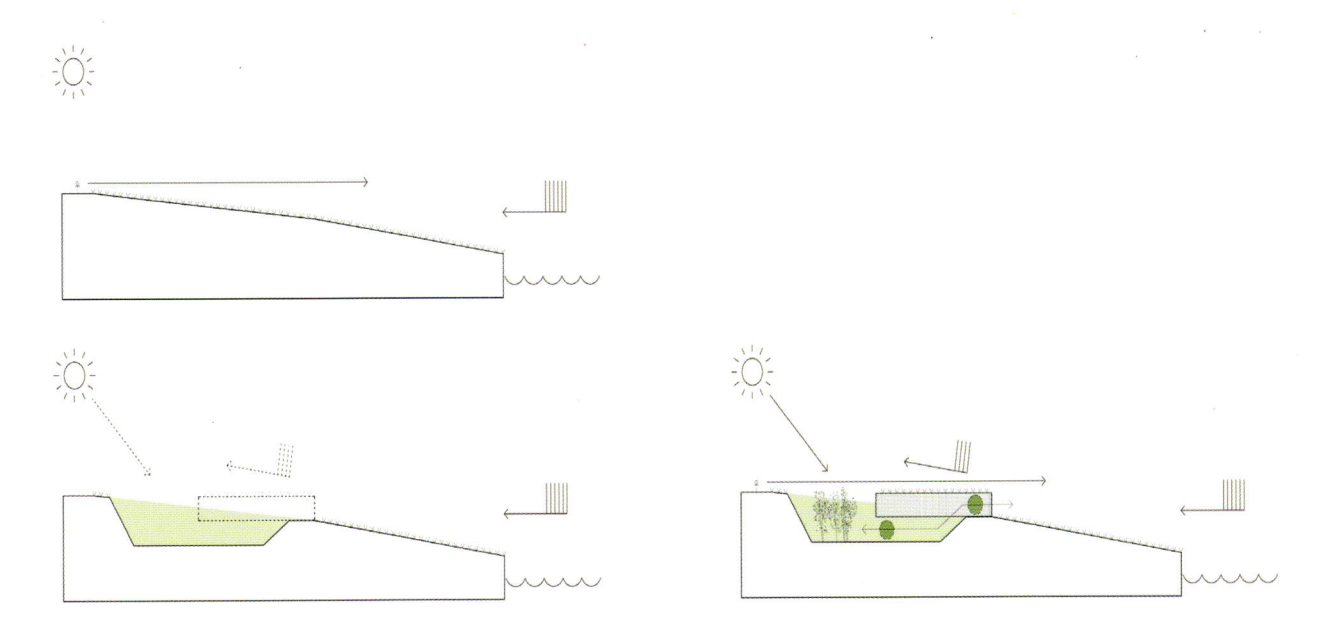

71 建築
Architecture

乱気流の家
風の通り道

TURBULENCE HOUSE
Between turbulences

スティーブン・ホール建築設計事務所
撮影：ポール・ウォーチョル

STEVEN HOLL ARCHITECTS
PHOTO: © Paul Warchol

アビキュー、ニューメキシコ ― アメリカ ― 2005

　建物の中央にぽっかりと開いた穴は、ニューメキシコをしばしば襲う暴風雨が自由にこの建物を通り抜けられるようにするためのもの。すべての部材がカンザスシティーで製造され、この地で組み立てられた。デジタルデザインによって設計された31種類のアルミニウムパネルと肋材は完璧に接合して、提案された空気力学的な構造を実現し、非常に高い熱絶縁係数を達成した。屋根の一部に張られた太陽光発電パネルからは、毎日1キロワットアワーの電力が供給されるが、それはこの住宅の通常の必要電力を十分満たしている。

A hole in the central part of this edifice allows the turbulent winds of this New Mexico area to pass through freely. The model was prefabricated in Kansas City and its ribbed aluminum dressing is comprised of 31 different digitally-designed panels that adapt perfectly to the aerodynamic shape proposed, achieving a highly coefficient thermal insulation. The roof is partially covered with Photovoltaic panels that supply 1kw/hour/day, covering all the basic electrical needs of the house.

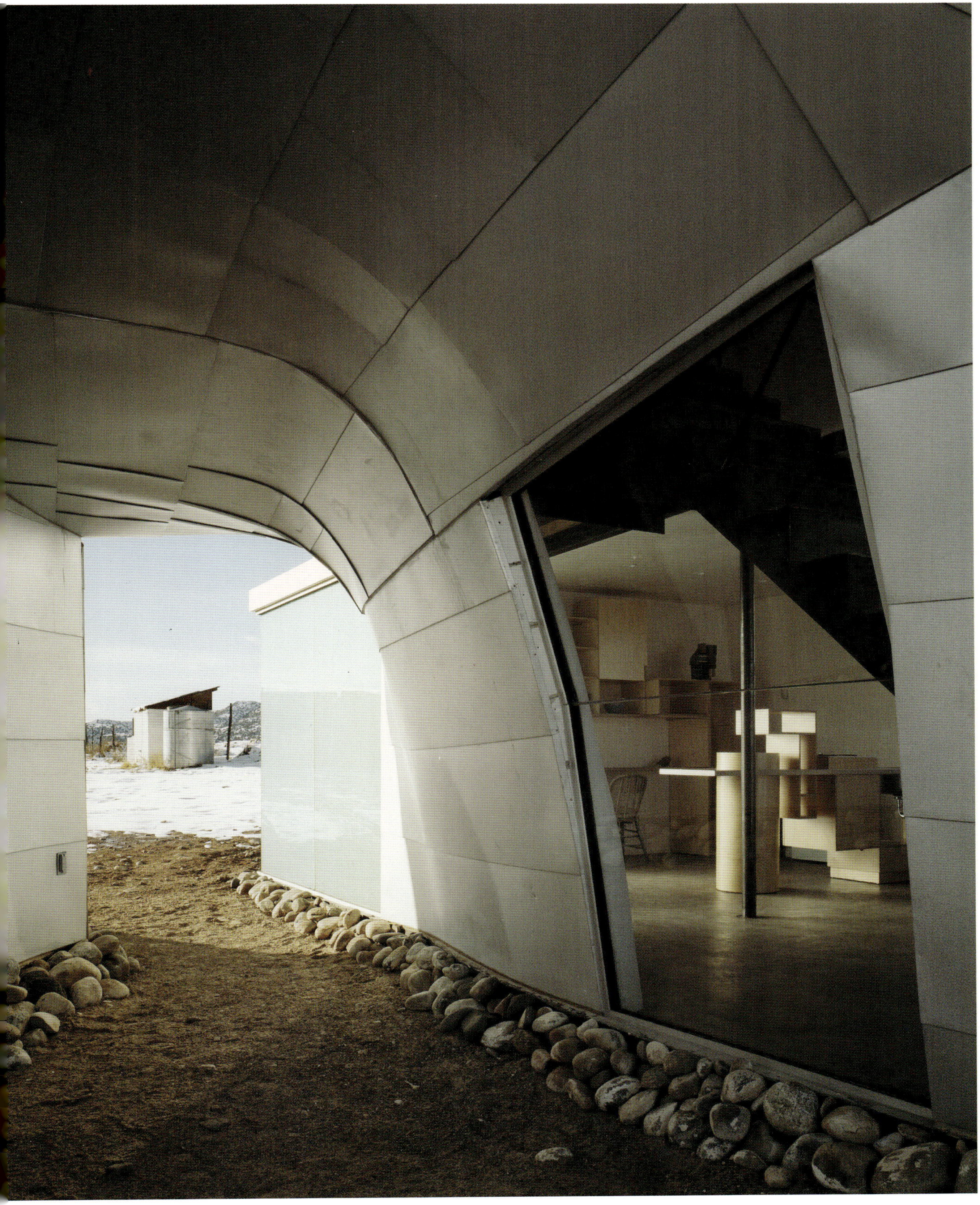

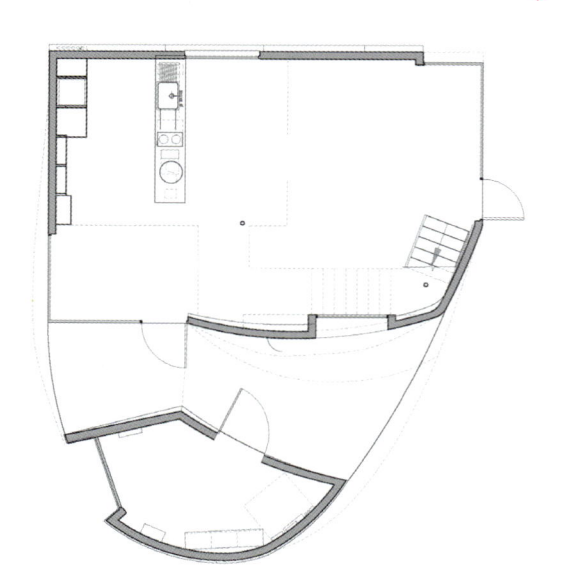

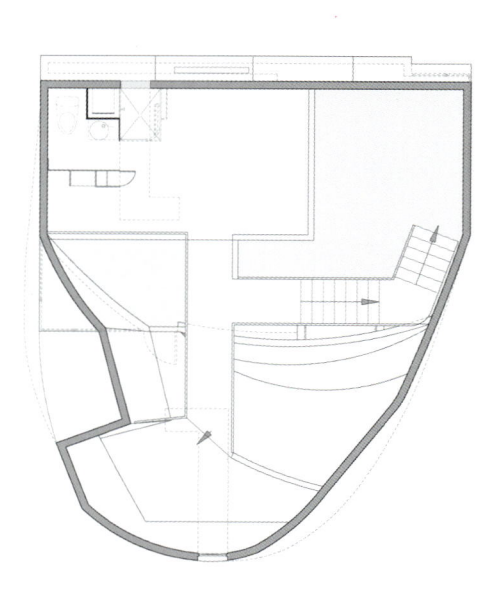

74 建 築
Architecture

自然に溶け込む色合いと小さくまとまった形は、時折訪れる雪景色とよく調和している。この孤立した住宅の近くには、異端の芸術家リチャード・タトルが建てた日干し煉瓦の家がある。

The neutral tones of this facade and its small dimensions adapt well with this occasionally snow-covered landscape. Near this enclave, the adobe homes made by artist Richard Tuttle can be found.

ブラウン・デュブイ邸
藁の美学

ヴェルナー・シュミット建築設計事務所
撮影：ヴェルナー・シュミット建築設計事務所、キャサリン・ワネク

ATELIER WERNER SCHMIDT
PHOTO: © Atelier Werner Schmidt, Catharine Wanek

BRAUN-DUBUIS HOUSE
The esthetic of straw

ディゼンティス ― スイス ― 2003

藁を使って家を建てるという考えはアメリカから学んだもの。アメリカではすでに20世紀初めにこの種の住居が建てられている。正真正銘の藁の家を建てるため、このスイスの建築家は実際に脱穀した後の藁だけを使った。それは安価で、手に入れやすく、断熱効果も高い。外部から見ると藁はどこにも見当たらないが、擁壁と屋根裏部屋の壁の下地は藁でできている。藁はビニールの紐で、ひと梱(こり)ずつ縛られ成形された。藁を積んだ後、それが十分定着するまで時間をとる必要があり、その間作業は中断した。

The idea to build with straw comes from the United States, where at the start of the 20th century buildings of this kind where already being built. True to form, this Swiss specialist made use of a product that is nothing more than agricultural residue, cheap and widely available, to create and thermally insulate this home.
It may not seem so from the outside, but the retaining walls and the attic have straw bases. The bales of straw are tied by hand with plastic straps. Once placed, work is delayed so that the straw can be given enough time to settle properly.

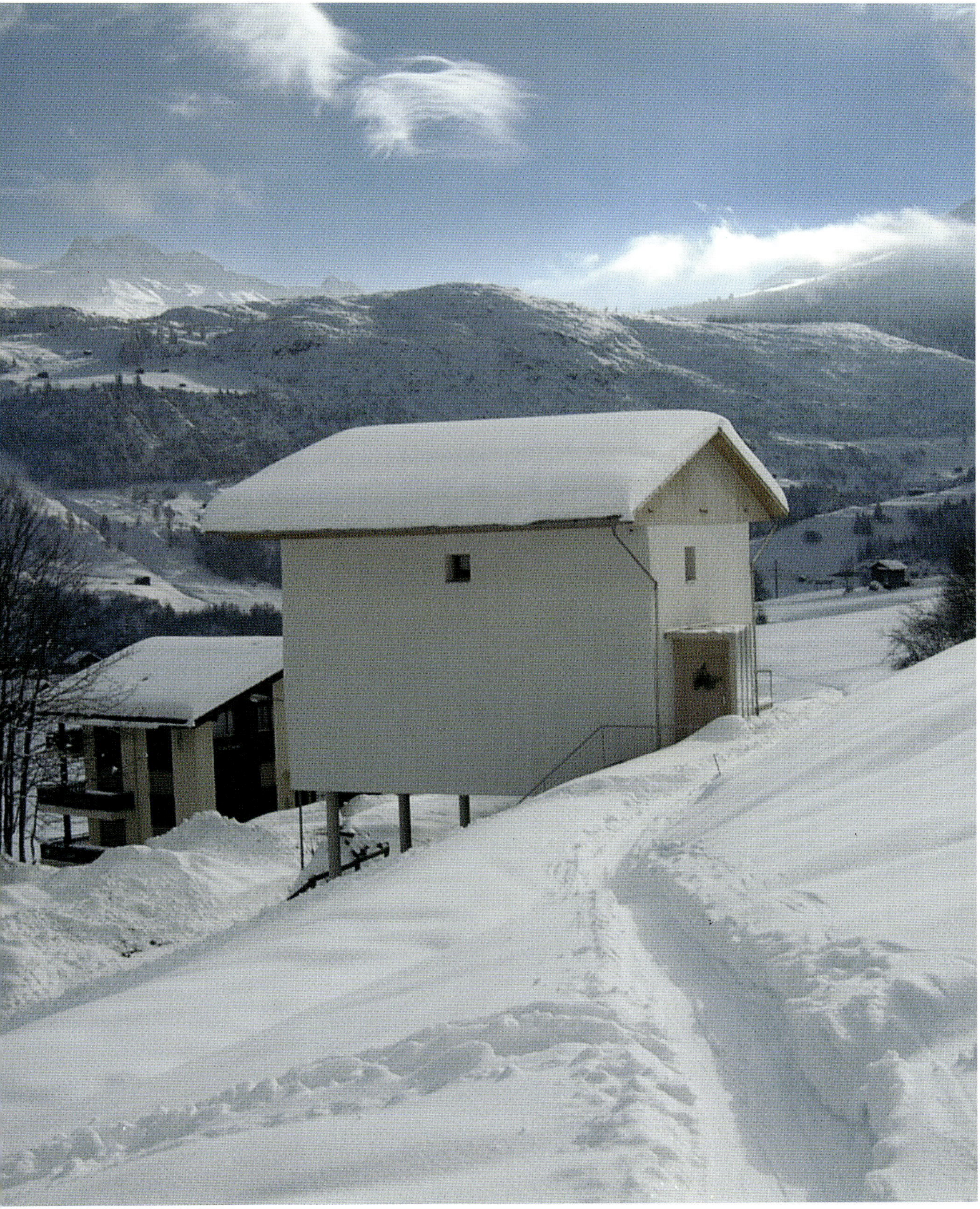

SITUATION M 1:500

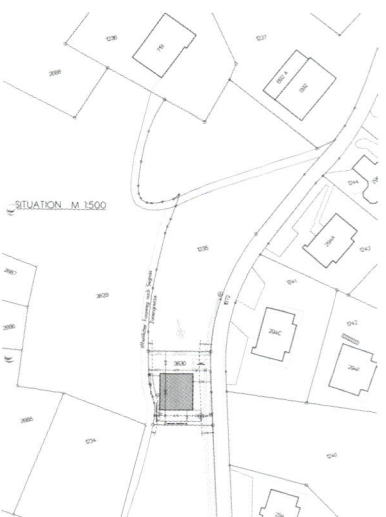

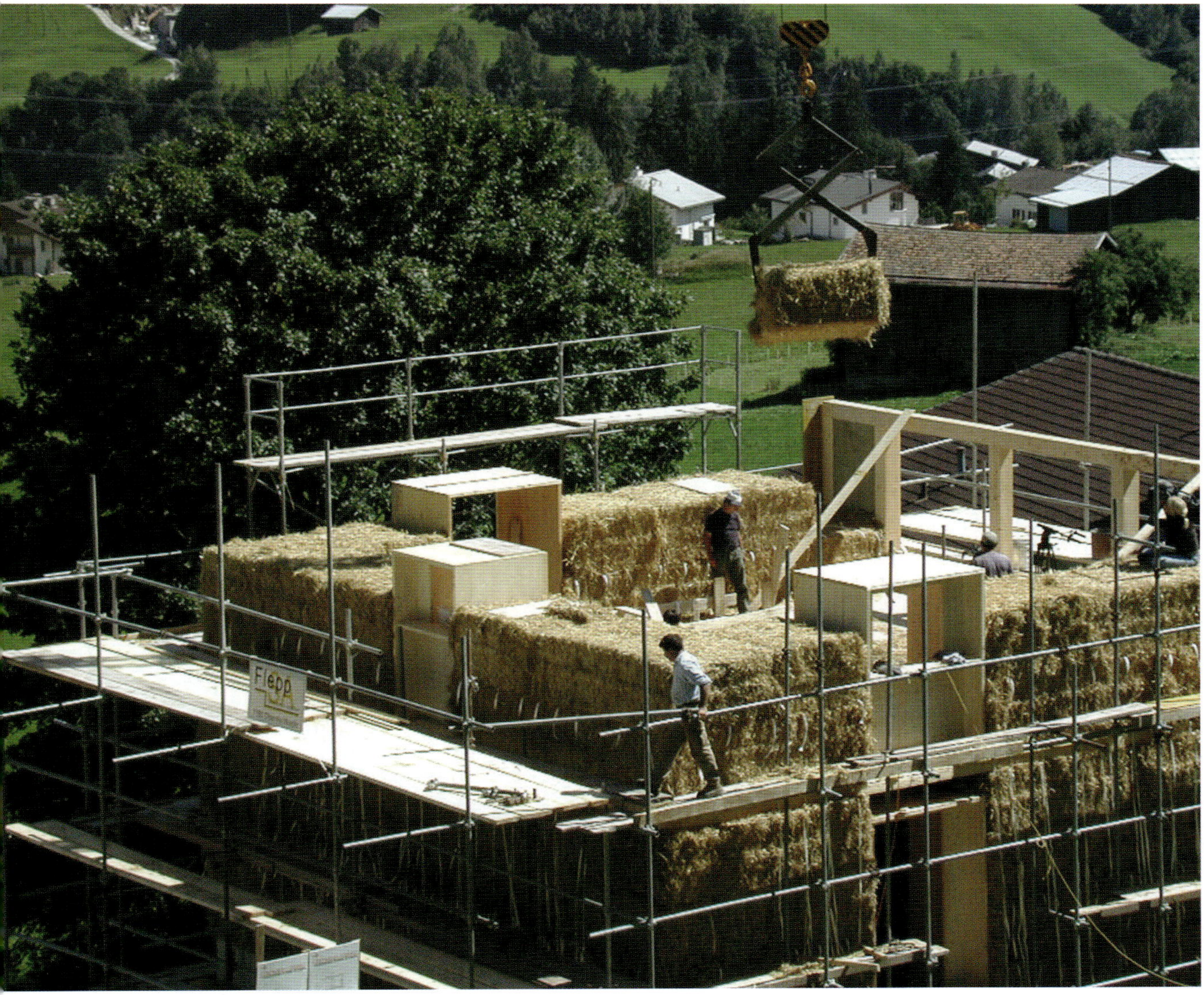
Flepp

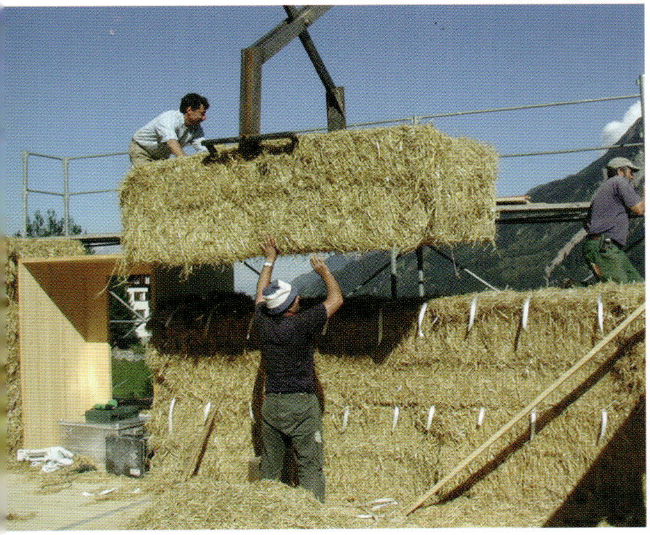

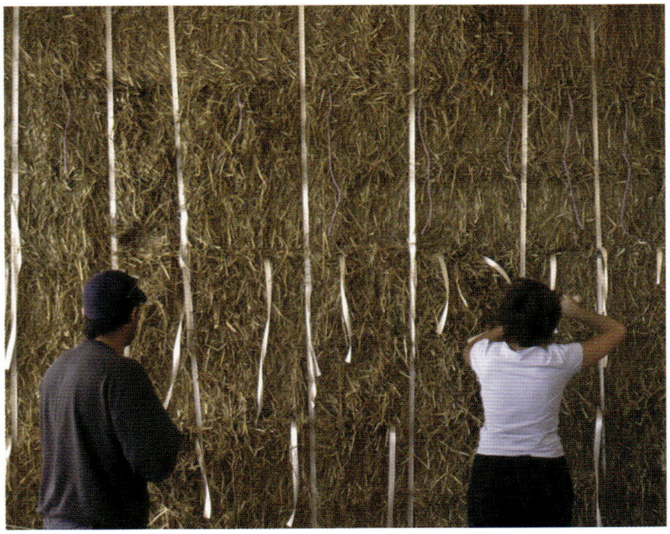

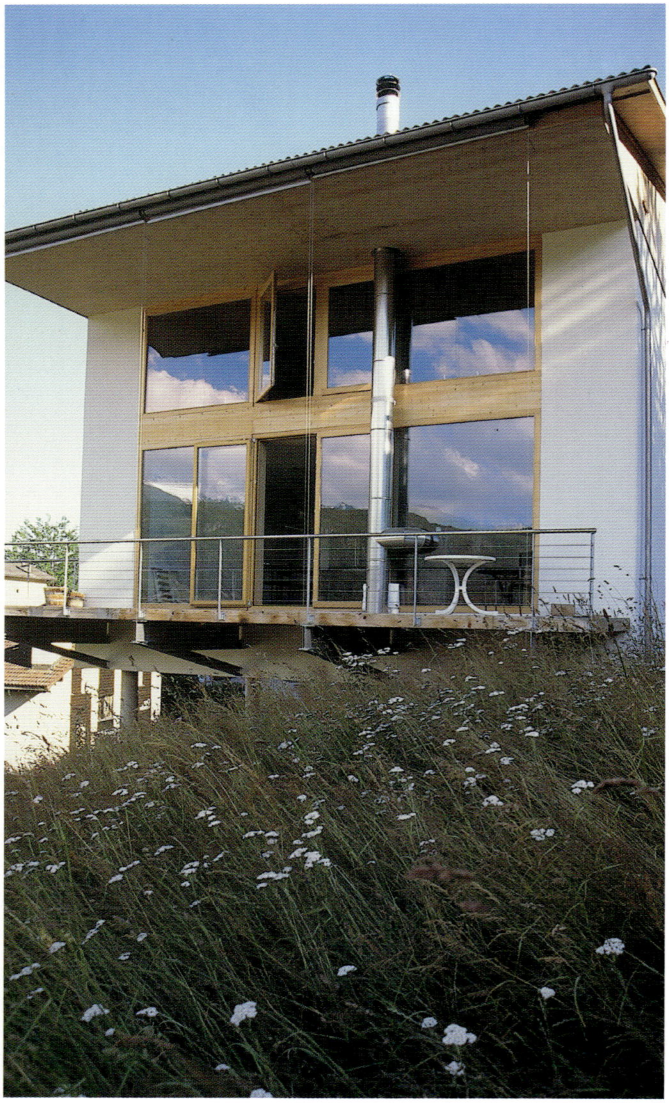
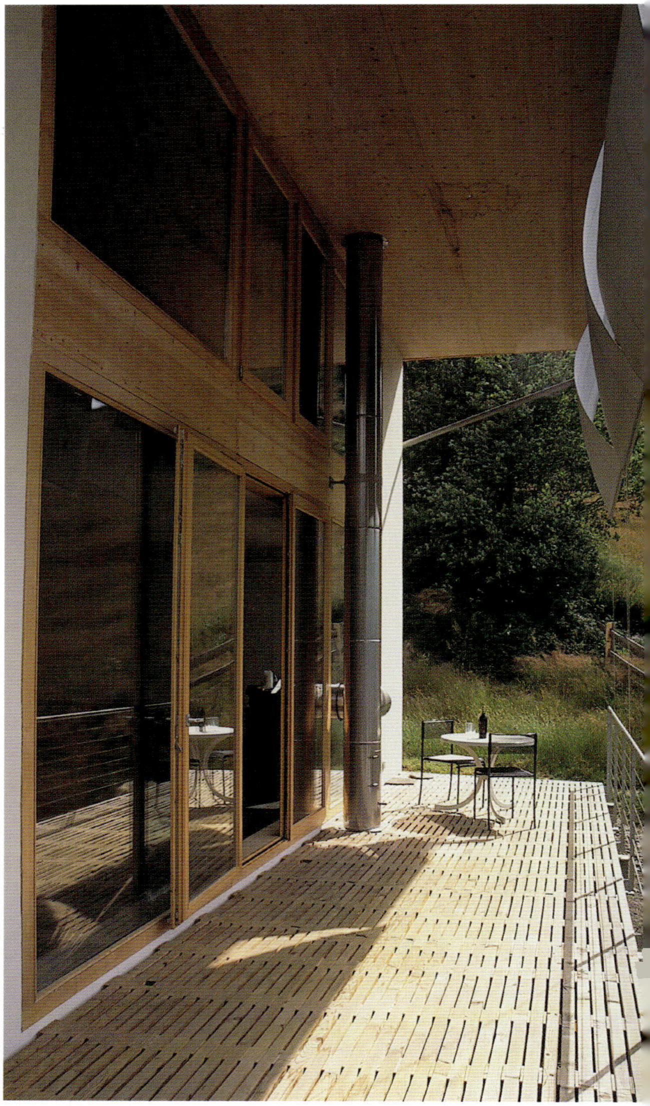
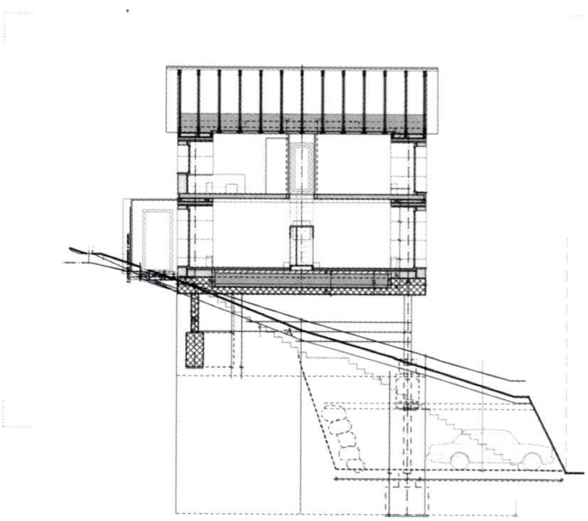
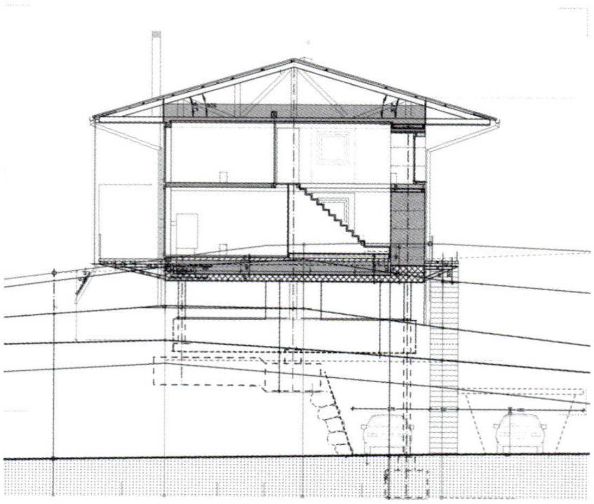

構造内部に詰め込まれた藁の存在は、住宅の外からも内からも見ることはできない。この住宅のもう1つの長所は、窓から眺める冬景色の素晴らしさは別にして、地震と暴風雪に強いことである。

The presence of straw in this structure is not visible from the exterior or the interior of the home. Another advantage of this house, apart from the picturesque winters, is its resistance against earthquakes and storms.

リギ・シャイデックの住宅
白銀の家

アンドレアス・フェーリマン―ガブリエル・ヘフラー
撮影：ヴァレンティン・ジェック

ANDREAS FUHRIMANN GABRIELLE HÄCHLER
PHOTO: © Valentin Jeck

HOUSE IN RIGI SCHEIDEGG
White color

リギ・シャイデック ― スイス ― 2003

　リギ・シャイデック村はスイス中部リギ山の麓にあるが、その山は古くから山の女王と呼ばれ、トレッキングの観光客で賑わうところである。村の他の家々とくらべて目立つその多角形の建物は、煙突型のマストを持った船に似ている。
　1階と2階の外壁を被覆している白い板が息を呑むほど美しく、冬、雪が積もると、丘の上に立つその白銀の建物は、地球と住居の統合の完全なる象徴となる。

The town of Rigi Scheidegg sits beside the Rigi Mountains, in central Switzerland, an area highly valued for its hiking trails. Standing out from the rest of the community, this polygonal edifice has a profile similar to that of a ship with a chimney-shaped mast.
The pale colored wood covering the walls on the first and second floor is a nice surprise, and during the winter snowfall, the combination of white and its position high on a hill turns it into a perfect symbol of earthly integration.

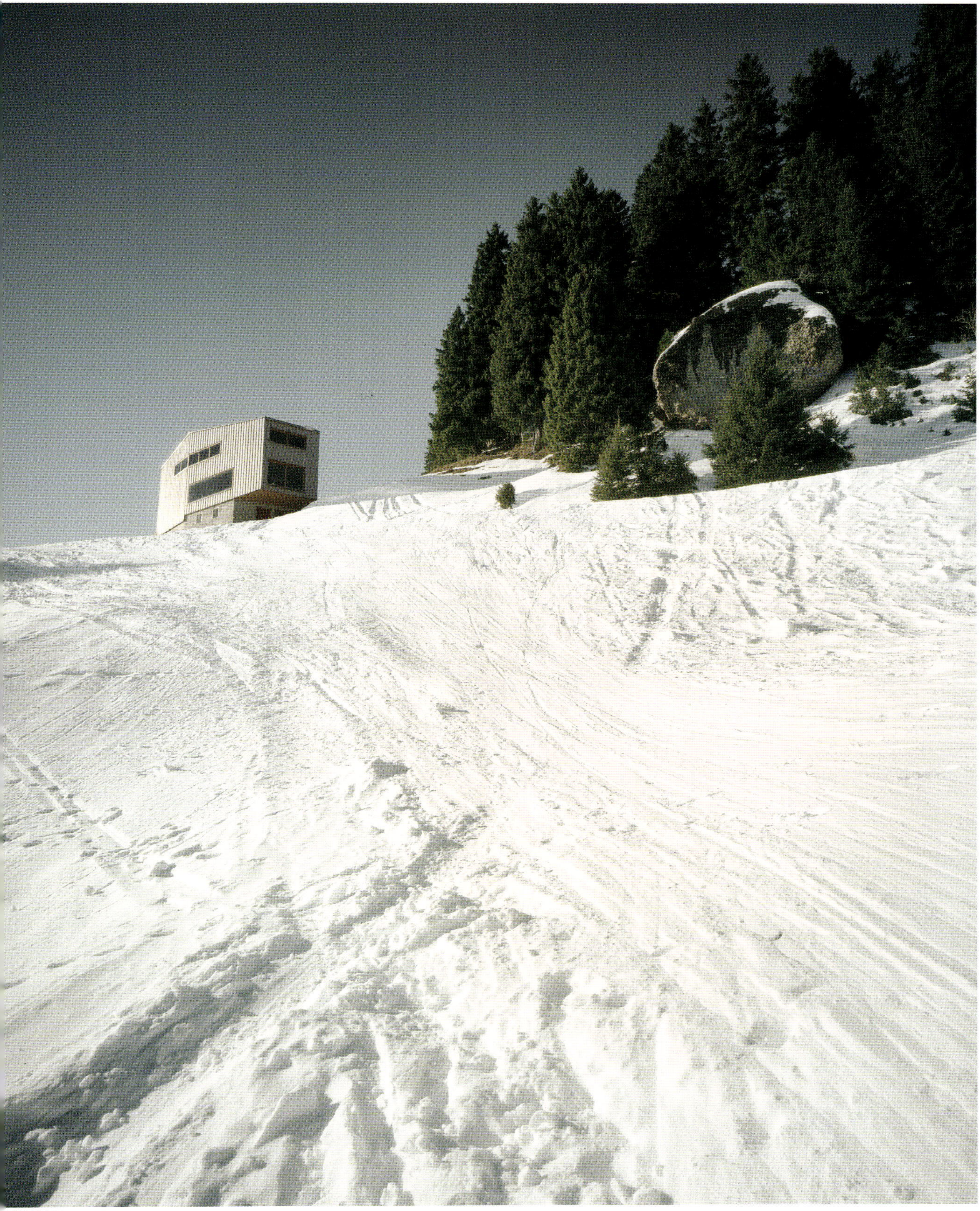

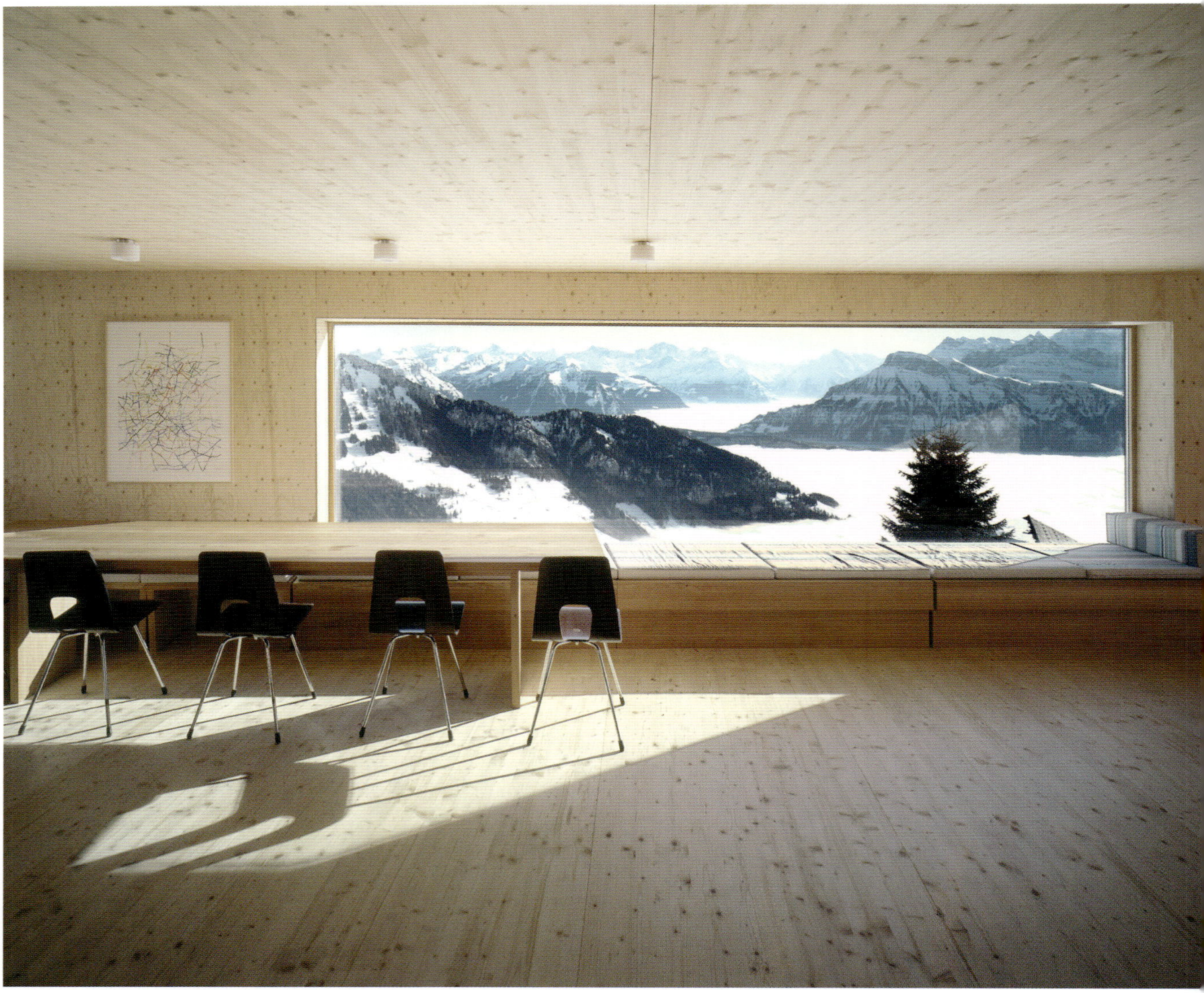

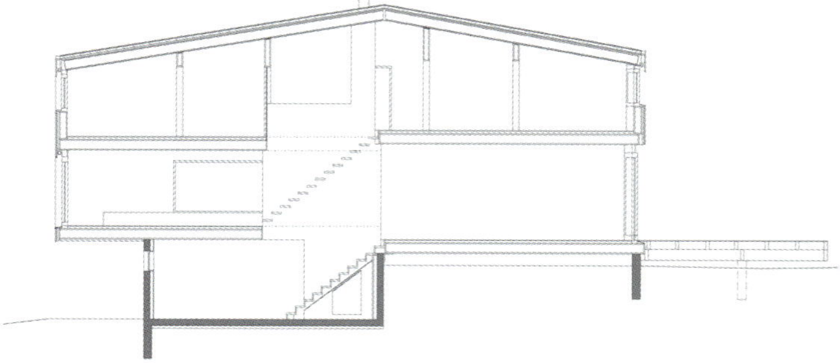

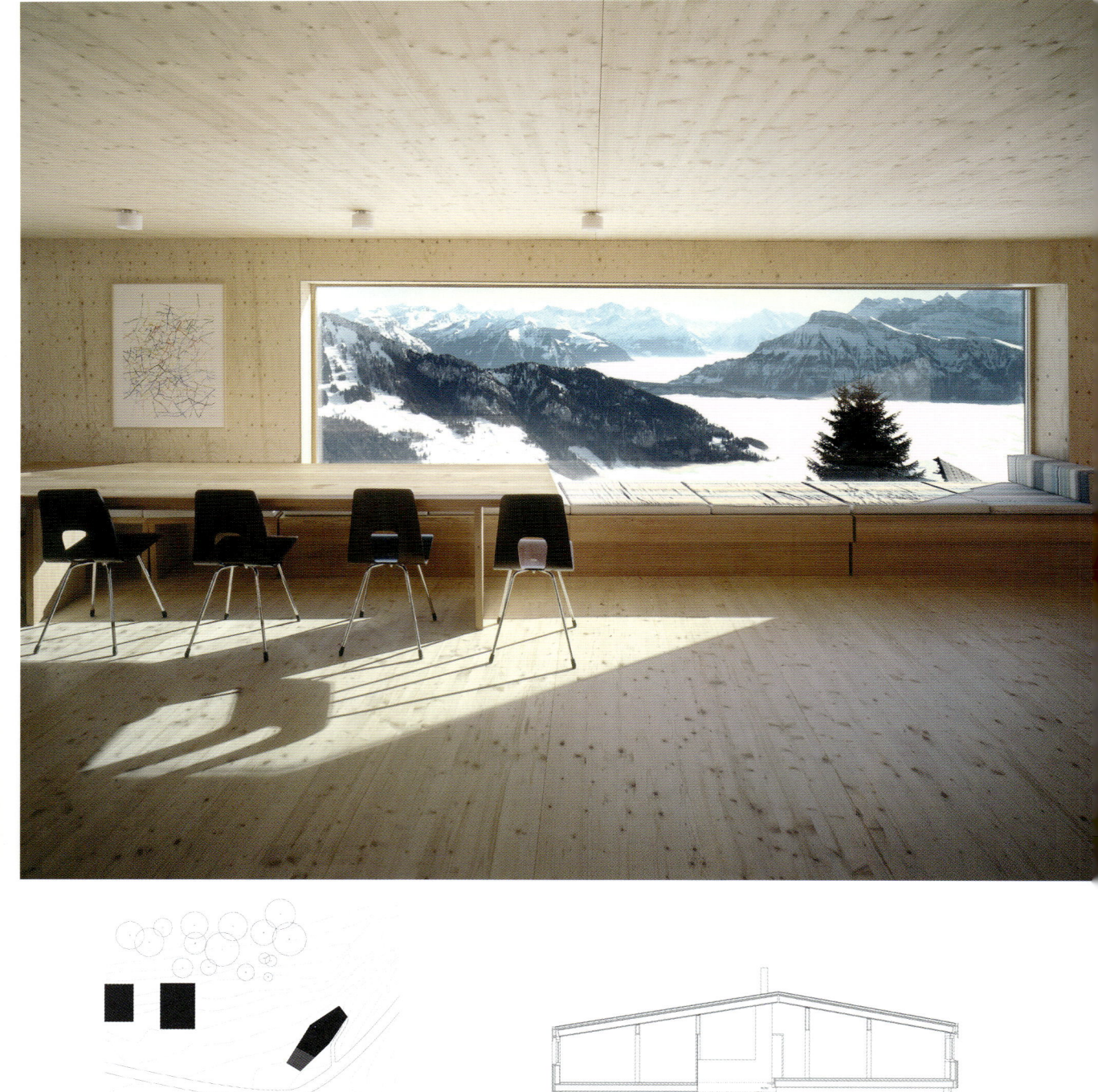

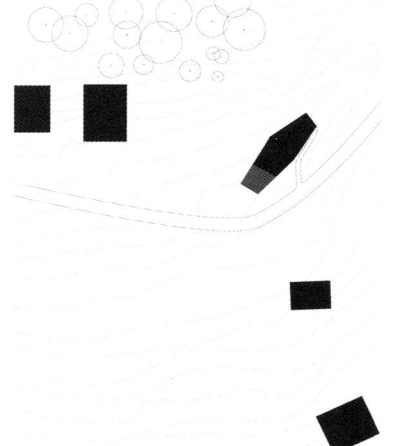

南面のテラスからは美しいアルプスの景色が一望できる。その眺望は、住居を崖に固定しているコンクリート基礎の上に突き出した、中空に持ち上げられている板張りデッキを越えて伸展していく。主入り口はその反対側にある。

The terrace on the south flank enjoys beautiful Alpine views, extending over a wooden deck suspended in mid-air and jutting out over the cement structure anchoring the residence to the cliff-side. On the other side, we find the main entrance.

ラ・レセルバの住宅
灼熱に耐える外皮

LA RESERVA HOUSE
Skin against the heat

セバスチャン・イラリャズバル
撮影：カルロス・エギグレン

SEBASTIÁN IRARRÁZAVAL
PHOTO: © Carlos Eguiguren

ラ・レセルバ、コリーナ、サンチアゴ・デ・チリ ― チリ ― 2006

　モジュラー住宅の建築手法を取り入れ、住宅は2個の角柱を直交させた形で造られた。コストは低く抑えられ、外皮の赤錆の色がフォルムによく調和して、ラ・レセルバの乾燥した荒々しい地形に融け込んでいる。建物は、比喩的に言うならば、この地の厳しい気候に真っ向から勝負せず、本題をそれたところで議論しながら、それをうまく利用している。地上4mの高さに持ち上げられた長尺の建物に起こることが予想される反響音を防ぐため、目地を広く取った板張りの吊り下げ天井や、天井・壁の下地にウールを詰め込むなどの音響対策が取られた。

With a cross-patterned floor plan, moderate cost and a structure based on modular architecture schematics, this house plays with rusty red colors on its exterior so that it may adapt to its dry and rural La Reserva surroundings. Metaphorically, the building makes avail of the climate's rigors as if engaged in a digressive argument. Certain acoustic measures have been taken to lessen reverberations that may occur in large square edifices over 13 feet high, such as a drop ceiling (interior) made of separate boards and filled with wool inside to serve as noise proofing.

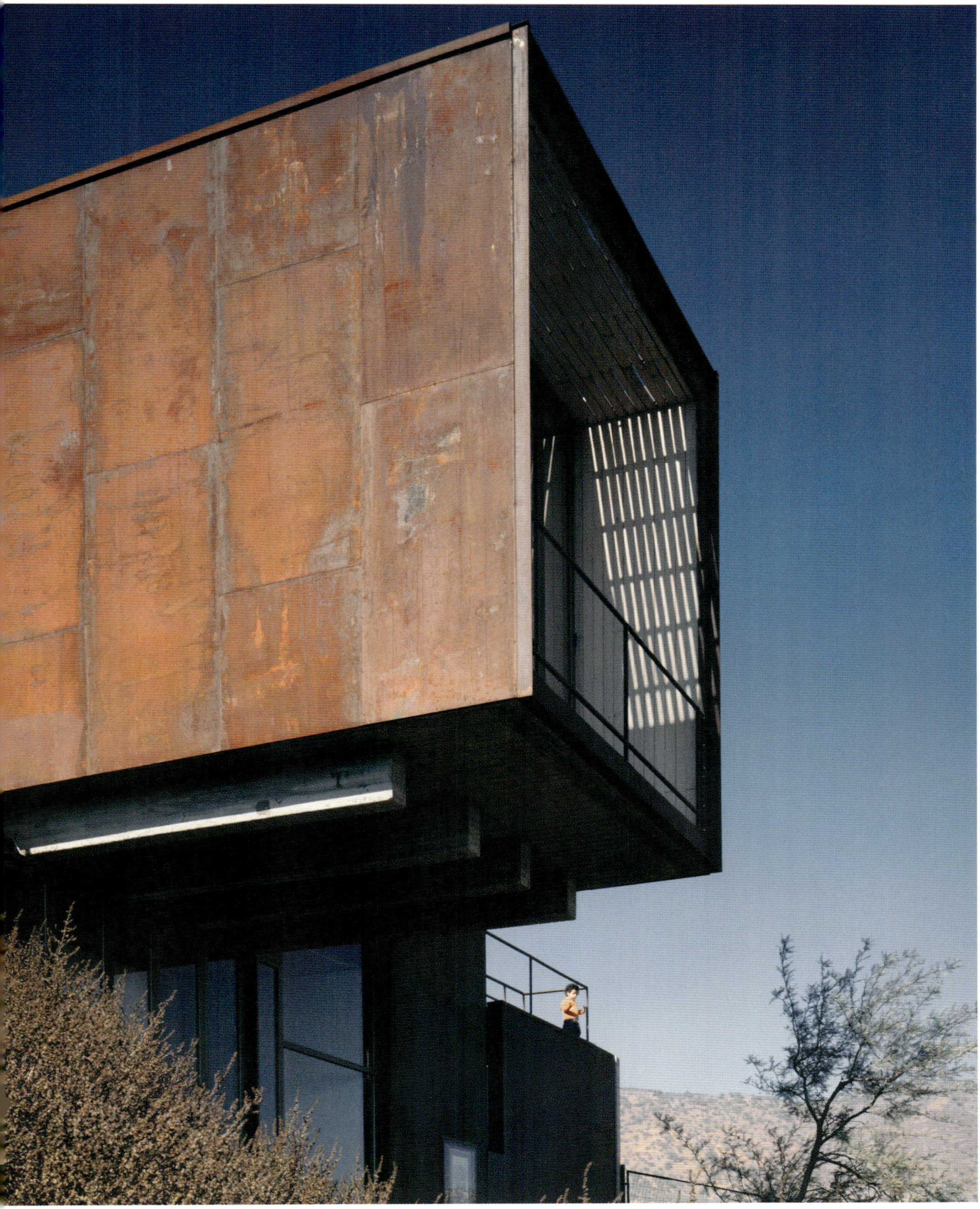

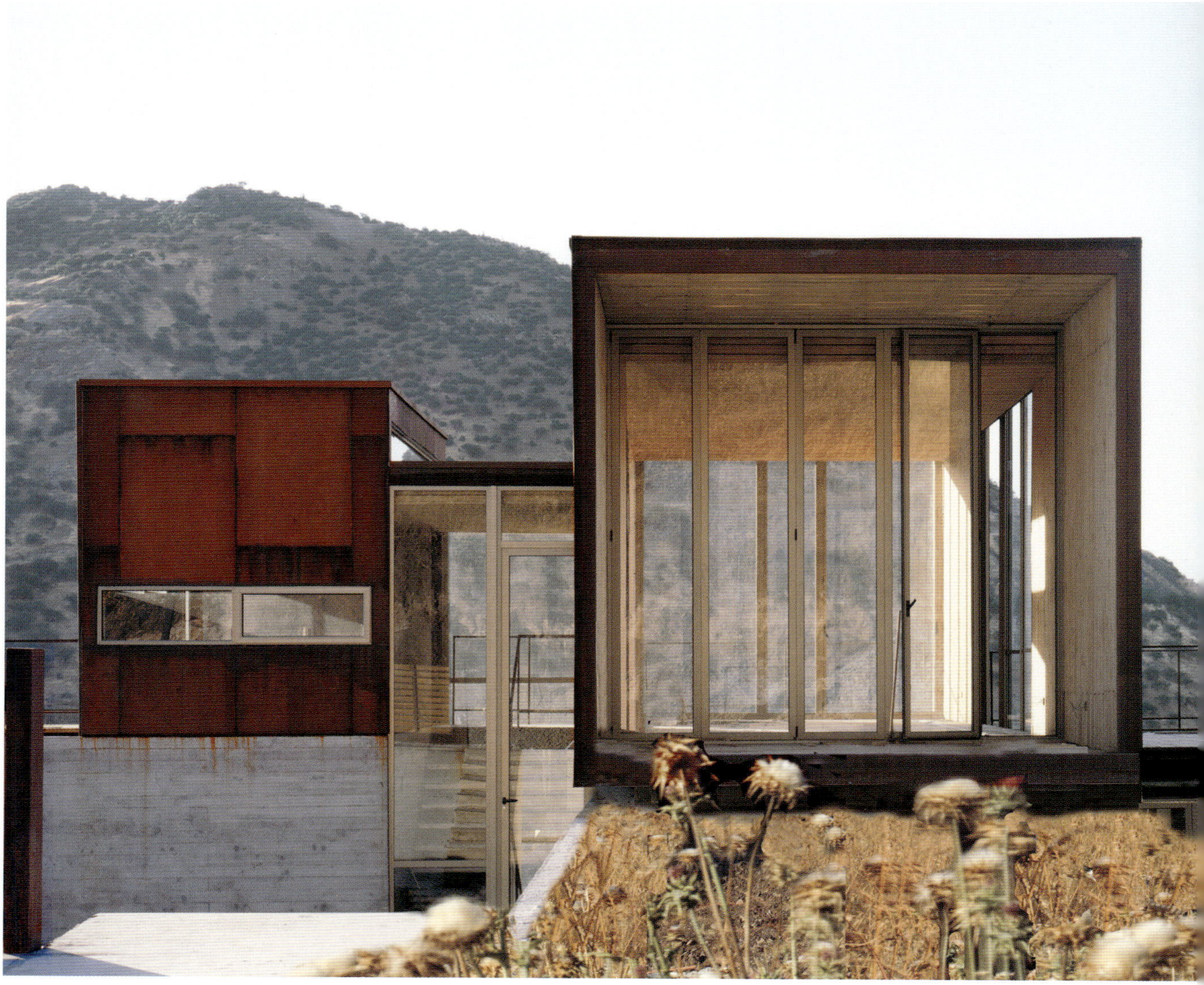

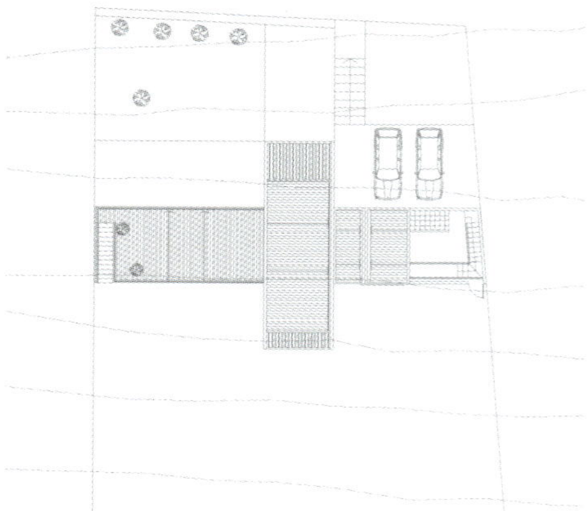

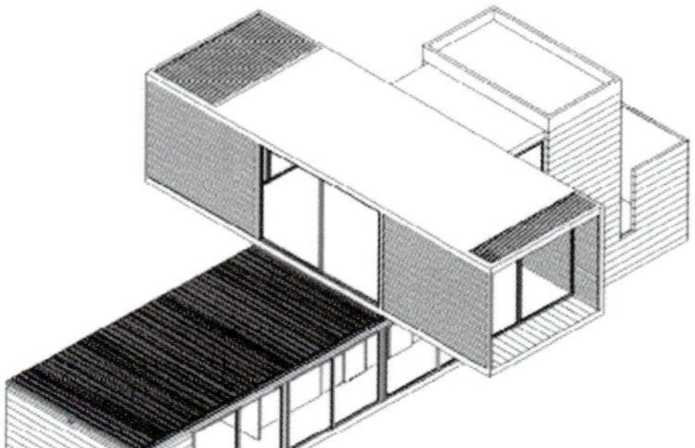

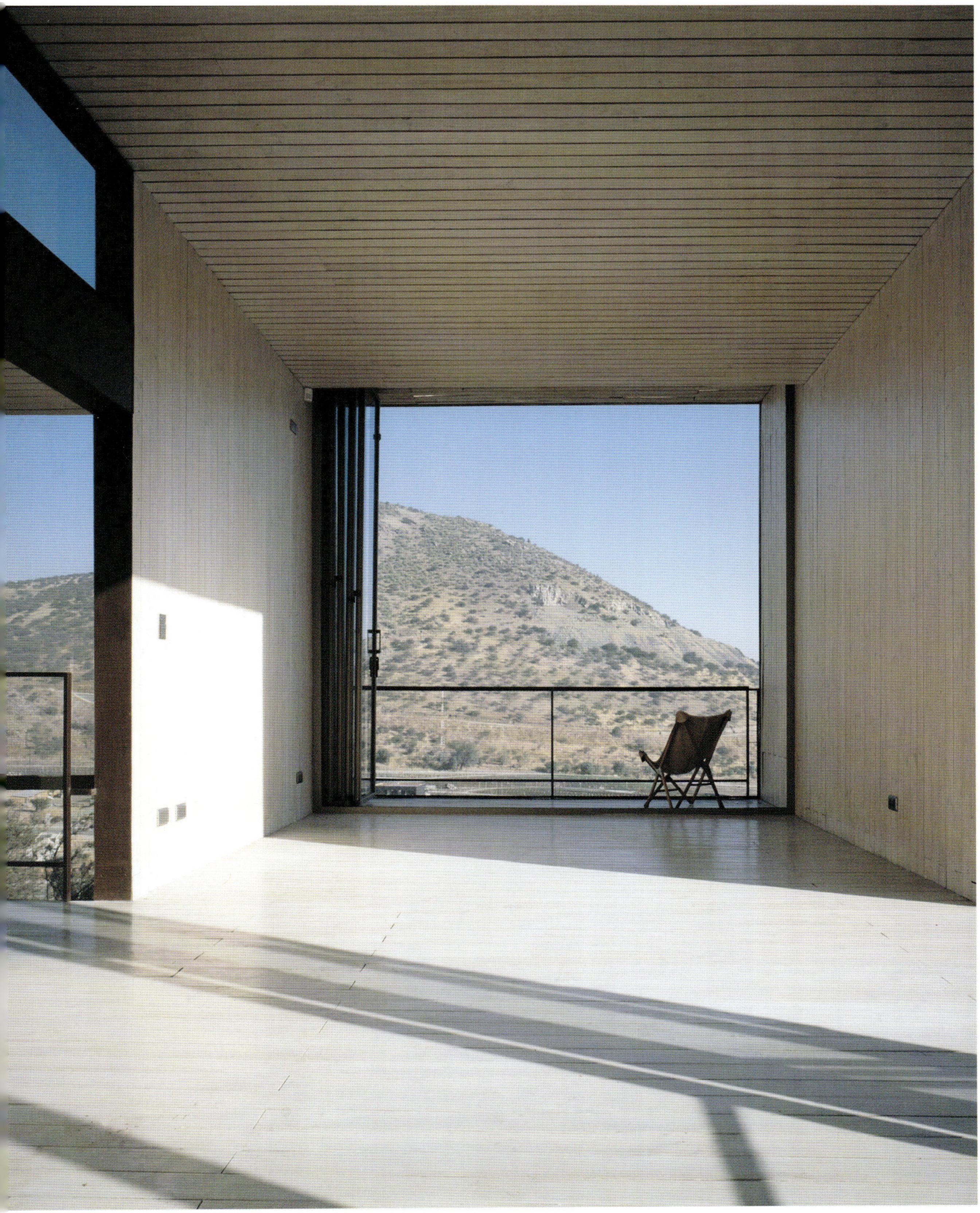

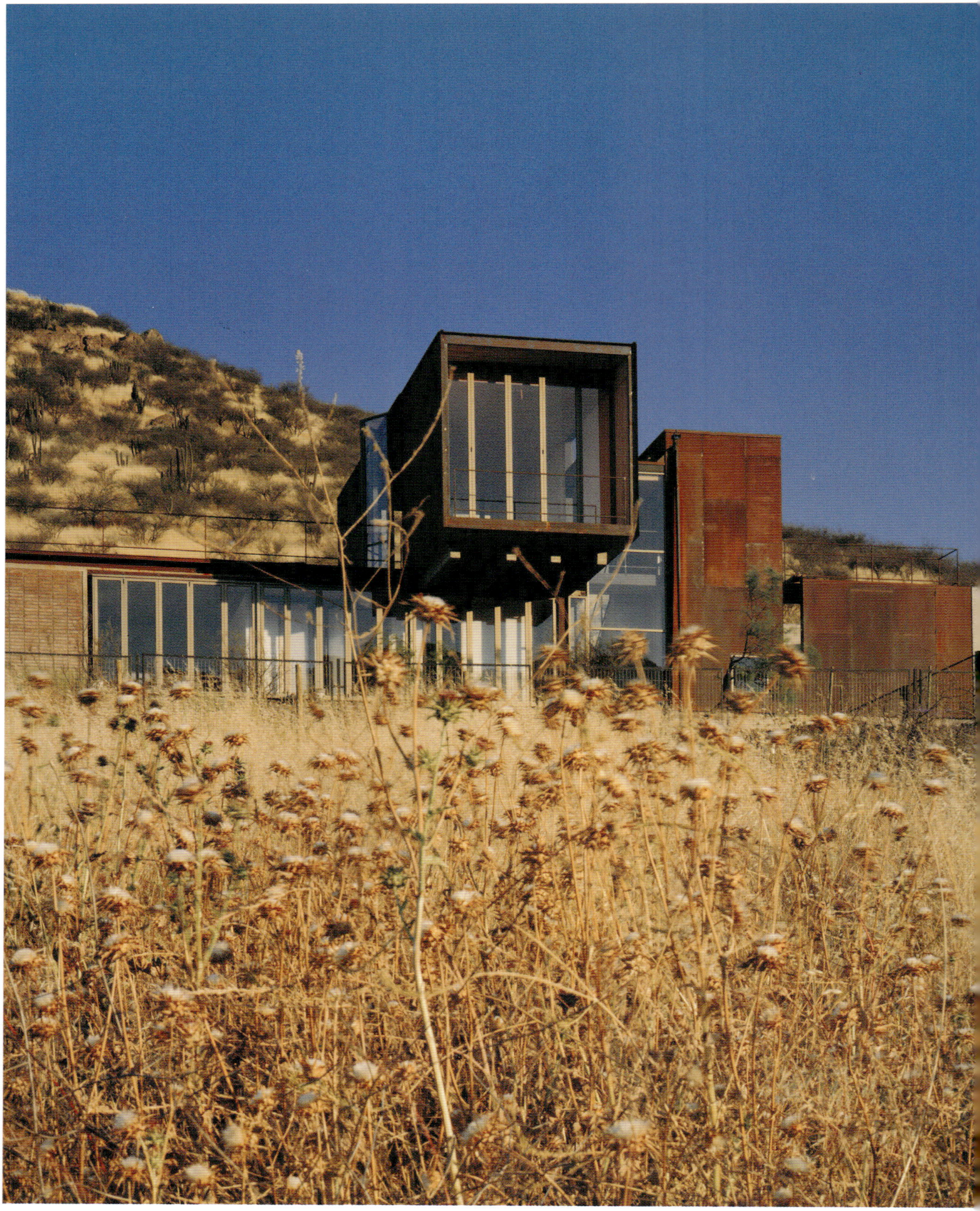

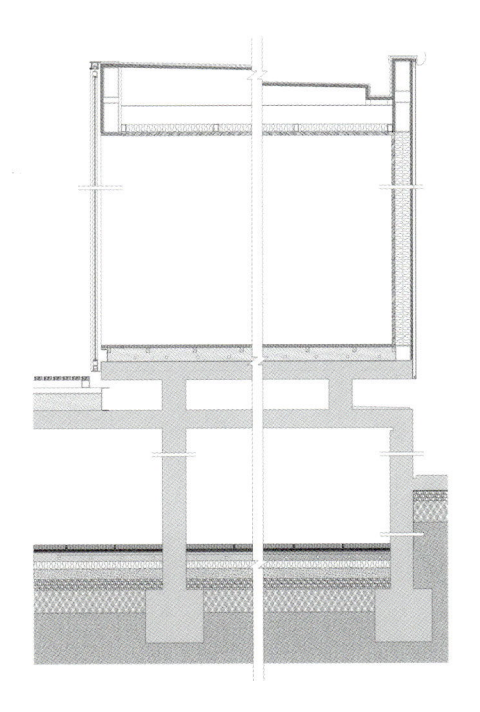

外皮の酸化鉄パネルは熱せられると温度は上昇するが、二重壁になっているため、空気対流が起こり、断熱隔壁となって内側の壁を冷やす効果がある。このようにしてこの住宅は、この地の灼熱の気候から自分自身を守っている。

The steel oxide panels make up a double-sided wall that can heat up and, once air is moved, create an insulating chamber, cooling the walls on the inside. This way the home can protect itself from the region's warm climate.

レンガウのロッジ
地形を克服して

ジョン・ジェニングス／ドライ・デザイン
撮影：アンディーヌ・ブロール

LENGAU LODGE
Refuge in the reserve

JOHN JENNINGS/DRY DESIGN
PHOTO: © Undine Prohl

バールウォーター、リンポポ州 — 南アフリカ共和国 — 2004

　幾分かは土着の建築から発想を得ながら、この住宅の哲学は、自然保護区に対する影響を最小限に止めるということで一貫している。ごみ処理、水の給排水はすべて施設内で行い、太陽光も能動的（太陽光発電パネル）に、あるいは受動的（建物の方角）に活用されている。自生植物の保護には最大の注意が払われ、建設中も地盤の掘削は行われなかった。敷地全体は、獰猛な番犬を置く代わりに、電気防護柵で守られている。砂岩の岩盤の上に形成されたこの辺りの地層に合わせて、この建物も砂岩の質感を基本にして建てられている。

The idea is partly inspired by vernacular architecture, the philosophy of making the smallest possible impact on a protected natural terrain. Waste and water are treated in situ, the use of sunlight is both active (solar panels) and passive (orientation); native vegetation is respected and no land movement occurred during construction.
The property was electrified as a measure of protection in lieu of the savage fauna. The geology in the area, formed by a sandstone foundation, gives the base of the buildings texture.

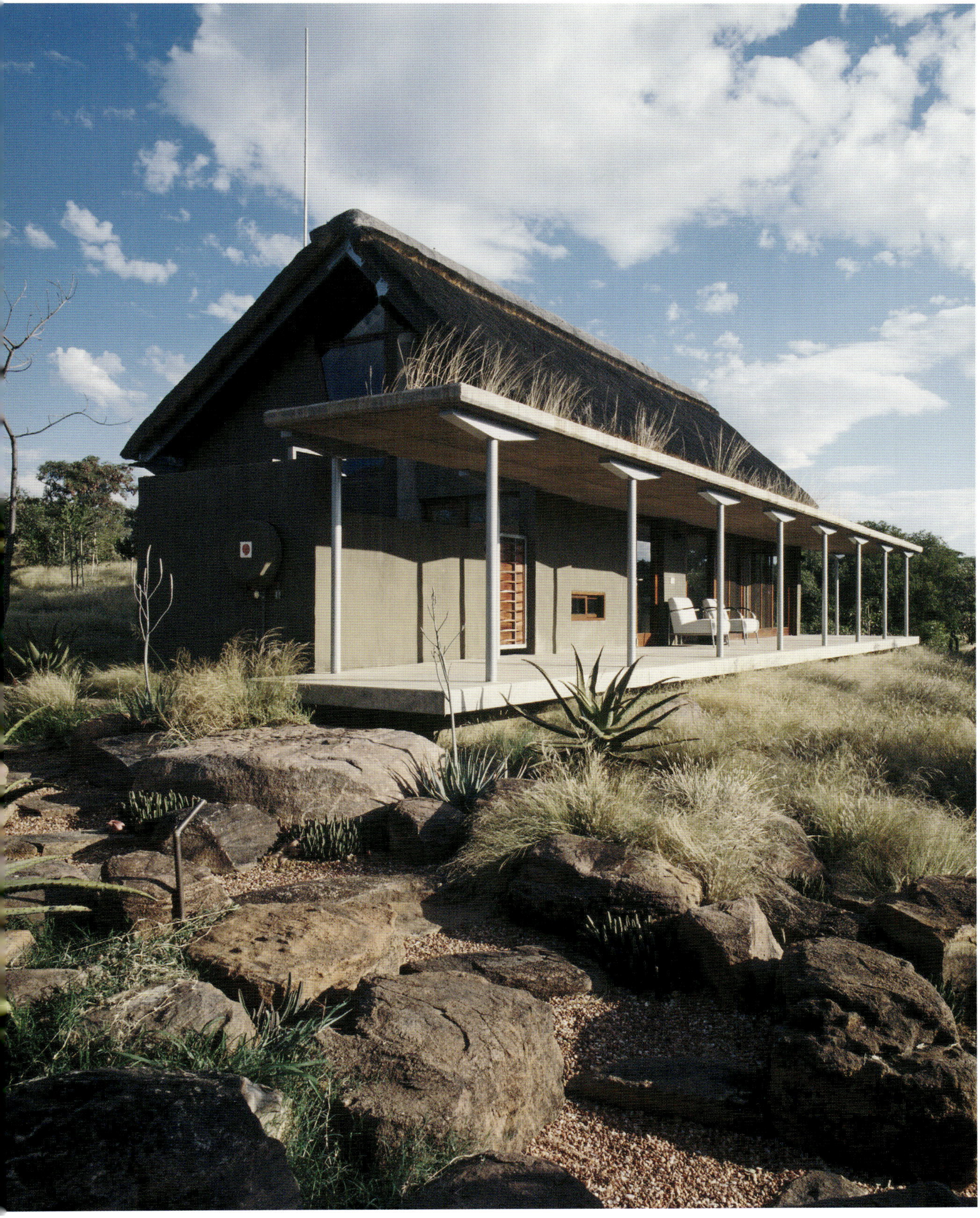

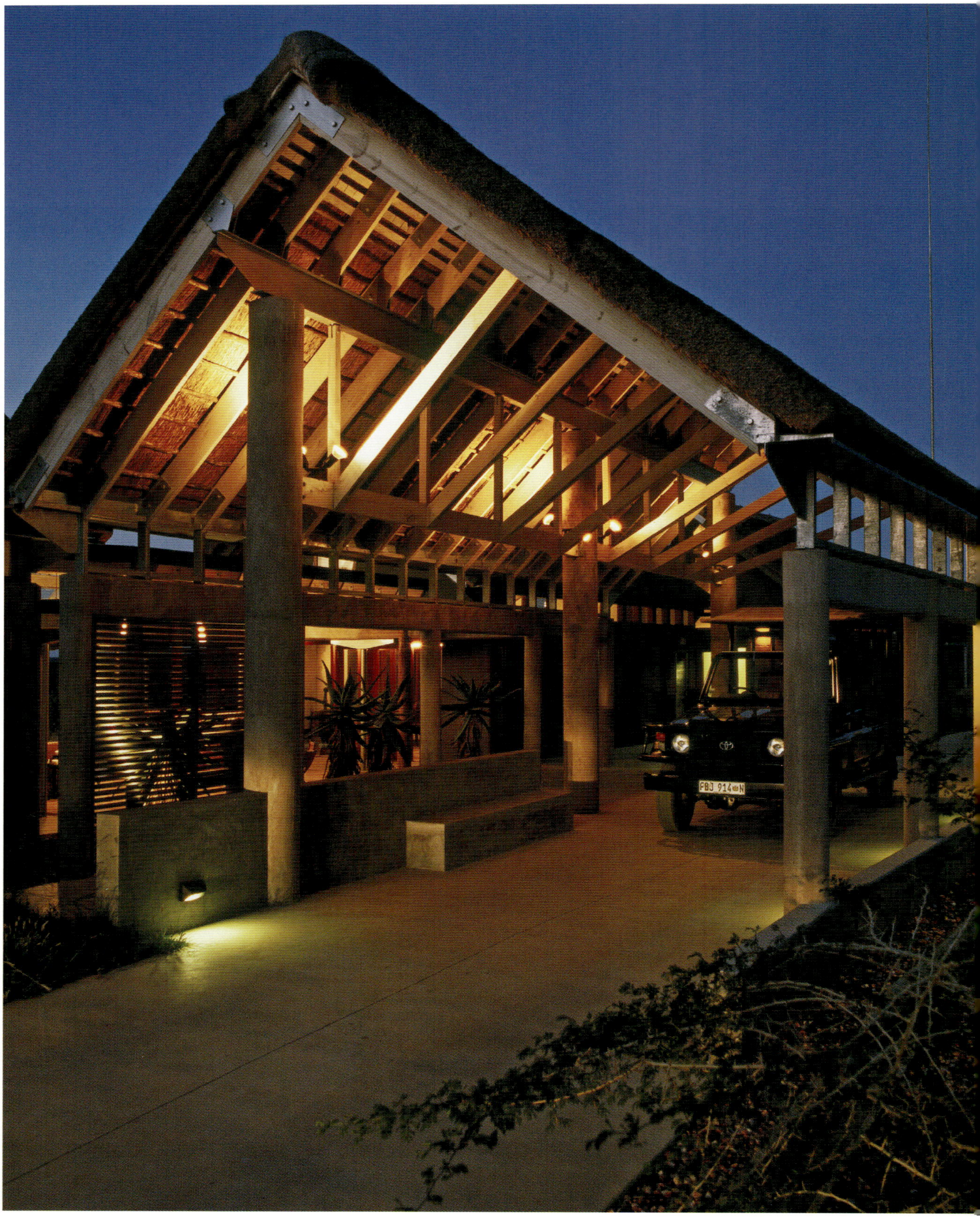

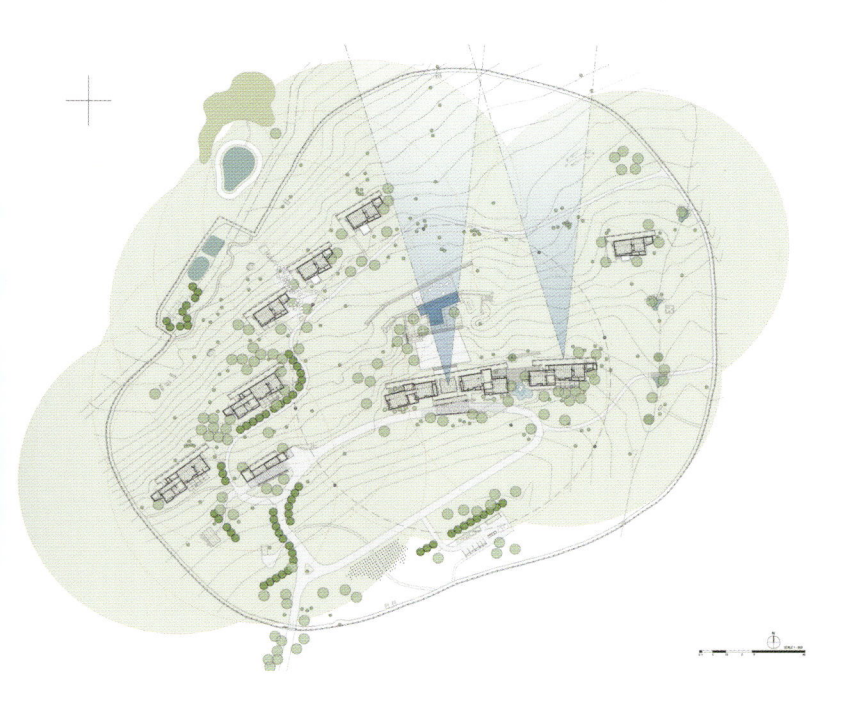

ドライ・デザインによって設計された9つの建物によって、5戸のシェルターからなる1区画が構成されているが、各区画は500haの敷地を持つ。通路と壁は、石灰岩、砂利、堆積岩などすべて地元産出の材料を用いている。

The nine buildings planned by Dry Design form part of a group of 5 shelters, with 500 hectares for each group. The paths and walls incorporate local natural elements, like limestone, gravel and sediment.

ベッドルームとして設計された5戸のシェルターには、それぞれ屋外シャワーが備えられている。すべてのシェルターが高台にあるという利点を最大限に生かして、ヨハネスブルクから車でわずか3時間の、この自然保護区の雄大なワイルドライフを存分に味わえるように設計されている。

Each one of the 5 shelters planned as bedrooms has its own open-air shower. They make avail of elevated areas that serve as scenic view-points of this nature reserve situated 3 hours from Johannesburg.

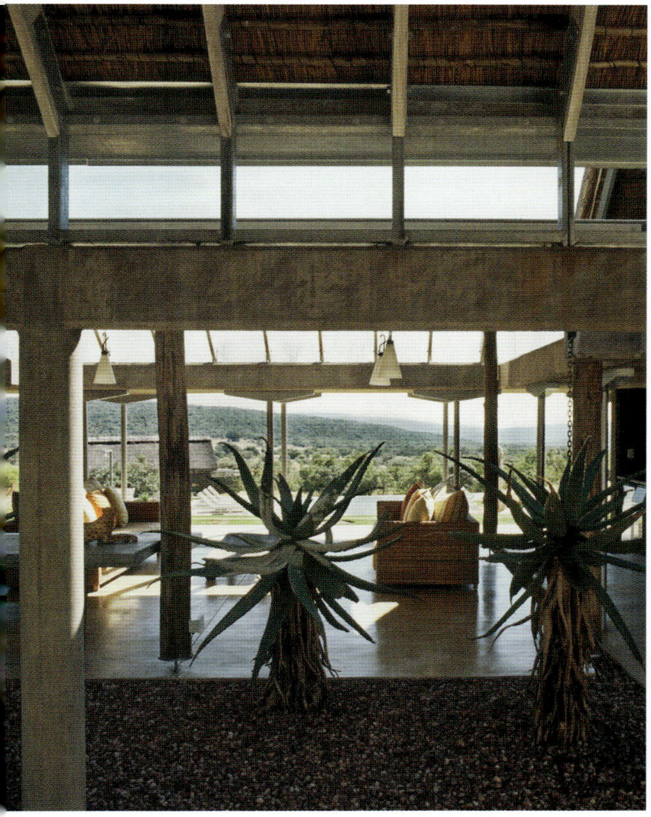
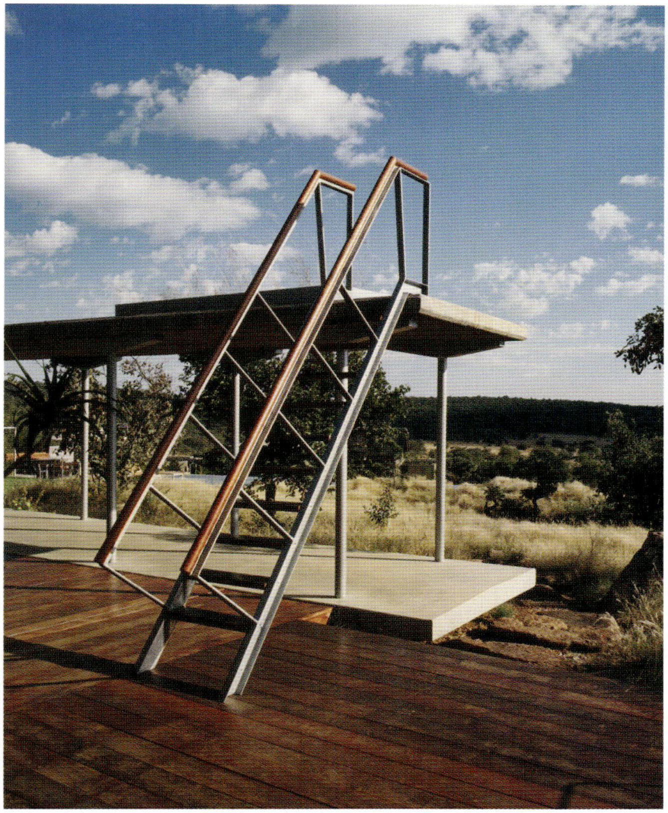
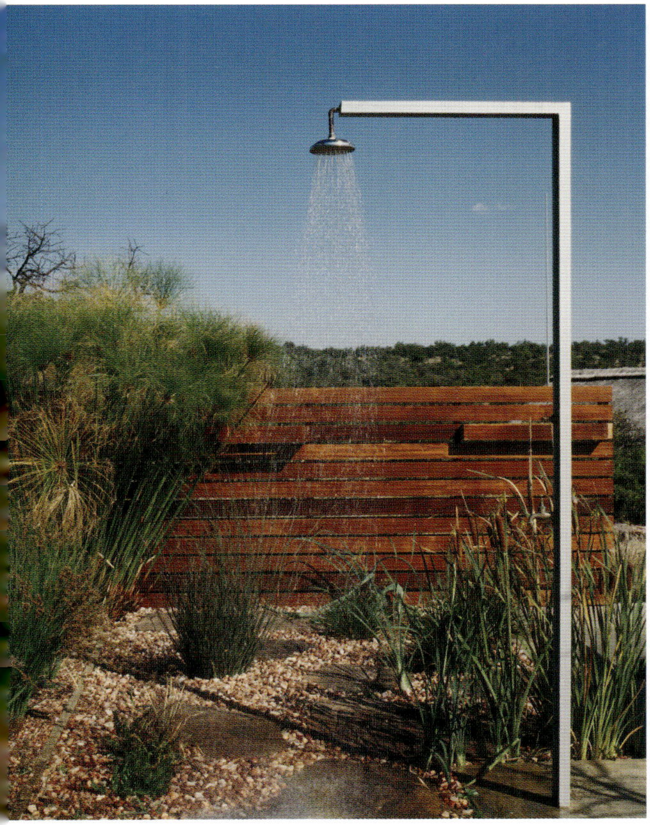
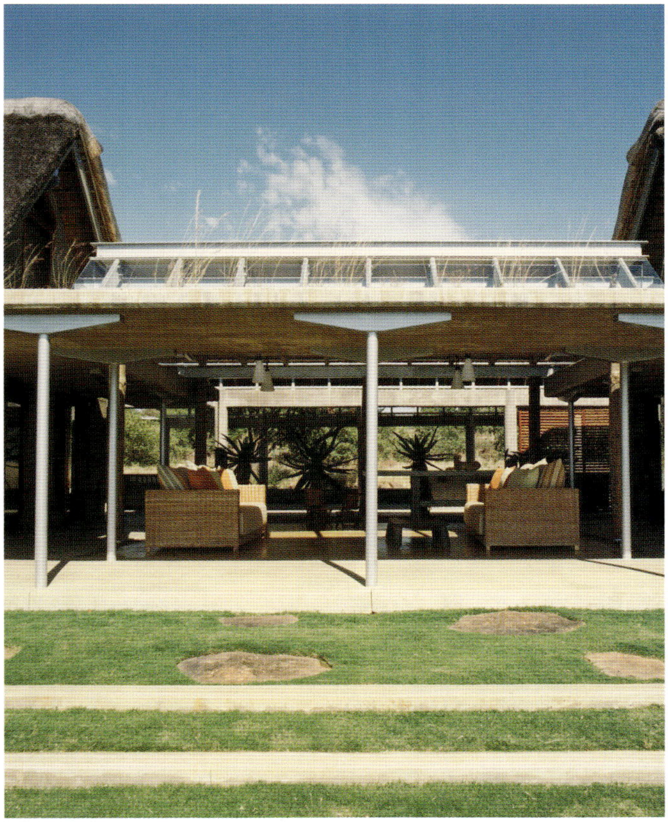

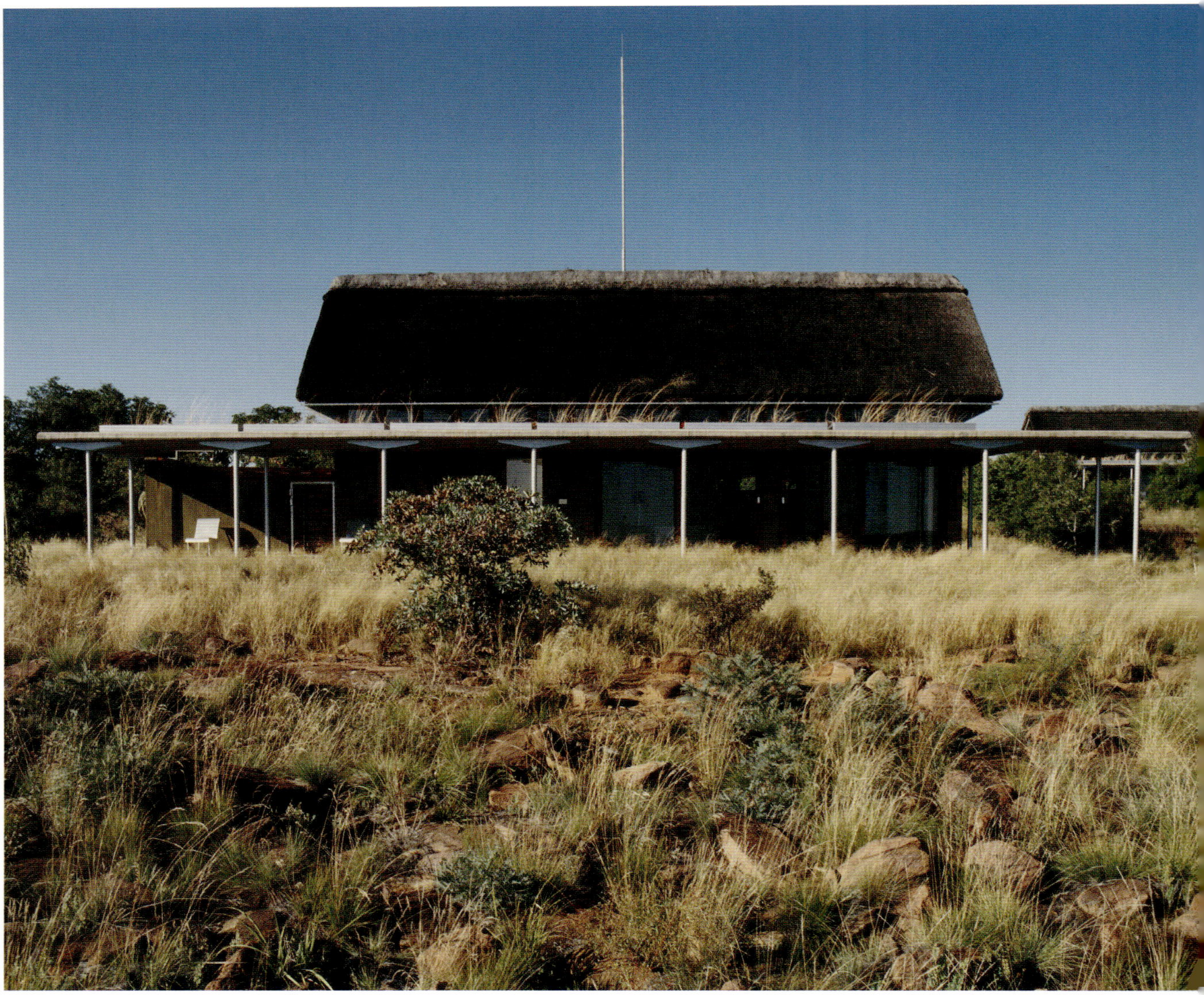

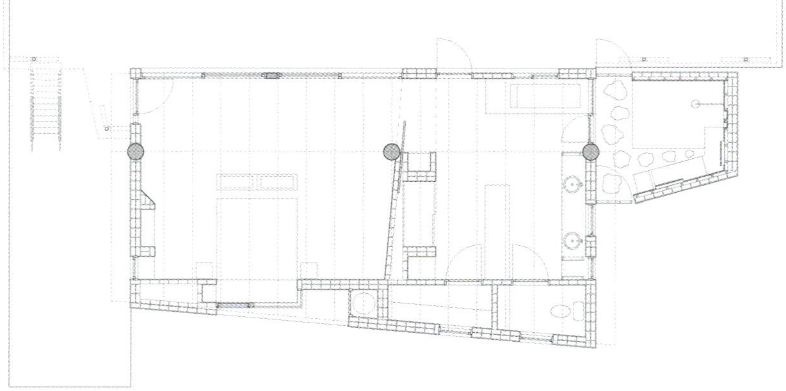

屋根は地元産出の木材を使った小屋組みの上をかや葺きにしているが、そのかや葺は15〜25年は持つと想定されている。この屋根は断熱効果が高く、雨水を分流するのに適している。セメントのポーチの上には、地元の植物が植えられている。

The roofs were raised upon this wood and straw structure calculated to last 15-25 years and act as thermal insulation and rain diverter. Above the cement porches, they planted local herbaceous plants.

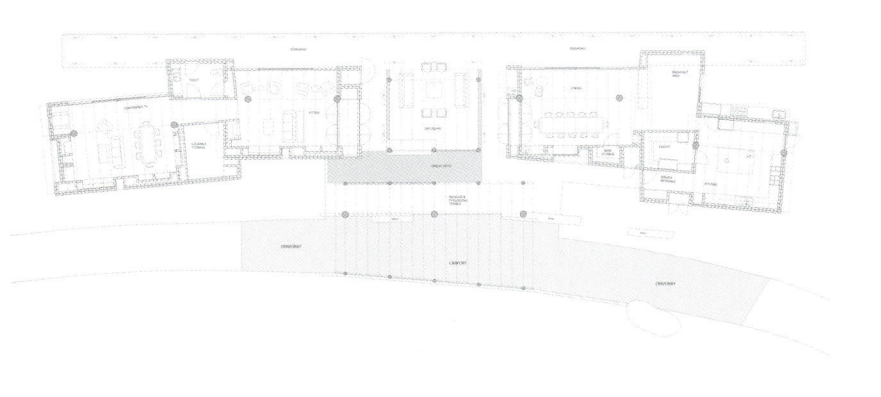

ストーン・ハウス
生気候学的勾配
バイオクライマティック

STONE HOUSE
The bio-climatic slope

三分一 博志 建築設計事務所
撮影：平井 広行

SAMBUICHI ARCHITECTS
PHOTO: © Hiroyuki Hirai

島根県 — 日本 — 2005

　礫石の小山に半分埋もれた住宅は、生気候学的設計がもたらす優位性を最大限生かしながら、建築の主な露出部分である広い木の屋根構造を大地から持ち上げるように出現している。夏、風は花崗岩の礫石の隙間で濾過冷却され、屋根に設けられた空間を通り抜けながら、各室の開口部を通して高温と多湿を和らげる。冬の降雪期には、綿密に計算された礫石積みの勾配のおかげで、雪はかまくらのような断熱層としての役割を果たす。

As if half-buried, this home seems to emerge from the ground with an ample wood roof as its principal appeal, taking full advantage of the virtues that stem from its bio-climatic design. Thanks to the openings in the rooms, wind can pass through these spaces, alleviating the high temperatures and humidity of the summer as it filters through the pulverized granite and the spaces made in the roof. During the winter snowfall, precipitation accumulates on these slopes, which serves as a layer of insulation.

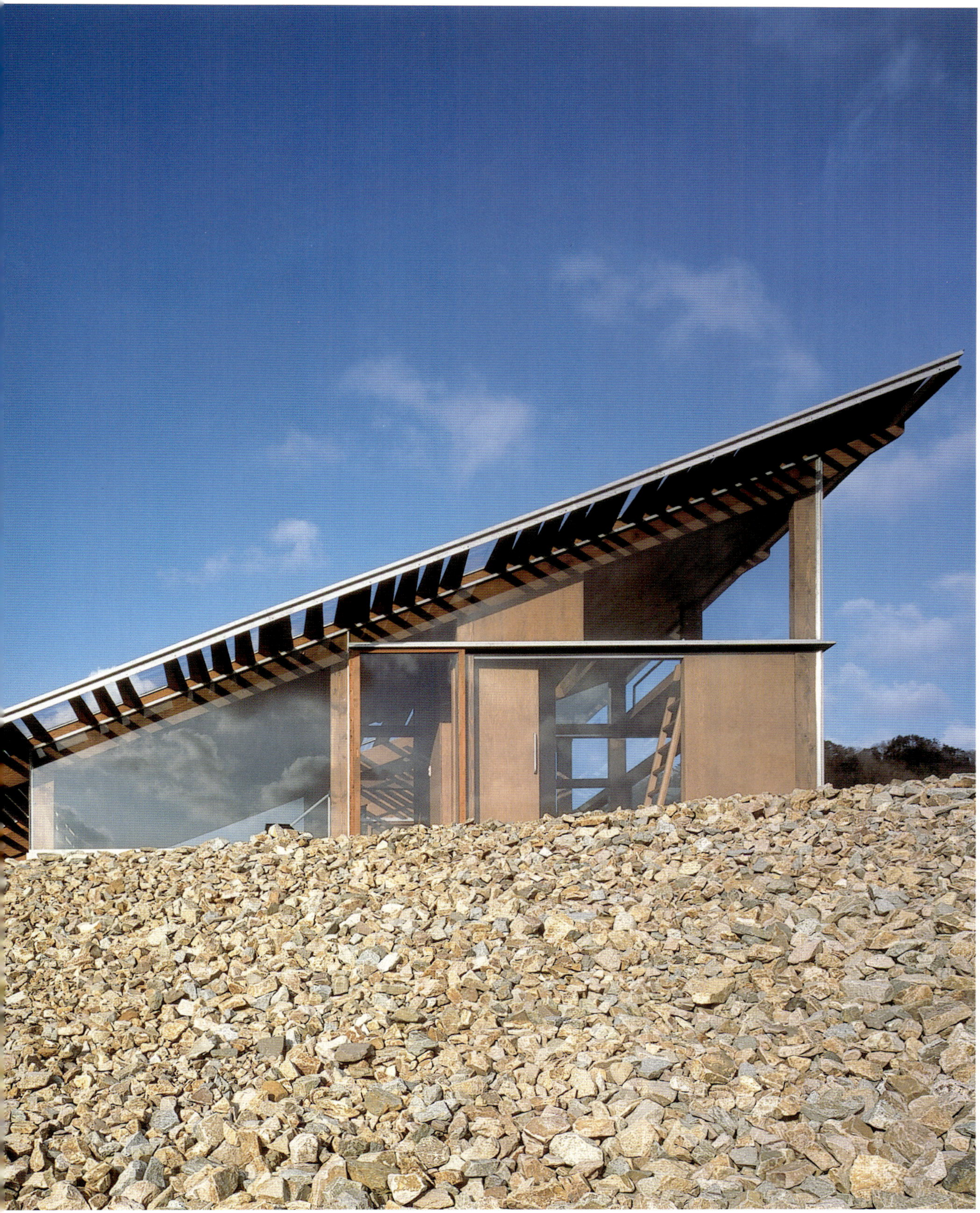

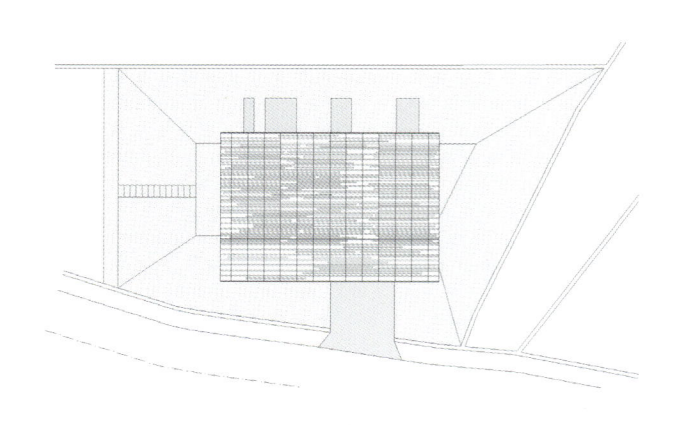

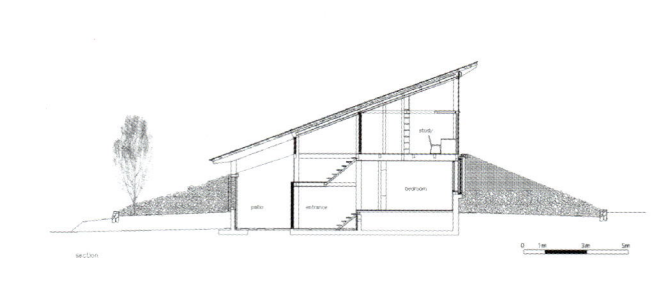

102 建 築
Architecture

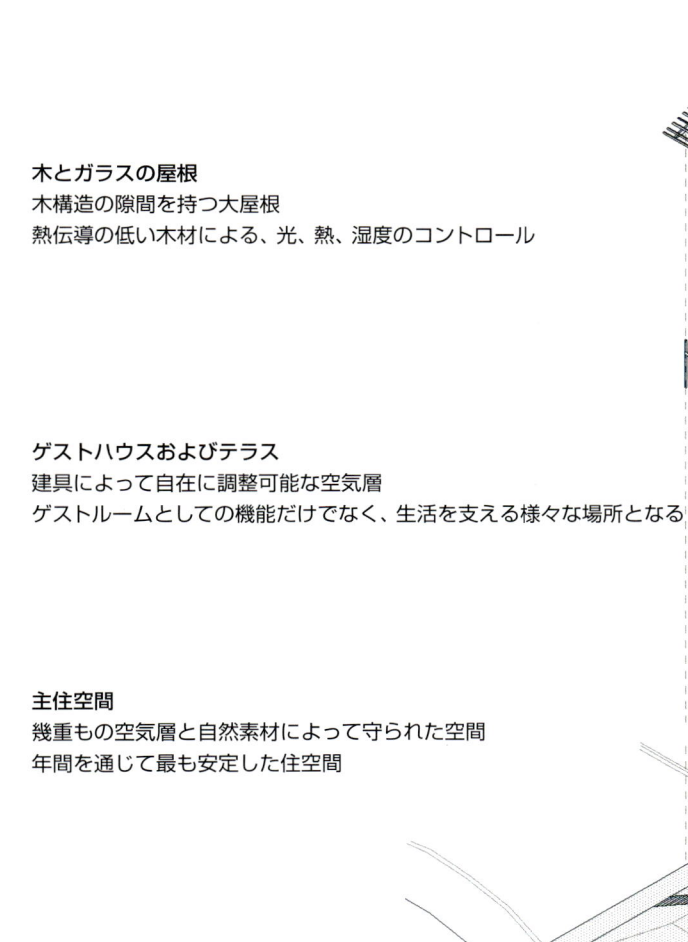

木とガラスの屋根
木構造の隙間を持つ大屋根
熱伝導の低い木材による、光、熱、湿度のコントロール

ゲストハウスおよびテラス
建具によって自在に調整可能な空気層
ゲストルームとしての機能だけでなく、生活を支える様々な場所となる

主住空間
幾重もの空気層と自然素材によって守られた空間
年間を通じて最も安定した住空間

空気と石の庭
砕石間の空気層

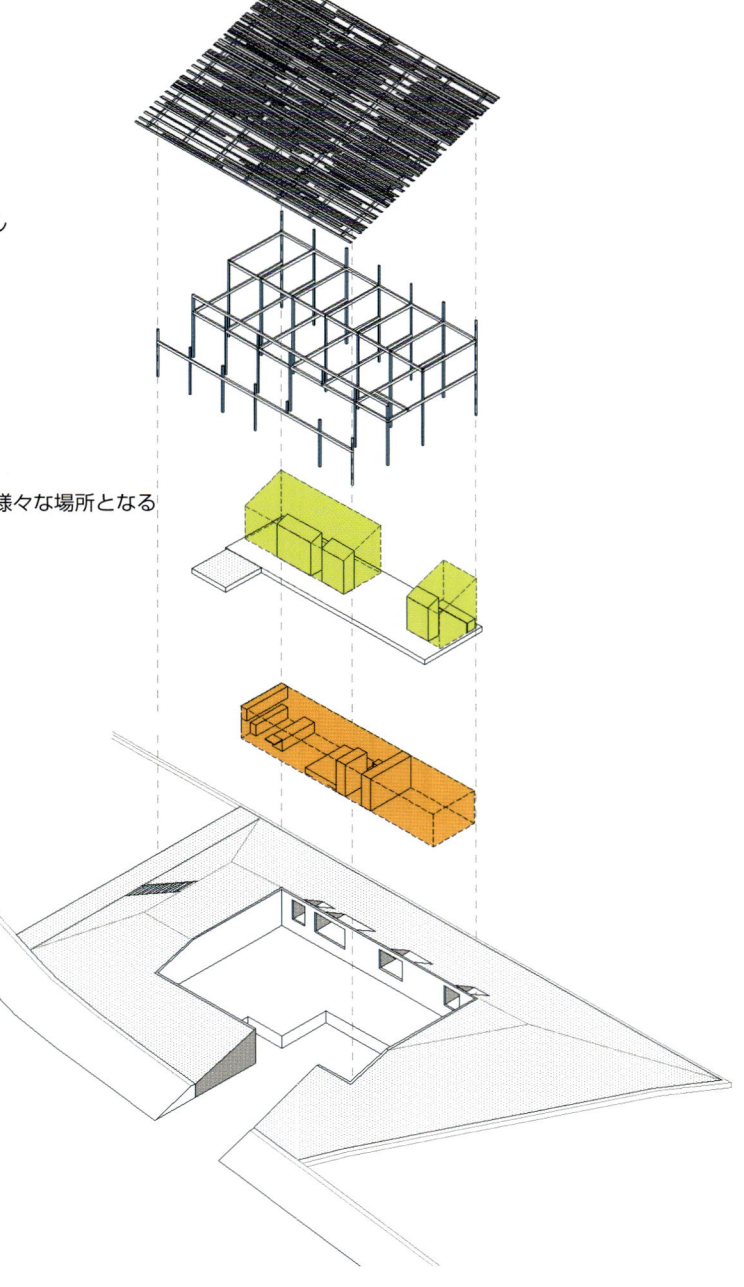

夏／開口＋砕石間空気層
木のドアと窓を開けると、
風は上層、下層とも全室を通り抜ける。
さらに木の屋根構造の隙間と砕石の隙間による
通風によって、高温多湿を和らげる。

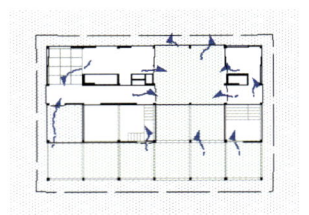

section
横断面図

upper floor / guest house
上層／ゲストハウス

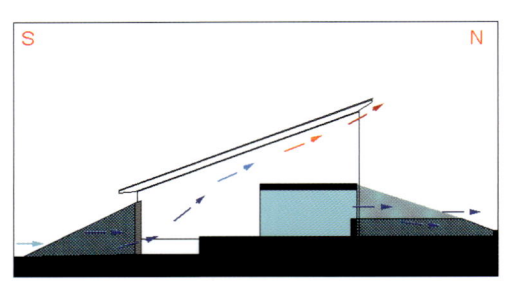

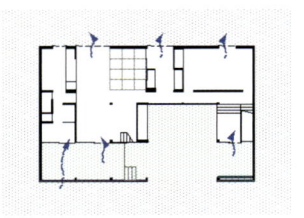

lower floor / main house
下層／主住空間

冬／閉めた状態
木のドアと窓を閉めると、
上層全体は下層主住空間のための空気層となる。
また砕石の上に雪が積もると、
それはかまくらのような空気の断熱層を形成する。
こうして下層の主住空間は、
幾重もの空気の層に覆われた空間となる。

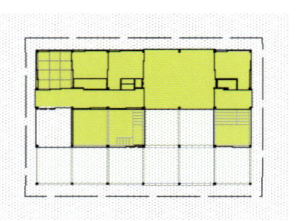

section
横断面図

upper floor / guest house
上層／ゲストハウス

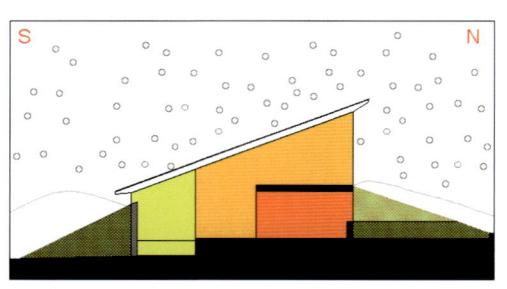

lower floor / main house
下層／主住空間

下層は家族のための住空間で、上層はゲストハウスとなっている。建築家は自然素材の可能性を最大限引き出しながら配置し、年間を通して快適な住空間を創造した。

The owners live on the bottom floor, while the top floor is reserved for visitors. The architect makes use of a natural material (stone) and its studied arrangement to properly acclimatize the rooms year round.

ヒュッテの家
環境効率の高い格納庫

スタジオNL-D
撮影：ハンズ・ヴァールマン／ヘクティク・ピクチャーズ

STUDIO NL-D
PHOTO: © Hans Werlemann/Hectic Pictures

HOUSE OF HUTS
The eco-efficient hangar

ブレダ ― オランダ ― 2006

　この地域に多く建てられているカタログ販売の廉価住宅に対するアンチテーゼとして、この先駆的住宅は、飛行場の格納庫から発想を得た独特の姿形だけでなく、環境効率の高い熱放射スキンによっても他と一線を画している。半円筒形のスチール製のスキン全体には、この構造体のために特に考案された最先端の冷暖房システムが張り巡らされている。構造体の重量が低く抑えられているため基礎は軽いものですみ、組立て工期も3ヵ月と従来のコンクリートやレンガの外壁と比べると格段に短く、優れたエネルギー効率を示している。

As an alternative to the economical homes sold in catalogues throughout the area, this prototype stands out for its physiognomy, which takes its inspiration from traditional airport hangars, and for its highly energy-efficient, heat-radiating walls. Its cooling system is distributed along the half-circle formed by the steel roof, an experimental system specifically conceived for this structure. The edifice's reduced weight allows for a light-weight foundation, and its quick assembly (3 months) represents significant savings in terms of construction time when compared to traditional cement or brick exteriors.

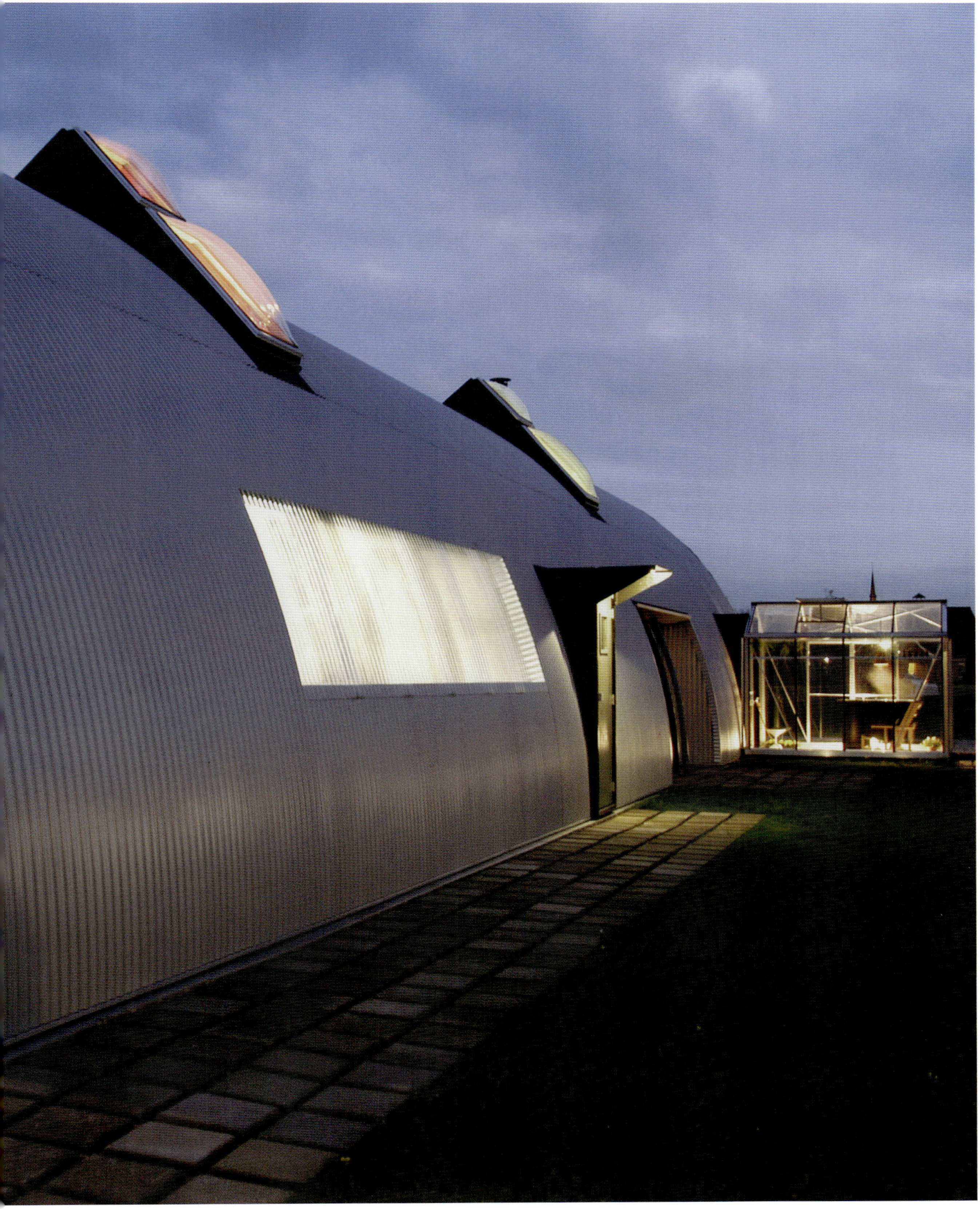

内壁とスチール波板のスキンの間に作られた隙間には、全長約1.8kmに達するビニル管が敷設され、冷暖房のための水を循環させている。南に面したガラス張りのファサードは、冬季は補助的な「受動」熱源として働く。

In the enclosure between the interior and exterior walls of this corrugated steel construction, almost 1.1 miles of piping brings water in for heating/refrigeration. A glass wall on the south side is an additional, "passive" heater during the winter.

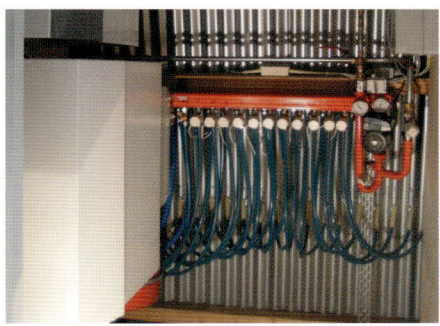

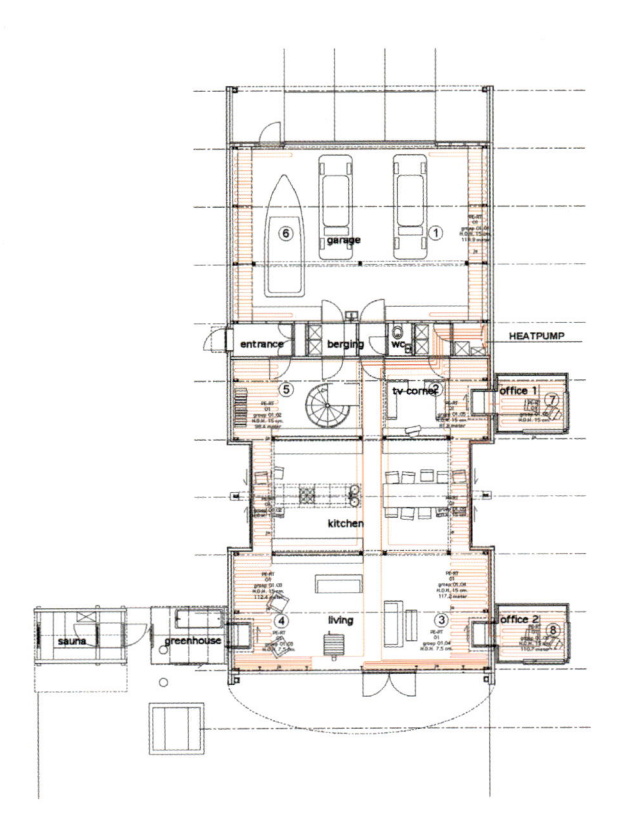

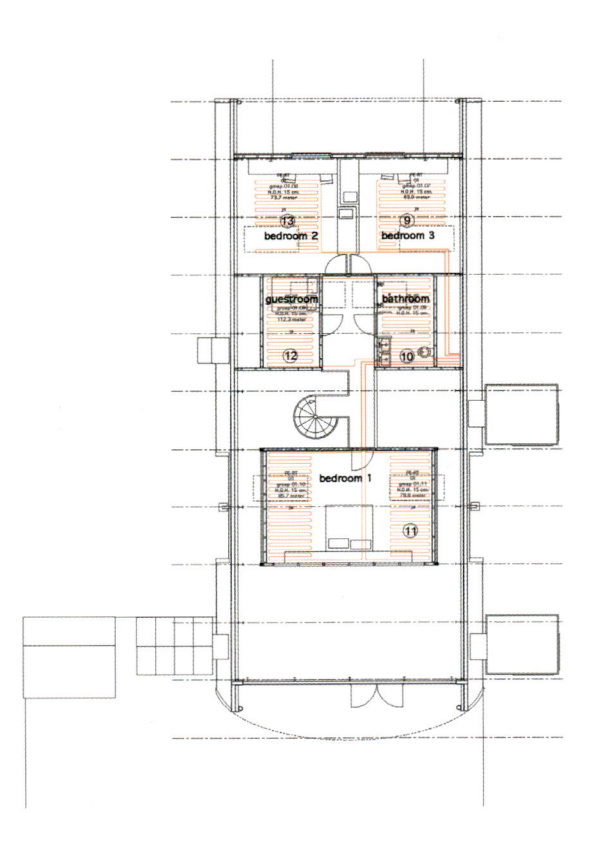

109 建築
Architecture

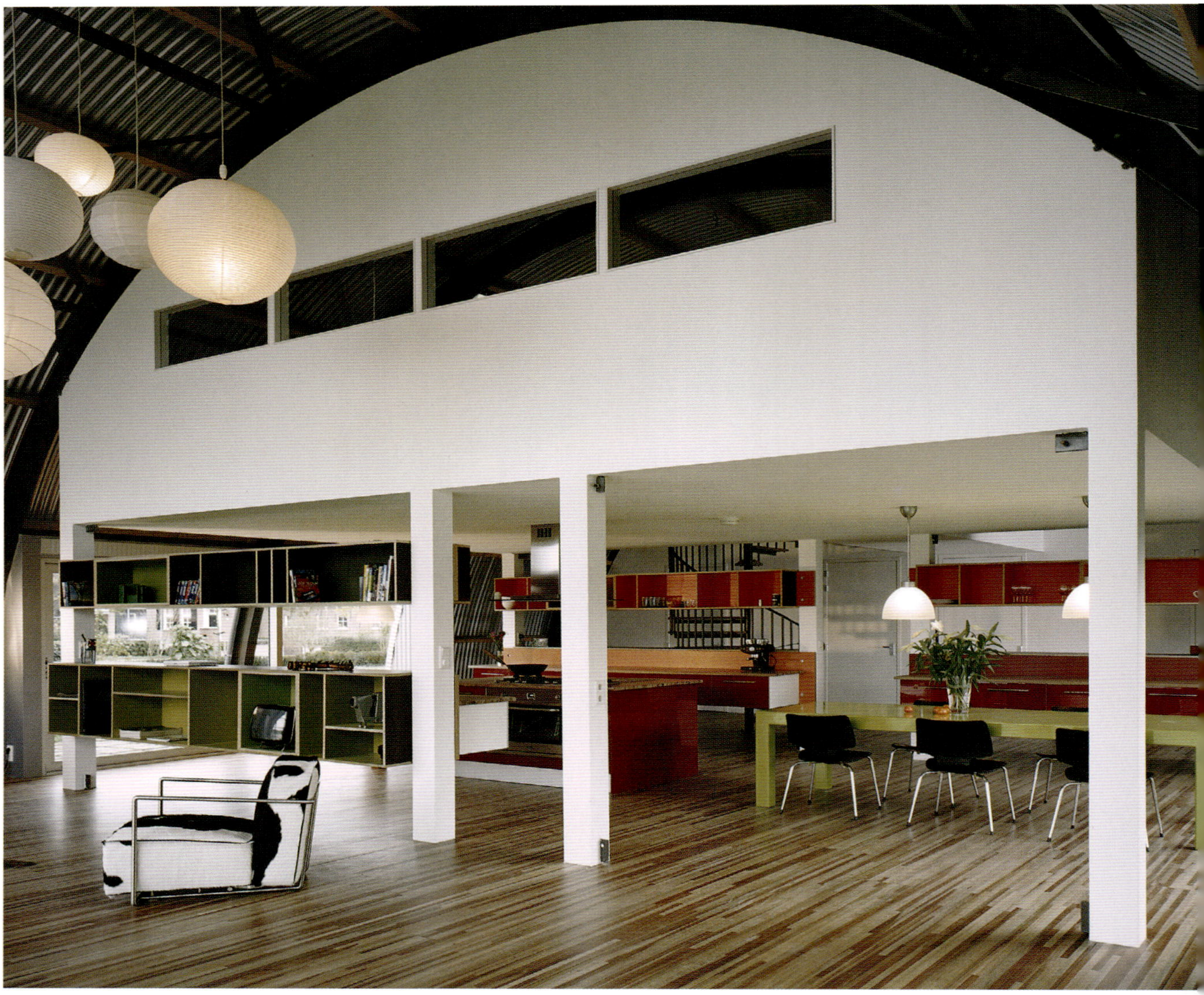

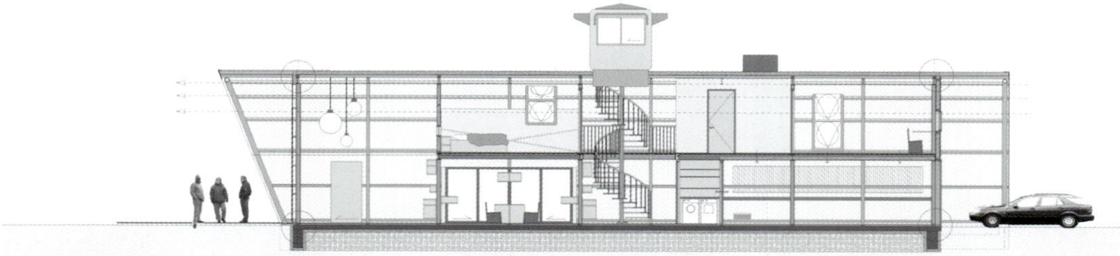

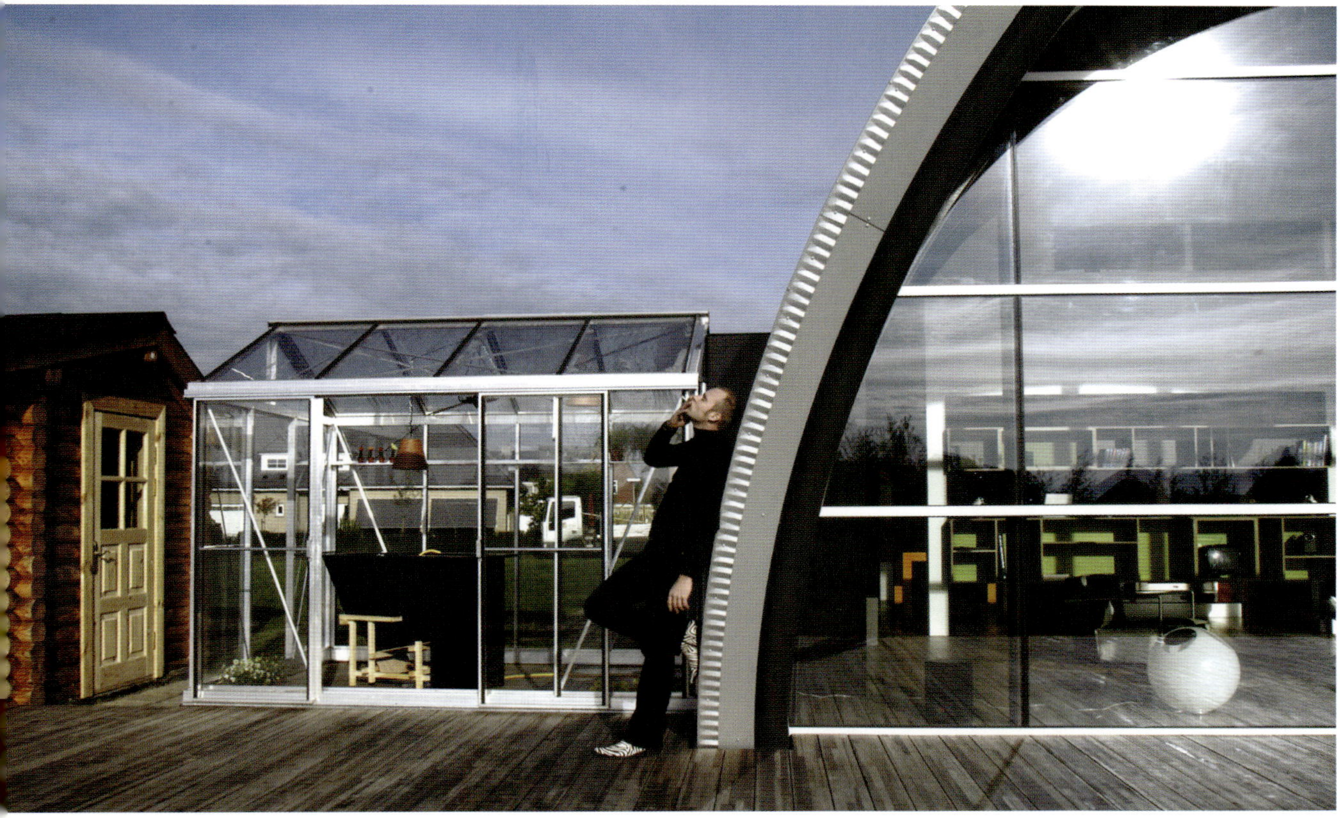

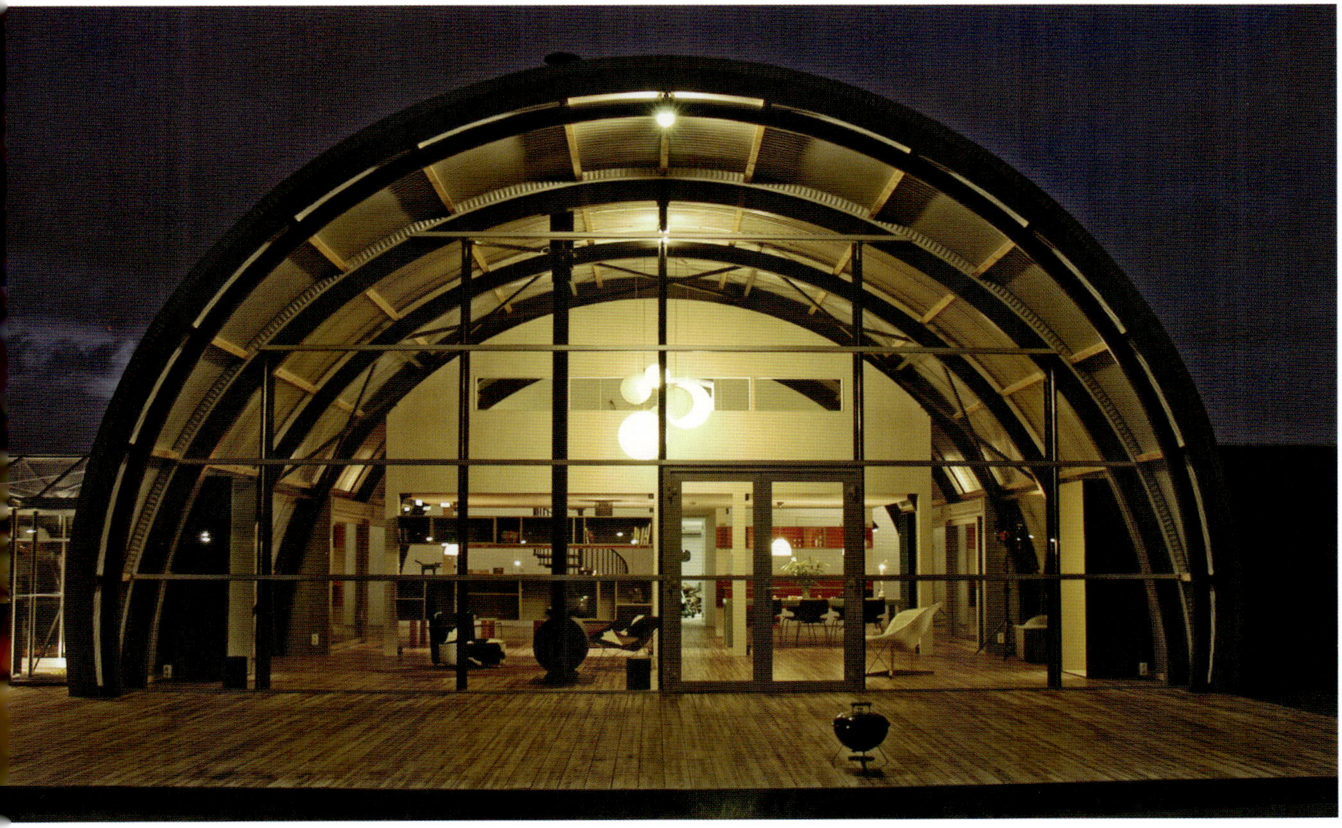

トーレス邸
ソーラー住宅

CASA TORRES
The solar home

ルイス・デ・ガリード
撮影：メイテ・ピエラ

LUIS DE GARRIDO
PHOTO: © Maite Piera

ナバッハス ― スペイン ― 2000

　南向きの方角、生気候学的(バイオクライマティック)設計、そして自然素材熱絶縁体の使用によって、この住宅のエネルギー消費量は、一般住宅の消費量のわずか10％程度ですむ。外壁材料にアーモンド殻を混合した環境負荷の低いパネルを使用することによって、全体の重量を軽減させ、搬入と組立ても容易にすることができた。その結果、工期は短縮され、建設費も低く抑えられた。自然素材熱絶縁体としては、麻とブラックコルクを用いた。温水と暖房の需要は、100％ソーラーエネルギーによってまかなわれている。

Debido a la orientación sur, a su diseño bioclimático y a su aislamiento e inercia térmica, esta casa consume tan solo el 10% de la energía que emplea una vivienda convencional. Utiliza paneles ecológicos de cáscara de almendra en el acabado de sus fachadas, de manera que se aligera el peso de la construcción y se facilita la instalación y montaje, con la consiguiente reducción de los tiempos y costes. Los aislamientos son de cáñamo y corcho negro. La vivienda se abastece de energía 100% solar, tanto para el agua caliente sanitaria como para la calefacción.

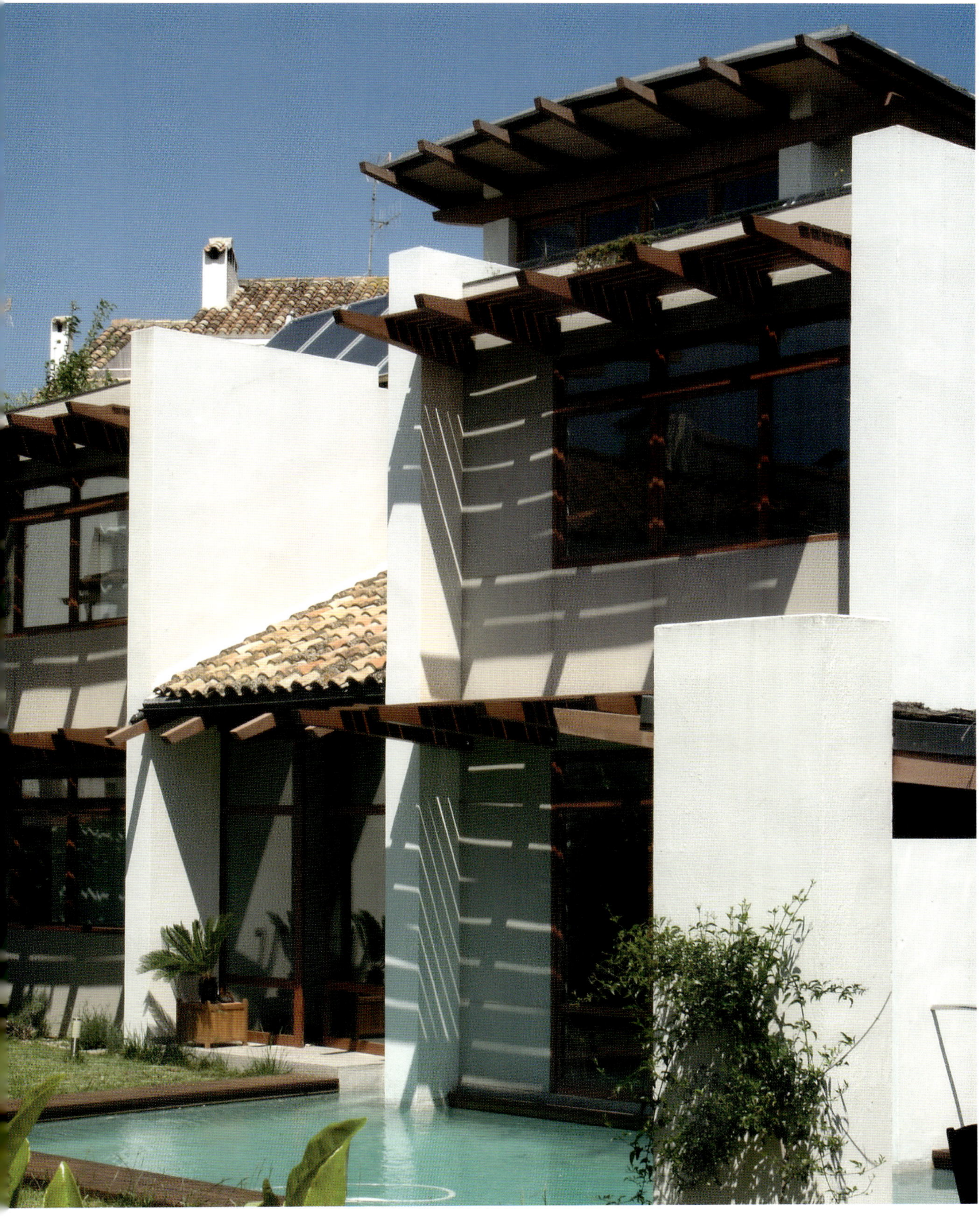

アーモンド殻は壁仕上げ材の中にも混合されている。生気候学的設計によって、室内全体にわたって自然換気が行われ、空調設備は一切使わずに快適な温度が保たれるようになっている。

Almond shells have been incorporated into the wall's finish. The bioclimatic design facilitates natural ventilation throughout the interior and permits an optimal climate without any need for air-conditioning.

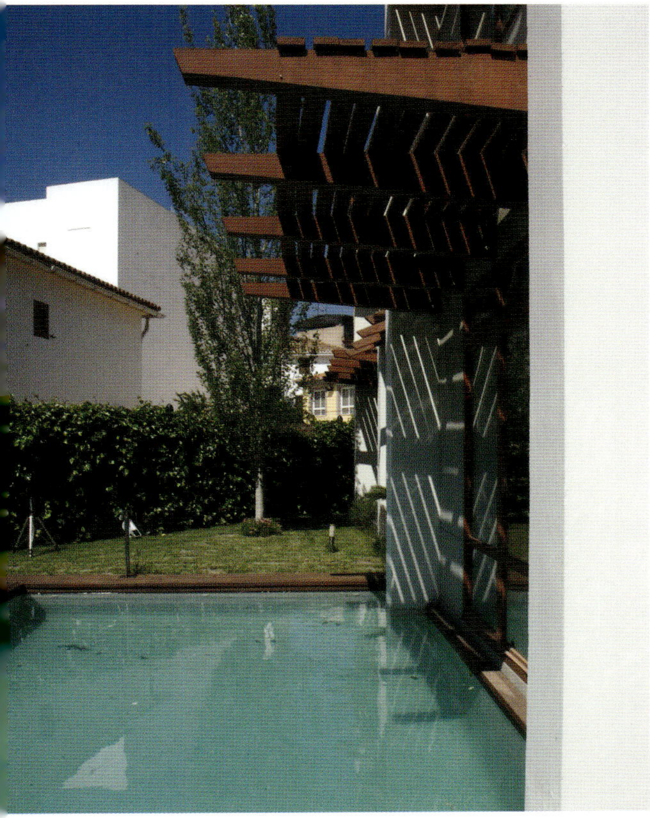

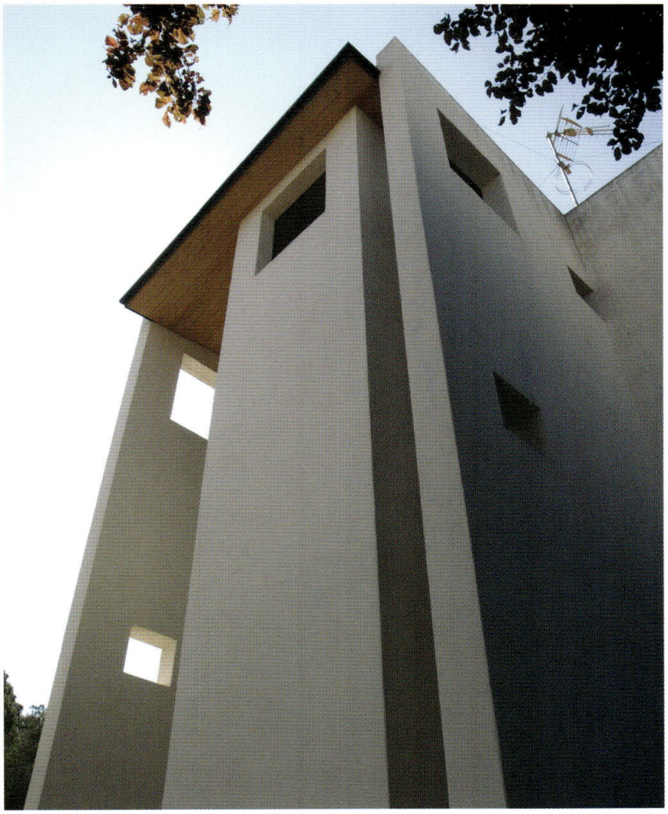

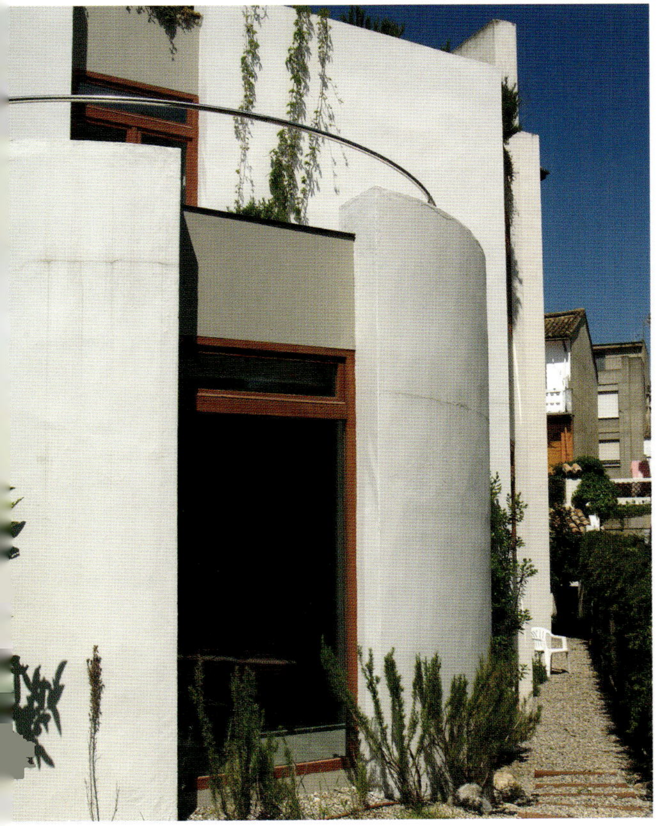

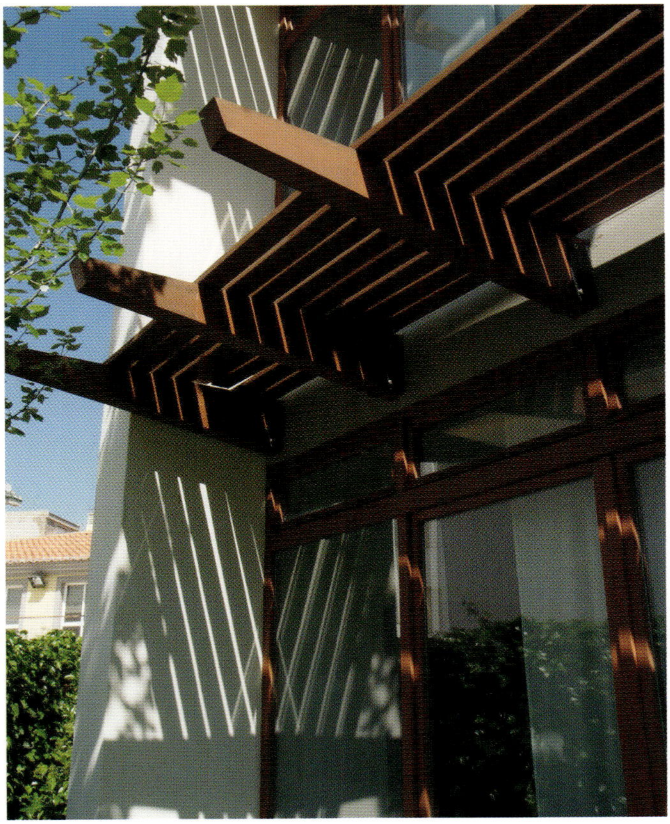

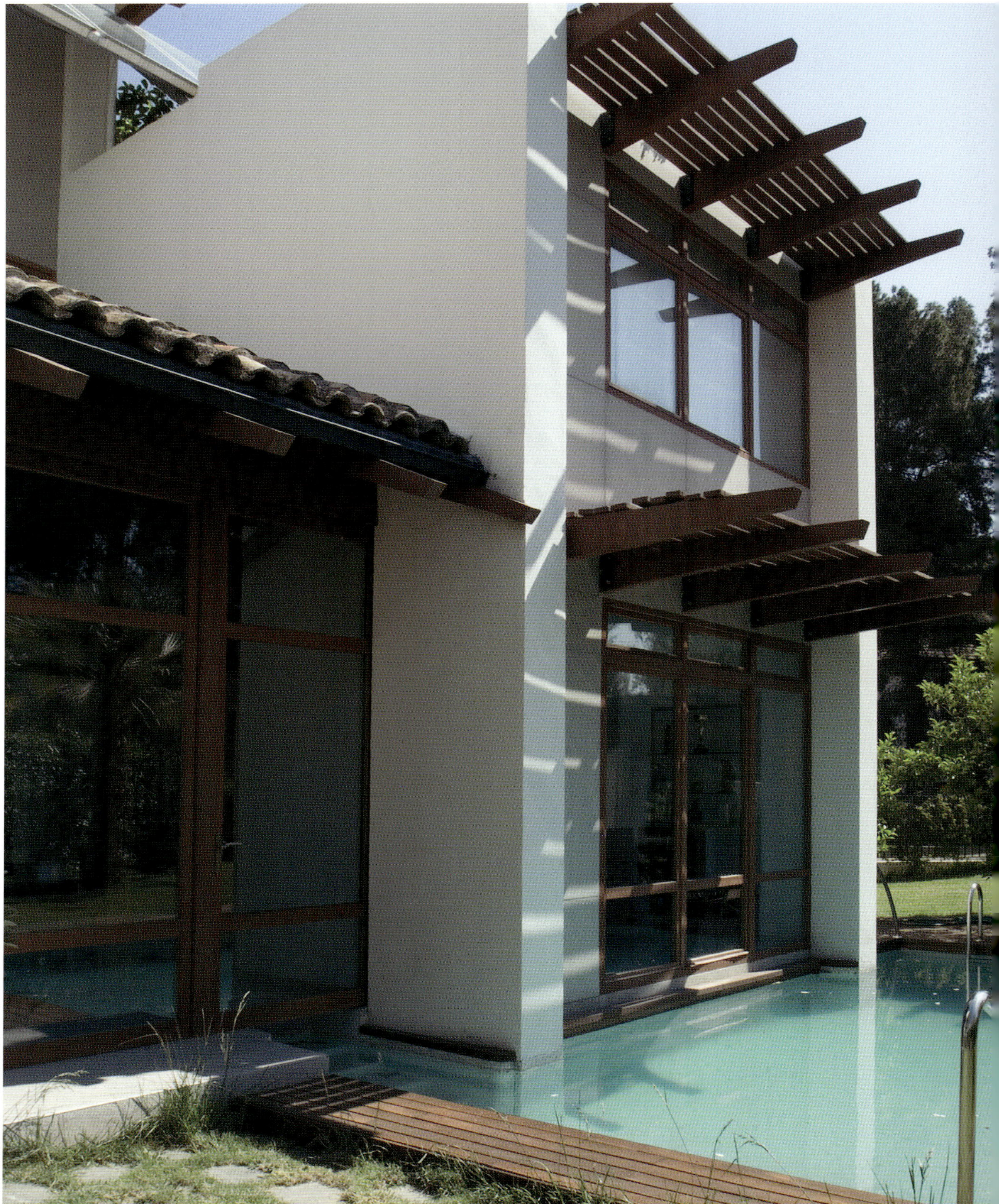

プールはソーラーパネルで温められているので、屋外にあるが年中温水プールにすることが可能だ。プールへは、家の中からも出入りができる。

The pool is heated with solar panels so that even though it is outdoors, it can be warm all year long. It can be entered from within the home itself.

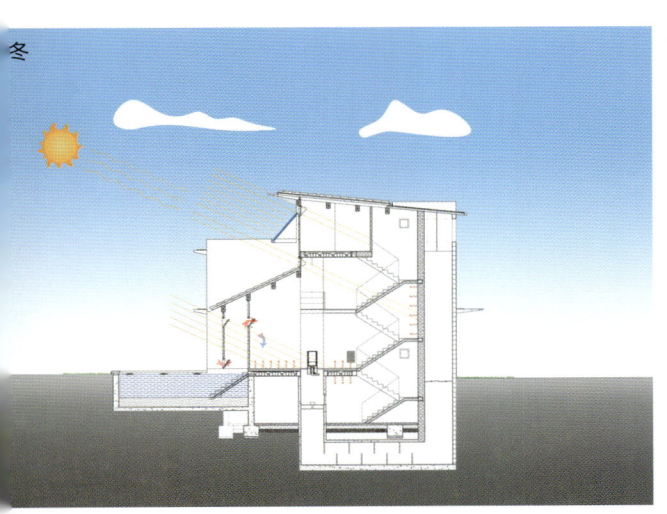

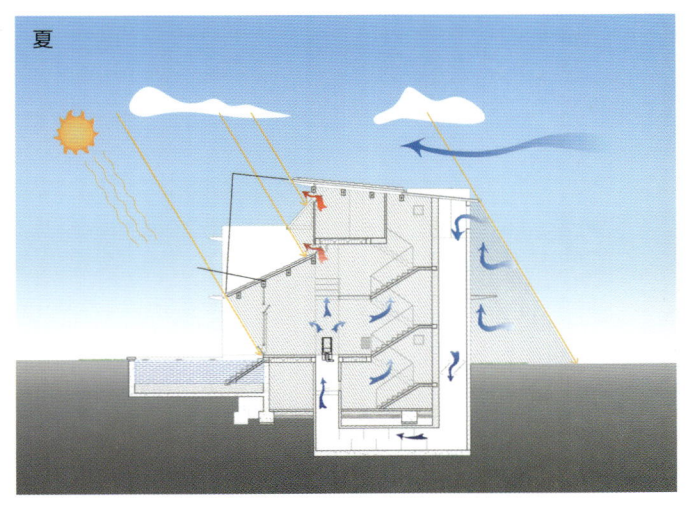

冬

夏

カンタロプスの住宅
プールにはさまれた窪地

ニコラ・トレマコルディ／NM建築設計事務所
撮影：アドリア・グーラ

NICOLA TREMACOLDI/NM ARQUITECTE
PHOTO: © Adrià Goula

HOUSE IN CANTALLOPS
Bunker between pools

カンタロプス ― スペイン ― 2004

　20世紀半ばの古い製粉所の間仕切り壁を利用してこの住宅は建てられている。古いものに対する尊敬の気持ちを失わず、しかも現代的である建築を目指して、住宅は周囲の木立を保存したままその内部に建てられた。設計にあたってもう1つ考慮しなければならなかったことは、時々この地域を襲う風速40mを超える北風で、そのため既存の外壁を二重防壁として利用した。耐力壁には多孔質のセラミック・ブロックと耐熱粘土を用いているため、環境ホルモンなどのアレルギー源のない健康住宅となっている。

This property conserves the original separation walls from an old mid-twentieth century mill. With respect for what came before, while defending the contemporary, this edifice was built inside preserving the already existing trees. Also noted were the strong north winds that can run through this area at up to 92 miles an hour, hence the use of the old walls as double-protection. For the load-bearing walls thermo-clay was used, a low density ceramic block with clay that ensures a healthy home, without toxicity or allergy.

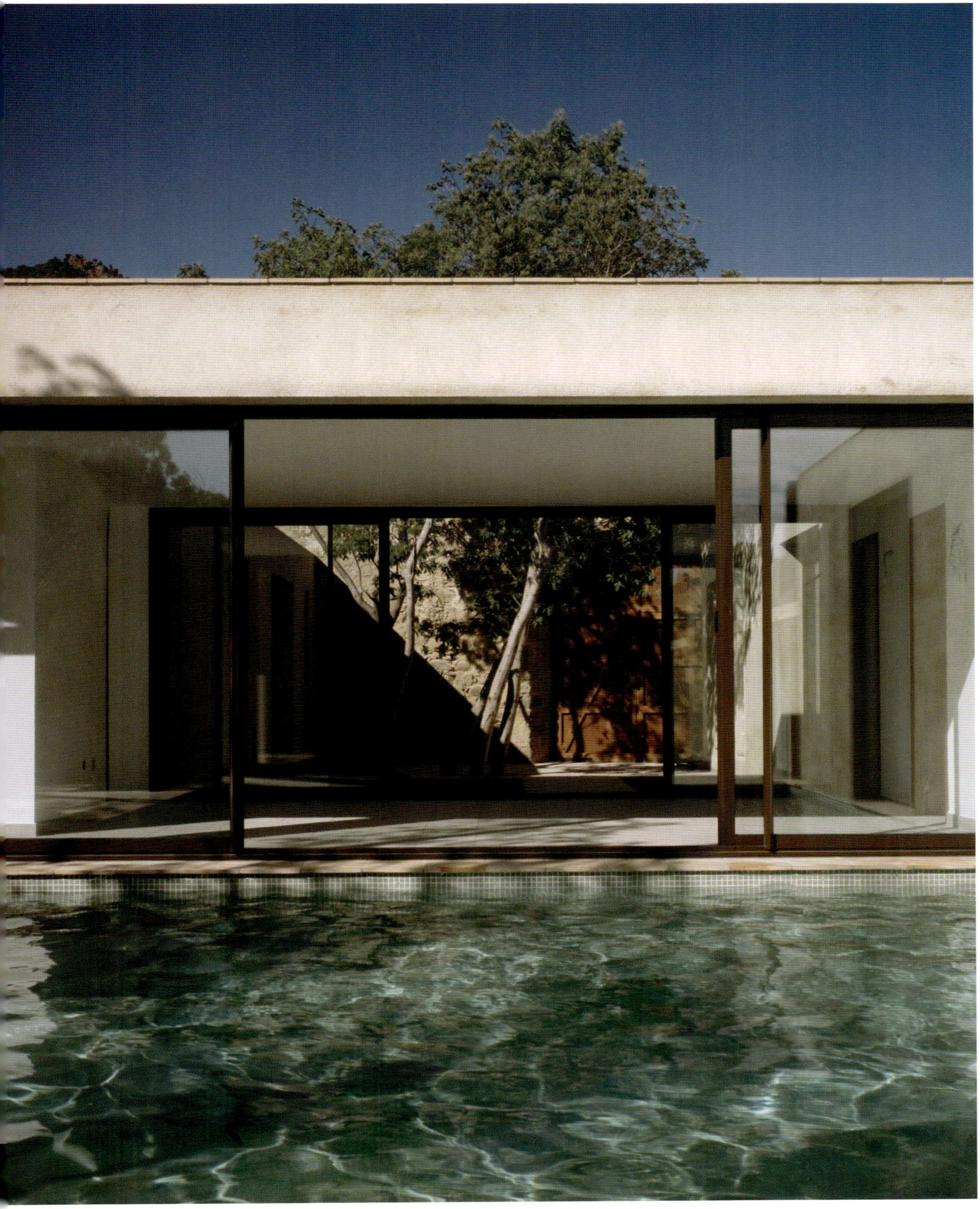

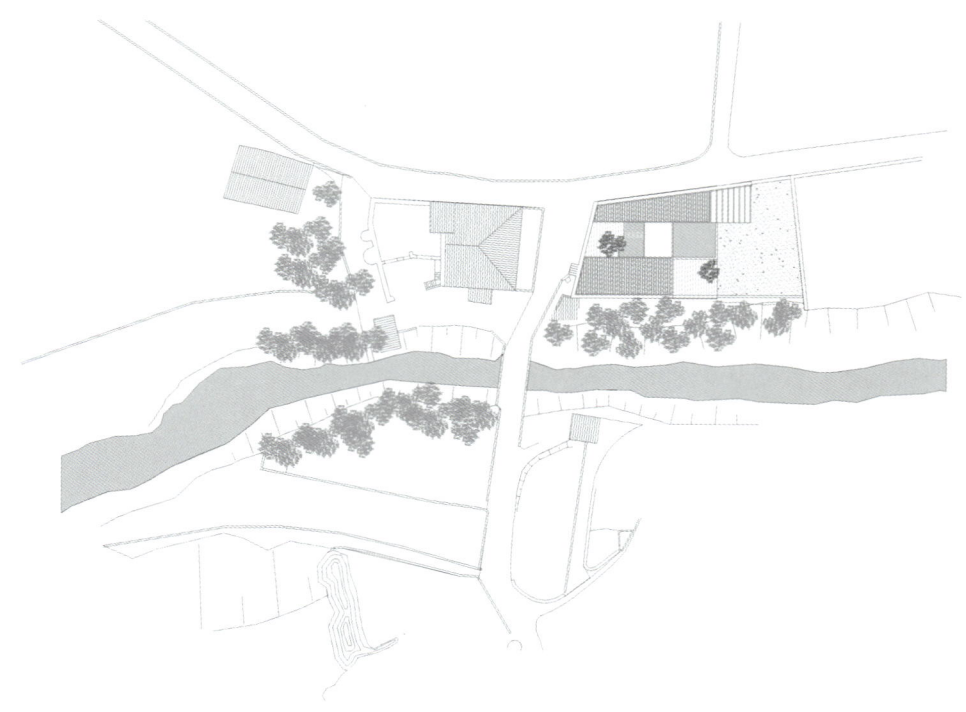

EMPLAZAMIENTO

paredes de calefaccion

células de conveccion

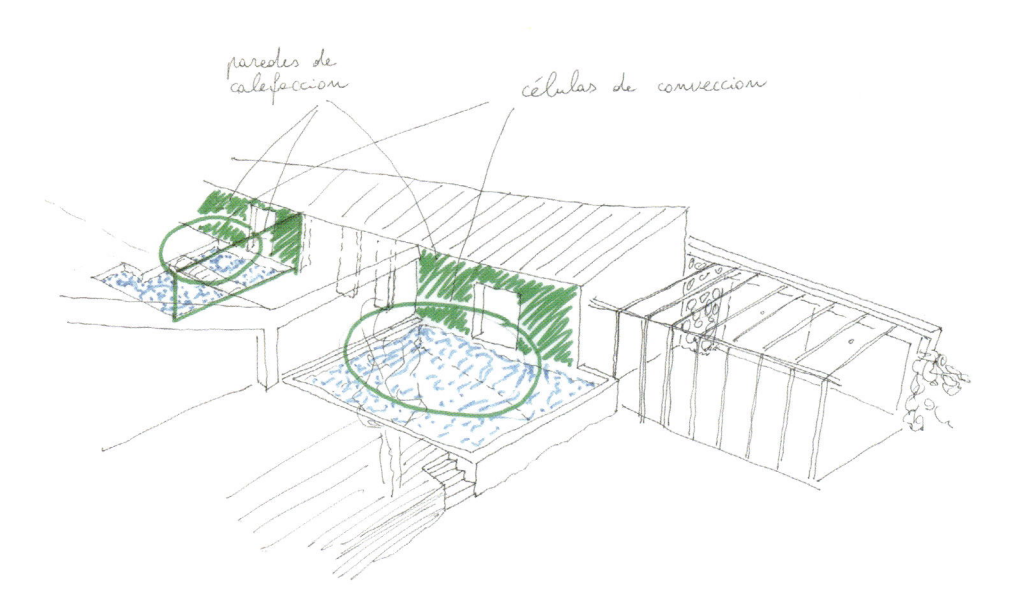

建 築
Architecture

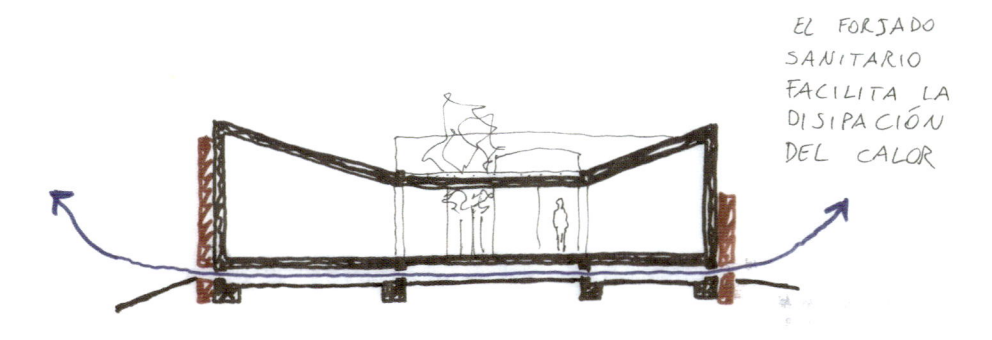

EL FORJADO
SANITARIO
FACILITA LA
DISIPACIÓN
DEL CALOR

水はこの住宅の生気候学的触媒として働いている。メインポーチの北と南の両側にある2つのプールが、対流を通じて空気循環を促進し、夏は熱を放出し、冬は蓄積する。

Water acts as a bioclimatic catalyst in this home. The two pools – one north and the other south of the main porch – promote air circulation through convection, so that it extracts heat during the summer and collects it in the winter.

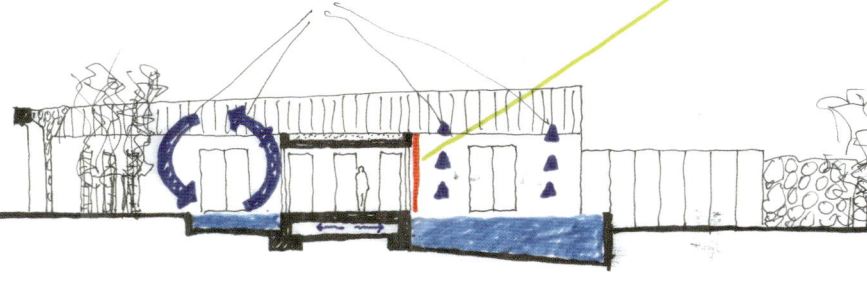

ハウス9×9
石の彫刻

タイタス・ベルンハルト建築設計事務所
撮影：クリスティアン・リヒタース

TITUS BERNHARD ARCHITEKTEN
PHOTO: © Christian Richters

HOUSE 9X9
Rock sculpture

シュタットベルゲン ― ドイツ ― 2003

　この縦横9m×9mのモノリス、石の彫刻のような住宅は、この人口15,000人の都市を覆う類型的な住宅に対する、視覚的、美学的アンチテーゼとなっている。簡素な美しさをたたえるモノリスは、環境負荷の低さでもこれからの住宅のあるべき姿を示している。堡籃(ほうらん)（石や土を詰めたかご）で造られた外壁は、重量28t、40,000個の礫石で造られているが、それらの礫石が住宅を生気候学的に保護している。夏と冬、礫石は空調設備をほとんど必要としないくらいに、室内の気温を快適に保つ。

With its monolithic and sculptured character and a 29 x 29 foot floor, this home was raised as a visual and esthetic counterpoint to the prevailing typology in this vicinity with 15,000 habitants. Its limited esthetic complies with ecological criteria. Its "gabion" style exterior is made with some 365 baskets holding about 40,000 stones and totaling 28 tons. This stone skin regulates the building bio-climatically, since in the summer and winter it provides a comfortable climate without barely any need for air-conditioning.

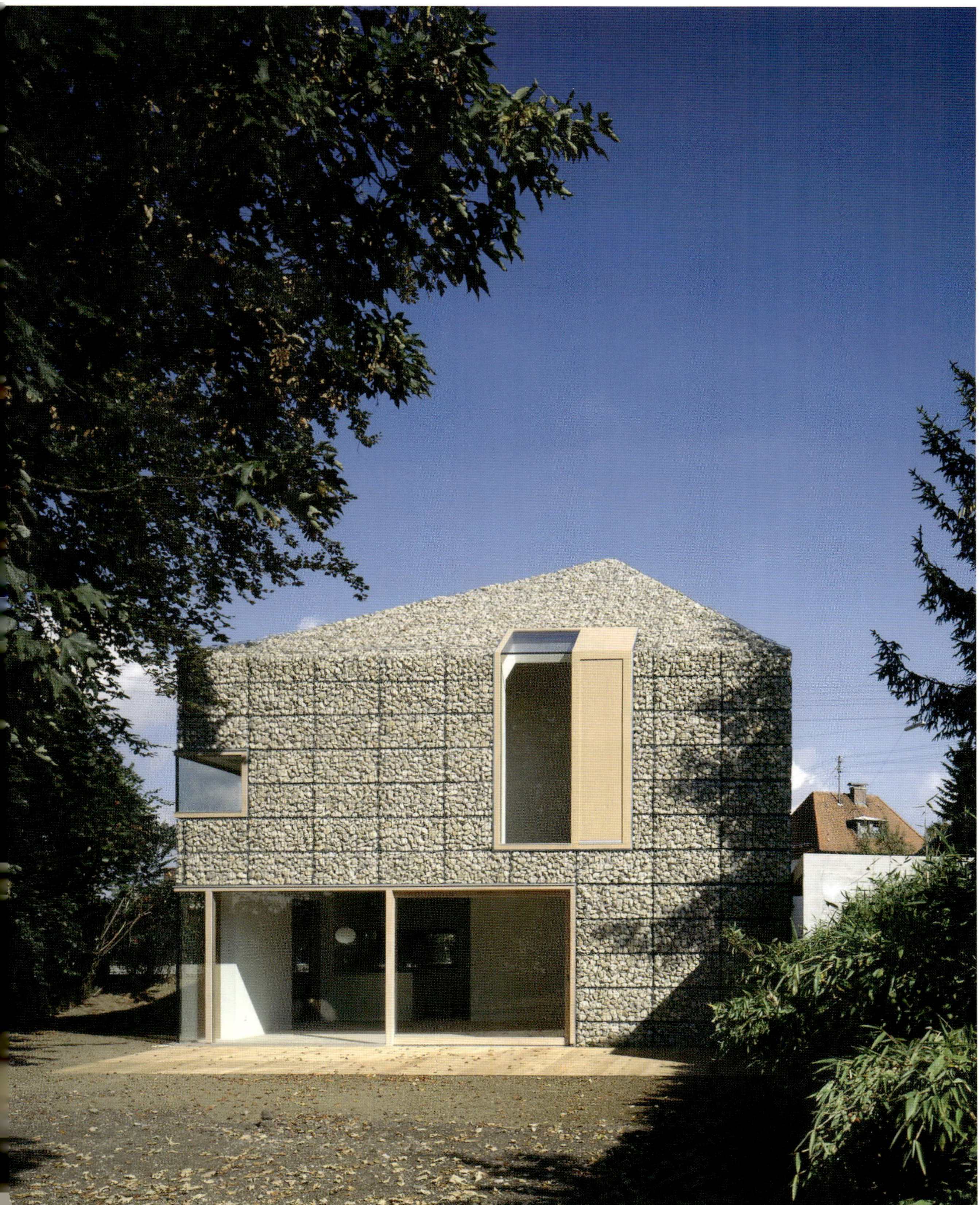

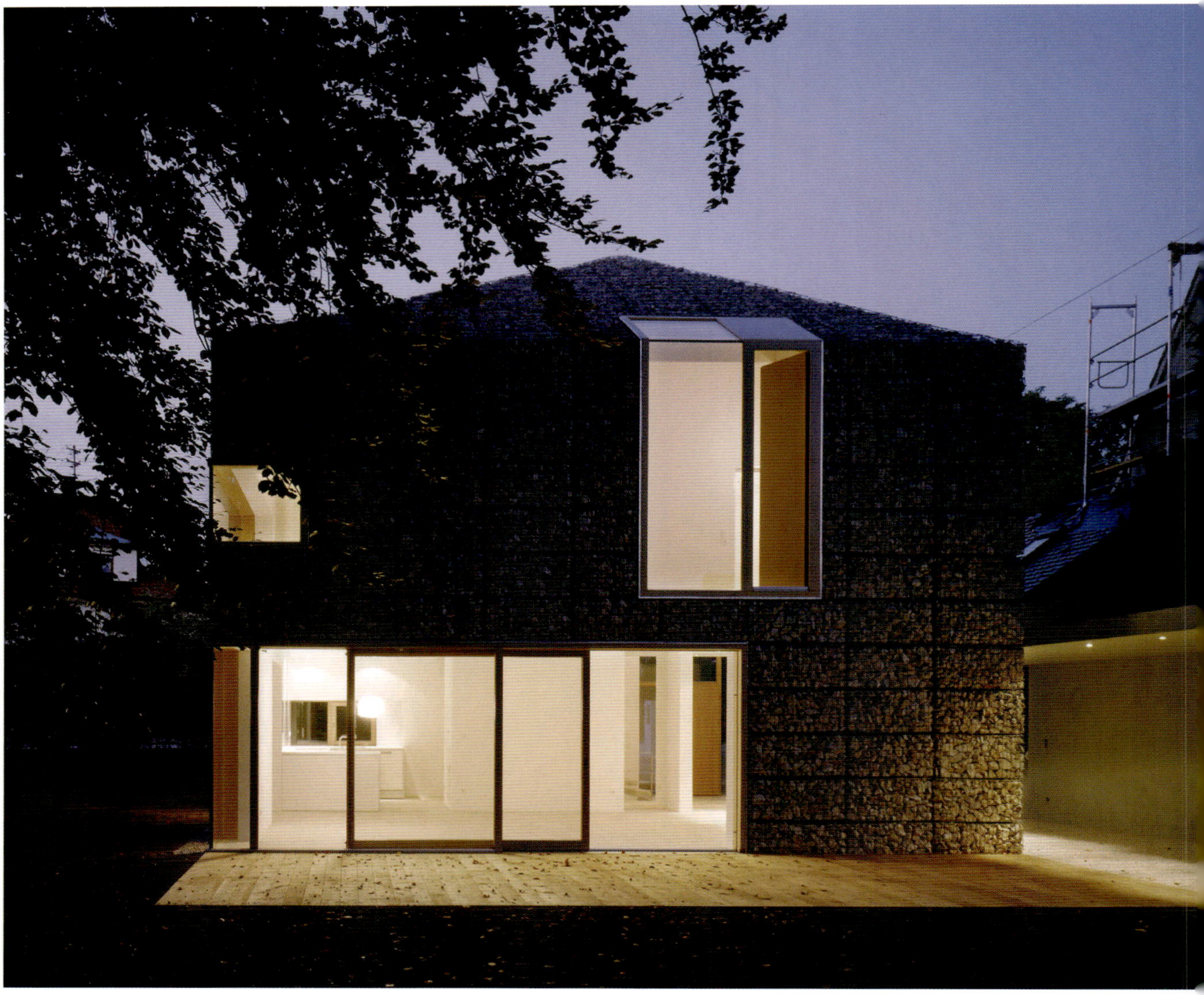

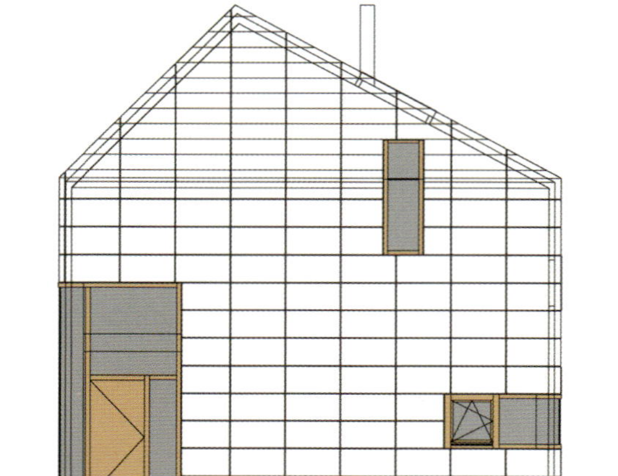

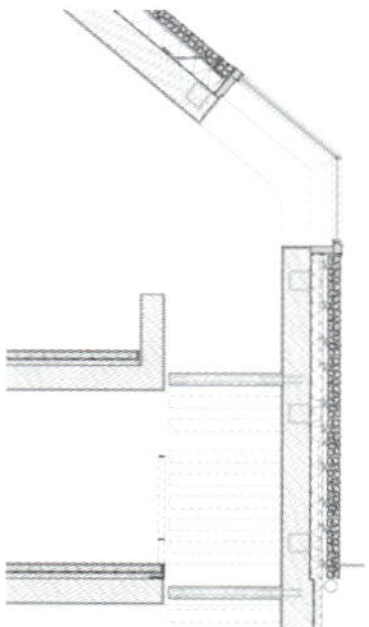

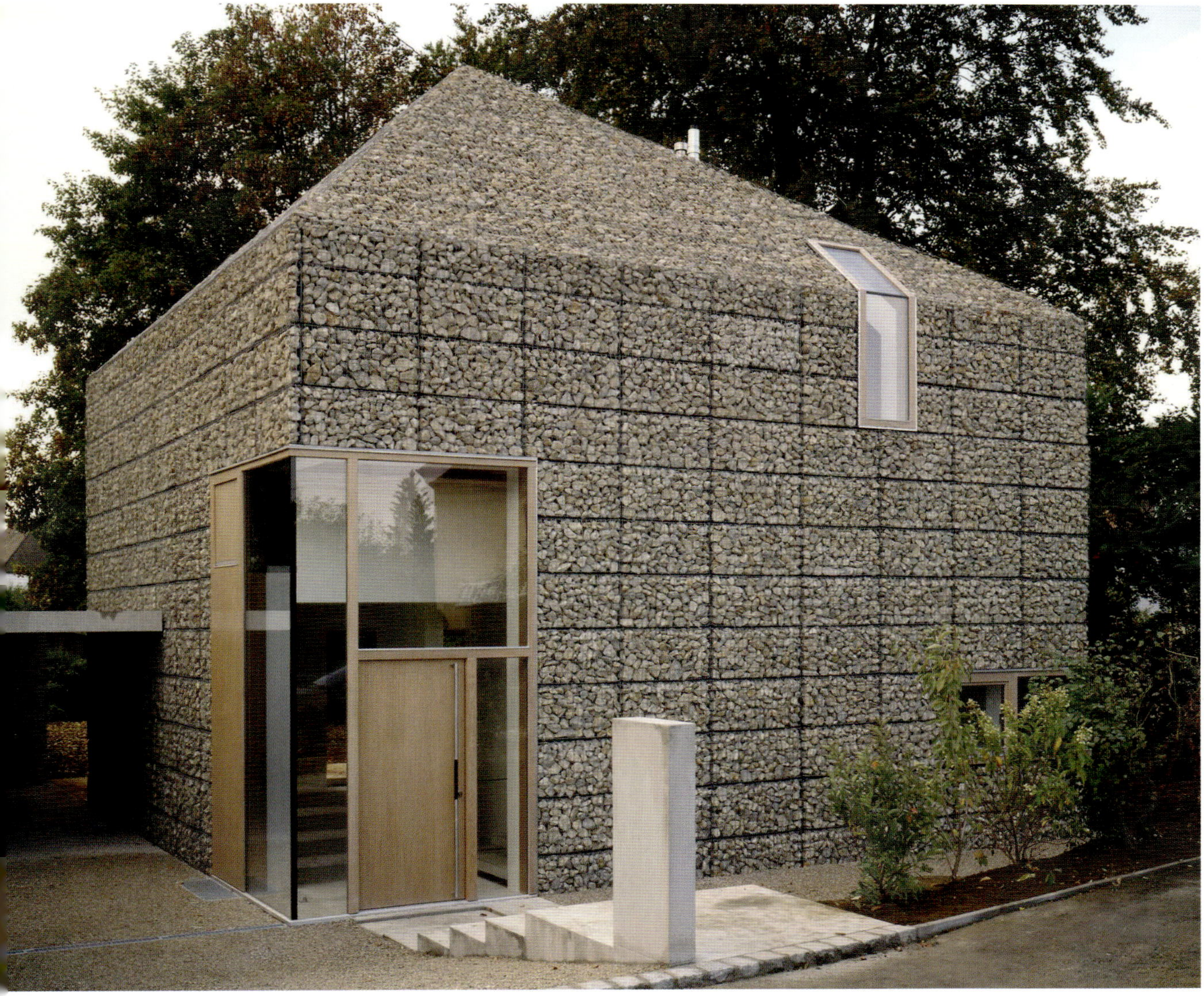

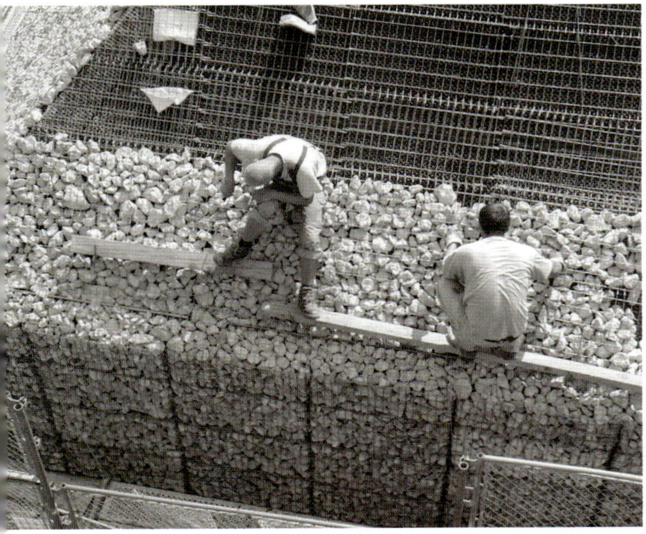

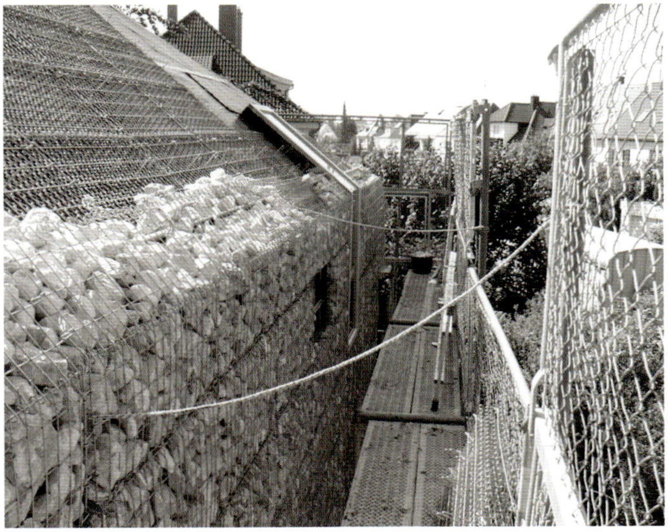

ピクセル・ハウス
画素化された外皮

スレード・アーキテクチュア＆マス・スタディーズ
撮影：キム・ヨングワン

SLADE ARCHITECTURE AND MASS STUDIES
PHOTO: © Kim Yong Kwan

PIXEL HOUSE
Pixilated skin

ヘイリ ― 韓国 ― 2003

　モノリス型住宅をもう1つ紹介しよう。建築家は以前から、デジタル画像の画素による連続性のあるデザインに強く惹かれていたが、この住宅ではついに9675個のレンガを用いて、外皮全体を画素化した。住宅は、不等辺四角形の平面の上に、1個1個のレンガの角を目立たせながら組積みされて建ち上がり、非定型の複合体を形成している。その独特の姿形と質感がこの住宅の存在感を高めている。一連の試みの最後の仕上げとして建築家が探求したものは、住宅を、発展した国土とその環境との間を結ぶ要衝とする最も自然な方法は何か、ということであった。

Another example of the monolithic spirit. The architects were inspired by the continuous design of pixilated digital imagery. For this they used 9,675 bricks to dress the walls. The house is seated upon a trapezoidal plane, with an elevated area where the juxtaposition of angulated bricks shapes an atypical compound that stands out for its textural and irregular character. Being the last home in its development, the architect sought out the most natural way to make it a passageway between the developed land and the environment around it.

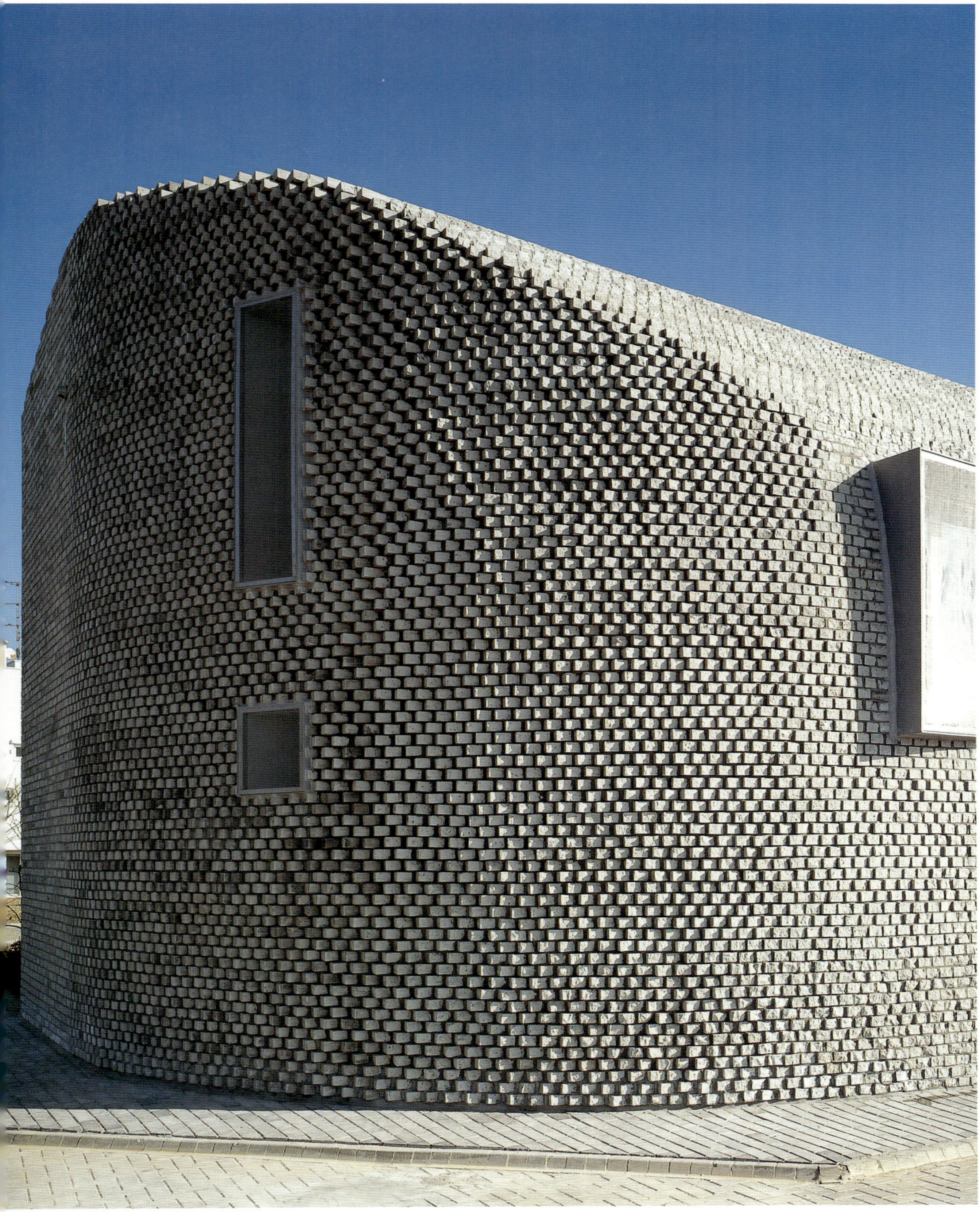

有機体を思わせる建築方法によって、物語性のある住宅が誕生した。住宅の背後に広がる広漠とした自然が建築家に、すぐ近くの丘から転がり落ちてきた巨岩のような住宅を建ててはどうかと暗示したのではないだろうか？

This is organic-looking architecture serving as a narrative model. The wild surroundings attached to the building's rear exterior suggested to the architects the idea of projecting an edifice that would look like a rock fallen from a nearby hill.

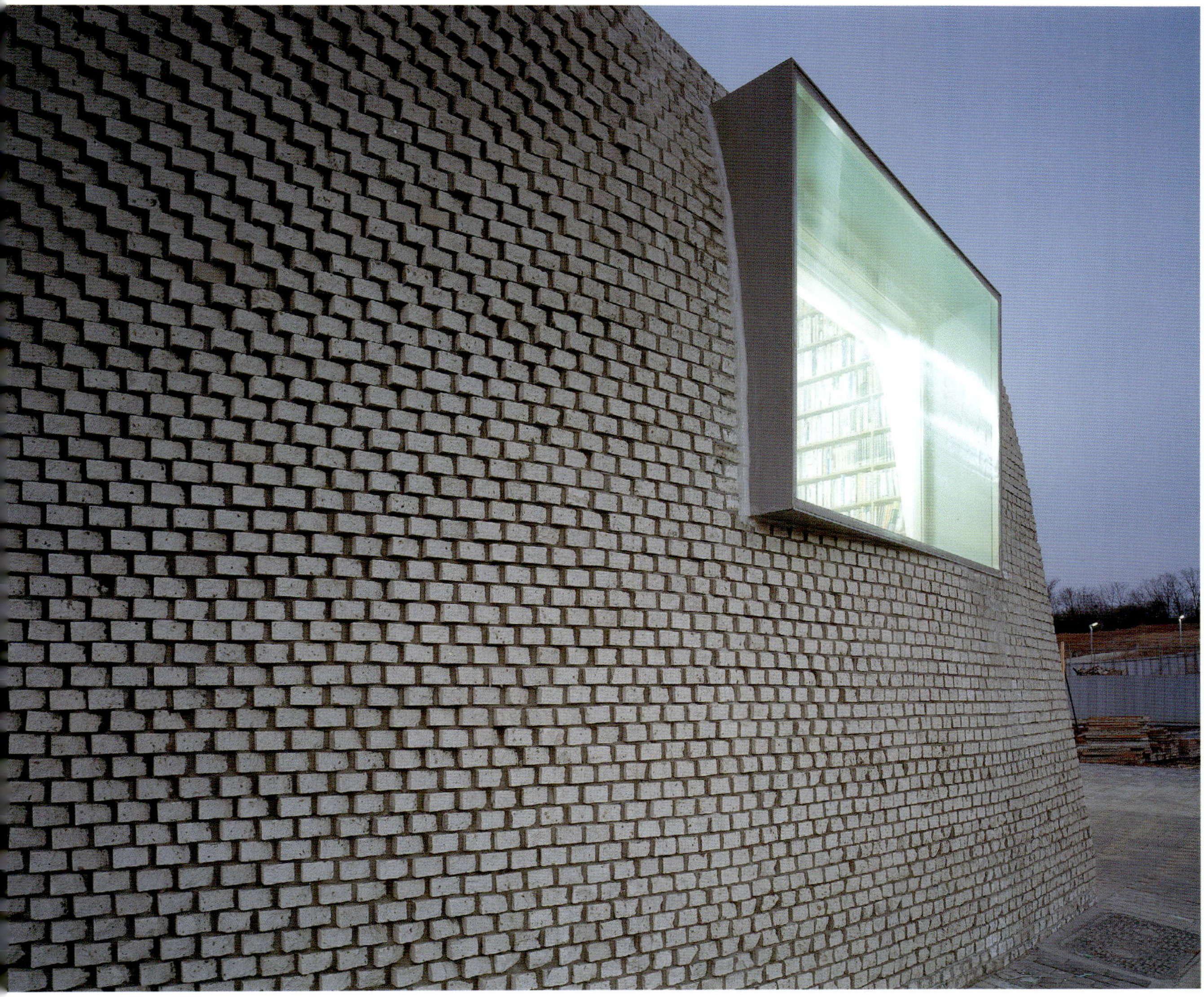

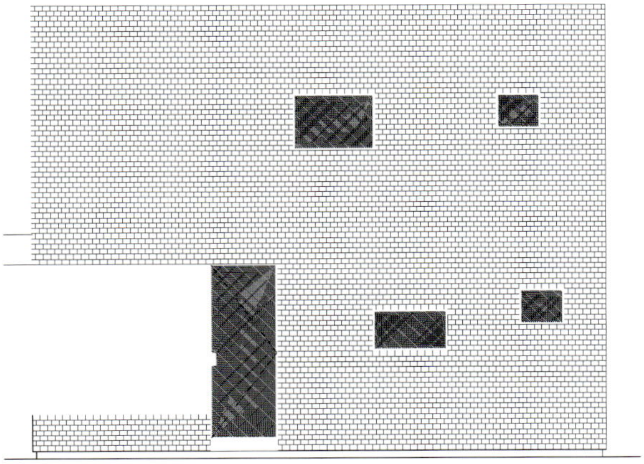

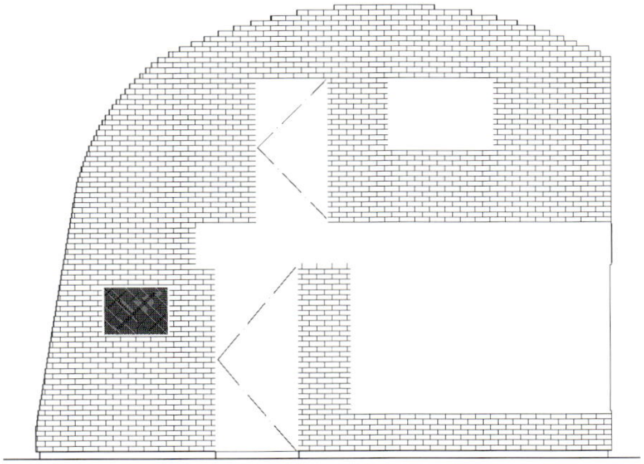

リアス・アルタスの住宅
リアス式海岸を見下ろして

J・トーレス & R・リャマサーレス／A-Cero
撮影：アンゲル・バルタナス

J. TORRES Y R. LLAMAZARES/ A-CERO
PHOTO: © Ángel Baltanás

リアス・アルタス ― スペイン ― 2003

HOUSE IN RÍAS ALTAS
The ria lookout

　モカクリーム色の石灰岩で完全に被われたこの住宅の設計には、2つの逃れられない前提条件があった。1つは空間的なもの（立地は、スペイン海岸法が開発を全面的に禁止している地域のすぐ隣に位置している）で、もう1つは概念的なもの（施主は、ガリシア地方の特色であるリアス式海岸を見下ろすことができる躍動感溢れる建物を希望した）であった。海岸線に向うなだらかな勾配を利用して、住宅は2層構造とし、半分地中に埋もれた格好になっている下層を広く取り、中庭を設け、入り口となる上層は小さく収めた。

The design of this home completely covered in crème-mocha colored limestone was decided by two inescapable pre-requisites: one spatial (the property is located beside land upon which Spanish Coastal Law has prohibited all development) and the other conceptual (the express desire that the edifice become a livable watchtower over these Galician rias). The terrain's inclination towards the sea allows the home to be built in two levels, one half-buried with an indoor garden, and another, smaller one at entry level.

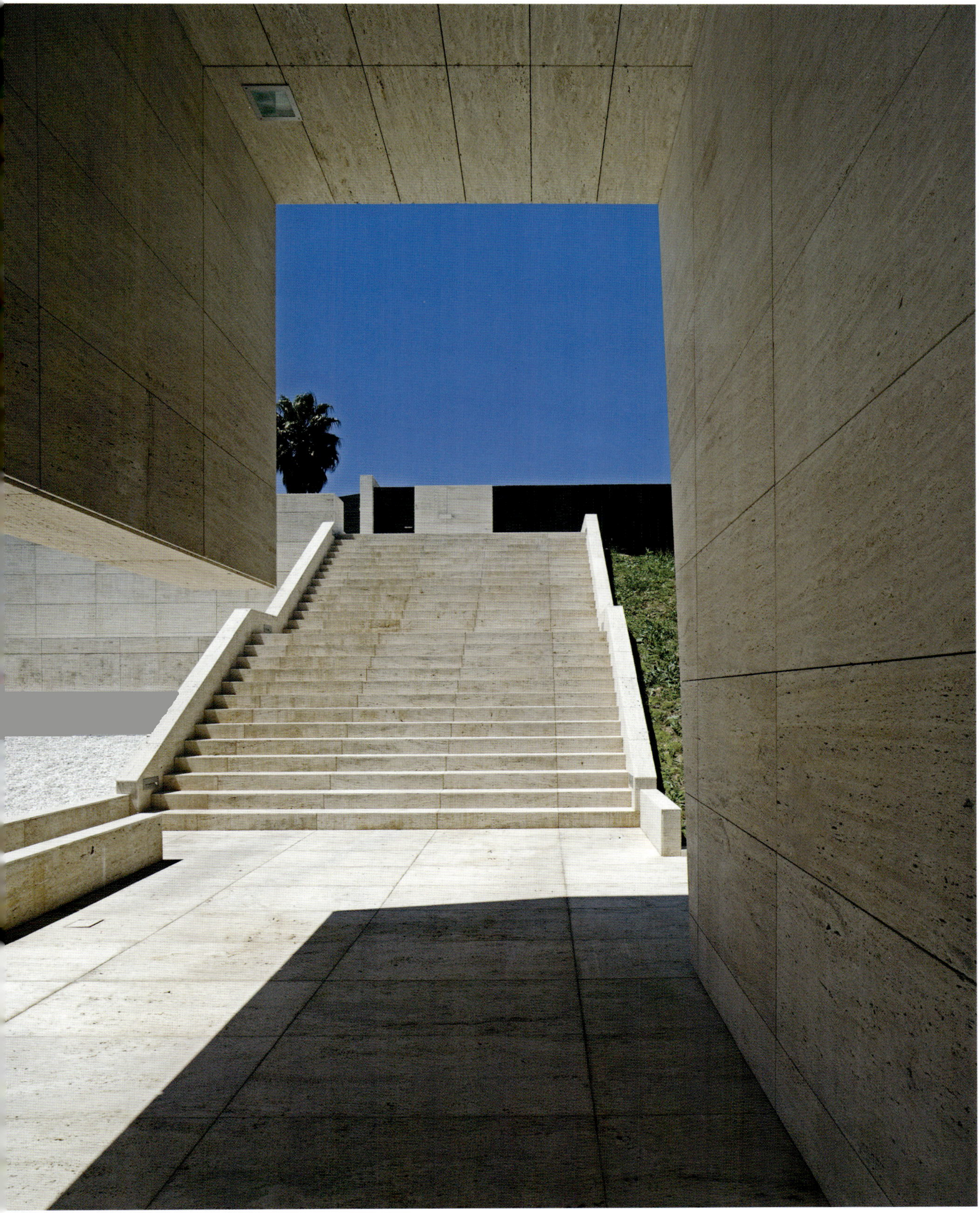

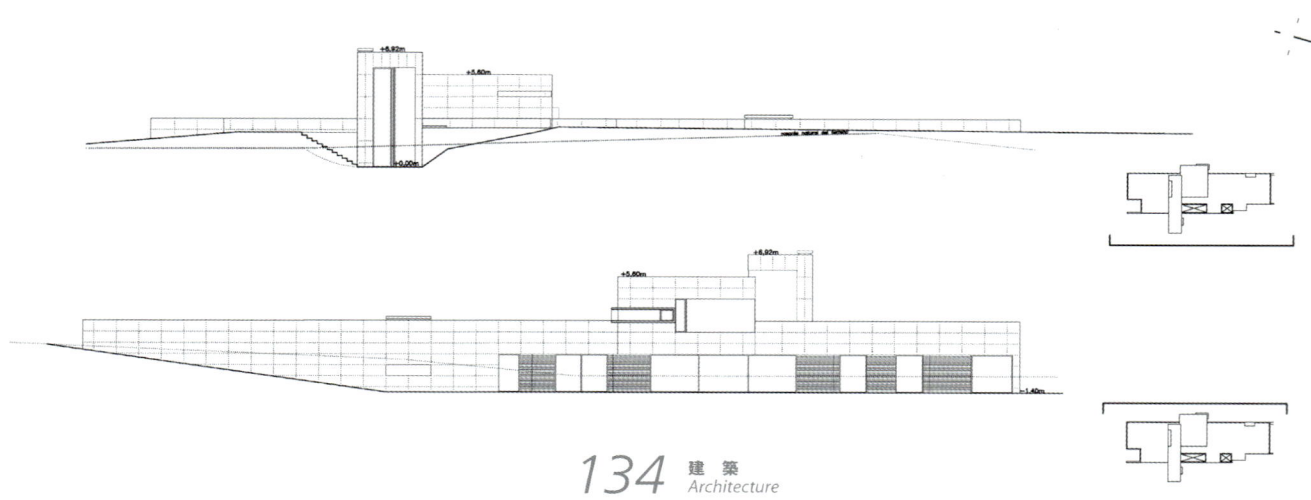

134 建築
Architecture

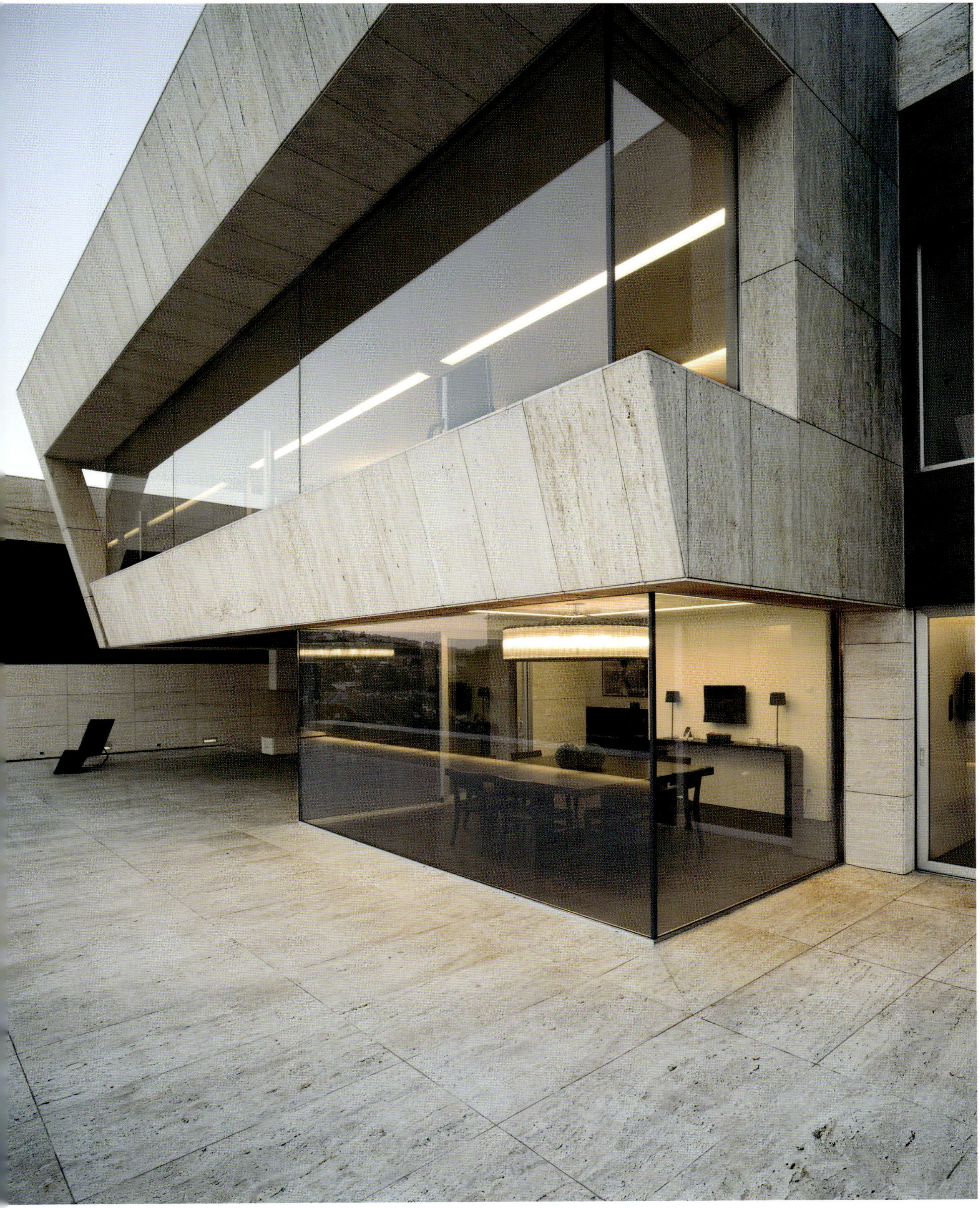

ワイルドキャット・リッジの住宅
標高2,800m

ヴォーサンガー建築設計事務所
撮影：トーマス・ダンガード

WILDCAT RIDGE RESIDENCE
At 9,200 ft altitude

VOORSANGER ARCHITECTS
PHOTO: © Thomas Damgaard

スノーマス、コロラド — アメリカ — 2004

　自然への侵襲を極力避けるという命題のもと、現地の地質学的調査が入念に行われ、住宅は尾根に沿うような形で建てるということが決定された。風化した岩を組んだ巨大な壁が、隆起した尾根の上を脊柱のように横ざまに走り、西側のリビングと東側のバスルーム、子供部屋の分水嶺になっている。冬と夏の室温調整には、60基の地熱源ヒートポンプが使われ、必要エネルギーの100％近くを満たしている。

Those involved proposed creating as little impact on the land as possible, studying the tectonic geography of the location and deciding upon an end result that would run parallel to the mountain crest. A large mossy wall, goes through this elevated terrain crosswise like a spinal column, and creates a dividing line between the living room on the west and the bathrooms and children's bedrooms on the east. For temperature control in winter and summer, 60 geothermal sources are used, providing almost 100% of all necessary resources.

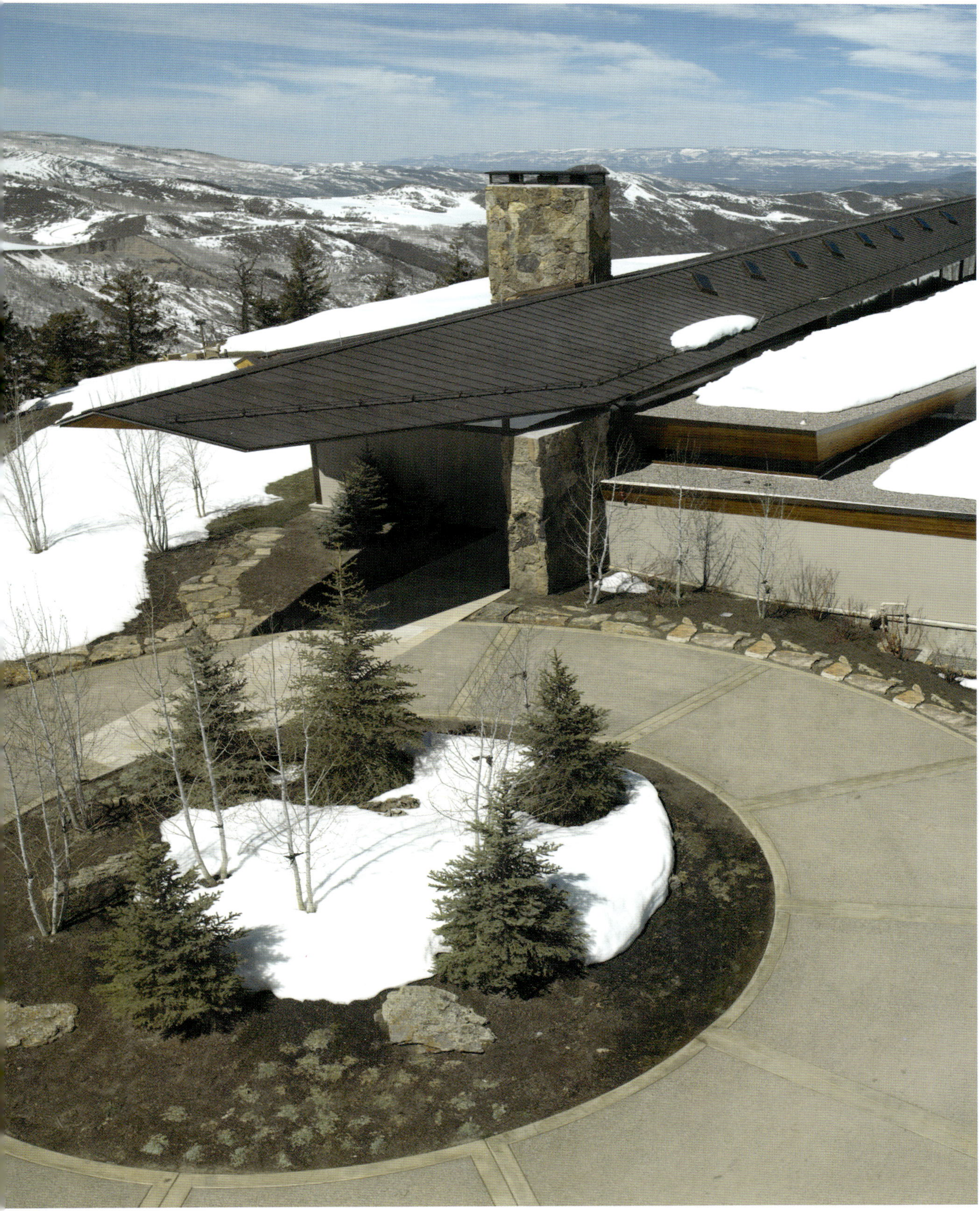

Site Plan

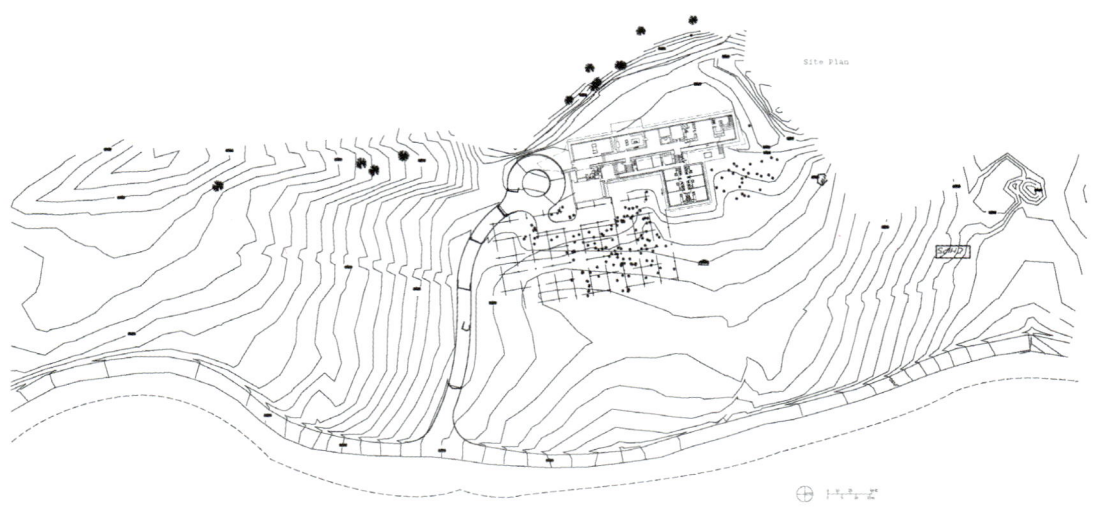

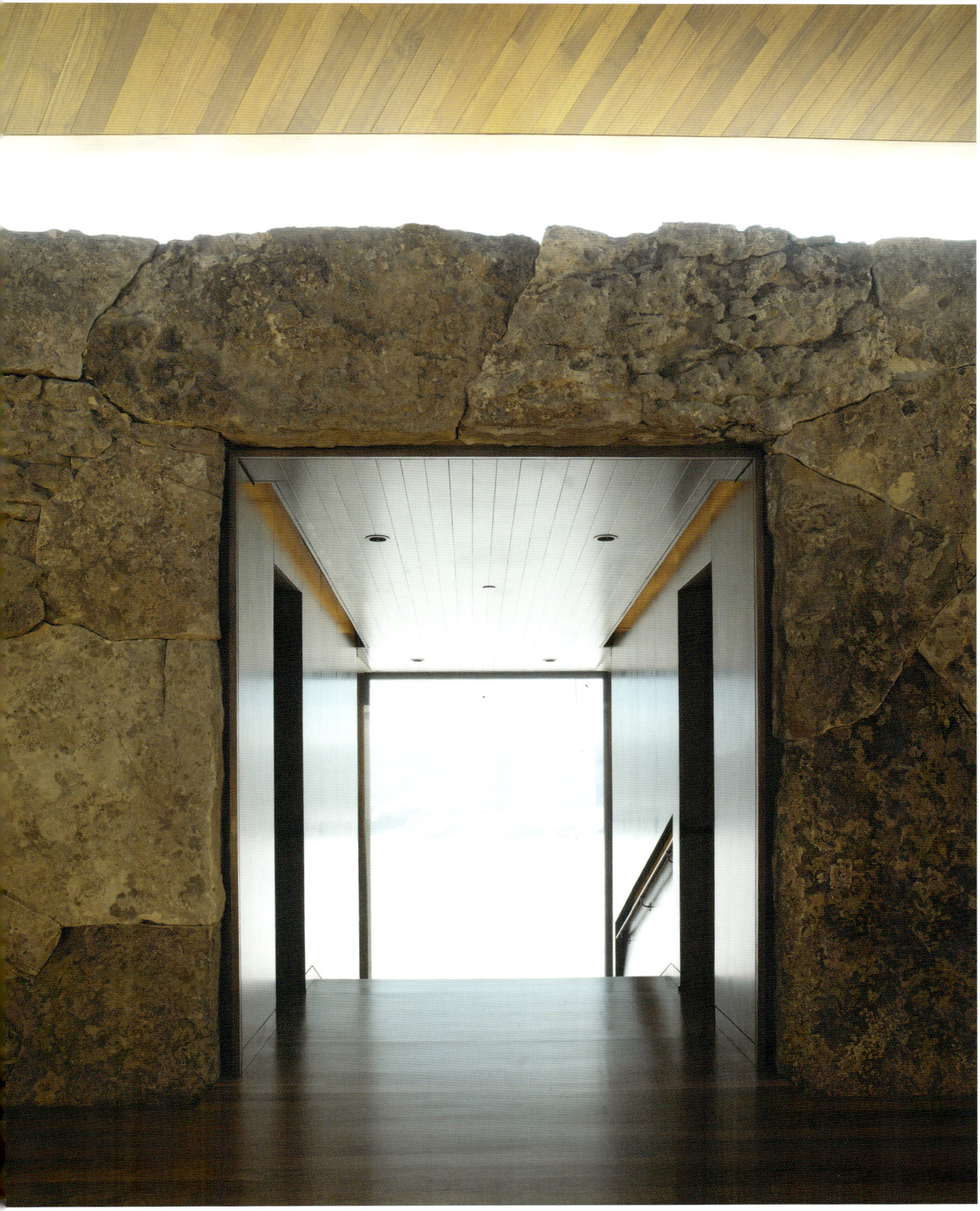

サルゾー近郊の住宅
小道の上の天然スレート

エリック・グースナール
撮影：フィリップ・ルオー

HOUSE NEAR SARZEAU
Slate on the path

ERIC GOUESNARD
PHOTO: © Philippe Ruault

サルゾー、ナント ― フランス ― 1999

　切妻屋根の2つの建物をガラス張りの渡り廊下が連結する、きわめて簡素な構成を持つこの住宅からは、不思議な詩情が漂ってくる。ファサードから屋根へと一体となった外皮は天然スレートで覆われ、そのくすんだ色合いが、壁越しに見えるオレンジ色を基調とした室内の生き生きとした生活感を一層きわだたせている。建物の外観はまわりの自然とよく調和し、2つの生活空間は、まるで小道の傍に無造作に置かれた2個の天然スレートのスラブのようだ。

The austerity of this project - basically composed of two units with gabled roofs connected by a glass catwalk - cannot hide its scenic poetry. The façade and roof are covered in slate, the dark tones of which contrast with the very much alive interiors where the color orange predominates throughout the walls. The outside of the edifice adapts well with the natural surroundings, as if the architect had achieved an analogy between two habitable spaces and two slabs of slate found beside the road.

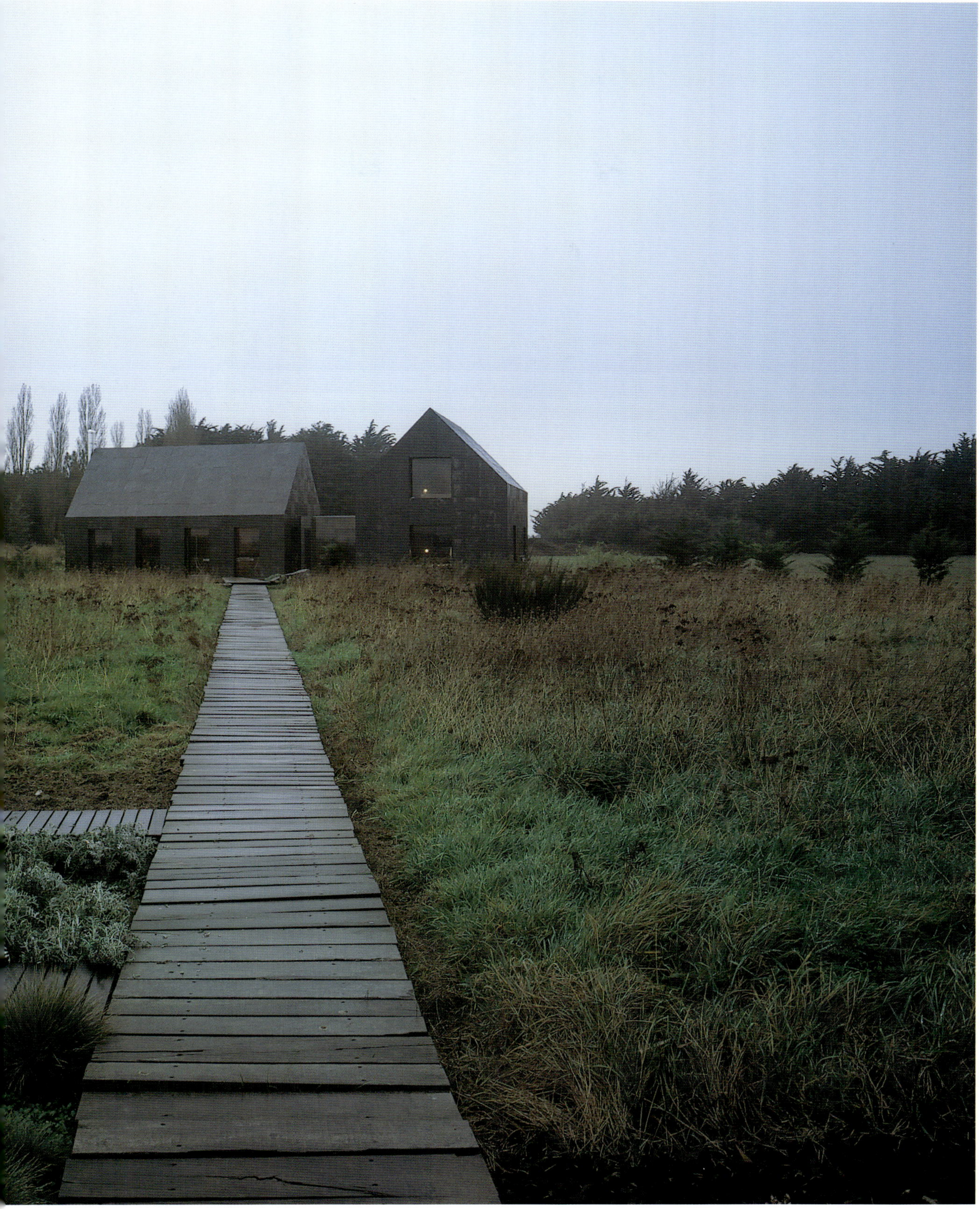

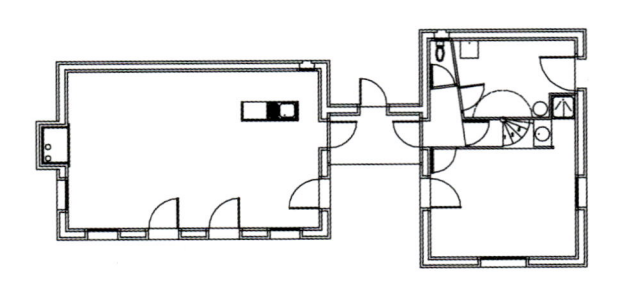

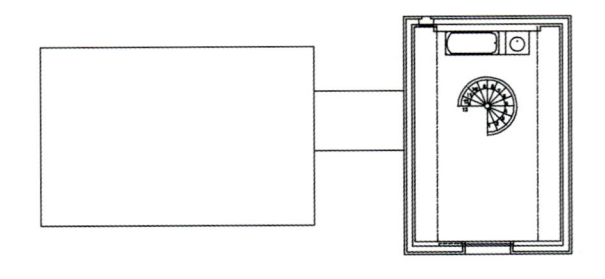

142 建 築
Architecture

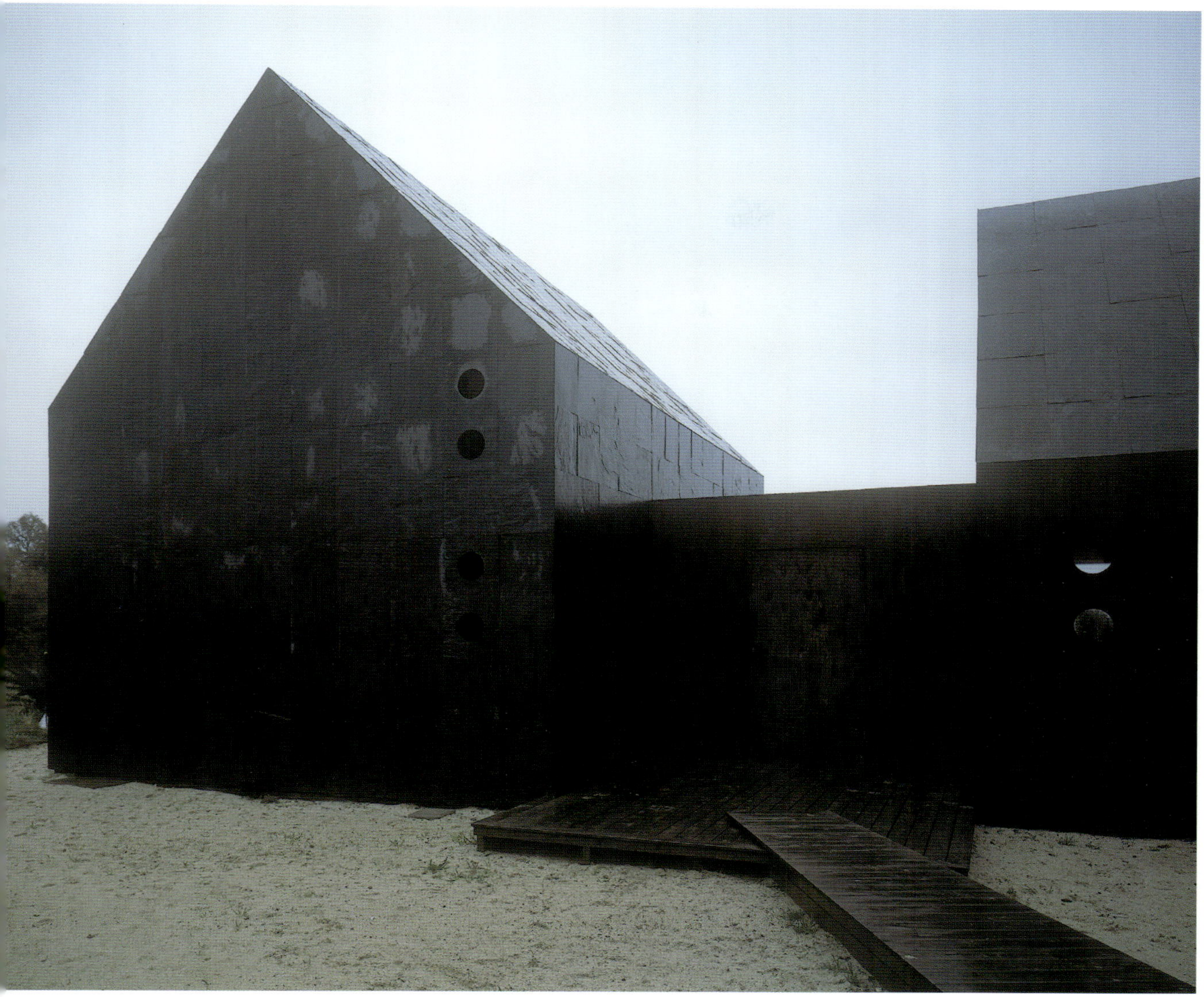

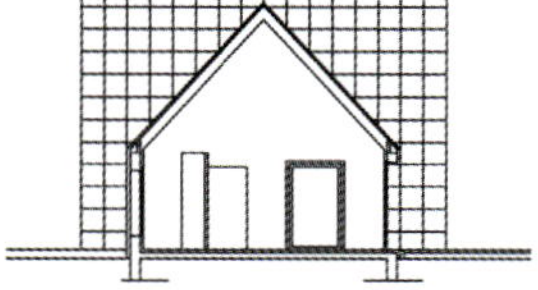

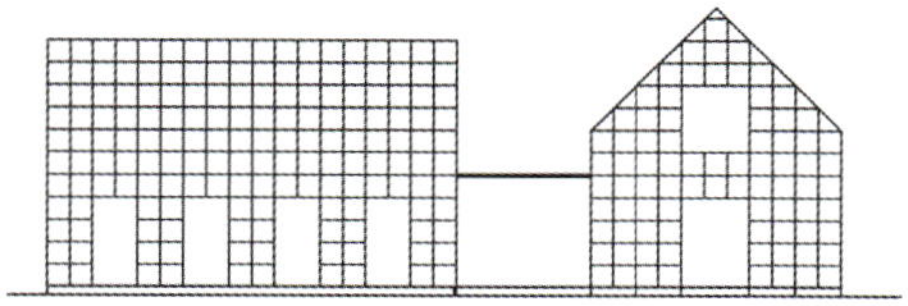

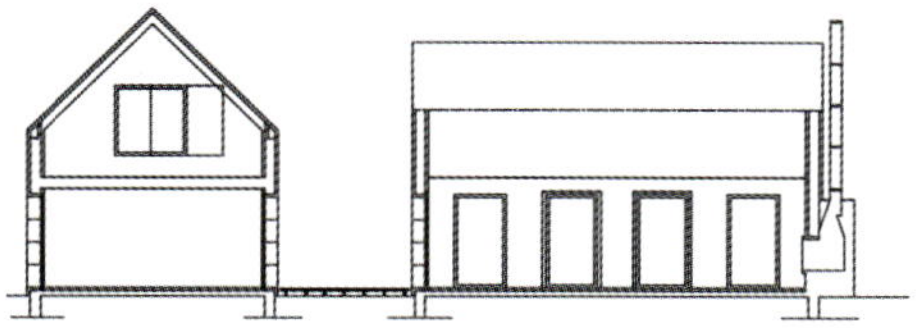

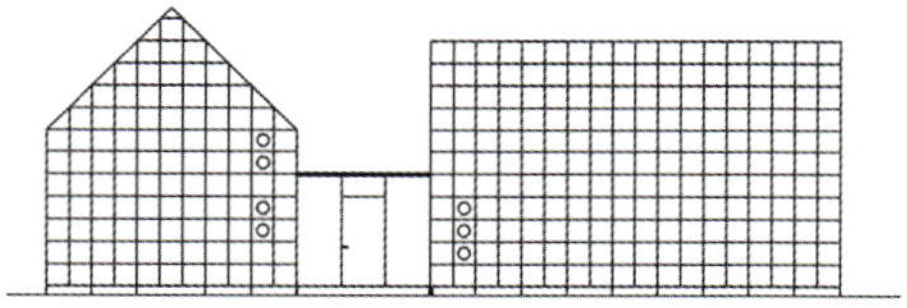

ミ・デリリオの住宅
海沿いの寺院

HOUSE OF MY DELIRIUM
A temple by the sea

ルイス・フローレス・アベジャン
撮影：ホアン・ヒッタース／サープレスエージェンシー

LUIS FLORES ABELLÁN
PHOTO: © Juan Hitters/Surpress

ラ・バーラ、プンタ・デル・エステ ― ウルグアイ ― 2005

　クライアントの強い個性を映して、この美しい海を臨む別荘は、堂々とした静かな美しさを湛えている。石、木、セメント、ガラスなどの材料にはいっさい塗装も仕上げもほどこされず、無垢な状態のままに置かれている。石は構造的要素として外壁となり同時に内壁となっている。壁面に厚く塗りこめられたプラスターが醸し出す強い存在感、構造が打ち出す独特の美学、それらにはネイティブ・アメリカンの民族性がにじみ出ており、住宅はまるでマヤ文明の寺院のようだ。

Induced by his client's strong personality, the architect planned a summer home with scenic views of the sea, monumental character and sober elegance.
The elements used – stone, wood, cement and glass – had no treatments or color changes at all. The stone was incorporated as a structural element on the outside and in the interiors. The walled surfaces – thickly plastered – and the imposing esthetic of the building insinuate a native-American ethnicity, as if it were a type of Mayan temple.

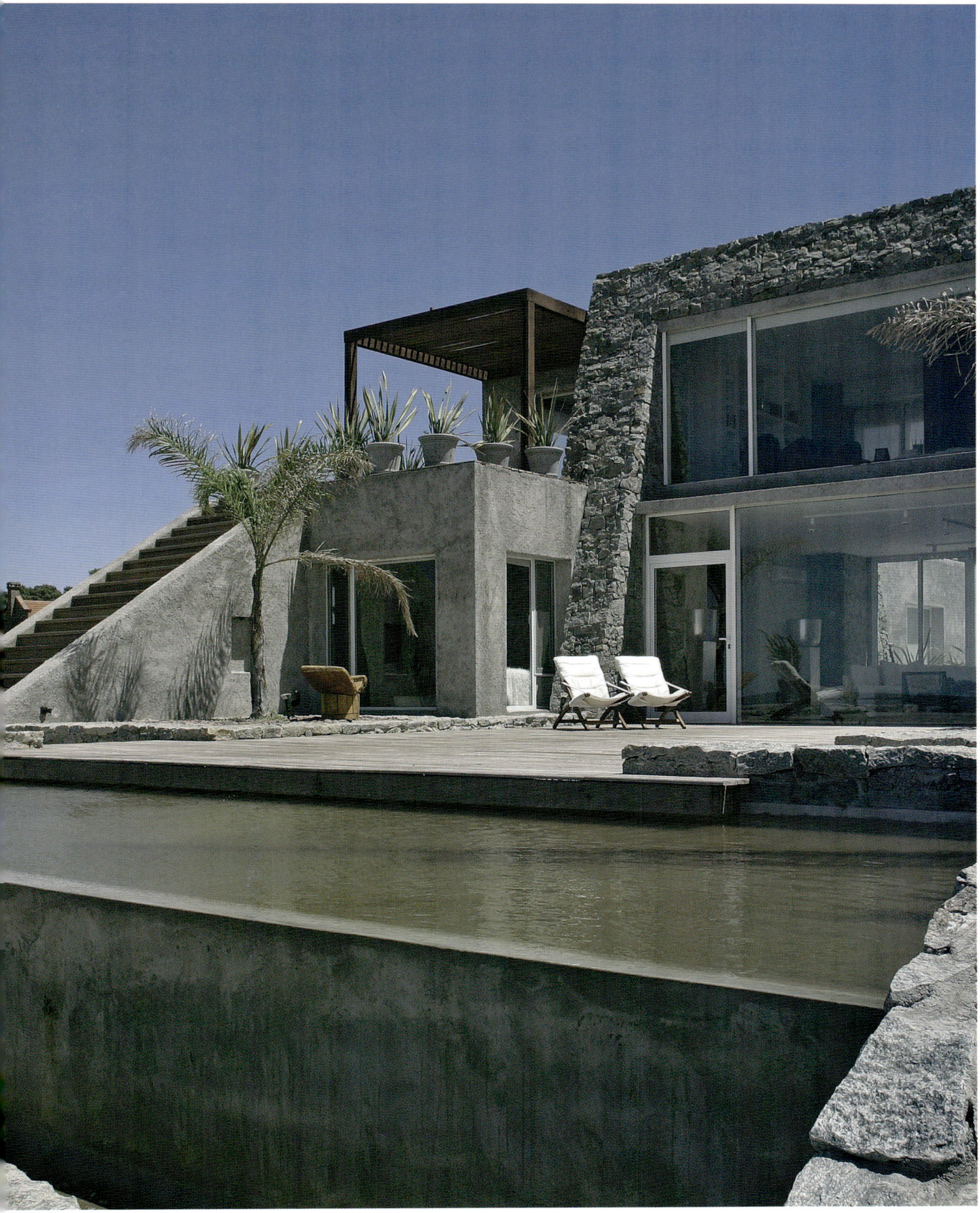

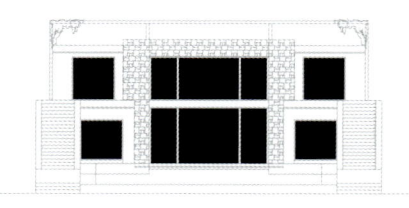

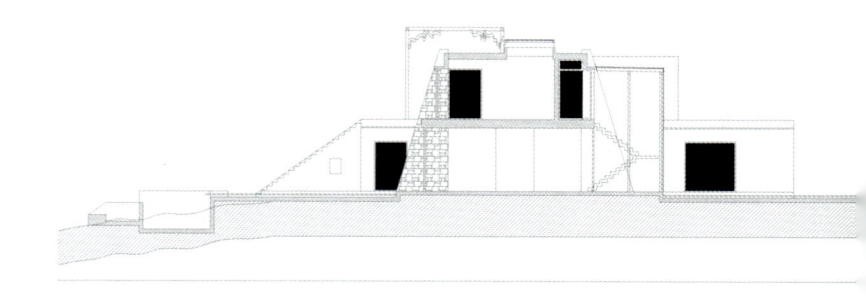

146 建築
Architecture

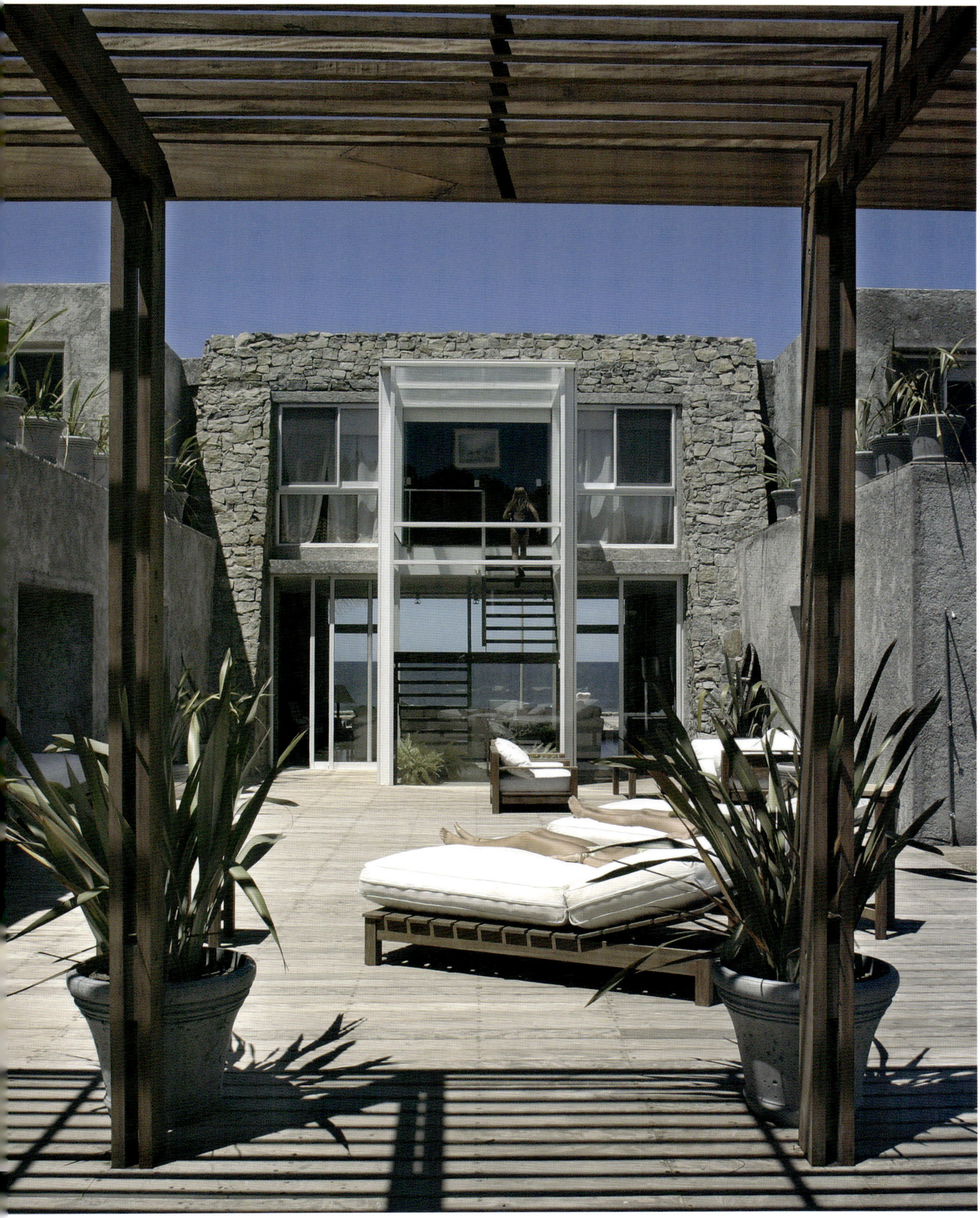

フリンダース・ビーチの住宅
アースカラー

サイモン・スワニー建築設計事務所
撮影：トレバー・マイン／マイン・フォト

SIMON SWANEY ARCHITECT
PHOTO: © Trevor Mein / Mein Photo

FLINDERS BEACH HOUSE
Earth color

フリンダース、ビクトリア州 ─ オーストラリア ─ 2004

　住宅はオーストラリアの気候風土によく適合している。この大陸の海岸線に沿って増殖している多くの巨大住宅とは正反対に、この住宅の設計思想は、無駄を削ぎ落とした耐用年数の長い建物を建てるということで一貫している。耐力壁と外壁には、セメントと土を混合した版築 (rammed earth) が用いられているが、それはほとんどメンテナンスを必要とせず、調湿調温にも優れている。版築による二重壁構造は、時折吹きつける強い海風から主住空間を護っている。

A house that has been adapted to the climate and characteristics of the land on which it sits. As opposed to the majority of the large homes that have proliferated along the Australian coast-line, the plans were drawn to construct a lean and durable edifice. The load-bearing walls and enclosure incorporate rammed earth, a mix of cement and soil, and need very little maintenance. The double-walled exterior of the property protects the main body from the occasionally strong coastal winds.

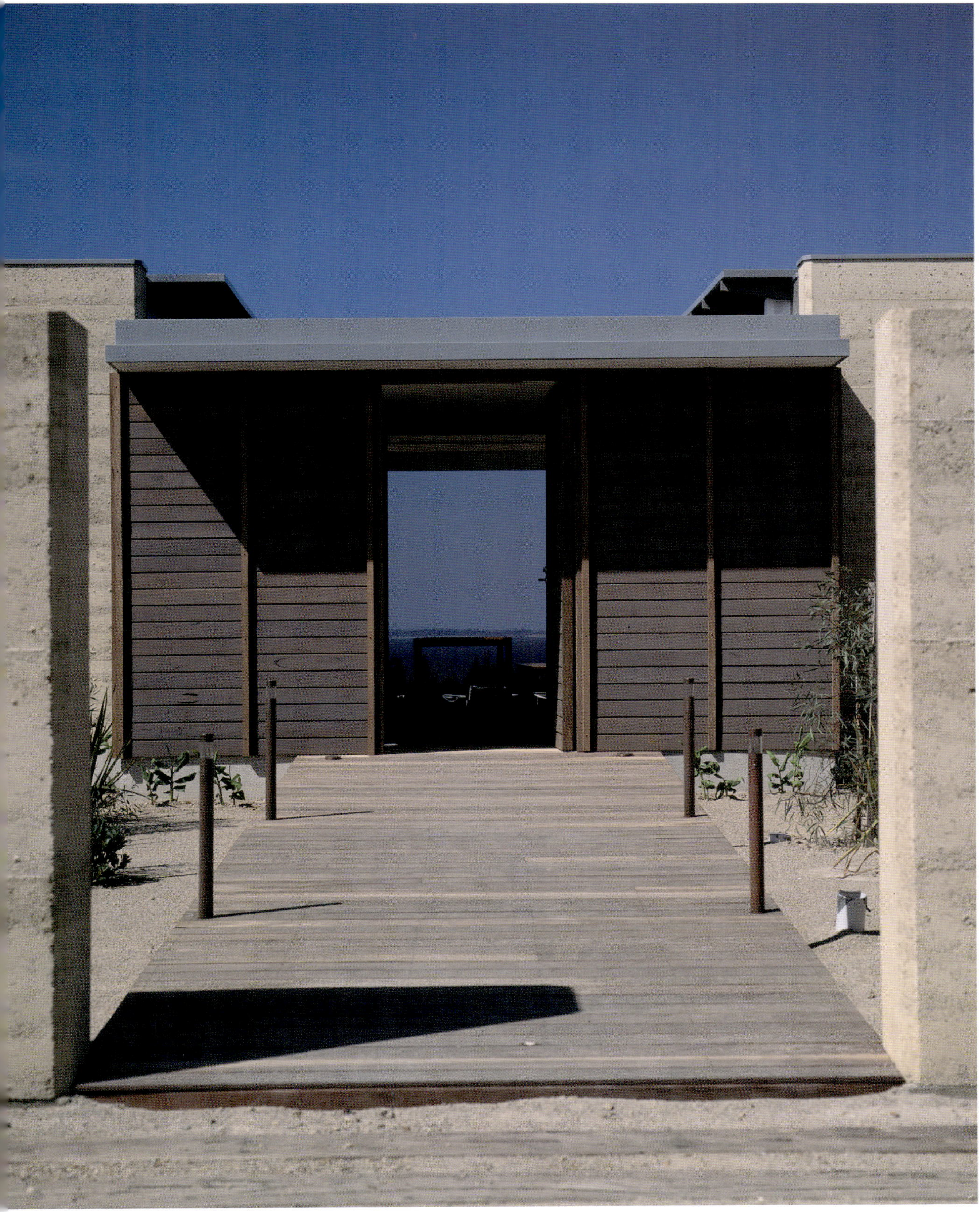

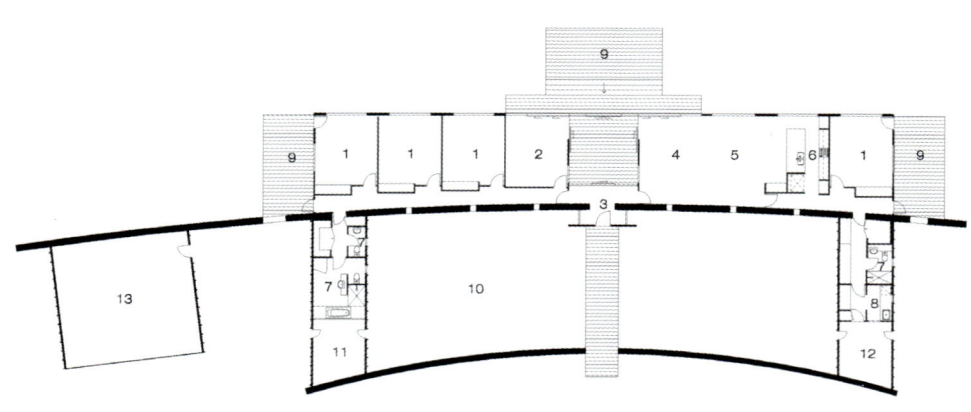

1. ベッドルーム
2. プレイルーム
3. 玄関
4. リビング
5. ダイニング
6. キッチン
7. バスルーム
8. ランドリー
9. デッキ
10. セントラルガーデン
11. 北向きの庭
12. サービスヤード
13. ガレージ

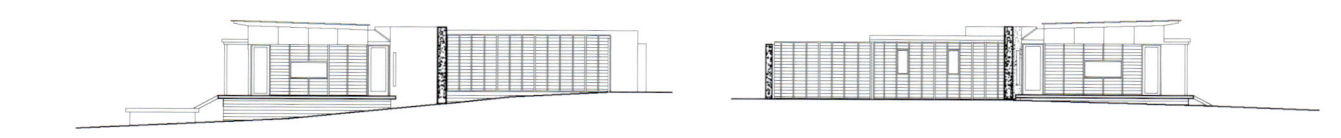

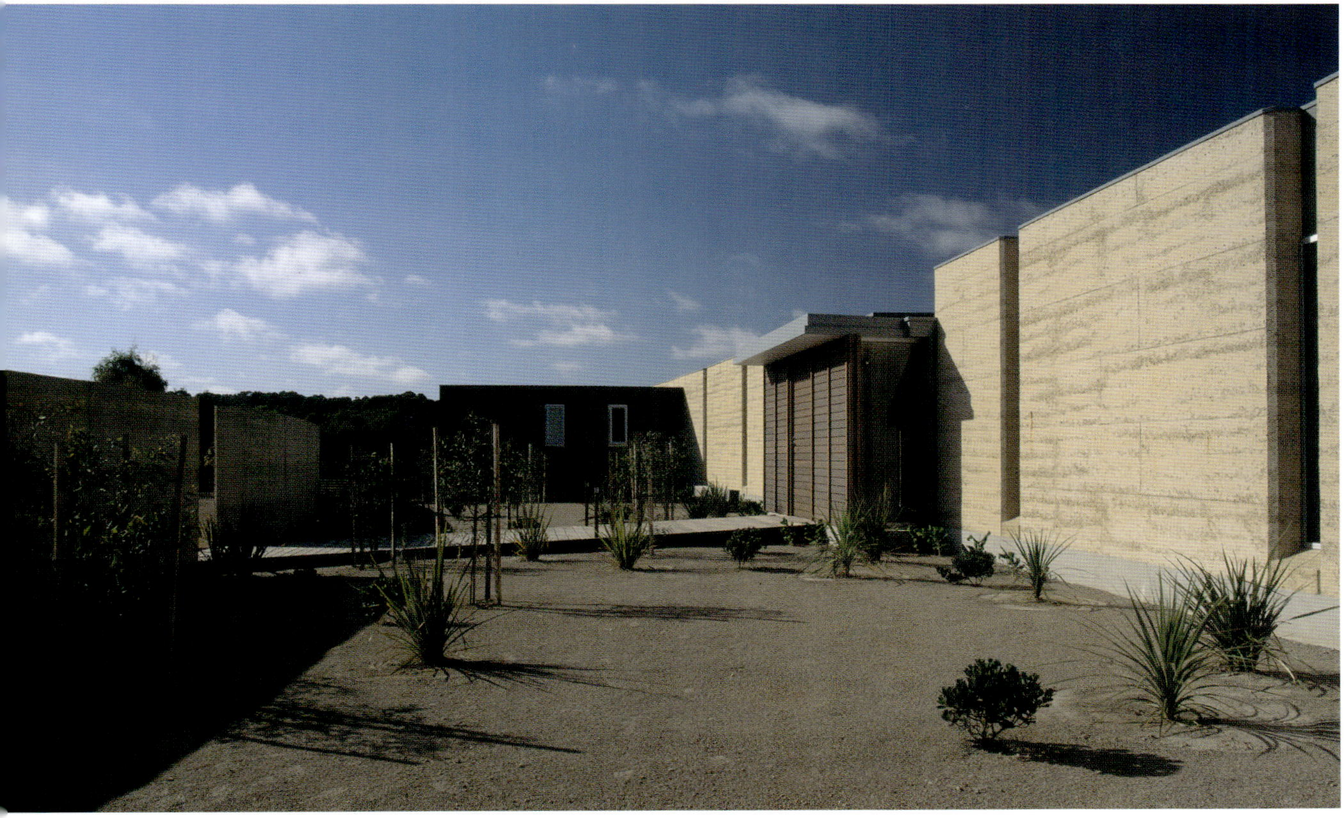

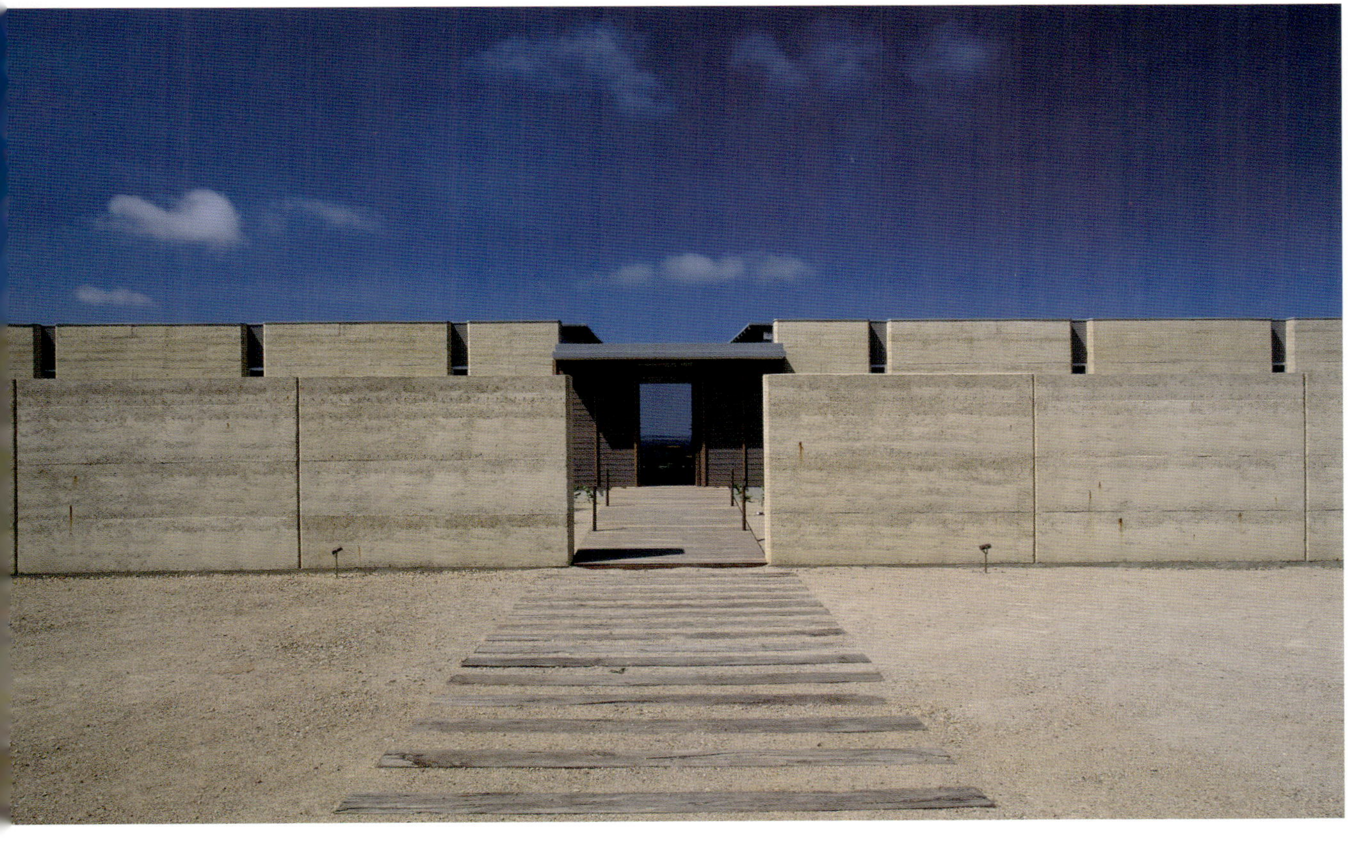

葡萄畑の住宅
土着的で現代的な
ヴァナキュラー　コンテンポラリー

VINEYARD RESIDENCE
Vernacular and contemporary

ジョン・ウォードル建築設計事務所
撮影：トレバー・マイン／マイン・フォト

JOHN WARDLE ARCHITECTS
PHOTO: © Trevor Mein / Mein Photo

モーニントン ― オーストラリア ― 2004

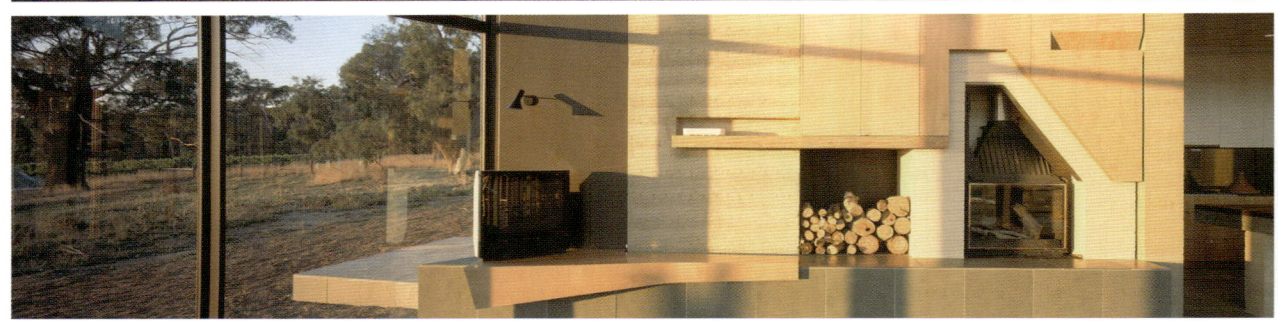

　版築など直接大地から譲り受ける材料を使いながら、建物は現代的線によって構成され、葡萄畑が広がる豊かな自然やモーニントン半島の土着の建物と、文脈を崩すことなくよく調和している。建築家は、ヴィンテージものの台木に新株を接木して独創的なワインを生み出しているオーストラリア・ワインの活気を、独特の隠喩（メタファー）を用いて表現したのだろう。生気候学的設計によって自然な室温調整や受動的太陽熱利用が図られ、化石燃料にあまり頼らないですむ住宅となっている。

The architect chose a modern line, achieving it through materials of partially earthen origin, such as rammed earth, and adapting them to this rural vineyard landscape and the vernacular architecture of the Mornington peninsula, without resorting to de-contextualization. Using his own metaphor, it's as if it were an attempt to graft strains of new wine with that of a vintage harvest. Its bioclimatic design incorporates natural ventilation, passive solar heating and low energy consumption.

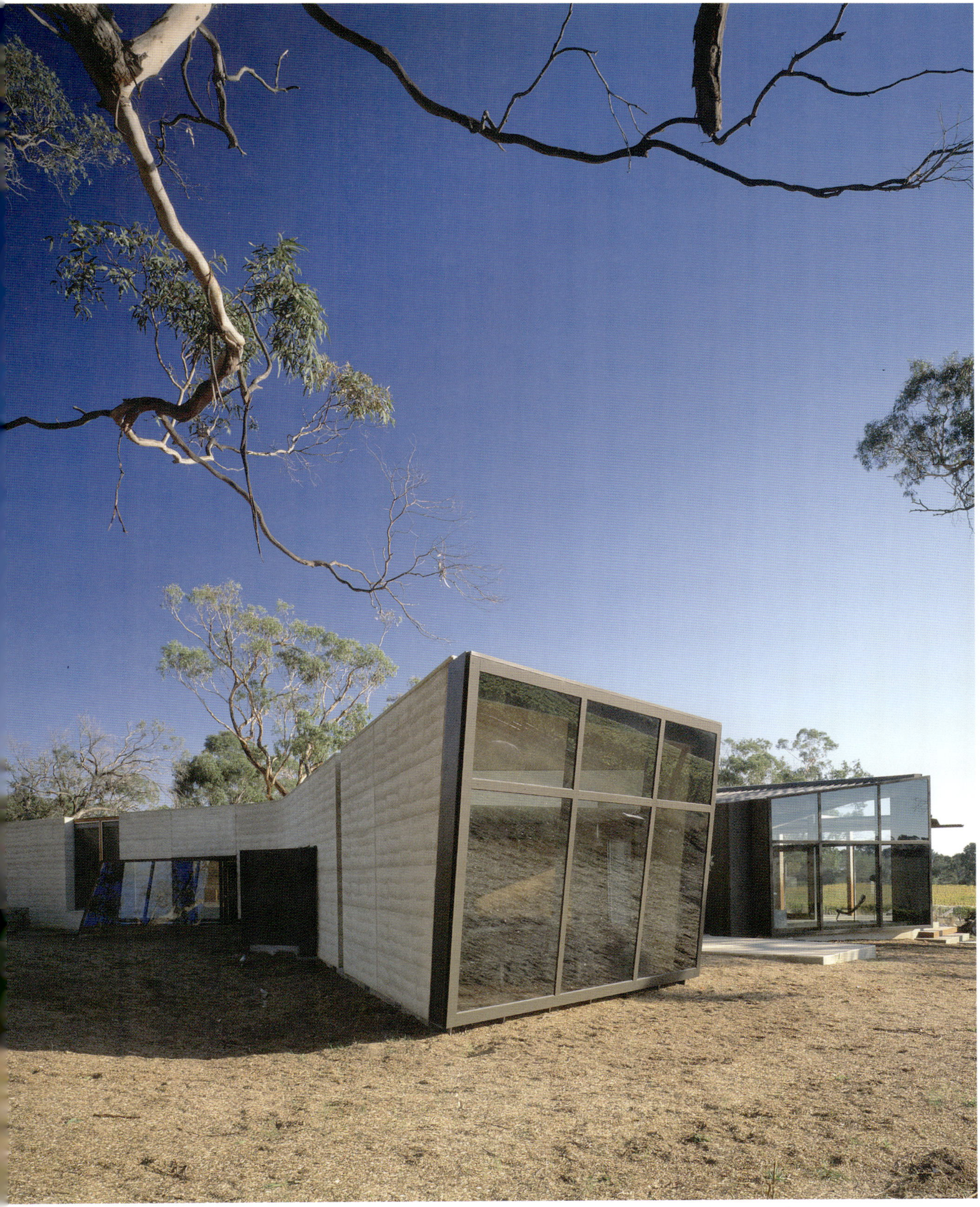

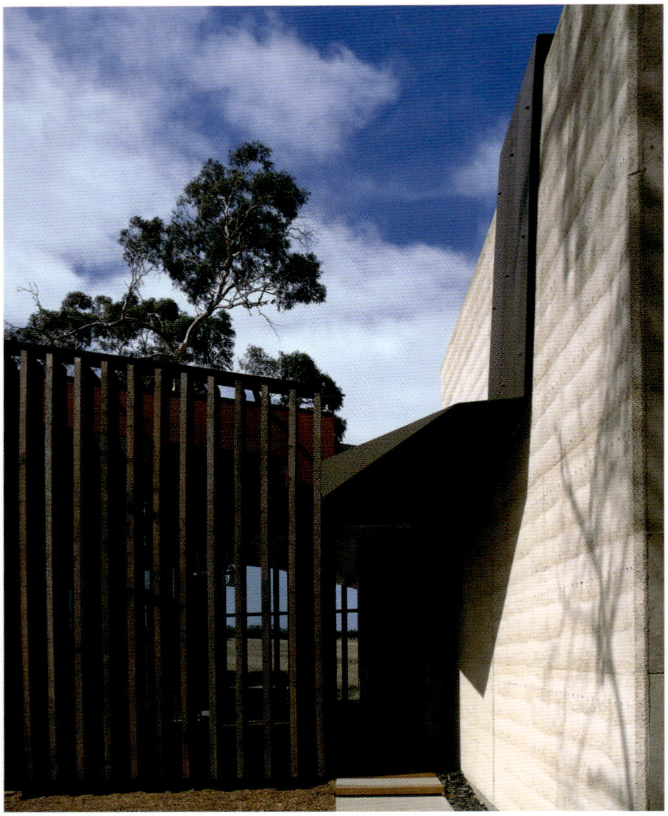

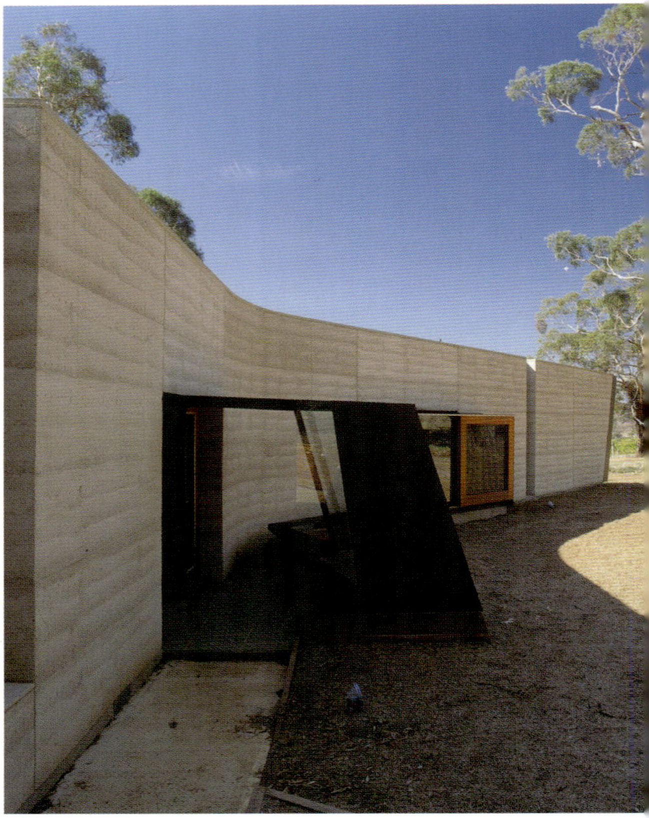

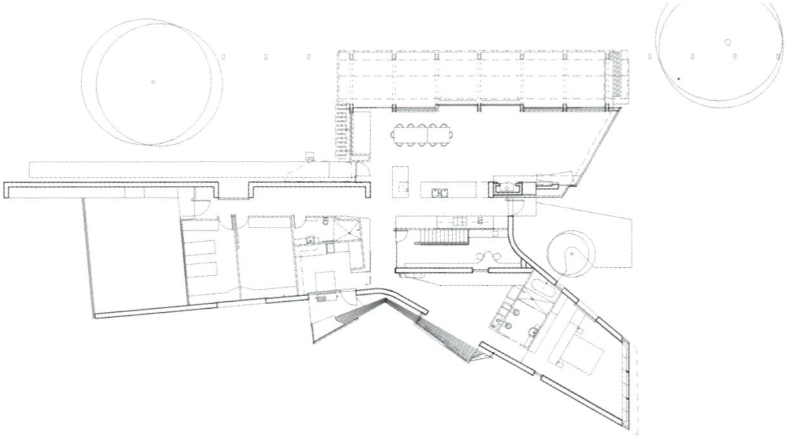

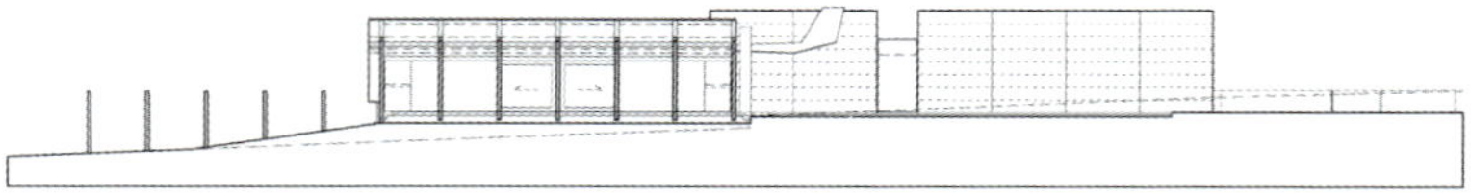

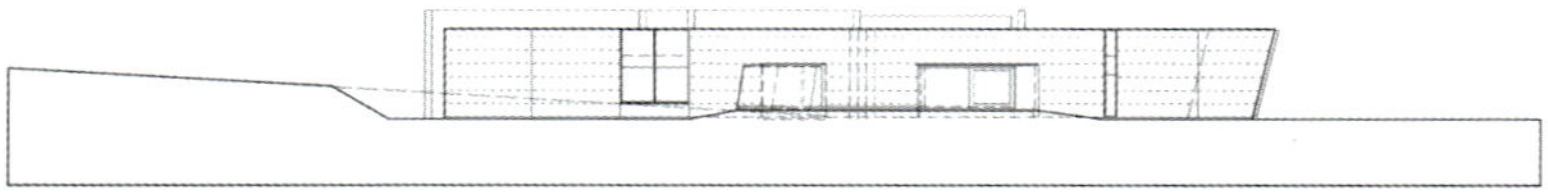

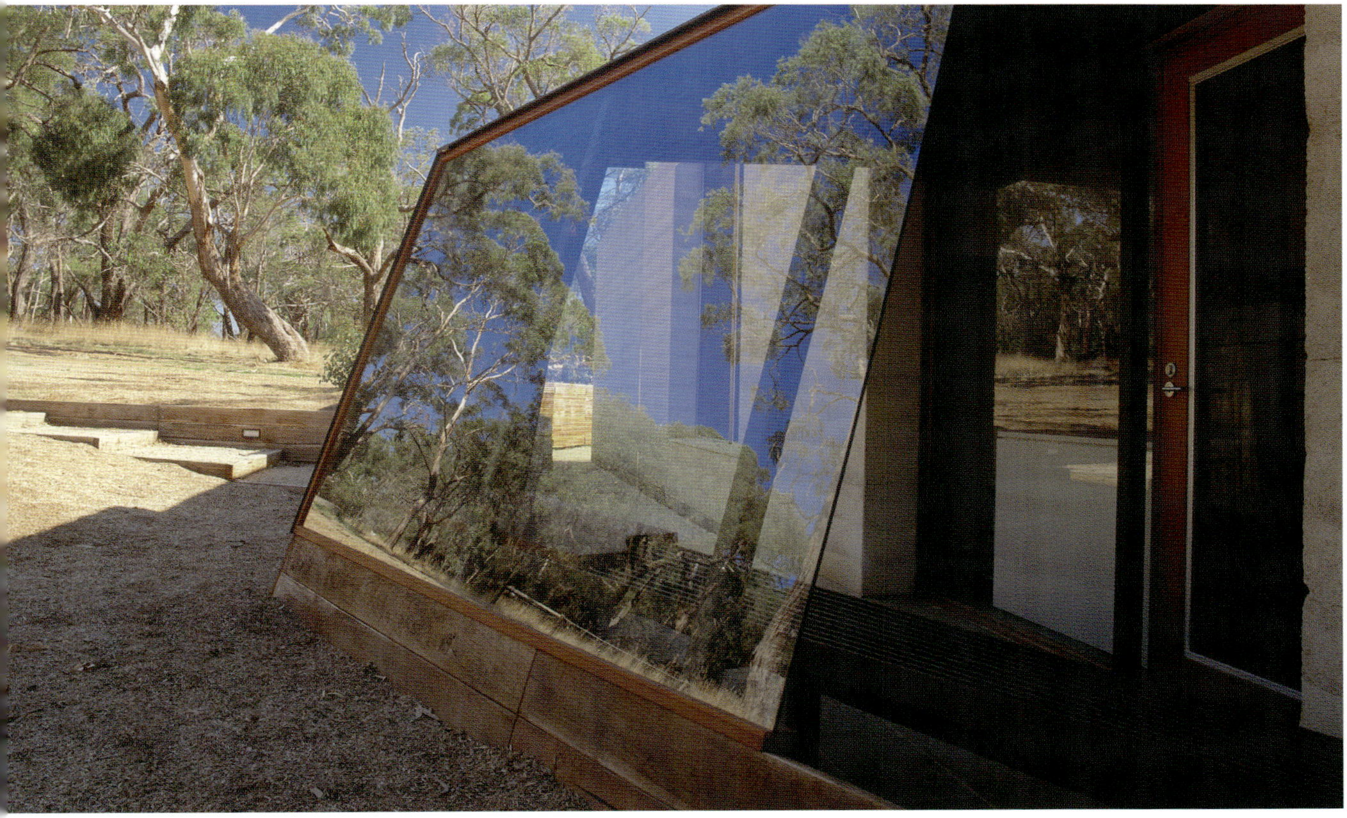

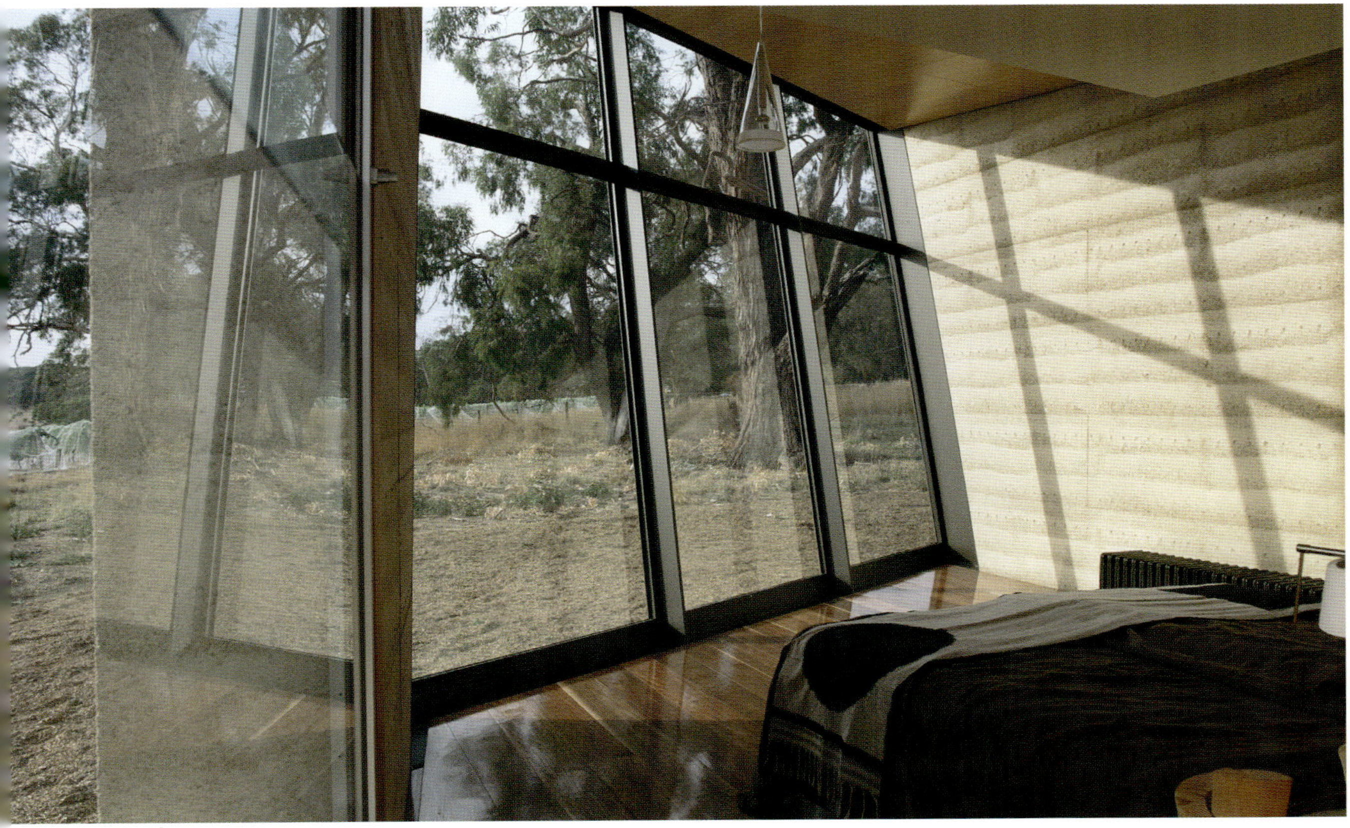

ポルケラ・デ・ロス・インファンテスのロフト
いなかの前衛

ヘスス・カスティージョ・オリ
撮影：アンゲル・バルタナス

JESÚS CASTILLO OLI
PHOTO: © Ángel Baltanás

LOFT IN PORQUERA DE LOS INFANTES
Rural vanguard

ポルケラ・デ・ロス・インファンテス ― スペイン ― 2006

廃墟を改築するという仕事を続けてきたカスティージョ・オリは、この激しく損壊した田舎の建物を用いて、革新と脱文脈化の狂喜に達した。元の石造の耐力壁と、窓の多く空いた2層のレンガ積みの構造物は手付かずのまま保存された。建物は質素な骨格と材料で造られているが、それは実験的精神を呼び覚まし、都市の工業的空間を連想させる。この住宅は、この地を永く覆っている農本主義的因習に対する現代的破戒を達成した。

With the aim of rehabilitating a ruin, Castillo Oli achieved a rapture of innovation and de-contextualization with this battered rural building, of which the original load-bearing masonry walls and the hollow double-brick construction were kept intact. A building of humble fabric and material, it awakens an experimental spirit and recalls the industrial spaces of urban architecture. It has achieved a contemporary transgression, considering the agrarian tradition of the location.

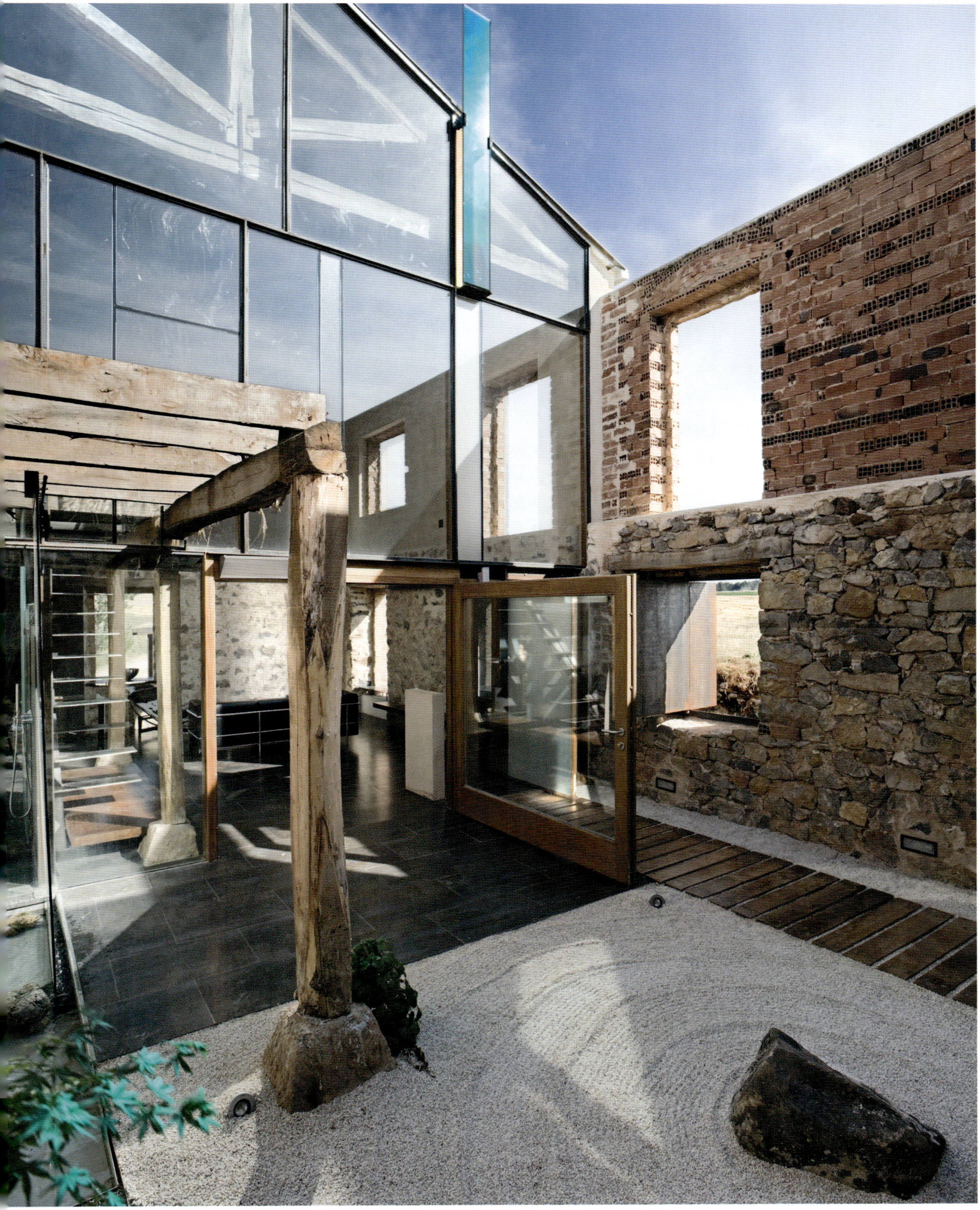

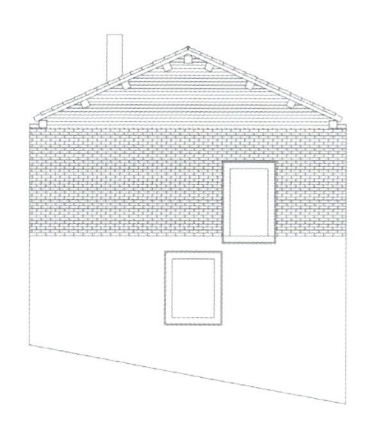

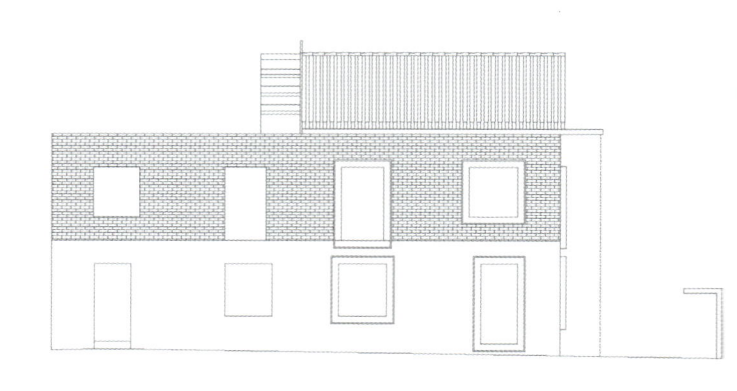

158 建築
Architecture

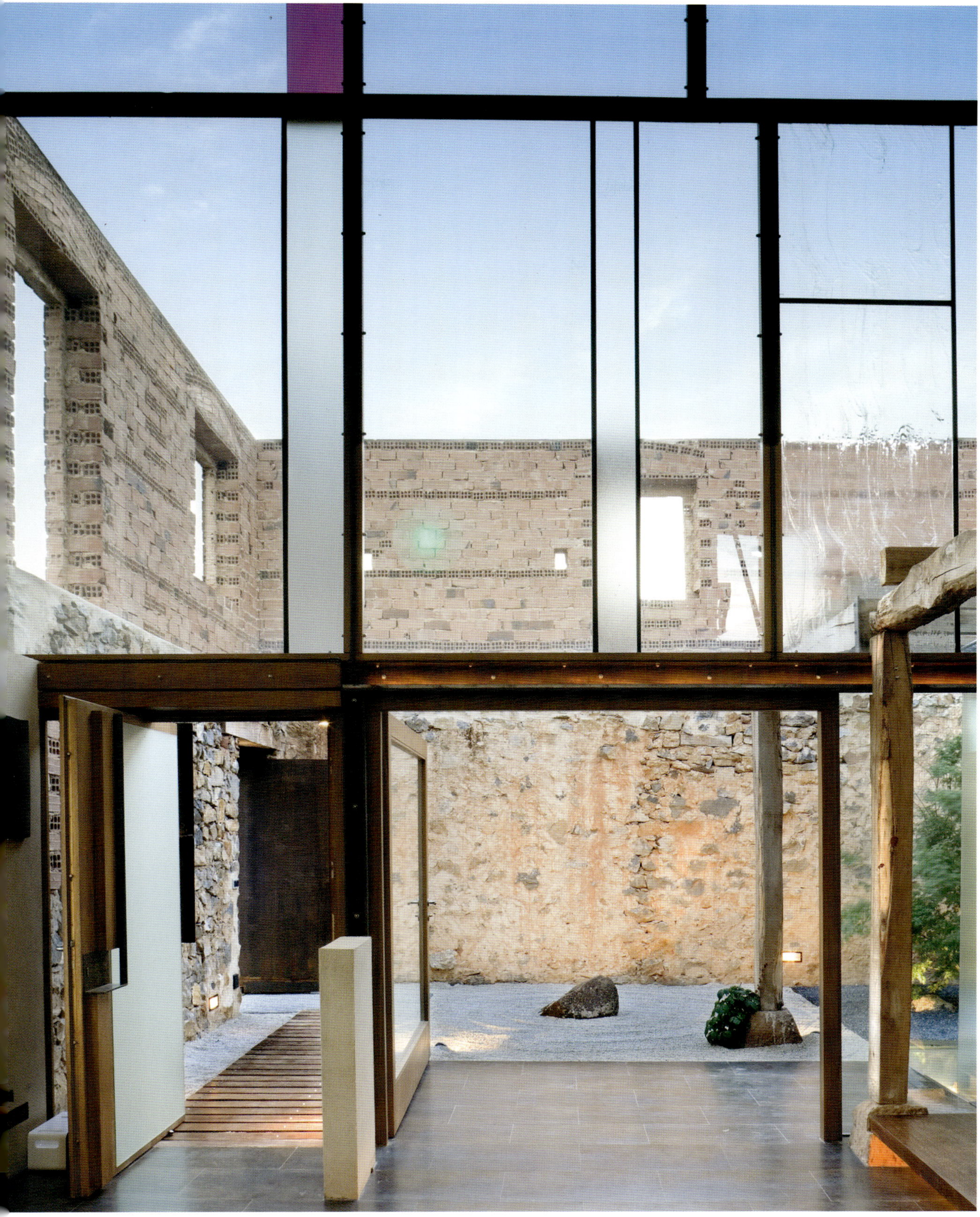

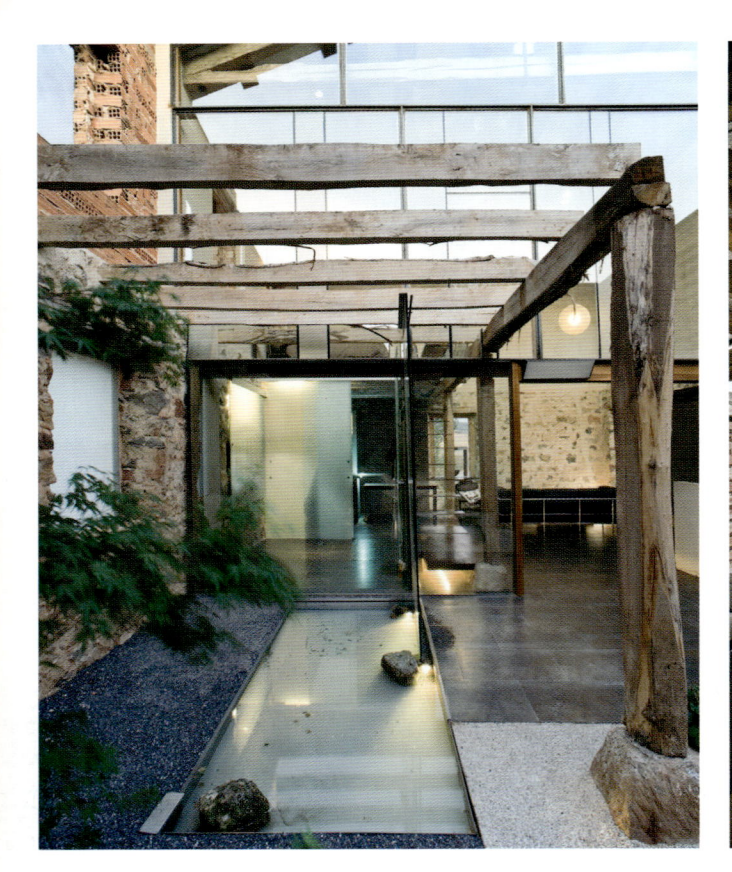

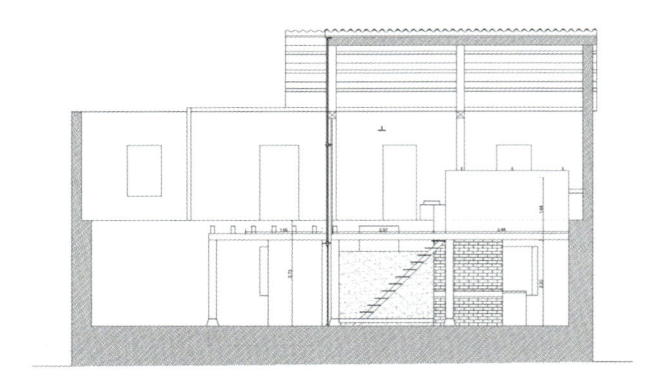

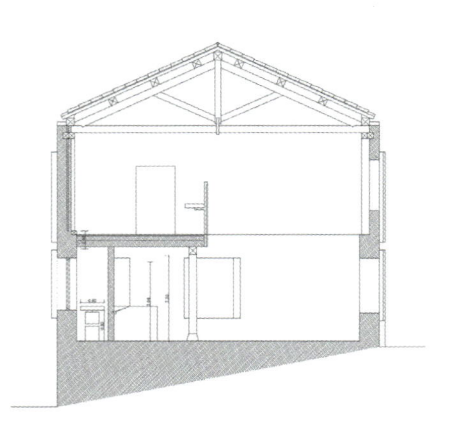

160 建築
Architecture

建築家は深みと存在感を増すため、わざと脱文脈化した材料を用いた。1階の元の石造の耐力壁は、室内に重厚な質感をもたらし、工場を思わせる内装に現代的な風趣を化合させている。

The architect meant for the use of de-contextualized materials to lend depth and presence. The original load-bearing mason wall on the first floor stamps texture into the interior, combining contemporary traces with a factory appearance.

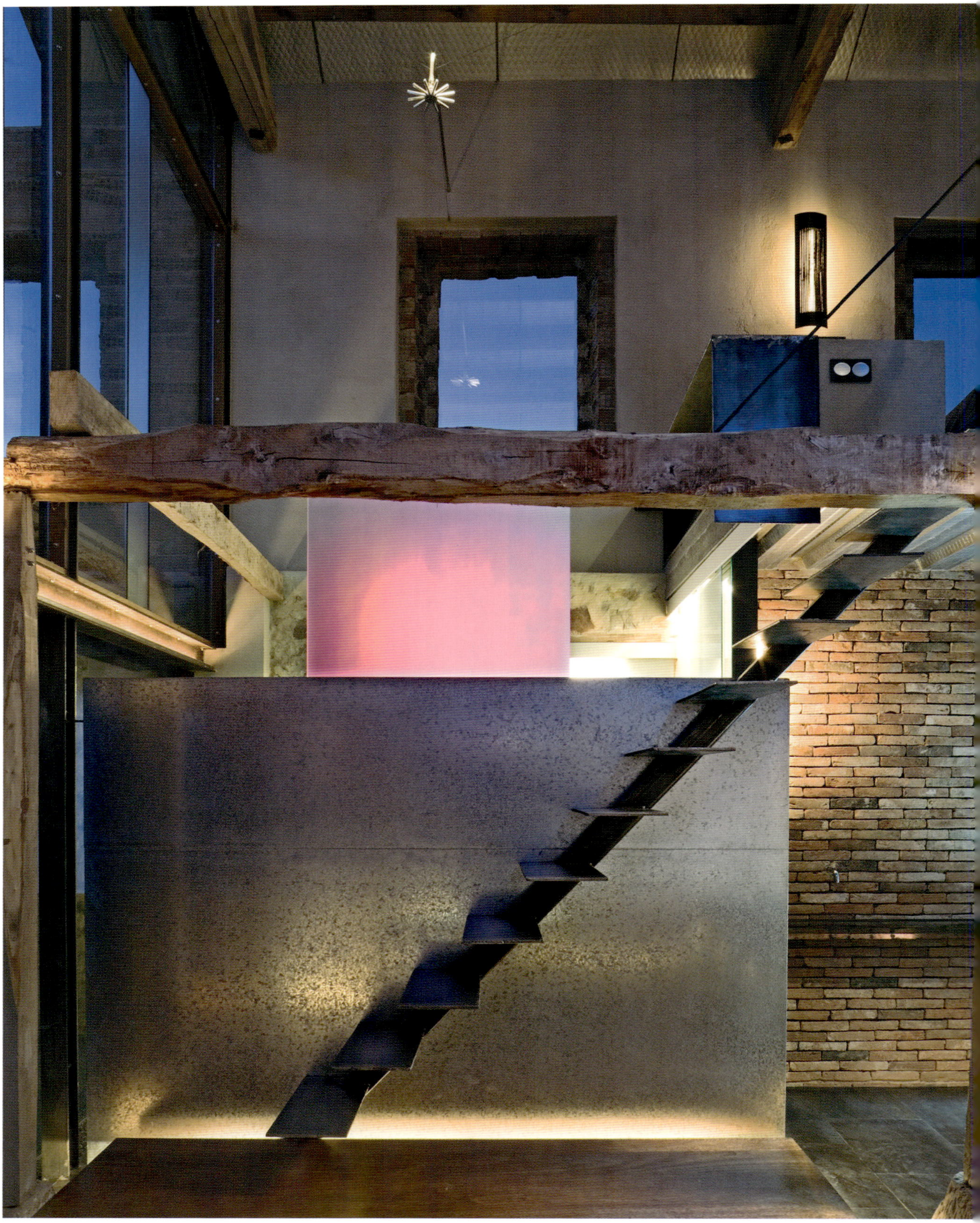

ファイブロセメント・シートや亜鉛メッキ鋼板、レンガ、木、エンボス加工アルミニウム、ホログラフィック・ガラスなどのあまり高価でない工業的材料が、古い、倉庫のような建物に現代的文脈を持ち込んでいる。

Inexpensive, industrial materials – like fibrocement sheets, galvanized steel plating, brick, wood, embossed aluminum or holographic glass – lend a contemporary context to an old warehouse type building.

第2部 インテリア

強固であるが、無限の建築的可能性を持つ地球素材、それらはわれわれの日常生活にその独特の個性を強く刻印する。それぞれのエレメント（石、日干し煉瓦など）は多種多様な色相、形、質感を有し、建物が置かれている環境に応じて、様々な装飾様式に適応する。磨きあげ研ぎ澄まされたミニマリスト的美しさから、質感の豊かさを強調する古風な、あるいは鄙びた表面仕上げまで、自然がもたらす高貴で優美な素材が示す無限の可能性をじっくり鑑賞していただきたい。

Solid by nature, but with an almost unlimited capacity for adaptation, the earth's materials imprint their character on our everyday settings.
Thanks to the great variety of tones, shapes and textures possessed by some elements (like stone or adobe); environments may acquire different decorative styles. From minimalist esthetics (which favor polished finishes) to those with a more antique, or rural cut (strengthened by a textural richness), the following pages illustrate the infinite possibilities of nature's most noble components.

ポルタス・ノヴァスの住宅

ヴィクトール・カニャス
撮影：ジョルディ・ミラレス

PORTAS NOVAS HOUSE
VÍCTOR CAÑAS
PHOTO: © Jordi Miralles

　コスタリカ半島に位置しているこの住宅は、起伏に富んだこの国の地形を再現している。主住空間は3つのユニットに分けられ、それぞれのユニットは漂礫の庭で囲まれている。その触感に満ちたおうとつのある表面は、建物を構成しているコンクリートとガラスの巨大な拡がりと対照的である。この漂礫の海を横切っているのは、チーク材でできた渡り廊下で、それは住宅の入り口である大理石と御影石でできた遊歩道(エスプラネード)へとつながり、そのまま大らかに太平洋まで延びている。

Situated on a Costa Rican peninsula, this building reproduces the staggered topography of the terrain. The principal body of the edification is divided into three units surrounded by a boulder garden. The highly textured surface contrasts with the huge expanses of cement and glass that form the building. Teak catwalks cross this sea of pebbles, connecting the marble and granite esplanades that form the entrance to this home which generously opens onto the Pacific Ocean.

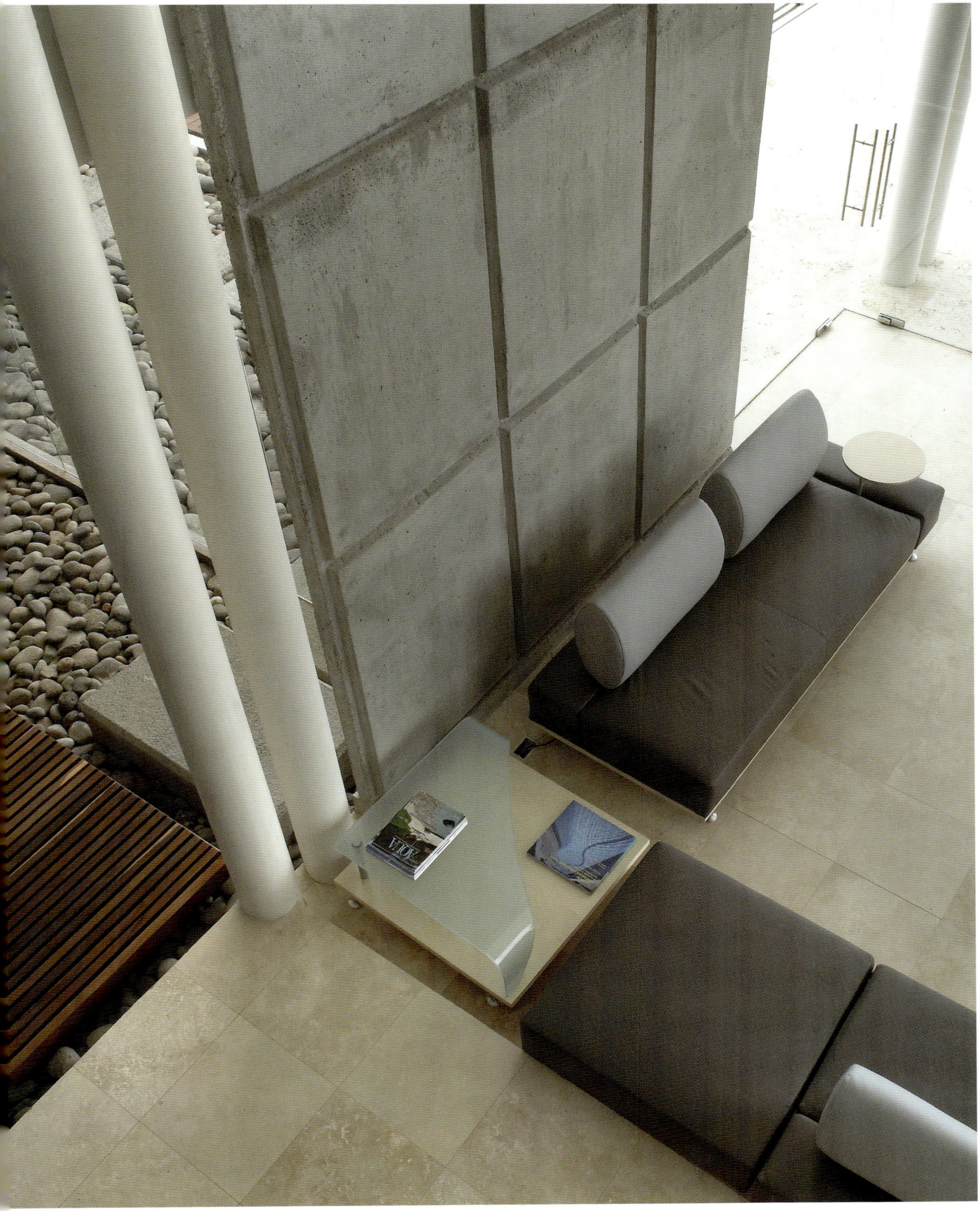

サバデルの改築住居

M2建築設計事務所
撮影：ホセ・エヴィア

REFORMING A HOME IN SABADELL
M2 ARQUITECTURA
PHOTO: © José Hevia

　サバデル旧市街の真ん中に位置する住宅の改築の話が出たとき、建築家は即座に、古い建物に残された伝統的な遺構を新しい建物の一部として組み込むことに決めた。なかでも、隣家との境界をなす住宅背部にある中庭の壁に、最も魅惑的なアンティークな要素を見いだした。下側3mまでの石積みを剥き出しのまま壁の土台にすることによって、侘びの雰囲気を漂わせる石造りの後土間（パーテール）ができあがった。

When the renovation of this house in the old center of Sabadell was proposed, the architect wasted no time in realizing the convenience of conserving some of the more traditional vestiges of the past in terms of fixtures, finding in the rear patio wall (shared with the neighboring building) the most attractive antique element yet. Lacking any covering on the wall below three meters high, a Zen-inspired parterre of rocks was built into the base of the wall.

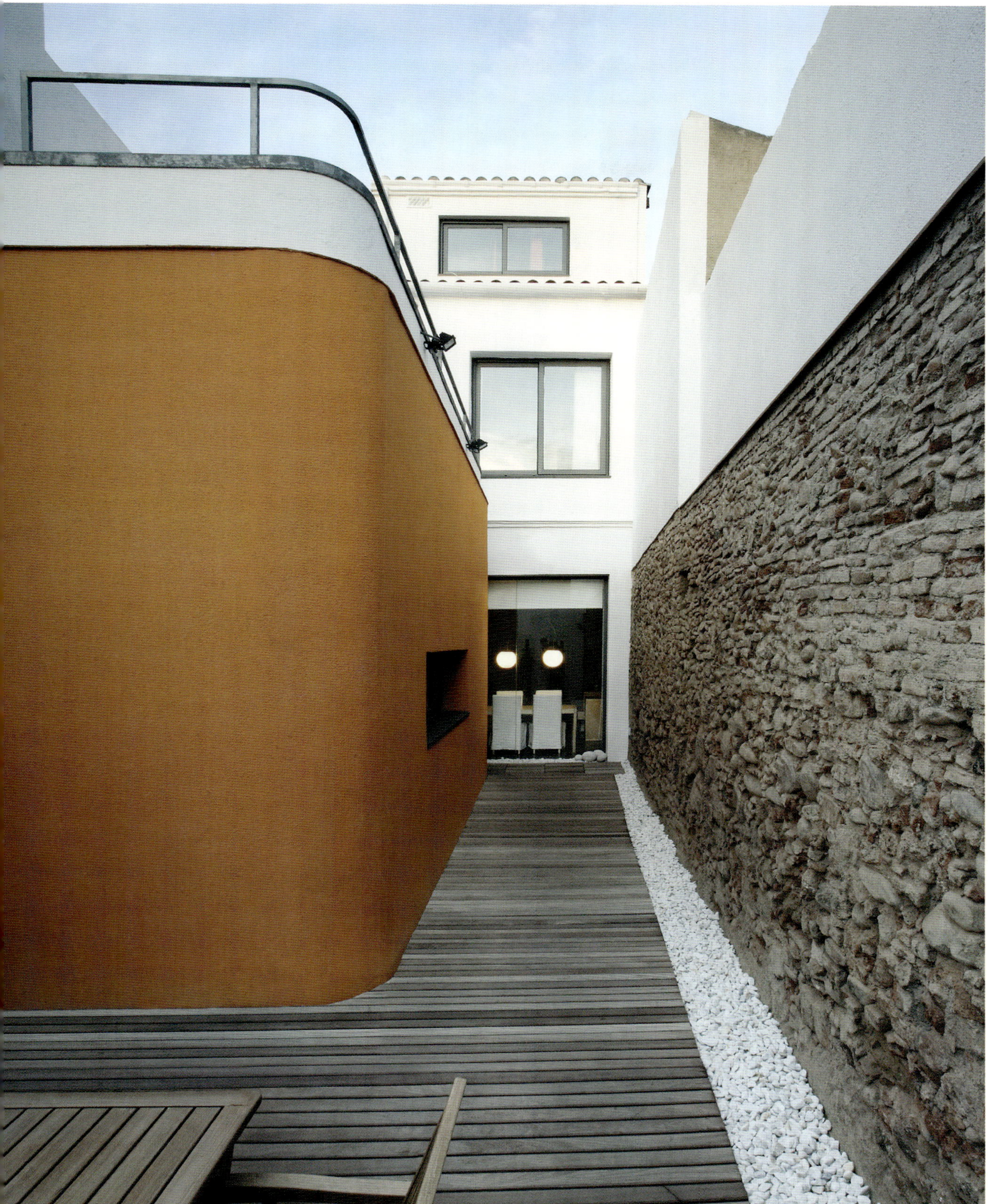

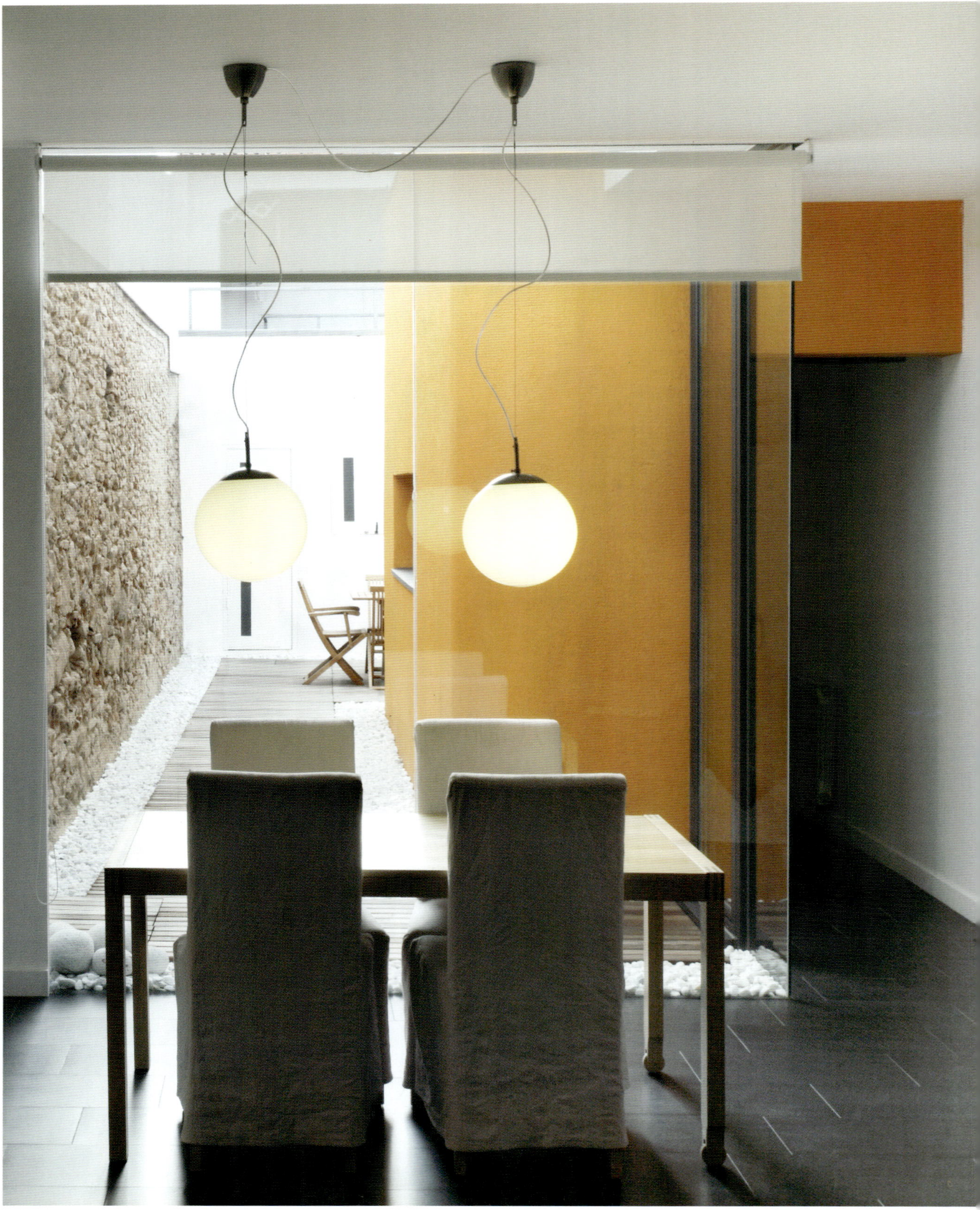

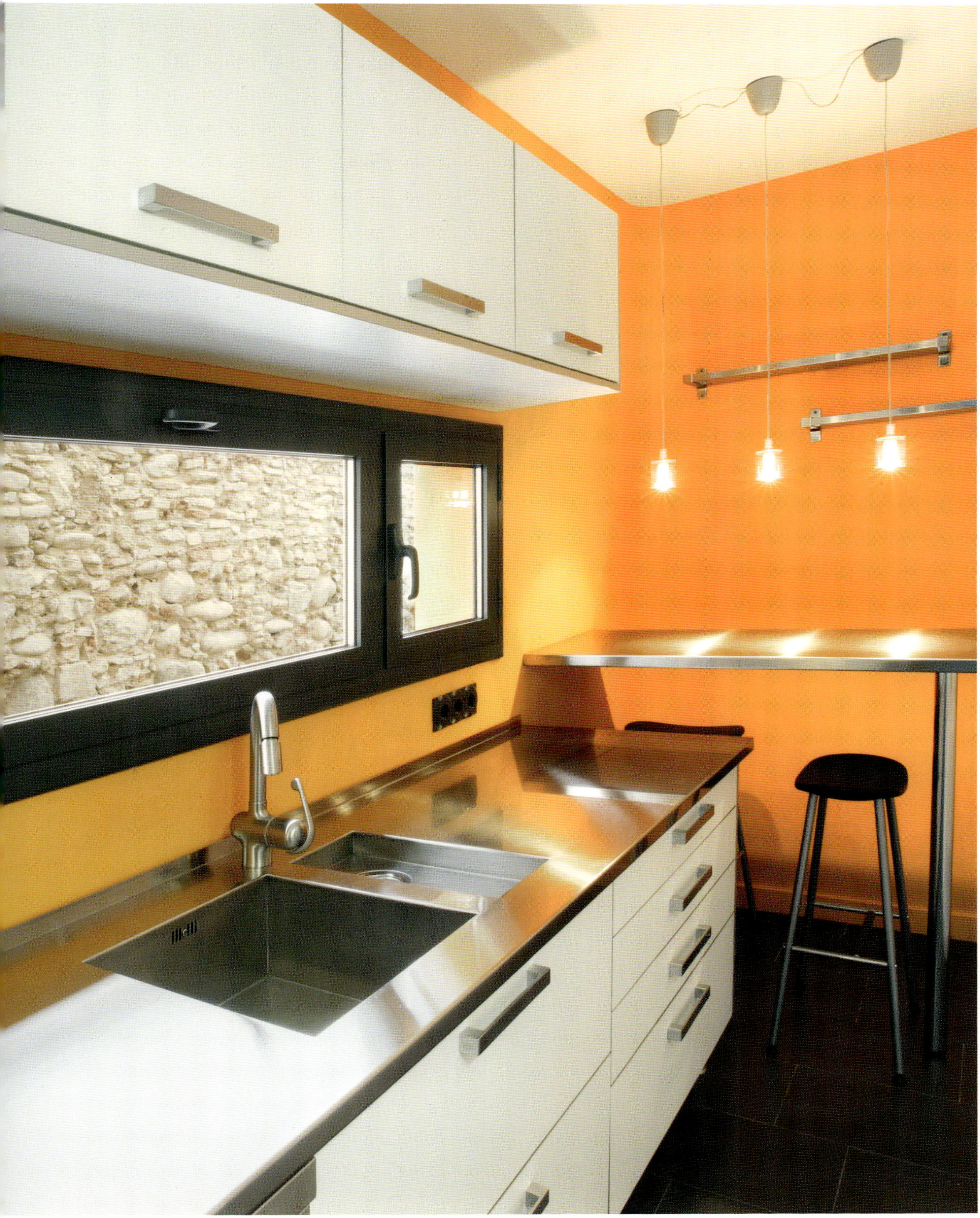

プッチェルダの住宅

カルレス・ジェルピ・アロヨ
撮影：ユーゲニ・ポンス

HOUSE IN PUIGCERDÀ
CARLES GELPÍ I ARROYO
PHOTO: © Eugeni Pons

　ピレネー山脈の麓に立つこの住宅の改築には、2種類の天然スレートがあれば十分だった。それは建物のほぼ全体を構成しながら、伝統的エレメントを現代建築の線と結合させた。淡い色合いの薄い切石がところどころに厚い切石を含みながら壁を構成し、暗緑色の天然スレートが、室内の床材と屋根葺き材の両方に使われている。これらのふんだんに使われている天然スレートの持つ熱絶縁効果により、1年の多くを雪に囲まれているこの住宅の内部は、意外なほどに暖かい。

Two types of slate were enough to almost entirely compose and redress this residence in the Pyrenees which combines traditional elements with contemporary architectural lines. The flat rocks of a lighter tone – also the thickest ones – form the walls, while the darker slate is used in the interior flooring and as an external layer for the roofing. The thermal insulation that this rock provides makes it suitable for a home that's covered with snow many months of the year.

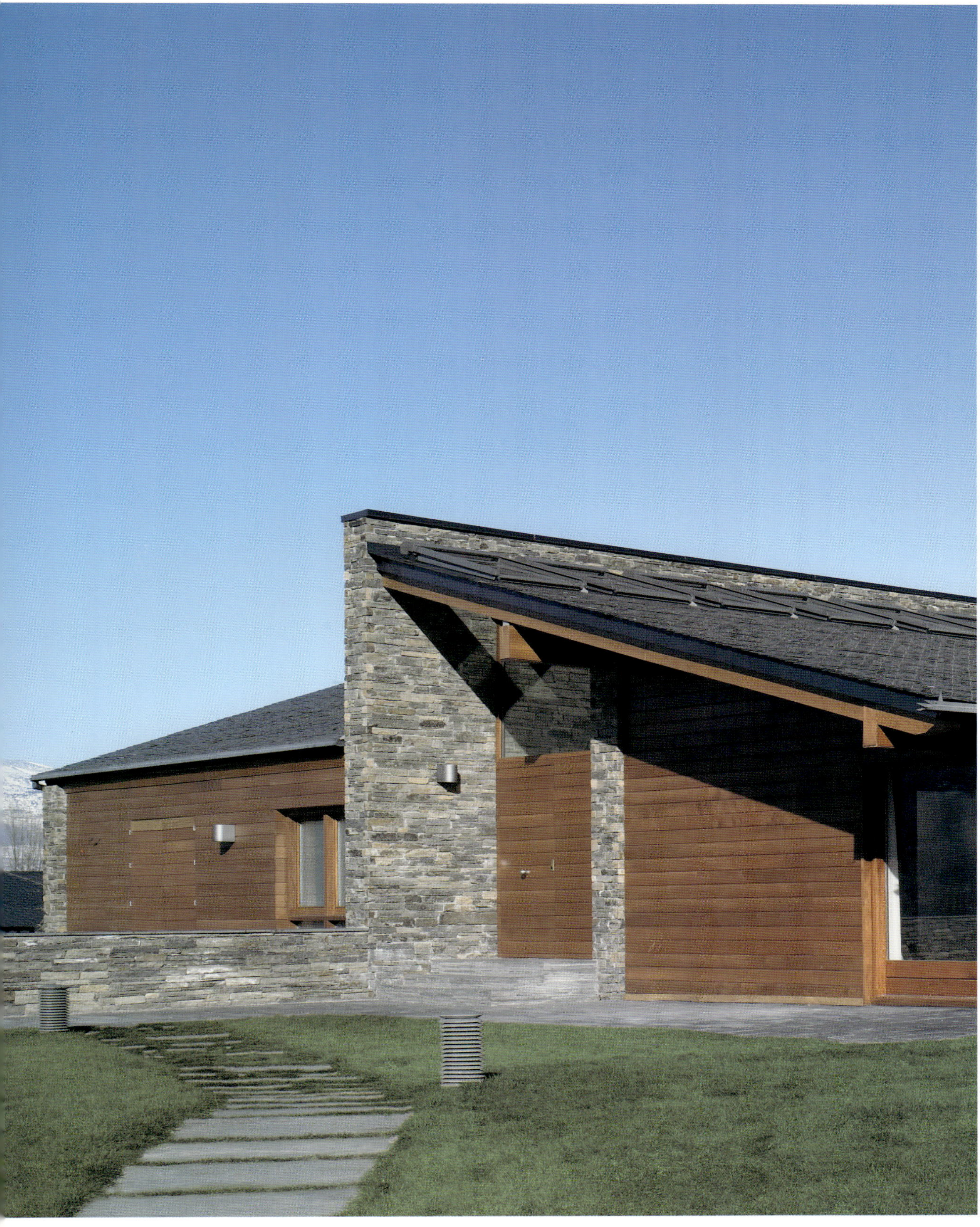

サン・ヴィチェンテの住宅

ヴィクトール・カニャス
撮影：ダニエラ・マッカデン／
サープレスエージェンシー

SAN VICENTE HOME
MARCELO DEL TORTO
PHOTO: © Daniela MacAdden/Surpressagency

　住宅は、それが置かれている広々とした平野にふさわしく、水平な面で定義されている。2つの主住空間を廊下が結ぶ構成となっていて、それぞれの空間は太陽の方角に基づいて設計された。地形を定義する地平線に平行になるように積まれた灰緑色の砂岩は、室内に重厚な質感をもたらし、木の暖かい無垢な線と対照をなしながら、豊かな装飾性を生み出している。

In accord with the vast and flat terrain upon which it's located, this house is defined by its horizontal plane. Composed of two central units connected by corridors, the spaces were built according to the sun's orientation. The arrangement of the gray sandstone rocks follows the predominating horizontal line, generating a texture that acquires a decorative value thanks to its contrast with the warm and pure lines of the wood.

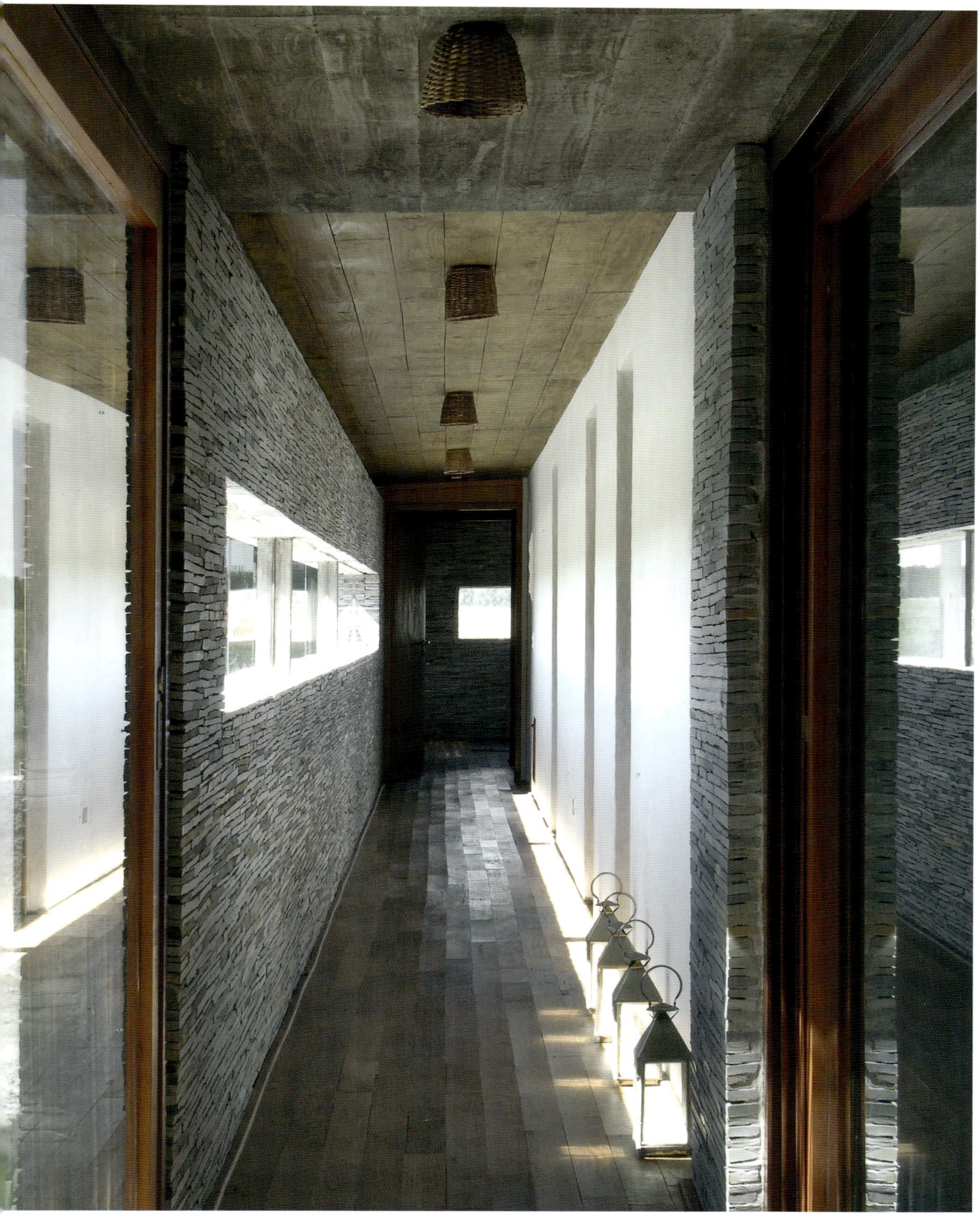

アストリッドの別荘

ウィンガーズ・アーキテクトコントロール
撮影：ジェームズ・シルバーマン

VILLA ASTRID
WINGARDHS ARKITEKTKONTOR
PHOTO: © James Silverman

　地形の高低差を大胆に利用して、住宅は山塊の一部をそのまま室内に導入し、擁壁とした。岩はその純粋な形状のまま1階の浴室、リビング、そして2階へ向う踊り場に出現し、建物を構成する幾何学的線、形、質感と対照的な姿を見せながら、それらと違和感なく融合している。ファサードに広く開けられた窓やガラスドアからも岩盤の露頭が眺められ、それがこの住宅の卓越した設計をいっそう際立たせている。

Thanks to the accentuated differences in the heights of the terrain on which this home was built, the mountain is introduced into the home and, naturally, acts as a retaining wall. The rock, in its purest state, bursts into the bottom floor bathroom, the living room and the entry way to the top floor, in contrast with the shapes and textures of the building's geometrical architecture. Seen through the large windows and glass doors, the rocky slope reinforces its prominence in the home's interior.

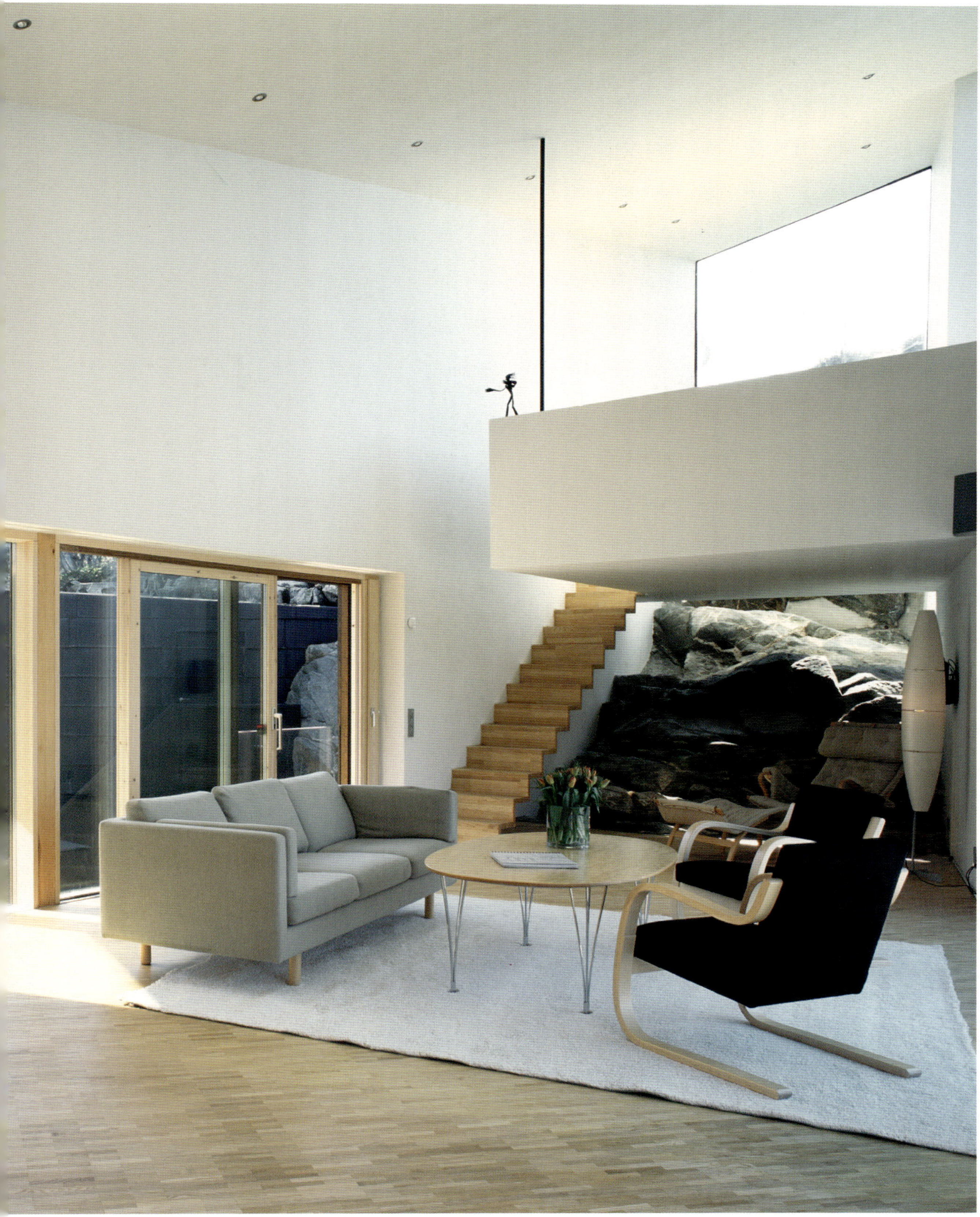

アル・マーレ

マーティン・ゴメス建築設計事務所
撮影：ホアン・ヒッタース／
サープレスエージェンシー
スタイリスト：マリアナ・ラポポルト

AL MARE
MARTÍN GÓMEZ ARQUITECTOS
PHOTO: © Juan Hitters (photos)/Surpressagency
Mariana Rapoport (stylist)

　石工職人の手練の技によって成型加工された25cmから70cm位までのさまざまな大きさの天然スレート・インゴットを見たとき、建築家はそれを使った壁をアルゼンチンのこの現代的な住宅の中心に据えようと決めた。壁は1階から3階までを貫いて立ち上がっているが、単純な繰り返しにならないように、どのようにインゴットを組積みするかに最大限の注意が払われた。片持ち階段の段板も、厚めの天然スレートを壁に組み込む形で作られている。

The careful cut given to these slate ingots (which fluctuate in length between 10 and 27 inches) by the artisan who made them, convinced the architect of the convenience of giving this wall center-stage in a modern Argentinean home. The wall runs along all three levels of the house, becoming its own puzzle where the pieces fit the hollows to create an unrepeatable sequence of shapes. The steps are somewhat thicker pieces of the same stone.

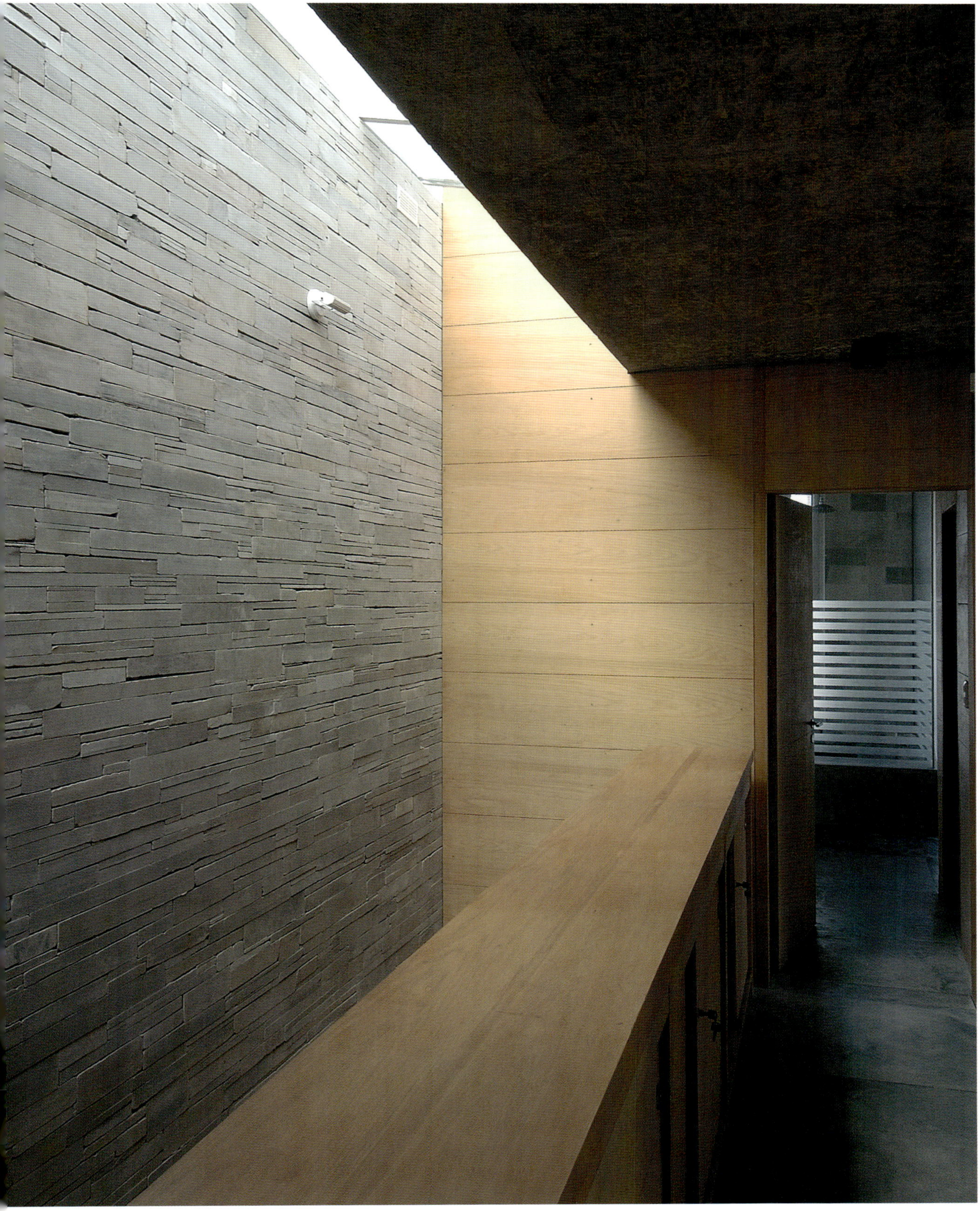

ベリマ通りの住宅

ウォーハ・デザイン
撮影：ティム・グリフィス

HOUSE ON BERRIMA ROAD
WOHA DESIGN
PHOTO: © Tim Griffith

　このシンガポールにあるシャレー風住宅の床と階段は御影石の板石で仕上げられているが、御影石が生み出す半音階の灰色と、まぶしく光る白のコントラストが、稀有な美しさを演出している。四角形で構成された 空間（クアドラングル）は、モノトーンで構成された独特の市松模様を見せているが、その模様はそのまま、鋼製の窓枠が作る不規則な格子模様へと連続している。天窓から光が注ぐ禅寺風の石庭が、室内と周囲の自然との関係を完結している。

The sheets of granite rock that were used as flooring and on the stairs of this Singapore chalet offer a chromatic scale of grays and reflective whites. The distinct tones in each quadrant form a kind of dark checkerboard, obviously replicated in the irregular grid formed by the metallic window frames. A Zen rock garden completes the connection between the home's design and the surrounding nature where the skylight is located.

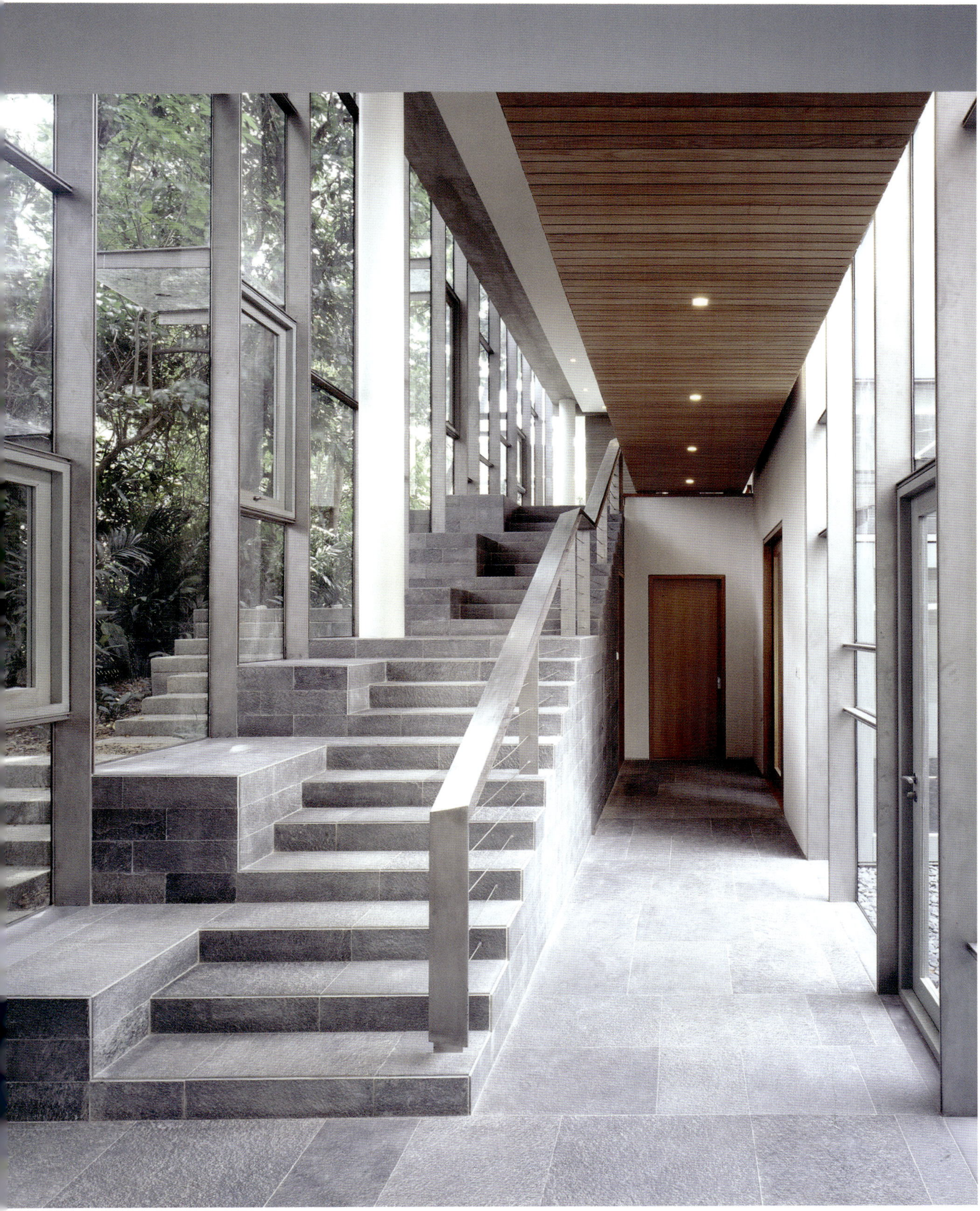

アベル邸

1100アーキテクト
撮影：ミカエル・モラン

ABELL RESIDENCE
1100 ARCHITECT
PHOTO: © Michael Moran

　1階フロアは優美な暗赤色の無垢の木板で被われ、しなやかな曲線を描いて上昇する回り階段の段板と2階フロアは、暗緑色の天然スレートの板石で被われている。窓から差し込む光を受けて柔らかな反射光を放つ研磨された天然スレートは、その上に置かれたアンティークなテーブルや椅子と共鳴し、乳白色の階段の蹴上げと美しいコントラストを作り出している。蹴上げと壁は同じ色で仕上げられ、感覚の連続性が生み出されている。

The floorboards on the lower floor are of elegant dark wood, while the steps on the sinuous staircase and the flooring on the second floor have been dressed with slate boards. Polished in such a way as to give off a certain shine when hit by the light from a window, this stone matches well with rustically inspired furniture and establishes an attractive contrast with the risers on the staircase, which have been painted the same color as the wall to lend a sense of continuity.

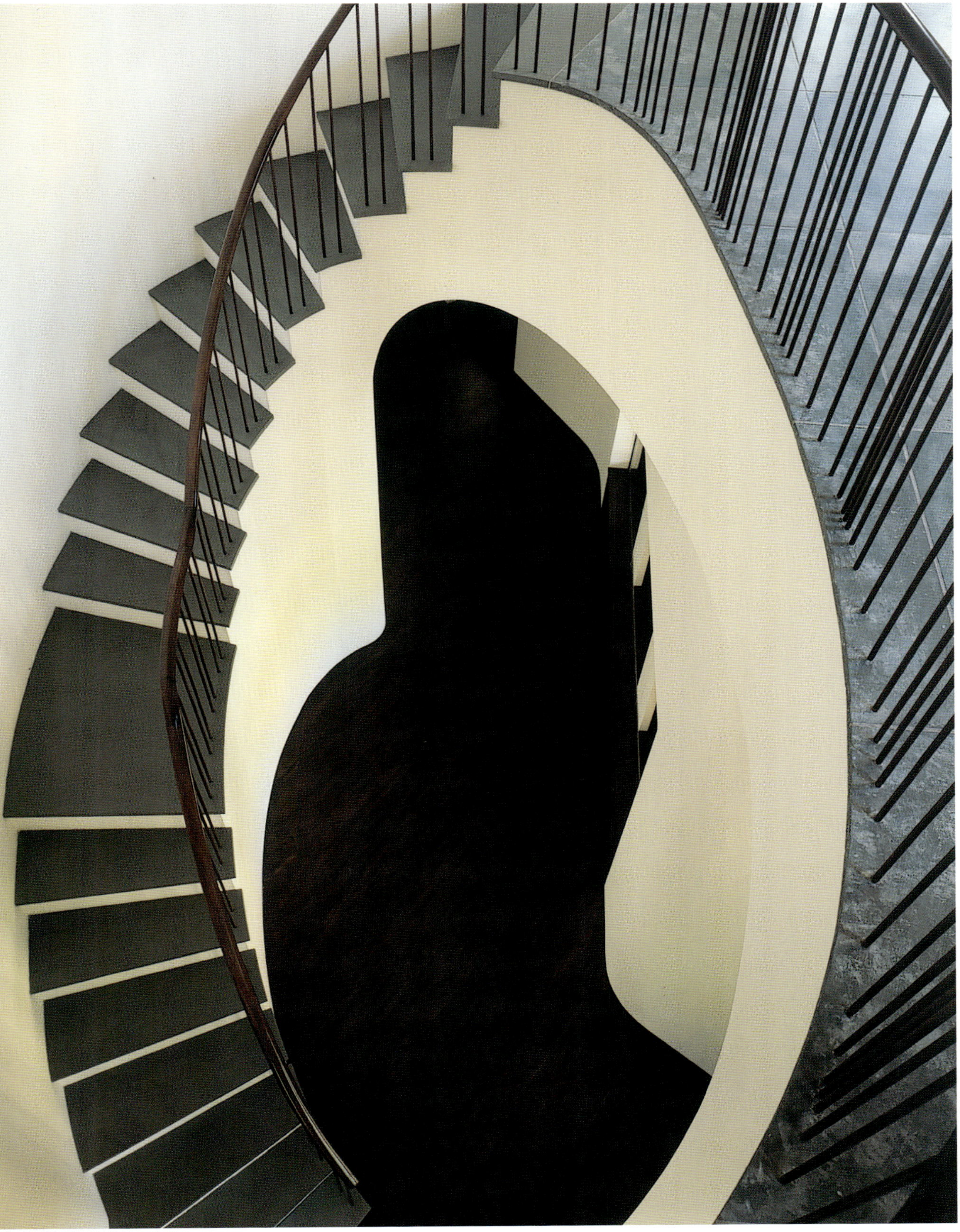

ブエノスアイレスの住宅

パブロ・サンチェス・エリア建築設計事務所
撮影：バージニア・デル・ジュディチェ

HOUSE IN BUENOS AIRES
PABLO SÁNCHEZ ELÍA (ARCHITECT) RENÉE ARMAS AND
RENÉE SÁENZ (STYLISTS)
PHOTO: © Virginia del Giudice

　住空間の中心的存在である螺旋階段の段板は、多孔性の大理石でできており、ブロンズ製の手すりと一体となって完璧な階律を生み出している。その周囲を段板がくだり降りる親柱もまた大理石でできており、ところどころに小さな壁がんが設けられ、彫刻が飾られている。素材も、装飾的要素も、すべてが古代ギリシャ・ローマの雰囲気を伝えるように選ばれていて、比類のない優美な空間が創りだされている。

A very porous marble was chosen for the steps on the spiral staircase presiding over this interior's decoration. A perfect match is made with the bronze banister. The column around which the steps descend is also of marble and has small niches built in for displaying sculptures. The selection of materials and ornamental elements inspire a Greco-Latin atmosphere of incomparable elegance.

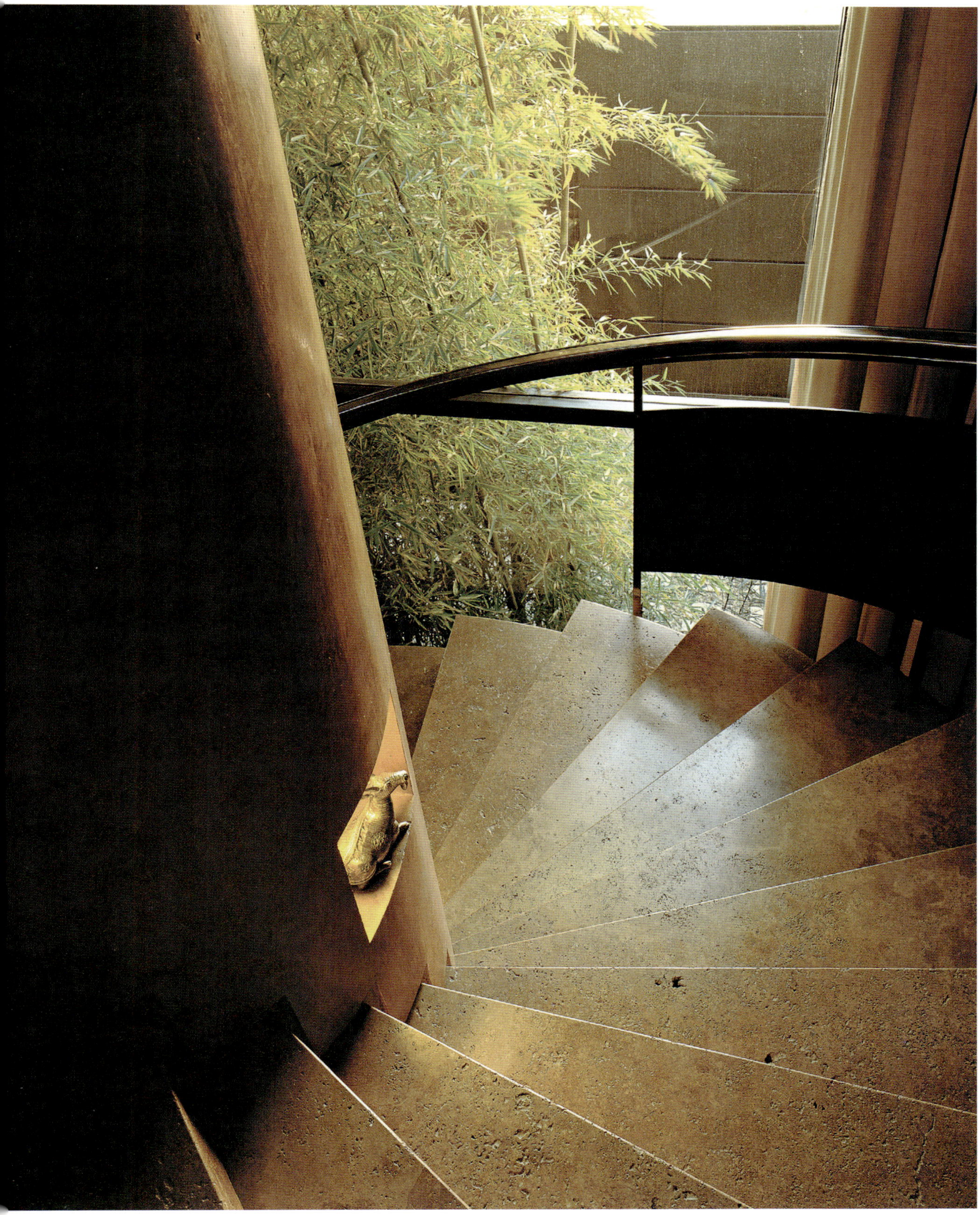

オストゥーニの住宅

スタジオ・トランジット
撮影：マッシモ・グラッシ

OSTUNI RESIDENCE
STUDIO TRANSIT
PHOTO: © Massimo Grassi

　かつての農村共同体が雨水を貯留するために使っていた巨大な竪穴の中という特殊な立地が、この住宅の特異性を定義している。剥き出しになった荒々しい岩肌の美しさに魅せられた建築家は、住空間を巨大なガラスパネルで囲むことに決めた。岩肌は巧妙な照明計画によって荘厳な輝きを放ち、それ以外の無駄な装飾を拒んでいる。地球の深奥部に抱かれていることを実感できる生活がここにある。

The placement of this home within an old tank – traditionally used in agricultural communities for collecting rainwater – determined the idiosyncrasy of this project. The attraction in exposing the stone convinced the architect that making a perimeter of glass panels would be suitable. With the right light, the stone walls would constitute the principal decorative element in a house that becomes a scenic look-out of geological observation.

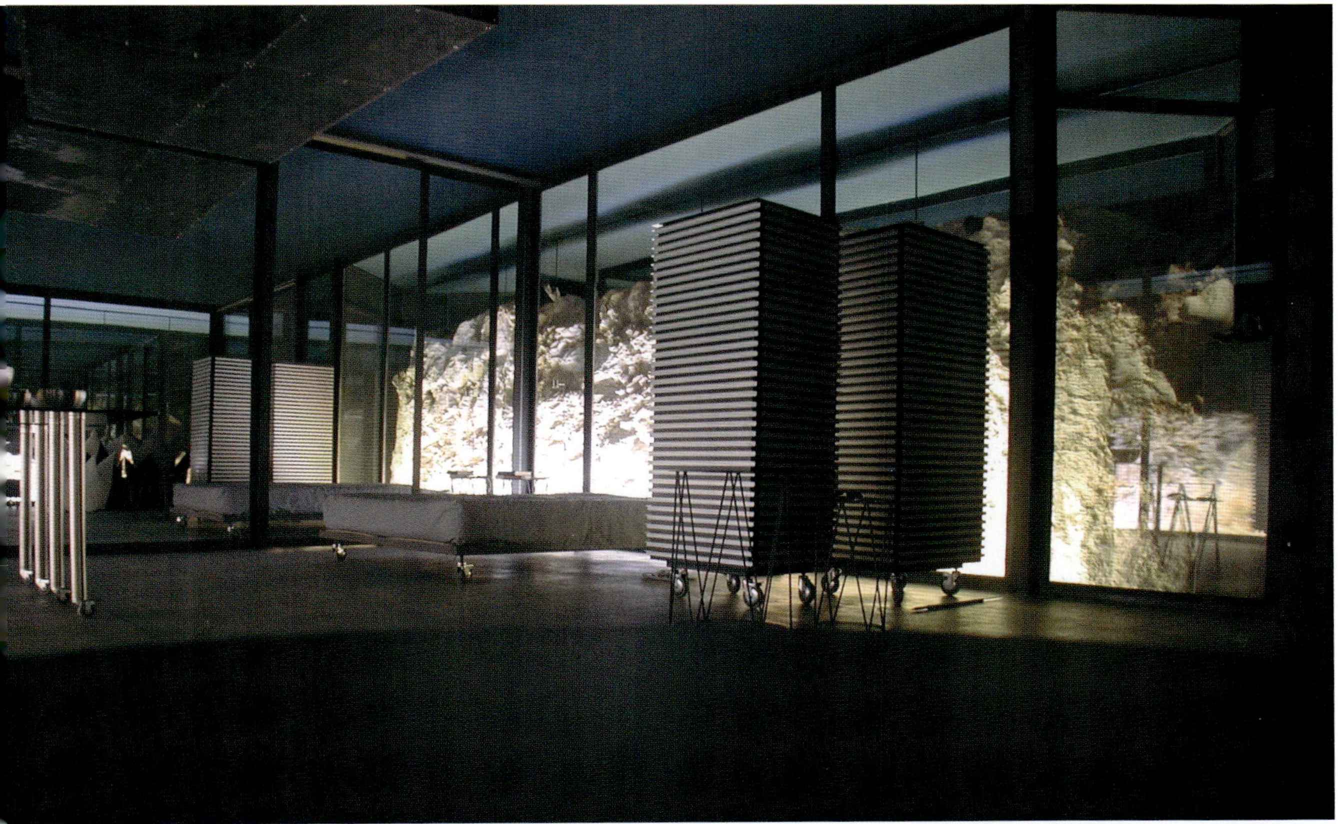

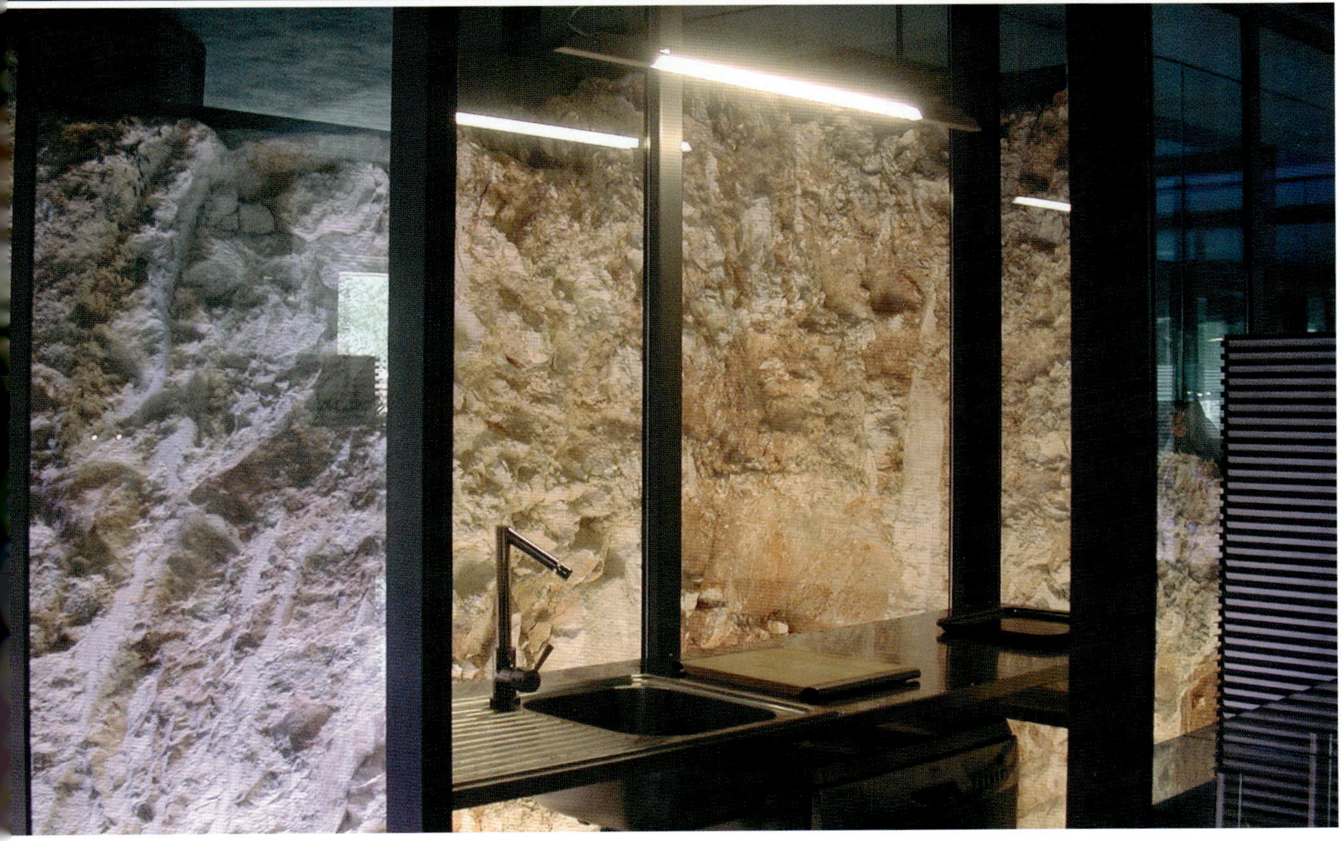

ヴィラドマの住宅

ベナサール・ノゲラ／アルバート・アウバッハ
撮影：ホセ・ルイス・ハウスマン

HOUSE IN VILLADOMAT
BENNASAR NOGUERA/ALBERT AUBACH
PHOTO: © José Luis Hausmann

　カタルーニヤの小さな村、アール・テンポルダーの古い納屋が、元の構造を残したまま住宅に生まれ変わった。村を囲む山々から掘り出された礫石の粗石積みで築かれていた壁面は、何も手を加えないままで上質の興趣に満ちた装飾的エレメントとなった。基礎石から立ち上がる切石積みの柱の上にはレンガのアーチが架かり、テラコッタの床と一体になって鄙びた優雅な空間を創り出した。家具、調度類も厳選され、暖炉煙突のスチールなど、使用される材料も慎重に吟味され、独特の美学が空間を満たしている。

This old barn in a small Alt Empordá town preserves its original structure. Stones of local orography continue to go unadorned on the walls – constituting a first rate decorative element – while the columns combine a stone base with rows of brick across the top. The floors, of unpolished ceramic, marry together with the rustic ambience inside. This is something also accomplished by the selection of furniture chosen and other materials used, like the steel chimney.

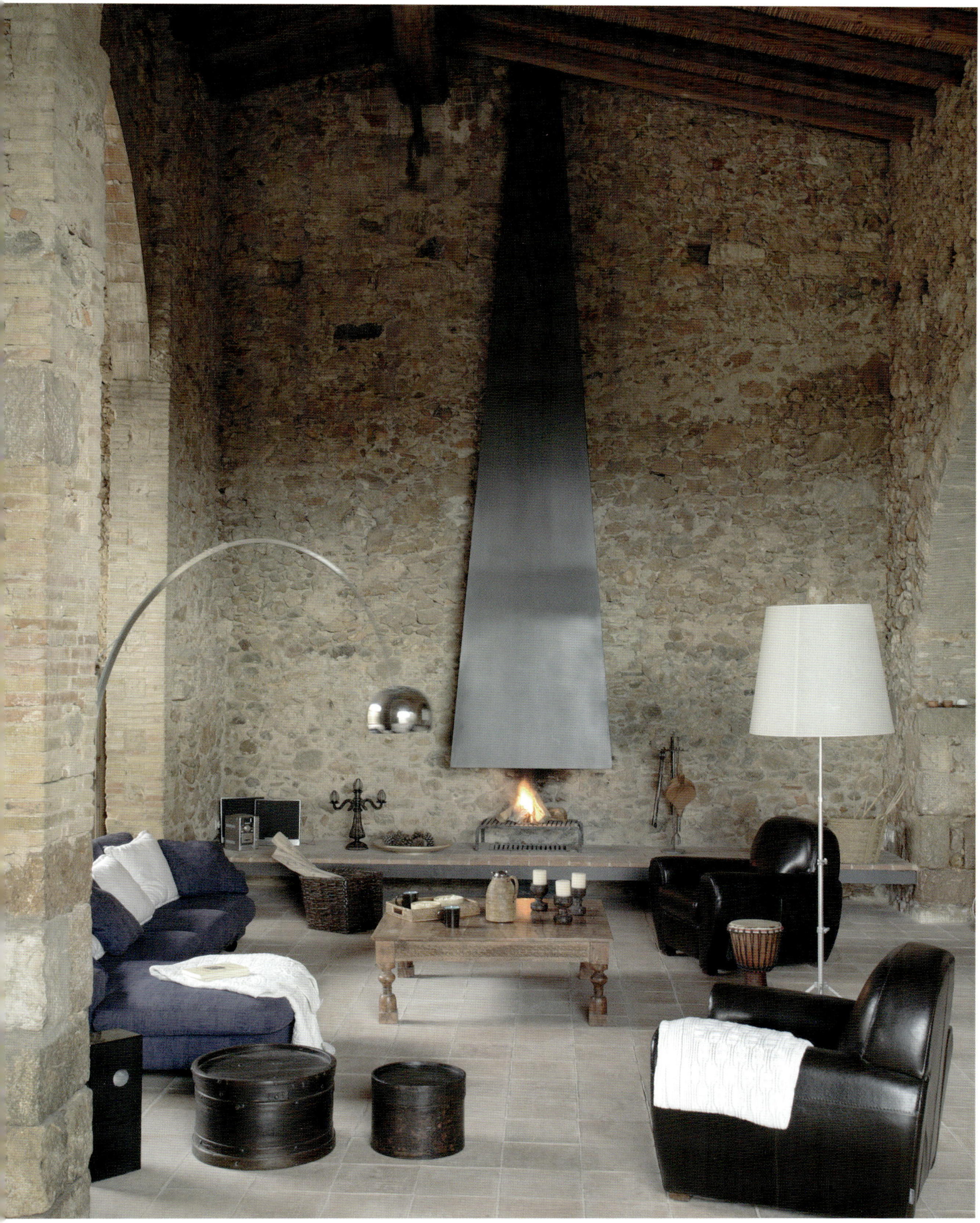

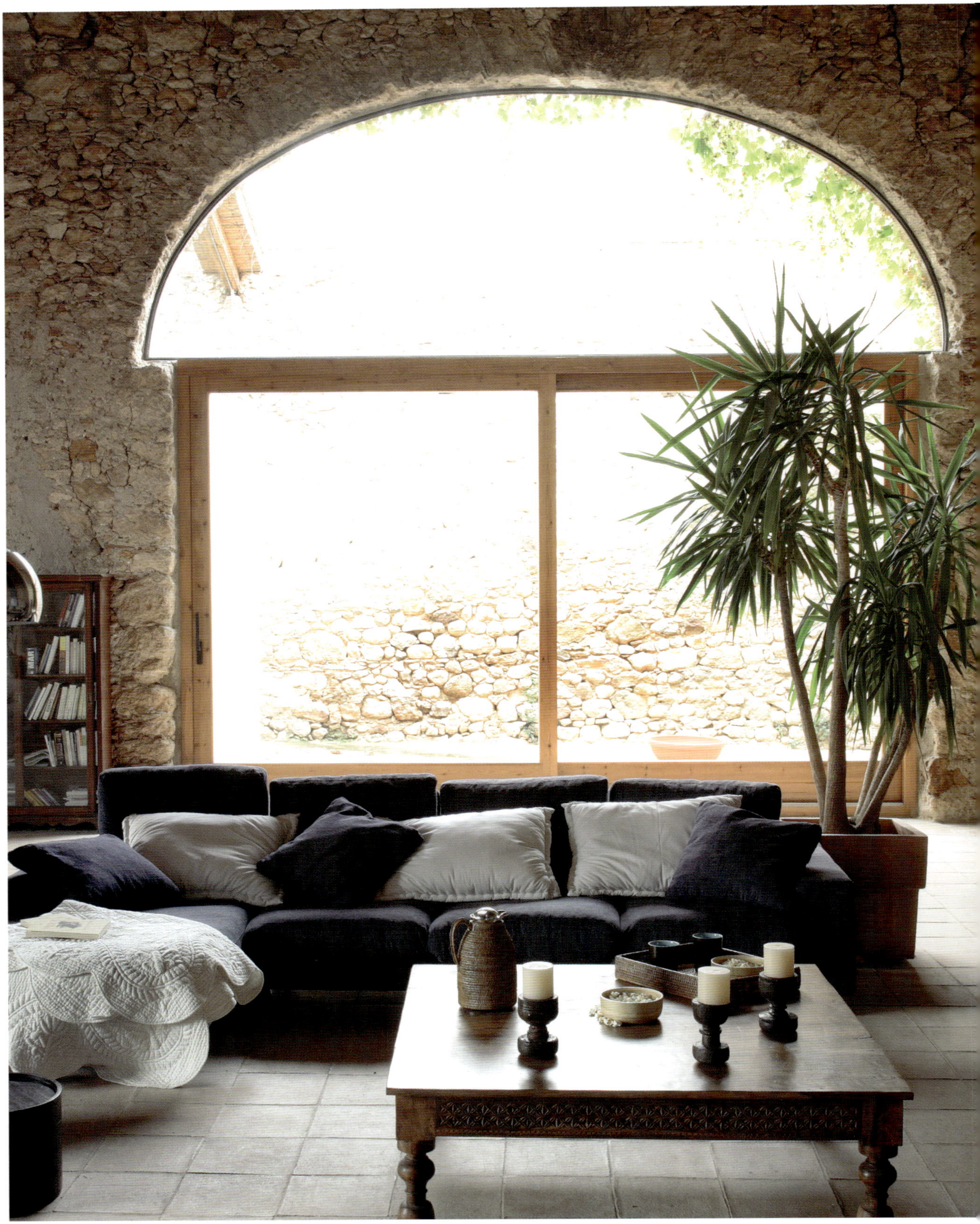

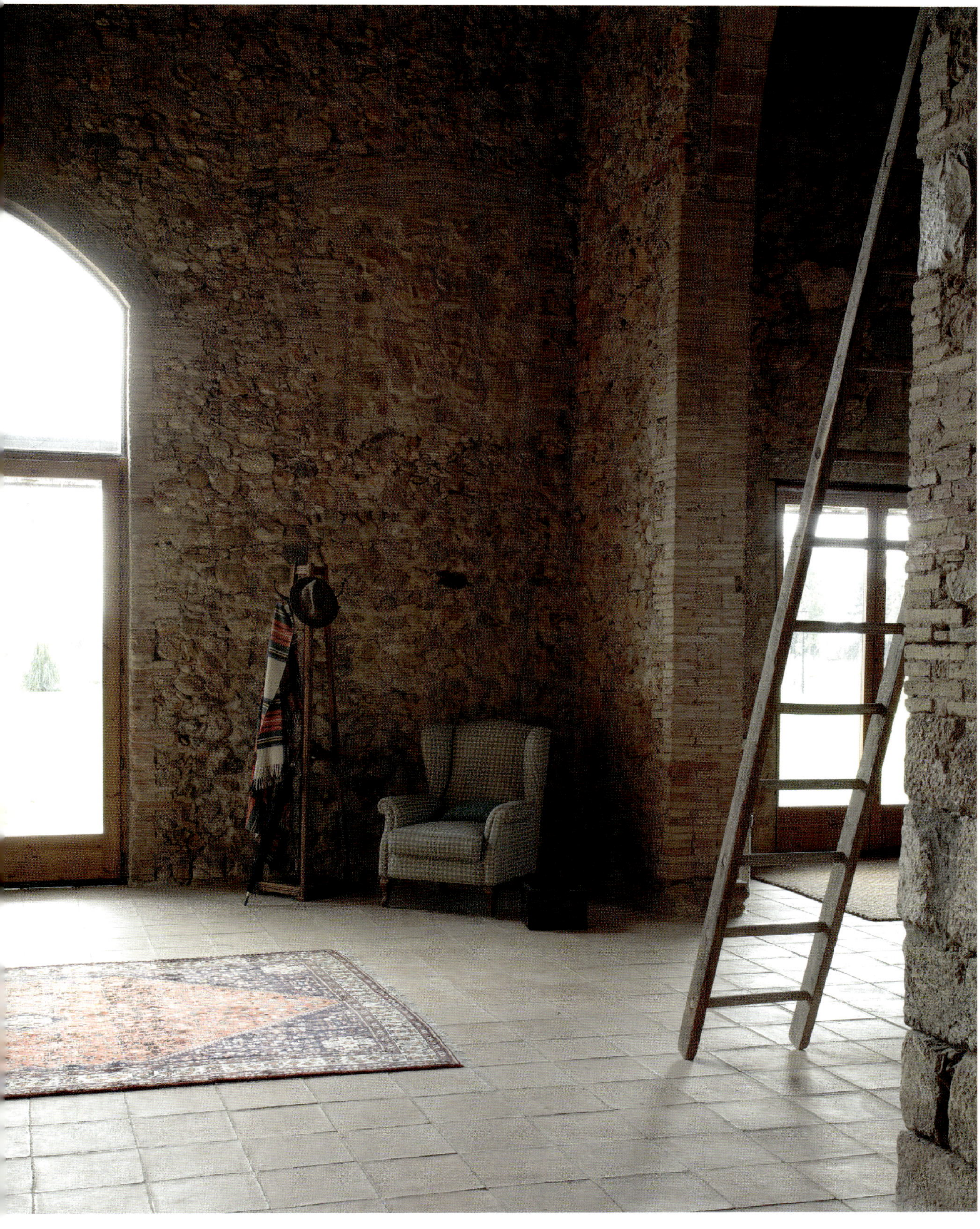

クーヴィオ・ヴァレーゼのロフト

シモーネ・ミケーリ建築設計事務所
撮影：S.M.A.H.

CUVIO VARESE LOFT
ARCHITECTURAL STUDIO SIMONE MICHELI
PHOTO: © S.M.A.H.

　建物は17世紀に築かれたもので、全体が粗面仕上げ切石積みで一体となった巨大な壁構造は、当時としては珍しいものではなかった。改築にあたってはこの壁の保存に最大限の注意が払われ、その結果、それは当時の北イタリアの建築技法を示す貴重な遺構ともなっている。壁は、なめらかな肌面を見せる新しい柱や梁に囲まれ、当時のレンガの組積法や石灰岩の切石積み技法を伝えながら、時間を超越した豊かな空間を生み出している。

This building dates back to the 17th Century, which is why the gigantic slabs of stone that pass for walls are not surprising. The greatest achievement in its renovation was the treatment given these walls, which now seem like archaeological samples of ancient methods of construction. Surrounded by smooth and newly built columns, these walls display ancient brickwork and practically white limestone, creating a scenic stone wall of great decorative value.

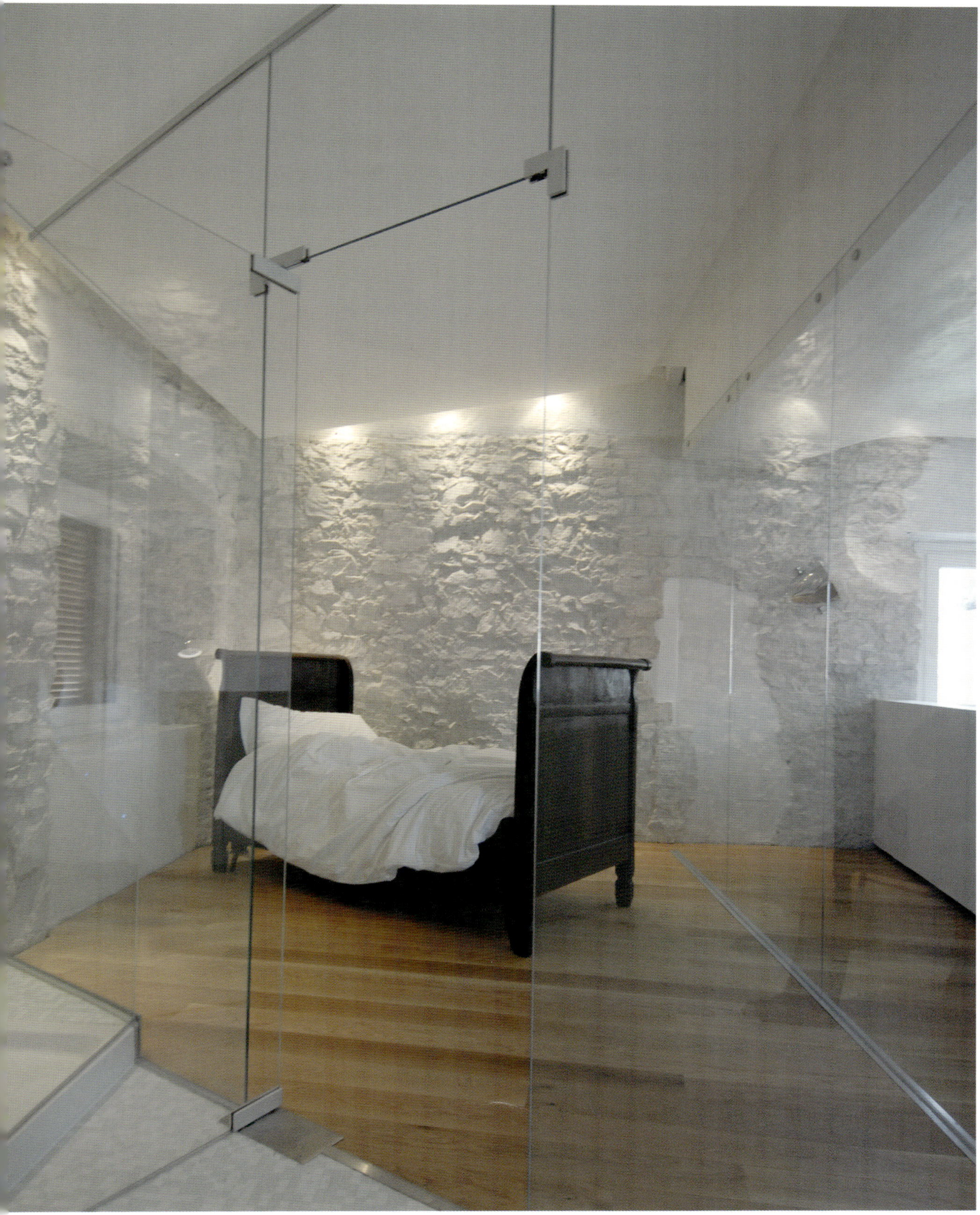

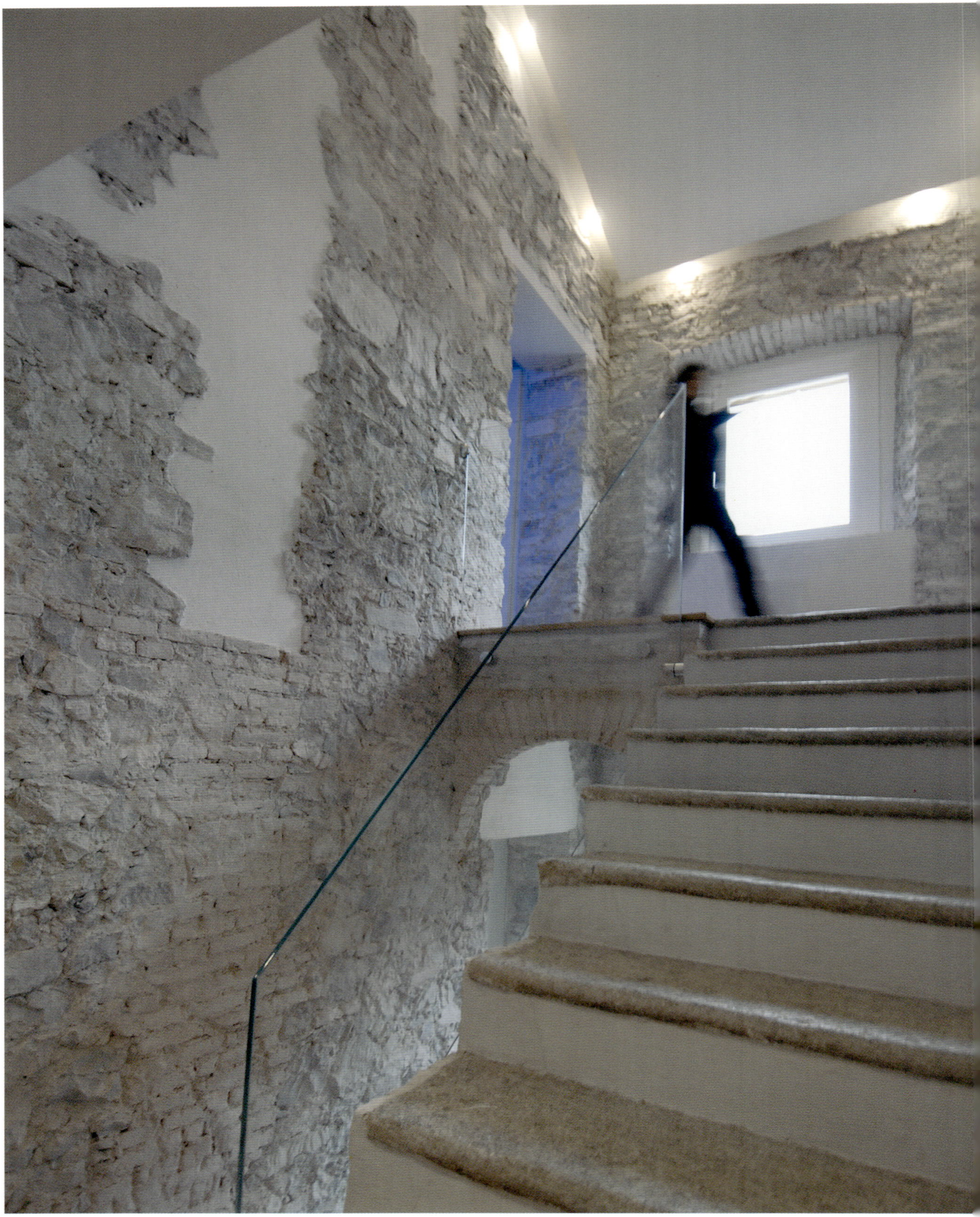

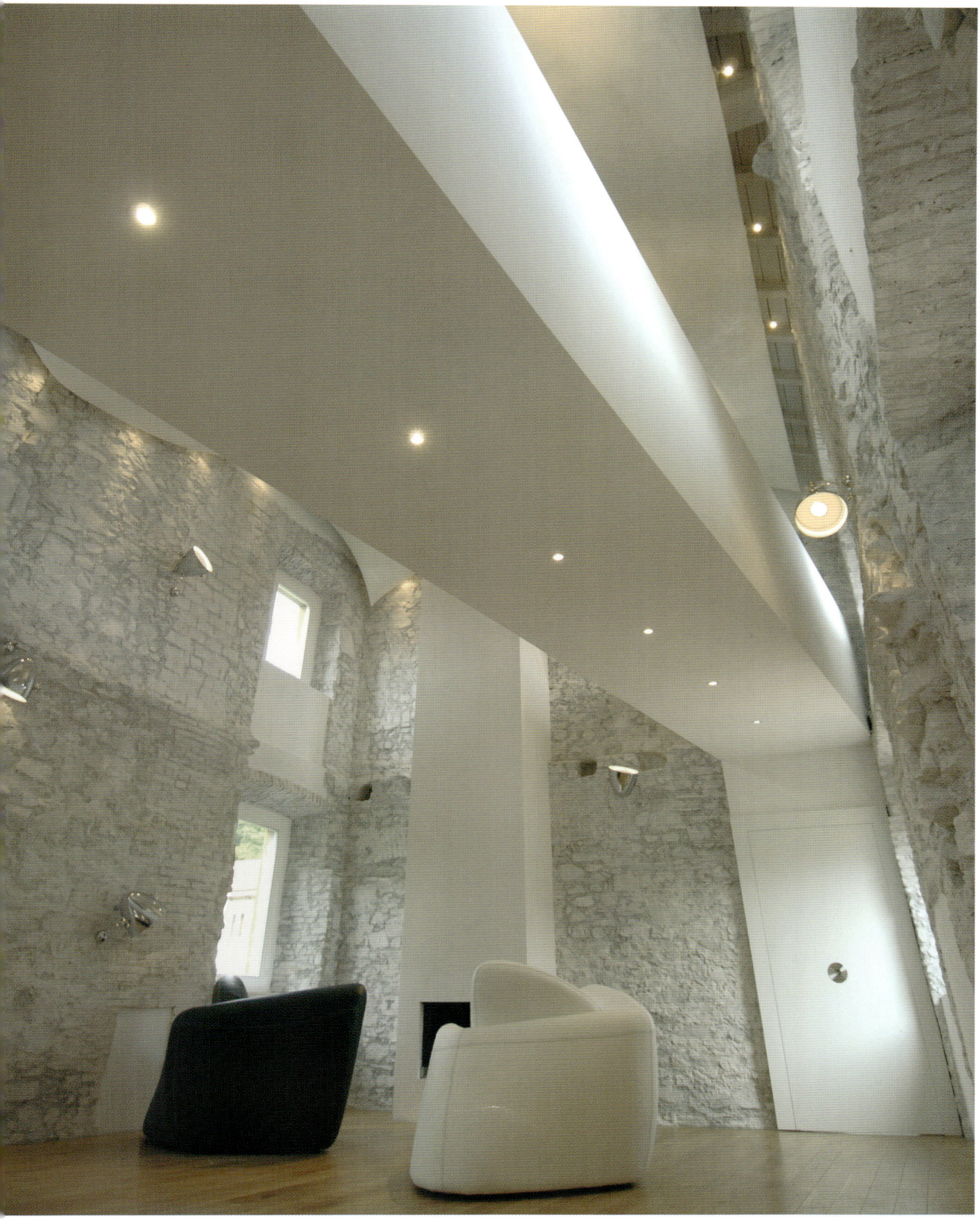

カルデテスの住宅

ジョルジュ・スビータ
撮影：ホセ・ルイス・ハウスマン

CALDETES HOME
JORGE SUBIETAS
PHOTO: © José Luis Hausmann

　1891年に建てられたこの海沿いの住宅の改築を建築家が引き受けたとき、それは住居というよりは廃墟であった。保存されていた2面の壁のうちの1面を、そのままの状態で露出させることにした。というのもその壁は、石、日干し煉瓦、セメントなどのさまざまな材料を不均一に複合させた独特の工法で造られており、それ自体が非常に価値の高いものだったからである。黒色酸化処理された鋼板で支えられている踏み板だけの片持ち階段がこの壁に固定され、2階へと上っているが、その渋い光沢は歴史を感じさせるこの壁を一層引き立たせている。

The architects undertook the renovation of this 1891 coastal house when the structure was in a state of ruin. Of the two walls that were kept, one was chosen to be left uncovered so that the entire construction process could be seen, which draws from an unequalled conglomerate of textures and materials like stone, adobe and cement. Steps leading up to the second floor were attached to this same wall. These boast a steel oxide finish that works well with the aged look of the wall.

Pulcinella
Pagliuccio.
Cucurucu
Scapino.
Cap. Grillo
Pantalon

ミナス通りのロフト

ウンルガール
撮影：ルイス・エヴィア

LOFT ON MINAS STREET
UNLUGAR
PHOTO: © Luis Hevia

　ロフトの改築にあたっては、床を白色セメントの金ゴテ仕上げとすることが決定された。外周壁の2段重ね粗面仕上げの花崗岩の基礎石はそのまま露出させ、床の色と合わせるように壁面も白色のプラスター仕上げとした。こうして出来上がったモノトーンの諧調にそって、キッチンテーブルもセメントで仕上げた。無駄を削ぎ落とした空間の中で、リビングルームの一画に置かれたテーブルの天然スレートの天板が、装飾的要素としてひときわ目を引く。

For the renovation of this loft, the floors were paved with artisanally-prepared white cement. Chromatically, these match with the white walls and the coarse granite bases tiered along the inside of the exterior wall. This abundance of grays begged for the cement composition of the kitchen table, and the inclusion of a single slate board in one corner of the living room becomes its only decorative element.

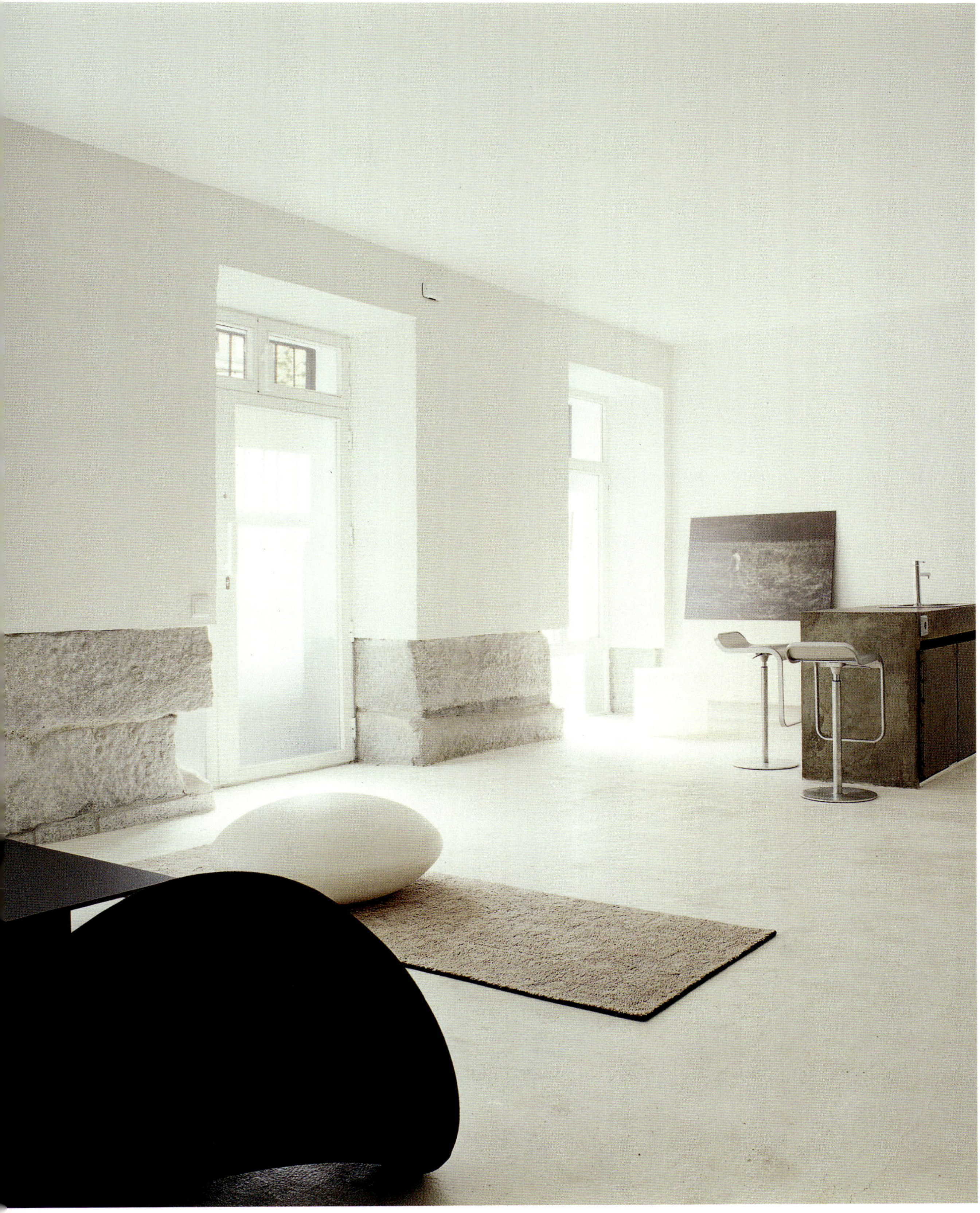

アイオルフィ邸

パガーニ・ディ・マウロ建築設計事務所
撮影：アンドレア・コルベッリーニ

AIOLFI HOUSE
PAGANI-DI MAURO ARCHITETTI
PHOTO: © Andrea Corbellini

　ゴルフ場の横にあるシャレー風住宅が誇るのは、3面の壁を被うオーストラリア産クオーツザイト・インゴットの石壁である。インゴットは現場で1枚1枚積まれたもので、白色、黄土色、灰色などの色が綾なす自然石の織物が、独特の優美な空間を現出させている。石は横目地を通した布積みとなっているが、出をランダムにしているため、質感に溢れた典雅なレリーフ壁となっている。これと同じ板石が、プール周りの床にも張られている。

Located beside a golf course, this chalet boasts Australian quartzite on three of its four walls. The stone planks, assembled in situ, vary chromatically and create an attractive web of whites, ochers and grays. The pieces of stone forming the walls reach different heights and make for an interesting relief. The same stone on the perimeter walls has been used to pave the area surrounding the pool.

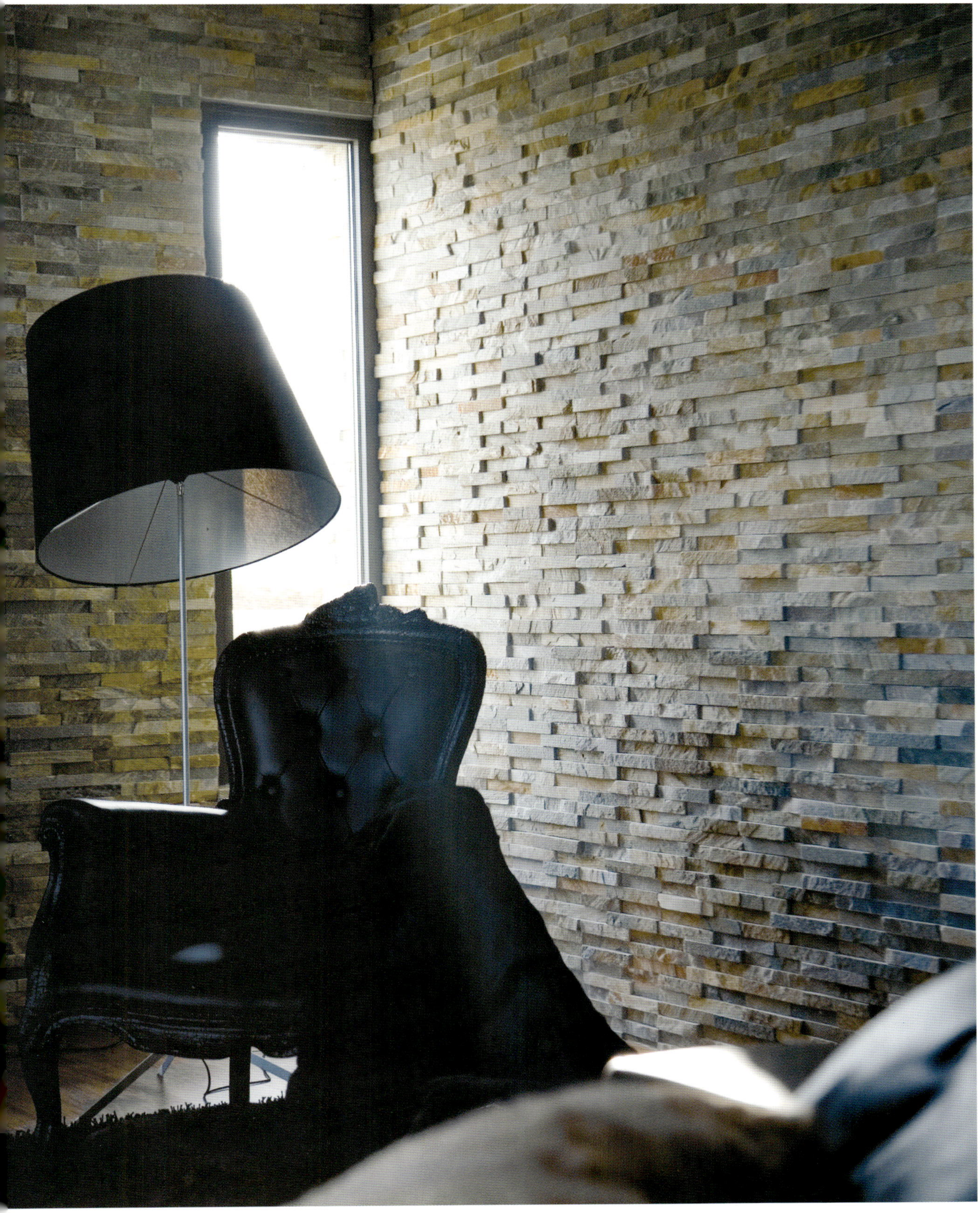

ムジェーヴの住宅

カルロ・ランパッツィ
撮影：レト・ガントゥリ／Zapaimages

HOUSE IN MEGEVE
CARLO RAMPAZZI
PHOTO: © Reto Guntli/Zapaimages

　この山荘が独創的なのは、それが建っているアルプス山脈とは必ずしも関係のない素材を使用しているところにある。天井と壁を横切る大きな梁とは対照的に、床は粗面仕上げの石灰岩の本石タイルが張られ、その一見無造作な配色の不均一性が、空間に不思議なリズム感を与えている。その石灰岩のベージュに導かれるように、カーキ色の家具や軽快な感じの革張り椅子が選ばれ、それらが暖炉のある壁を被う銀箔に微妙な色影を投げかけている。

The originality of this refuge comes from a selection of materials not necessarily associated with the mountains. In contrast with the thick beams running along the ceiling and walls, the floor is composed of slabs of unfinished limestone, with its rugged patchiness well highlighted. The beige-gray color of the stone invites the use of ocher colored furniture – as is the case with the light leather fabric on the chairs – working well with the silver dressing on the chimney.

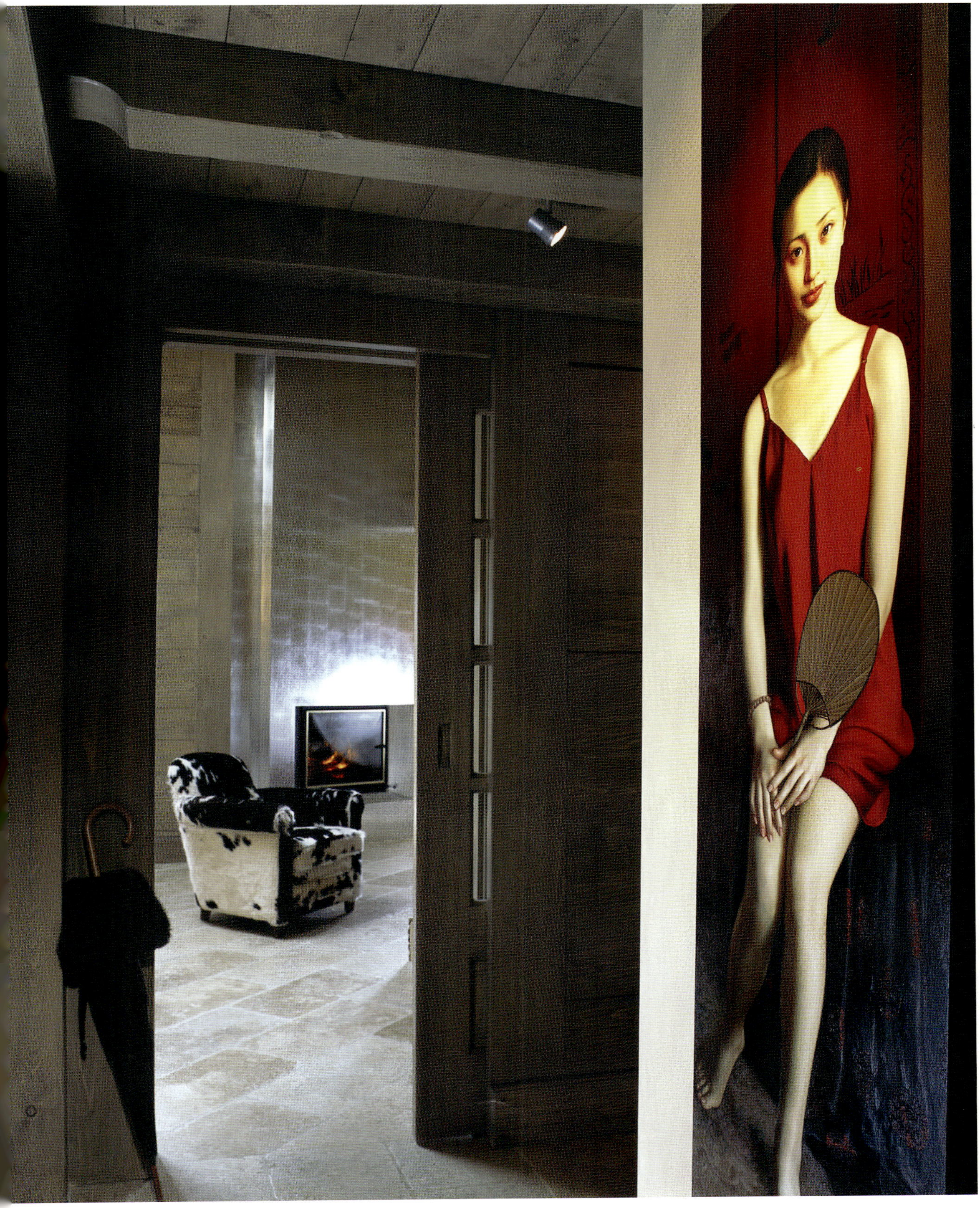

Pペントハウス

クラウディオ・シルヴェストリン
建築設計事務所
撮影：マッテオ・ピアッツァ

P PENTHOUSE
CLAUDIO SILVESTRIN ARCHITECTS
PHOTO: © Matteo Piazza

　ペントハウスが建築家の手によって、コート・ダジュールの素晴らしい眺望を見下ろす静謐な空間へと変貌させられた。通風を良くするために間仕切り壁を撤去したことによって、空間をある種の統一感が満たしている。螺旋階段のまわりに築かれた石灰岩でできた円筒形の壁が、圧倒的な表現力で空間を支配している。同様に強い存在感を漂わせているのが半球状のバスタブで、それはミニマリスト的でありながらも、中世の城郭を偲ばせるこの空間に、同意を表明している。

This penthouse has been converted into a calming and serene space, with enviously panoramic views of the Côte d'Azur. The space has acquired a certain unity thanks to the removal of interior walls to facilitate circulation between its spaces. The large cylindrical limestone wall around the spiral staircase imposes itself through its expressive force. Equally powerful is the stone tub shaped like a shell, recalling unquestionable modernity with a nod towards the ancient history architecture.

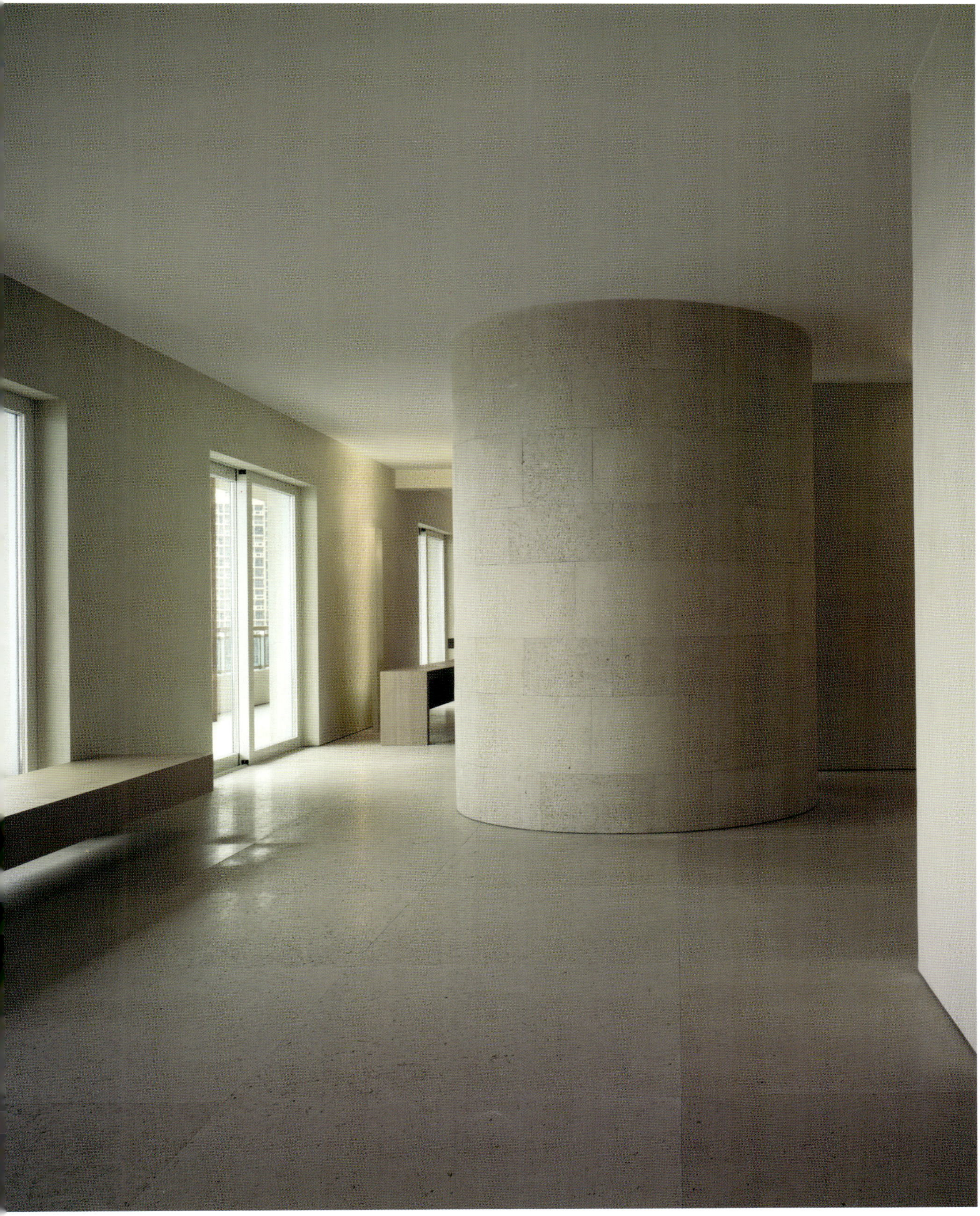

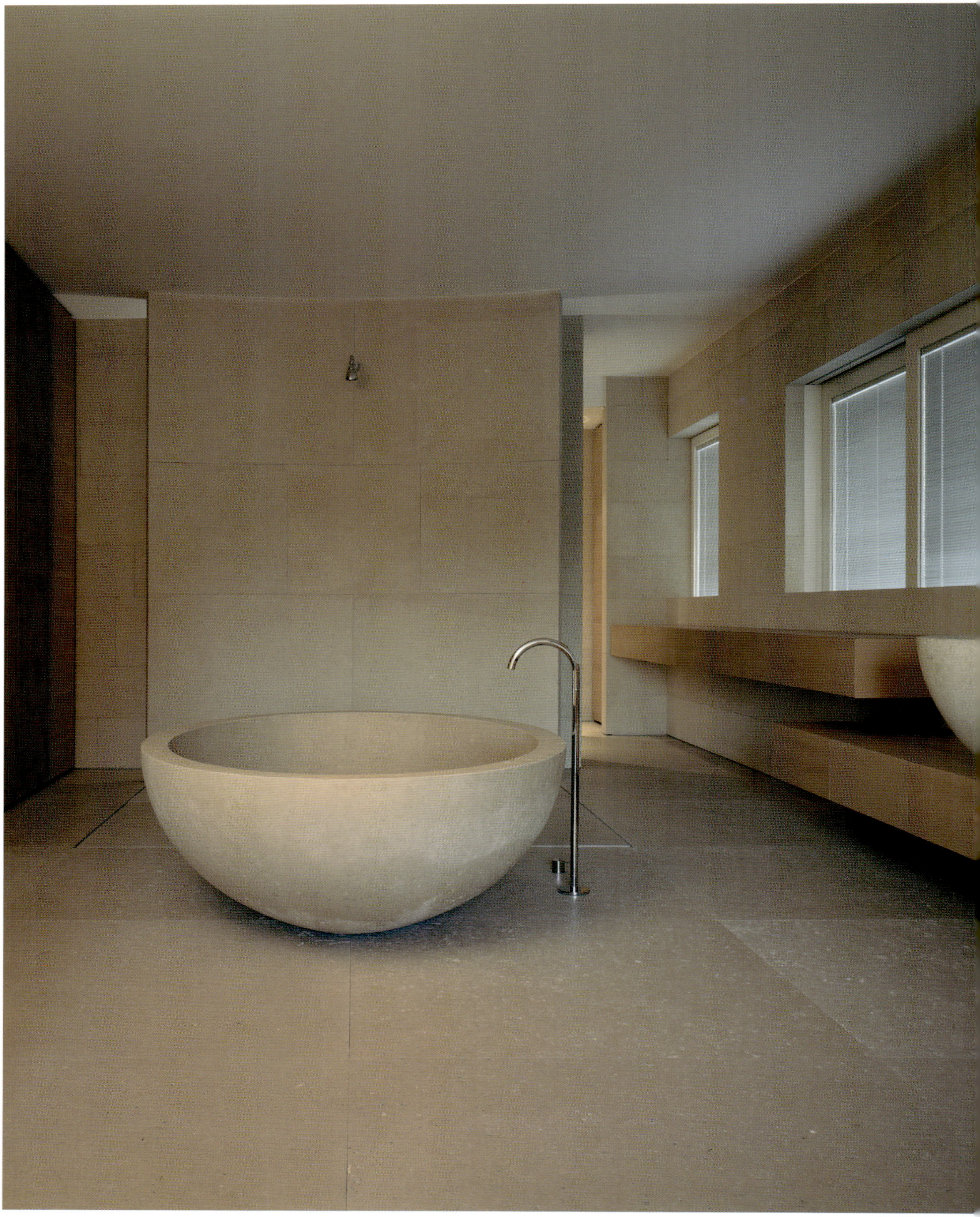

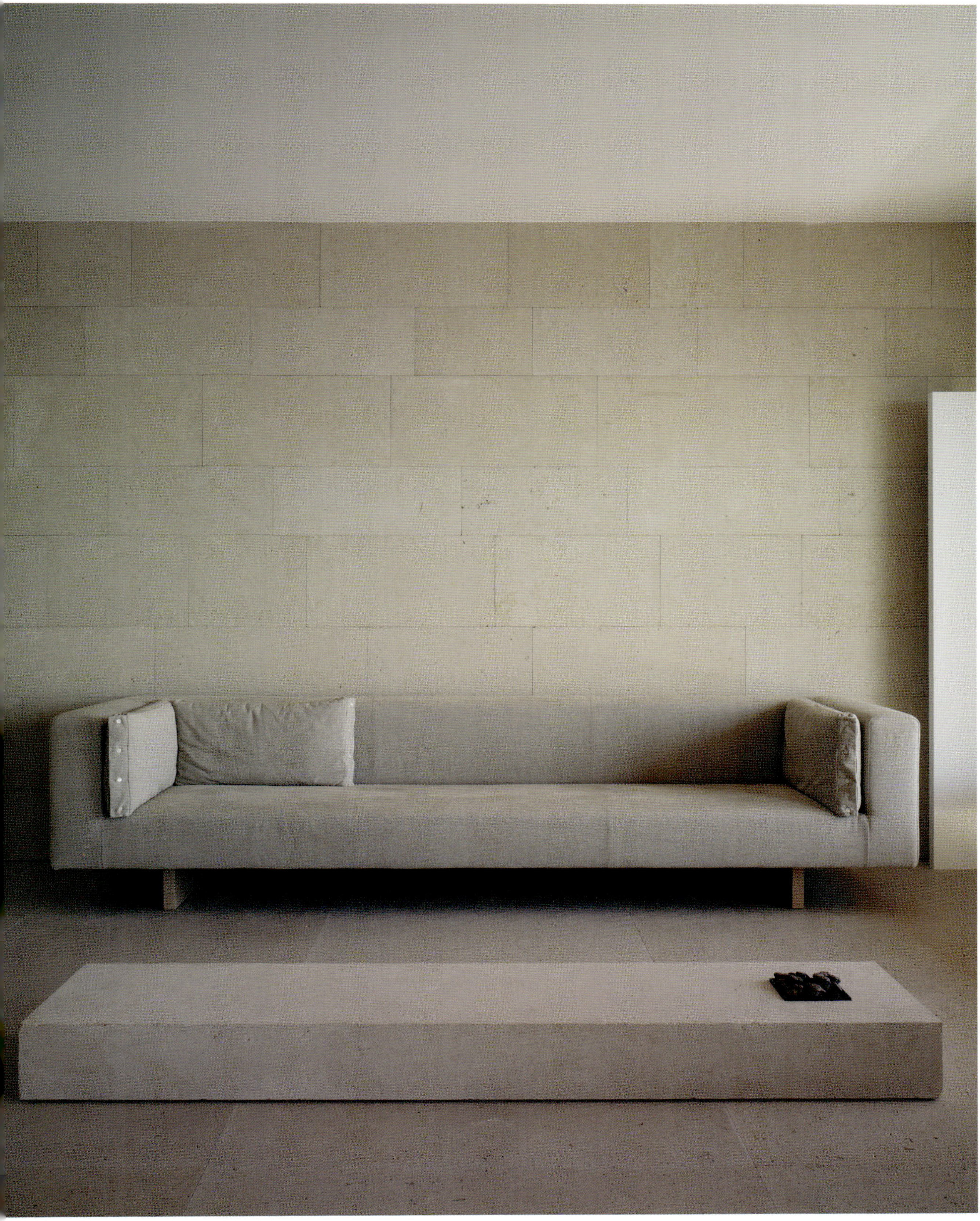

ポダール邸

所有者
撮影：マイケル・フリーマン

PODDAR HOUSE
OWNERS
PHOTO: © Michael Freeman

　この格調高いインドの住宅を特徴づけるものは、伝統文化に根ざした建築様式と、照明や塗装など細部の現代的仕上げとの組み合わせである。床の黒御影石には、東洋的思想を表象した幾何学模様が象眼細工され、コンクリート・レンガの組積壁の間には、床と同じ黒御影石の板石がアクセントに嵌め込まれている。これらのどっしりとした重量感のある素材と、天井を覆う軽快なチーク材とのコントラストが、空間を劇的に演出している。

The interior of this elegant home in India combines traditional culture architecture with modern solutions in fixtures, lighting and coating. The floors, of dark granite, are inlaid with a geometric design of marked oriental inspiration, while the walls combine concrete bricks with sheets of the same stone used for the floors. The contrast of these materials with the light teak protecting the ceiling is spectacular.

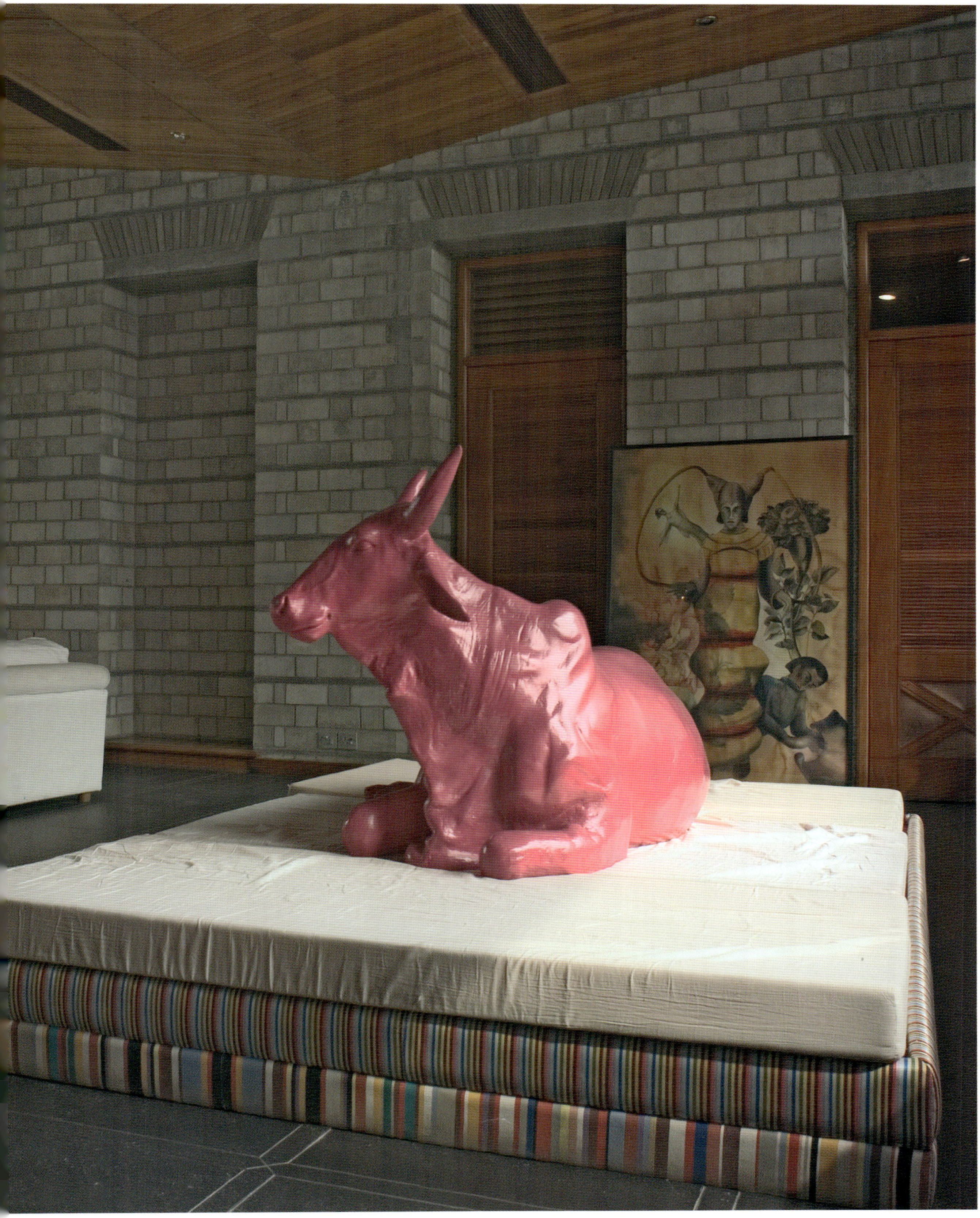

ポジターノの別荘

ラッツァリーニ・ピカリング建築設計事務所
撮影：マッテオ・ピアッツァ

VILLA POSITANO
LAZZARINI PICKERING ARCHITETTI
PHOTO: © Matteo Piazza

　現代的デザインの家具類を古典的な素材とその処理にうまく調和させながら配置することによって、気品に満ちた簡潔な室内空間が現出した。なかでも特に目を惹かれるのは、屋外で用いている砂岩と同調させた、自然な色の砂岩プラスター仕上げの柱とアーチ、そして18世紀に製造された伝統的なヴィエトリ・タイル。ユニークなのは、そのタイルを床や壁に張らずに、テーブルや天蓋などに張っているところである。

The interiors in this villa demonstrate a sublime simplicity in their unison of modern design furniture with classic materials and arrangement. Highlighted are columns and arches with natural colored sandstone plaster – the same stone used in the exteriors – and the traditional Viatri tiles, dating back to the 18th century. The uniqueness, in this case, stems from their use not as a wall or floor surface but as a surface for tables and canopies.

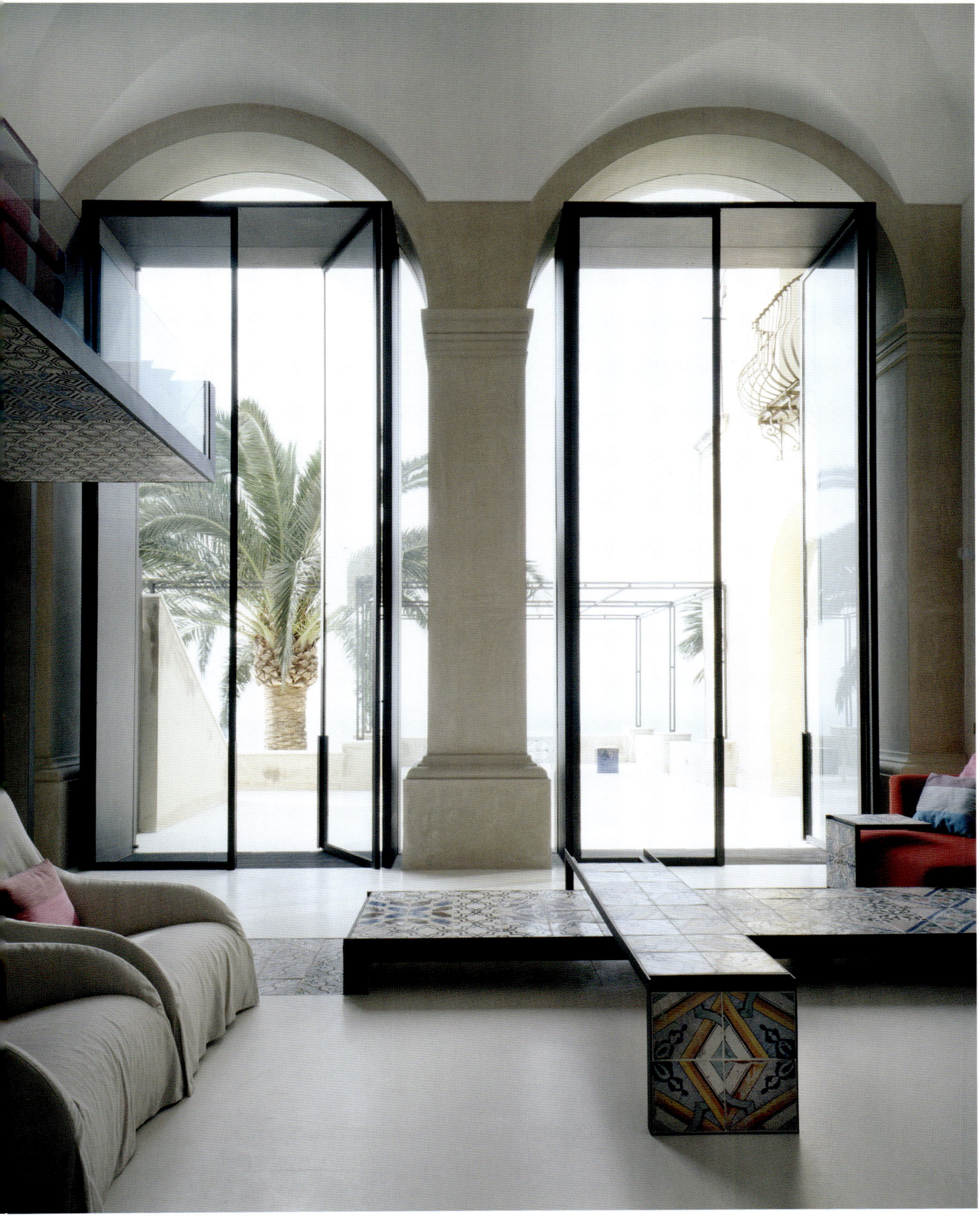

ビアジョッティ邸

所有者
撮影：レト・ガントゥリ／Redcover

BIAGIOTTI RESIDENCE
OWNER
PHOTO: © Reto Guntli/Redcover

　服飾デザイナーのラウラ・ビアジョッティは、5年間かけて、この中世の屋敷を自宅兼本部事務所として自らの手で改装した。最も見ごたえのある部屋がこのダイニングルームで、中世風とバロック風のフレスコ画が壁と天井を飾り、さまざまな大理石を組み合わせて作られた印象的なテーブルが陶製タイルの床の上に置かれ、壁には穴の多くあいたトラヴァーチン大理石の炉額が嵌め込まれている。生み出された空間は、家具によるドラマというよりは、彫刻化された多重奏と言うべきであろう。

For five years, designer Laura Biagiotti worked on the renovation of this medieval villa so she could make it her residence and the headquarters of her business. The most spectacular room is the dining room, where medieval and baroque frescoes are accompanied by an impressive table of different types of marble, ceramic floors and a very porous Travertine chimney. The result, more than a play of furniture, seems like a sculptured ensemble.

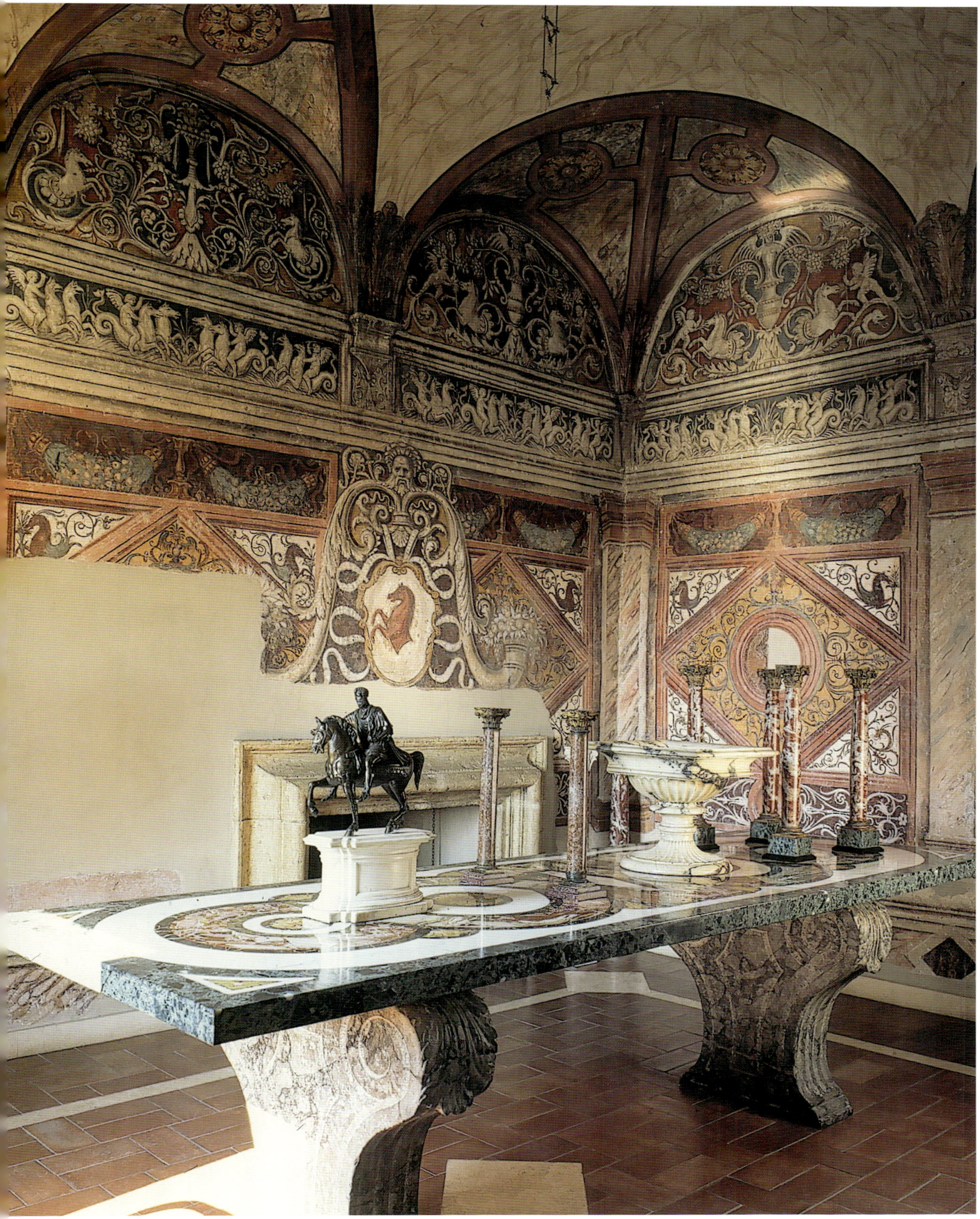

フロリダの住宅

プレストン・T・フィリップス建築設計事務所
撮影：レト・ガントゥリ／Zapaimages

FLORIDA RESIDENCE
PRESTON T. PHILLIPS ARCHITECT
PHOTO: © Reto Guntli/Zapaimages

　フロリダ、パームビーチという大西洋岸にありながら、この住宅は伝統的な地中海風デザインの特徴を色濃く持っている。明快な現代アートの作品が、古典的な姿形を持ち古代ローマを連想させる優美に彫り出された大理石のマントルピースなどの、時代を超越した要素と組み合わされている。その大胆な組み合わせが、大理石スラブの床と一体となって、独自の印象的な空間を創造している。

Though situated on the Atlantic coast – in Palm Beach, Florida – this residence reflects many of the traditional characteristics of Mediterranean design. An impressive contemporary art collection is combined with timeless elements, like the elegantly sculpted marble chimney, classically shaped and Latin-influenced. Its combination with the slabs of marble flooring is truly impressive.

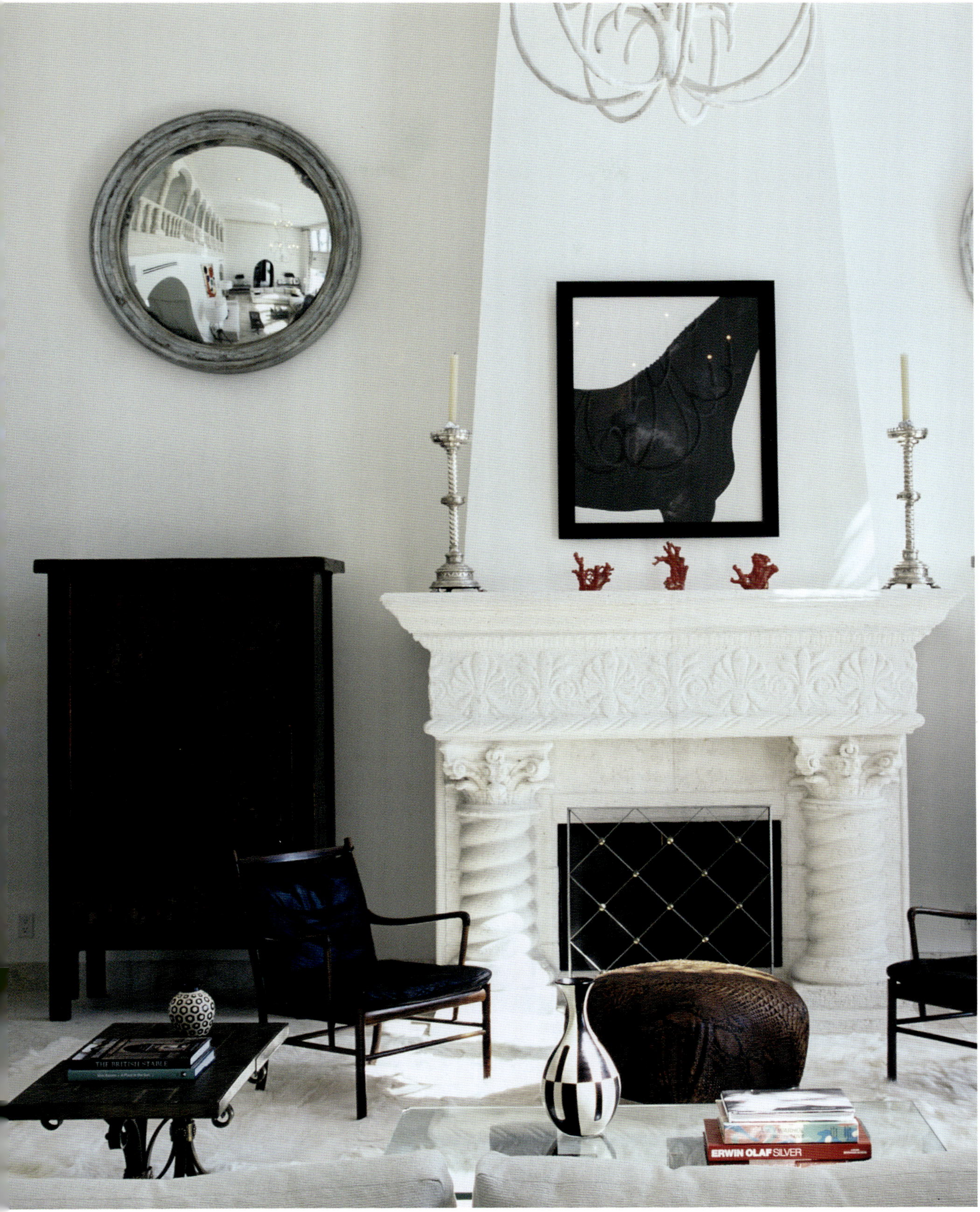
THE BRITISH STABLE
ERWIN OLAF SILVER

カンビの集合住宅

パガーニ・ディ・マウロ建築設計事務所
撮影：マッテオ・ピアッツァ

CAMBI APARTMENT
PAGANI-DI MAURO ARCHITETTI
PHOTO: © Matteo Piazza

　この住居は、建立を西暦700年代にまで遡ることができるフィレンツェのある歴史的建造物の頂塔の中にある。静寂感の漂う現代的で落ち着いた雰囲気を醸しだしているのは、床や壁の仕上げである。ブラジル産ブラックストーンの大判の本石タイルを、横目地を巧妙に目立たせながら張りつけているキッチンの壁が、ヘアライン仕上げのステンレス製フードなどの現代的デザインの厨房機器の背景として存在感をきわだたせている。赤い炎と黒の図式は、リビングルームの、炉床と黒く塗装したオーク材の大きな炉額の間にも繰り返されている。

With this sober and contemporary style, this loft in the cupola of a building from the year 700 owes a large part of its chic appearance to the dressings in the home's main areas. The Brazilian black stone – applied in large horizontal plates – in the kitchen stands out against the steel ventilation hood and fixtures. The same schematic is repeated in the large, black-colored oak fireplace on the living room floor.

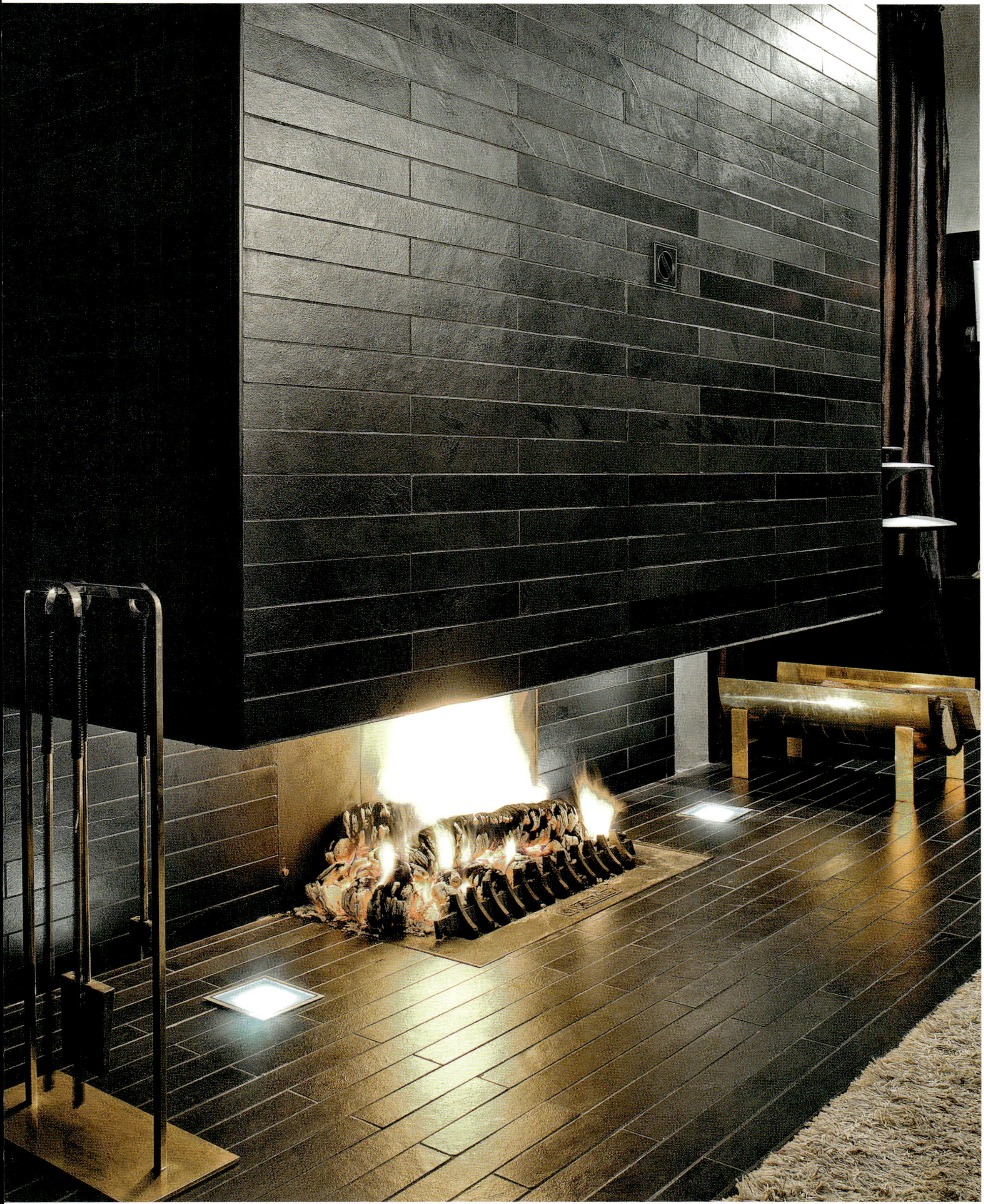

アルゼンチンの海浜住宅

マネイロ・ヴァスケス建築設計事務所
撮影：ホアン・ヒッタース／
サープレスエージェンシー
スタイリスト：マリアナ・ラポポルト

COASTAL ARGENTINA RESIDENCE
MANEIRO VÁZQUEZ ARQUITECTOS
PHOTO: © Juan Hitters (photos)/Surpresseagency,
Mariana Rapoport (stylist)

　壁のすっきりした直線でカットされた石灰岩本石タイルが、この海岸沿いの住宅の大きな魅力の1つである。表面の手で触りたくなる豊かな質感と、黄土色から金色へと微妙な移り変わりをみせる色調が、床の縁甲板とテラスの上の作業台の木の色と美しく調和している。そのアーストーンは全体を邪魔するどころか、逆に厨房設備の抑制されたグレーの色調に豊かな色彩を添えている。

The clean cut of the limestone on the walls of this coastal home is one of the principal attractions here. With its rugged aspect and tonal variations running from ocher to gold, this stone goes marvelously well with the wooden floorboards and the plank work-surface used on the terrace. The earth tones don't disrupt the whole; to the contrary, they lend a colorful note to the muted grays of the kitchen fixtures.

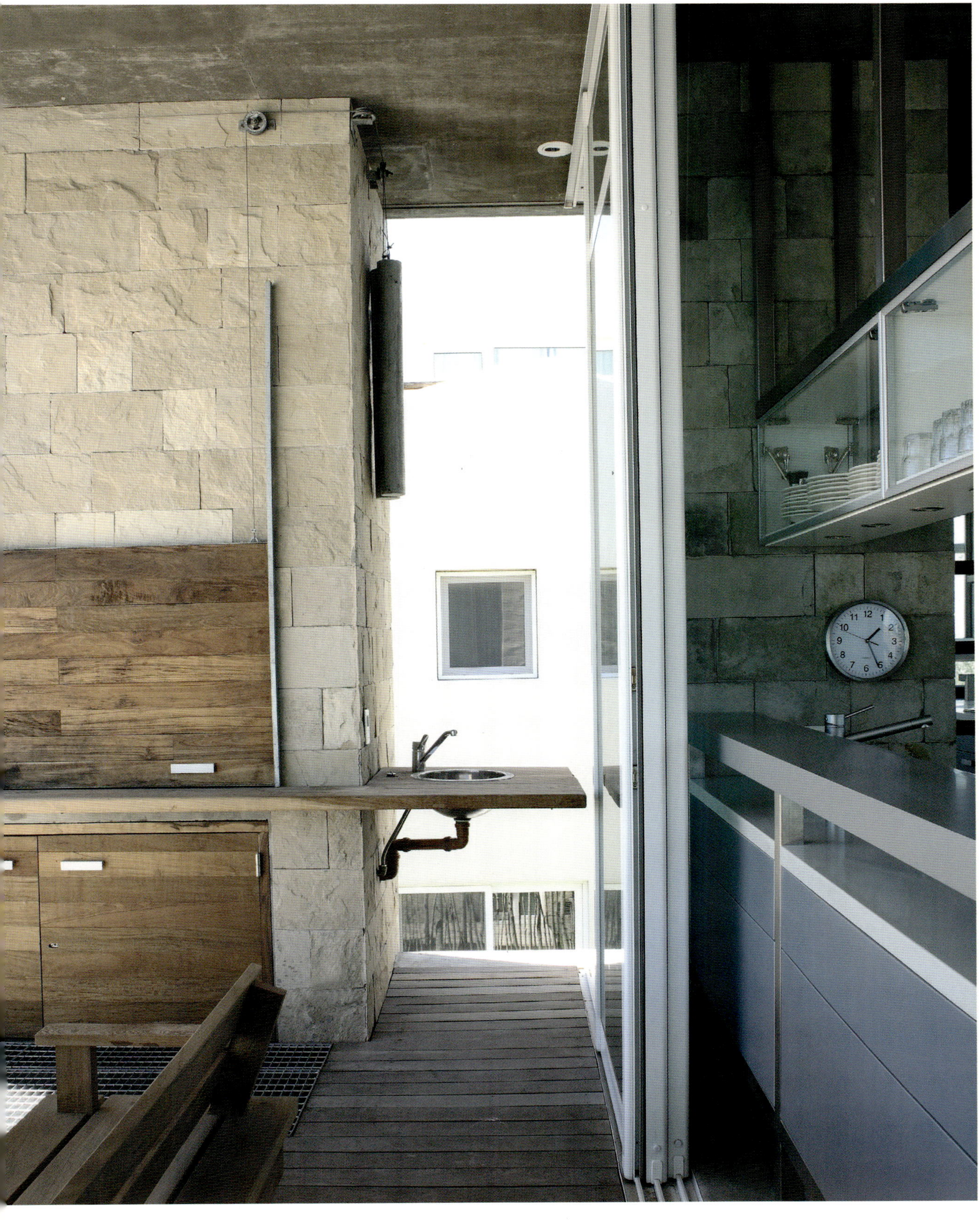

ラック邸ロフト

ラック・ビンスト／
クレパン・ビンスト建築設計事務所
撮影：A・フォン・アインジーデル／
Inside／Cover

LUC'S LOFT
LUC BINST/CREPAIN BINST ARCHITECTURE
PHOTO: © A.Von Einsiedel/Inside/Cover

ラック・ビンストは、彼自身の実験的精神をある種の演劇的手法で表現したいと考えた。そこで思いついたのが、キッチンをダイニングルームの海に浮かぶ大きな白く輝く大理石の島にすることであった。そこではすべてのものの表面が光を反射していることが重要だった。おのずと照明の概念も決まり、床から上向きに照らす青色蛍光灯の光が、島全体を劇的に浮かび上がらせることとなった。

Luc Binst intended to synthesize his experimental will with a certain theatrical spirit. In the kitchen and dining room, the architect conceived an island of huge dimensions dressed in shiny white marble. It was important that these surfaces be very reflective, hence this room's concept of illumination, so that the blue neon tones from the floor could alight upon everything in spectacular fashion.

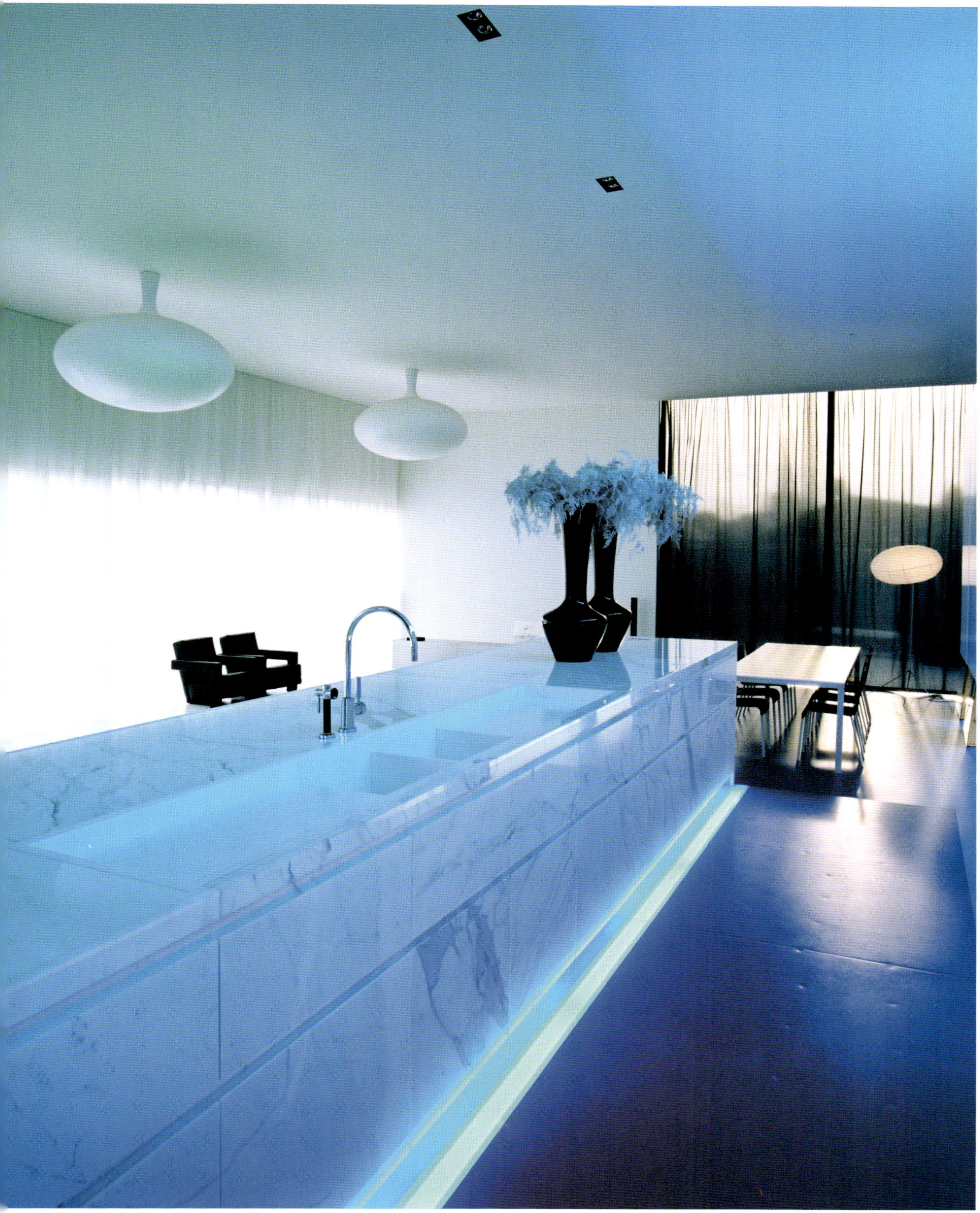

イズリントンの住宅

クラウディオ・シルヴェストリン
建築設計事務所
撮影：サラ・ブリー／owi.bz

ISLINGTON HOME
CLAUDIO SILVESTRIN ARCHITECTS
PHOTO: © Sarah Blee/owi.bz

近年、機能性が良く、斬新な設計を可能にすることから、アイランド・キッチンの人気が高まっている。長いキッチンカウンターの天板に使われているのは、イタリアのレッチェ大理石で、この住宅のいろいろな場所の床材としても多く用いられている。その高潔な白は、住宅の基調をなす白色とよく調和し、ひときわ輝いて見える。キッチンカウンター全体が無駄のない簡潔な線とフォルムでデザインされているため、大理石の縞模様が美しく浮かび上がっている。

In recent years, an unstoppable rise in kitchen islands has been observed due to their functionality and ground-breaking design. The Lecce marble used for the long kitchen counter-top and many of the floors throughout this home capture one's attention, chosen to match the predominantly white colors of the house. The simplicity of line and form with which this unit has been designed highlights the impressive streaks throughout.

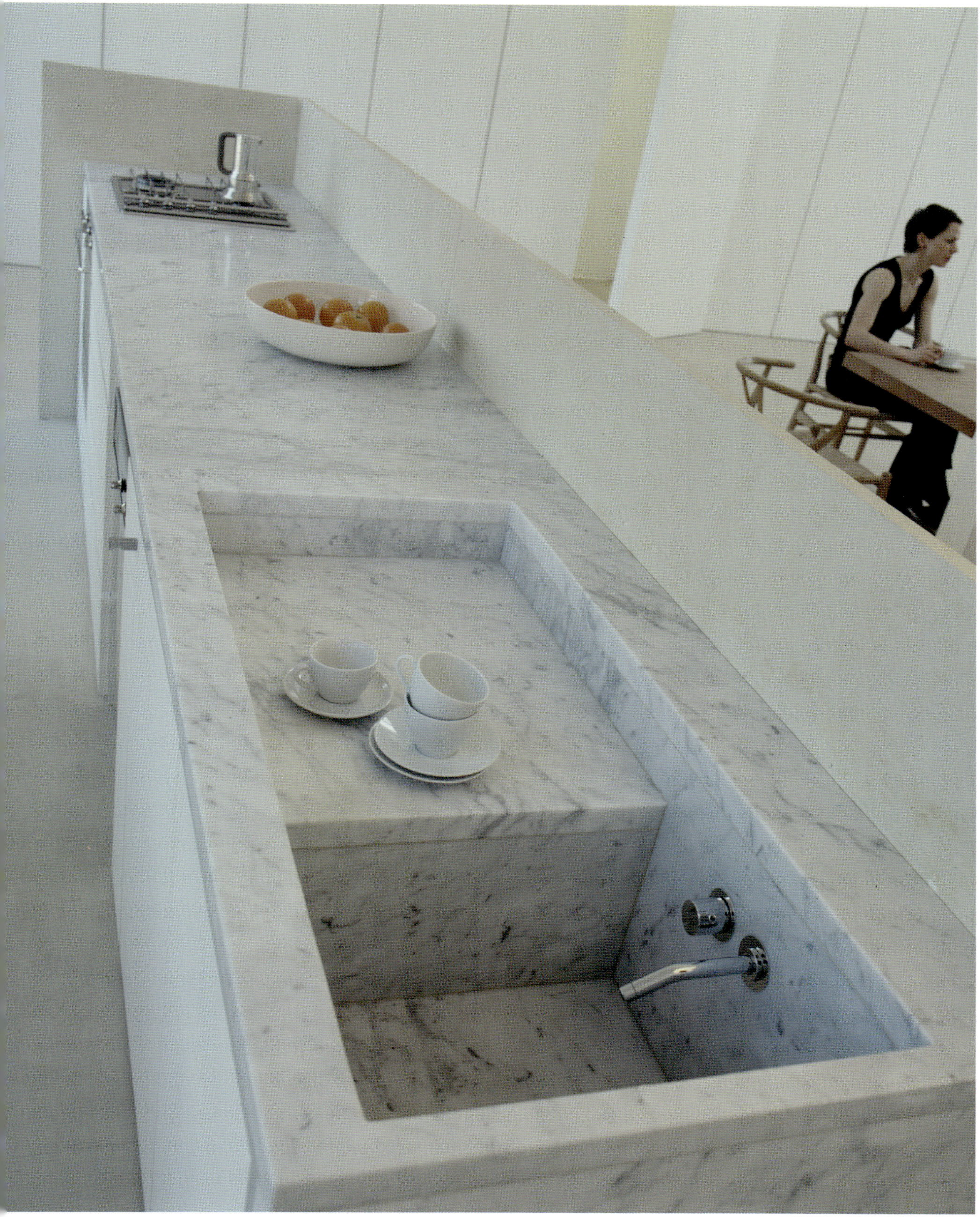

ラ・アデュアナの住宅

マーティン・ゴメス建築設計事務所
撮影：ダニエラ・マッカデン／
サープレスエージェンシー
スタイリスト：マリアナ・ラポポルト

LA ADUANA HOUSE
MARTÍN GÓMEZ ARQUITECTOS
PHOTO: © Mariana Rapoport
(stylist) Daniela Mac Adden/Surpressagency

　鉱物成分の違いによって現れる大理石の微妙な色合いを強調するため、建築家はキッチン全体を最も地味なやさしい色で統一することにした。その自然な色を背景にして、カウンタートップと壁面のカラーラ大理石の黒い縞模様が、地の白や灰色から鮮明に浮かび上がっている。その大理石は配膳場所も定義し、食器棚横の主人のための小さなオフィスとの仕切りになっている。

Of the various colors found in marble due to its mineral composition, the architect of this house opted for the most elegantly sober color in the kitchen. In this natural-colored ambiance, the black stains against the white and gray Carrara marble provide a perfect contrast with the counter-top and its bordering wall. In addition, the marble helps to define the preparation area, separating it from the small office beside the cupboard.

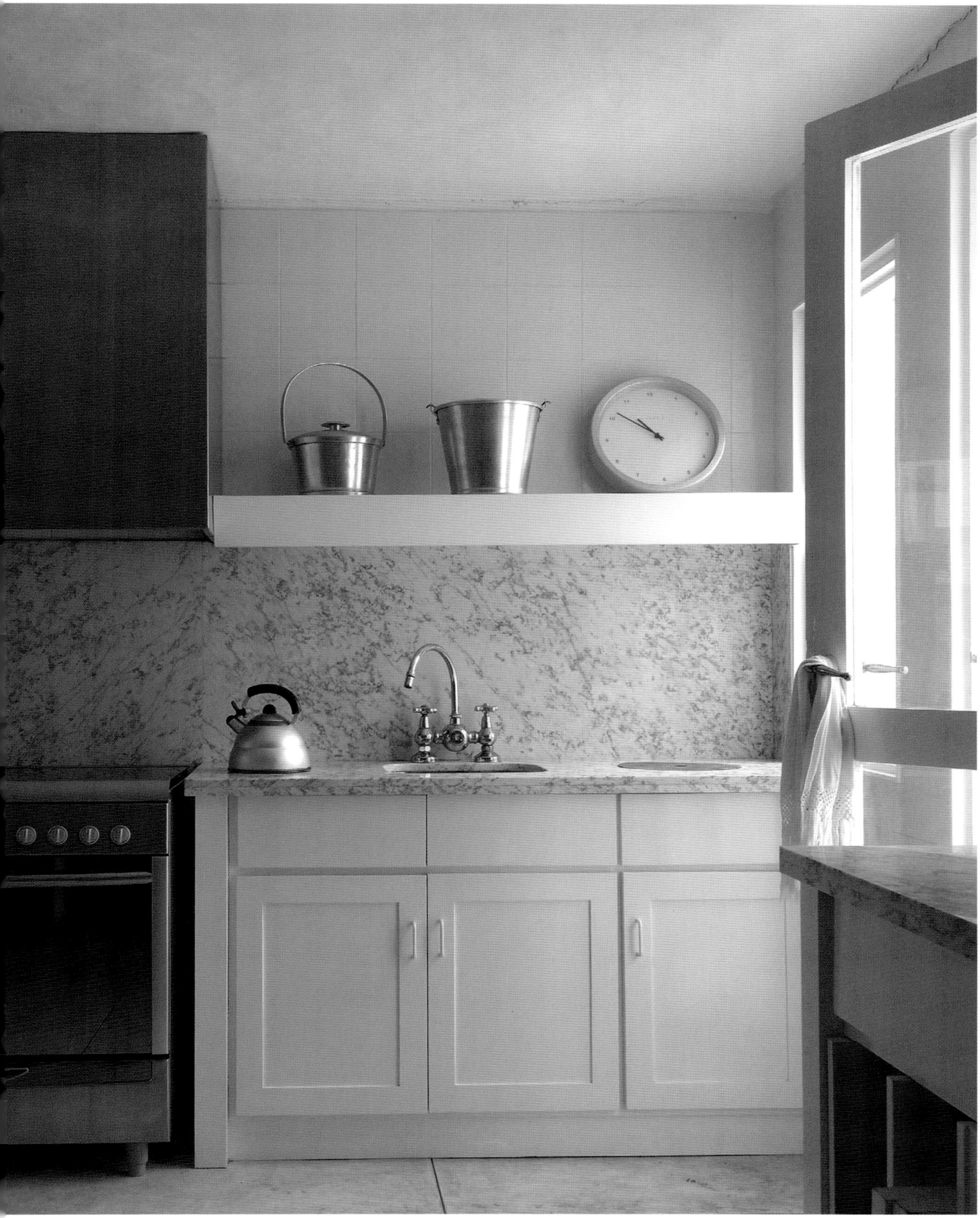

マドリードからの天然スレート

ペドロ・ボニーラ
撮影：ルイス・エヴィア

SLATE FROM MADRID
PEDRO BONILLA
PHOTO: © Luis Hevia

「コントラスト」という概念がこのバスルームを截然と定義している。マドリード近郊のセントラル山地から切り出した天然スレートが、柔らかな温もりをたたえる木肌と対位法を構成して空間を支配している。

チェリー無垢板の滑らかな表面が、天然スレートの思わず触れたくなる豊かな質感を背景に、いっそう清々しく感じられる。これほど視覚的に力強い男性的な空間が、たった2つの素材だけで構成され、住宅の他の空間と画然と区別されているとは、まったく見事としか言いようがない。

The word "contrast" superbly dominates any description of this bathroom. The slate extracted from the sierras around Madrid serve as a counterpoint to the delicately warm ocher color of the fixtures.
The cherry wood's smooth surface seems even smoother against the richly textured slate. Both materials compose a masculine area of such visual power that these alone serve to separate the area from the rest of the house.

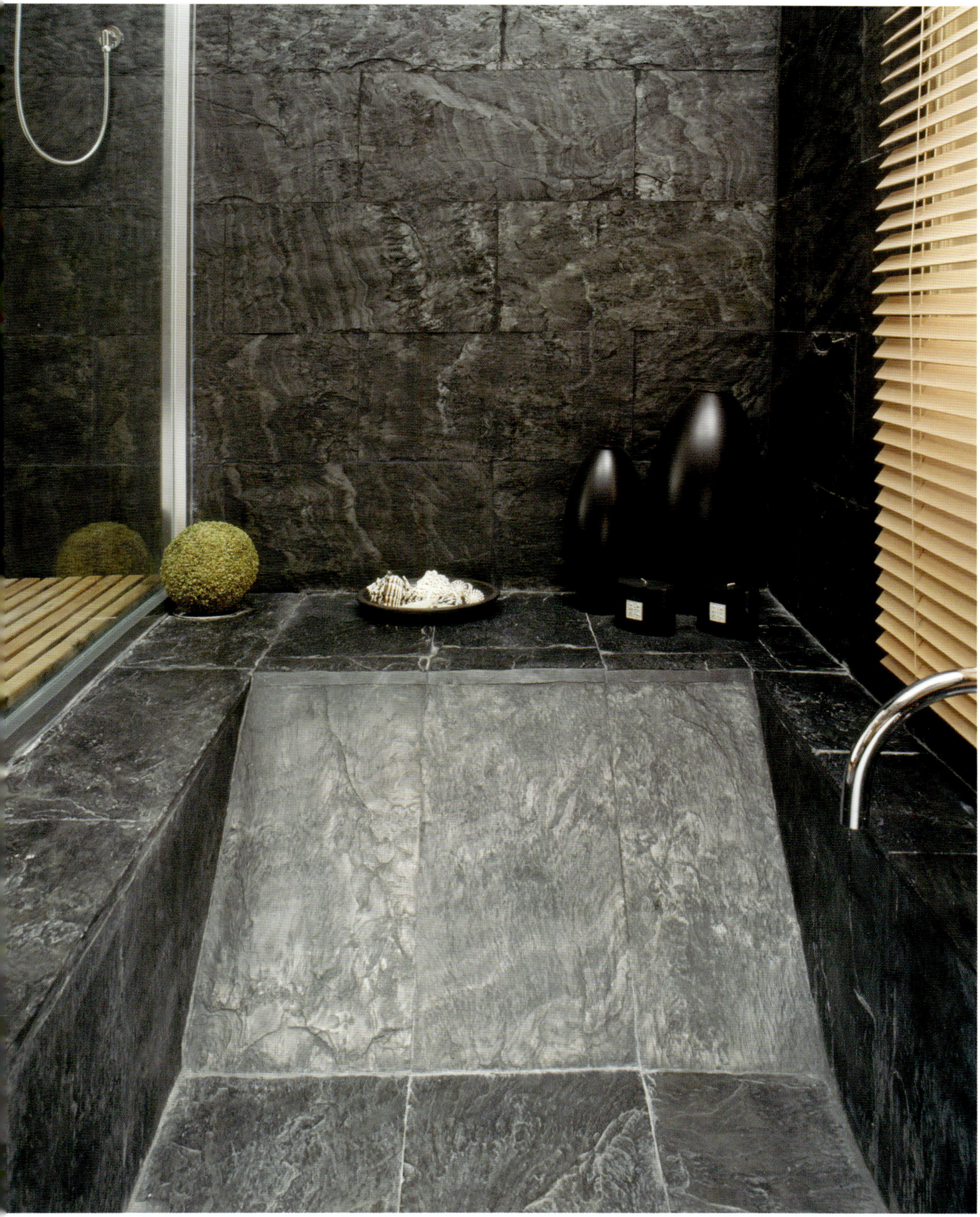

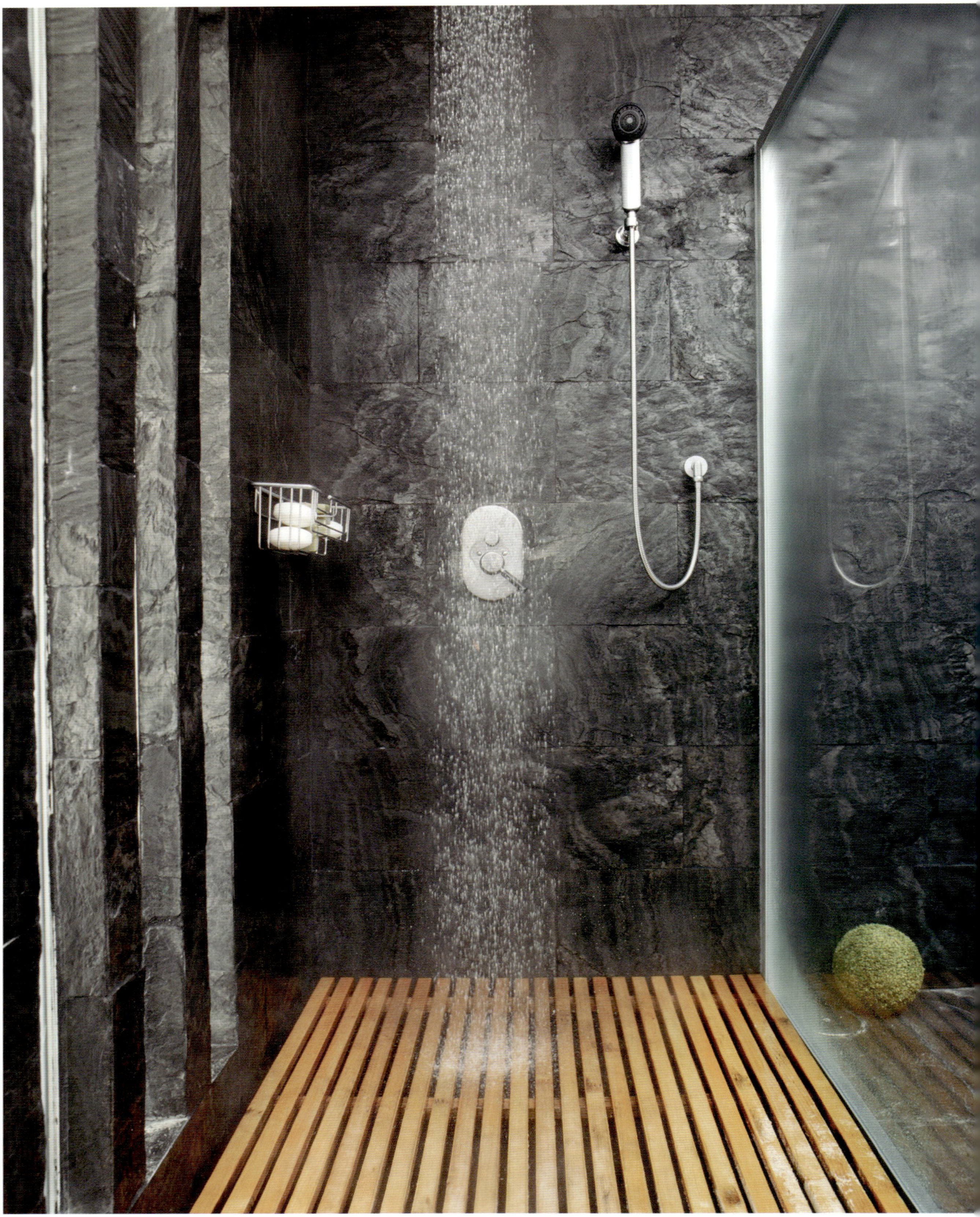

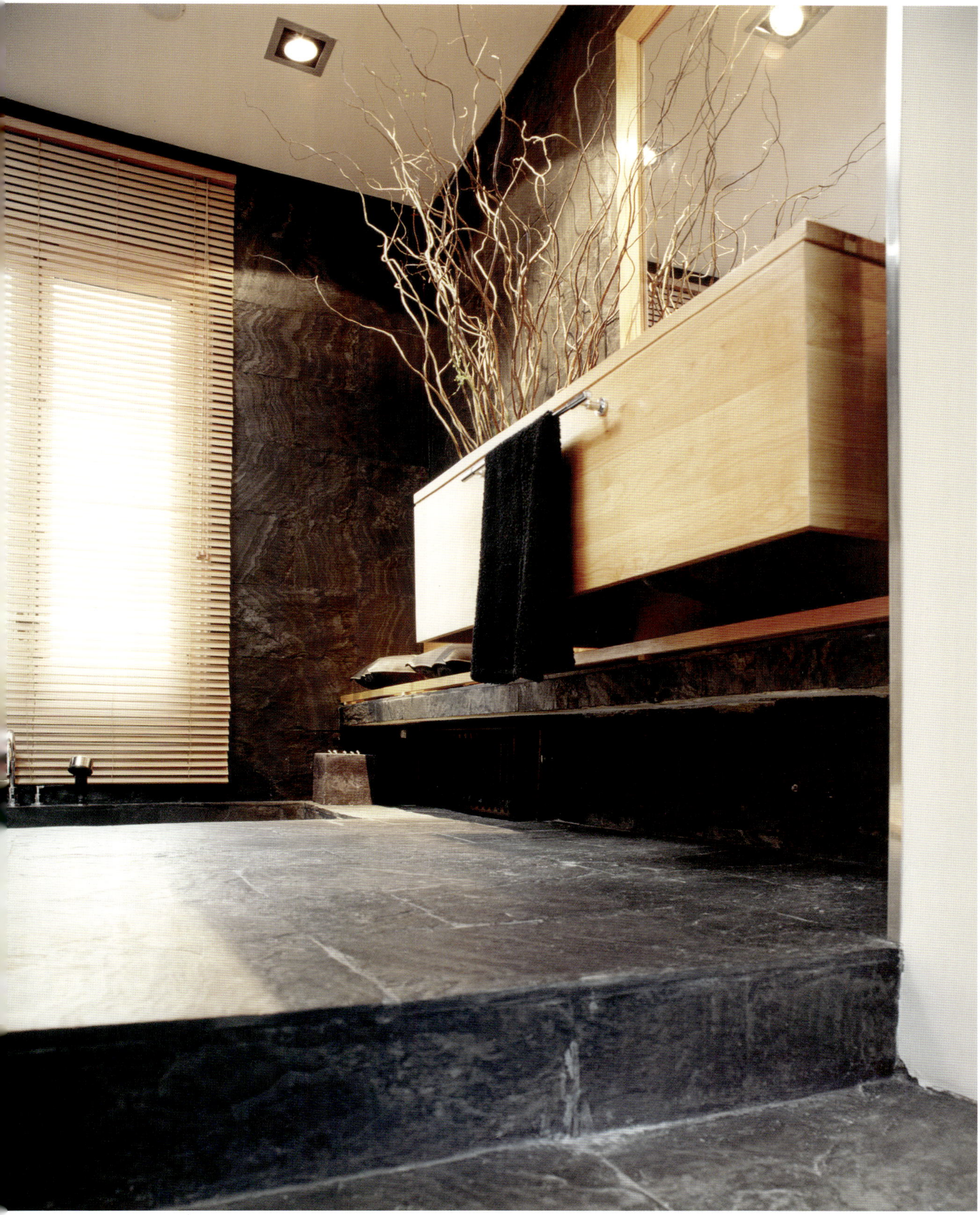

カルデス・デ・モンブイの住宅

アントニー・グラウ・ギルバー／
エウセビ・グティエレス
撮影：ホセ・ルイス・ハウスマン

HOUSE IN CALDES DE MONTBUI
ANTONI GRAU I GIRBAU/EUSEBI GUTIÉRREZ
PHOTO: © Jose Luis Hausmann

　住宅のオーナーは、自ら設計監督してバスルームを改築することにした。大理石のバスタブを修復し、同じ材料を用いてそれ以外の場所も仕上げることとした。こうしてマカエル大理石の本石タイルが壁と床に張られ、バスタブと統合されて、一体の彫刻作品のようなバスルームが完成した。大理石で被われた白い空間は、自然光に満ち溢れた豊饒なひと時を約束している。反対側の壁は黒でまとめたが、大理石の輝きのため、それが全体の光度に影響することはなかった。

The owner of the house chose to oversee its restoration himself, recovering the marble bath and using the same material for the rest of the bathroom. This way, the slabs of Macael marble that cover the walls and floors become unified with the bathtub, as if one complete sculpture. These generate a well lit area within the room, amplifying the natural light. Thanks to this reflective power, it's possible to have a black wall on the opposite side without affecting the overall luminosity.

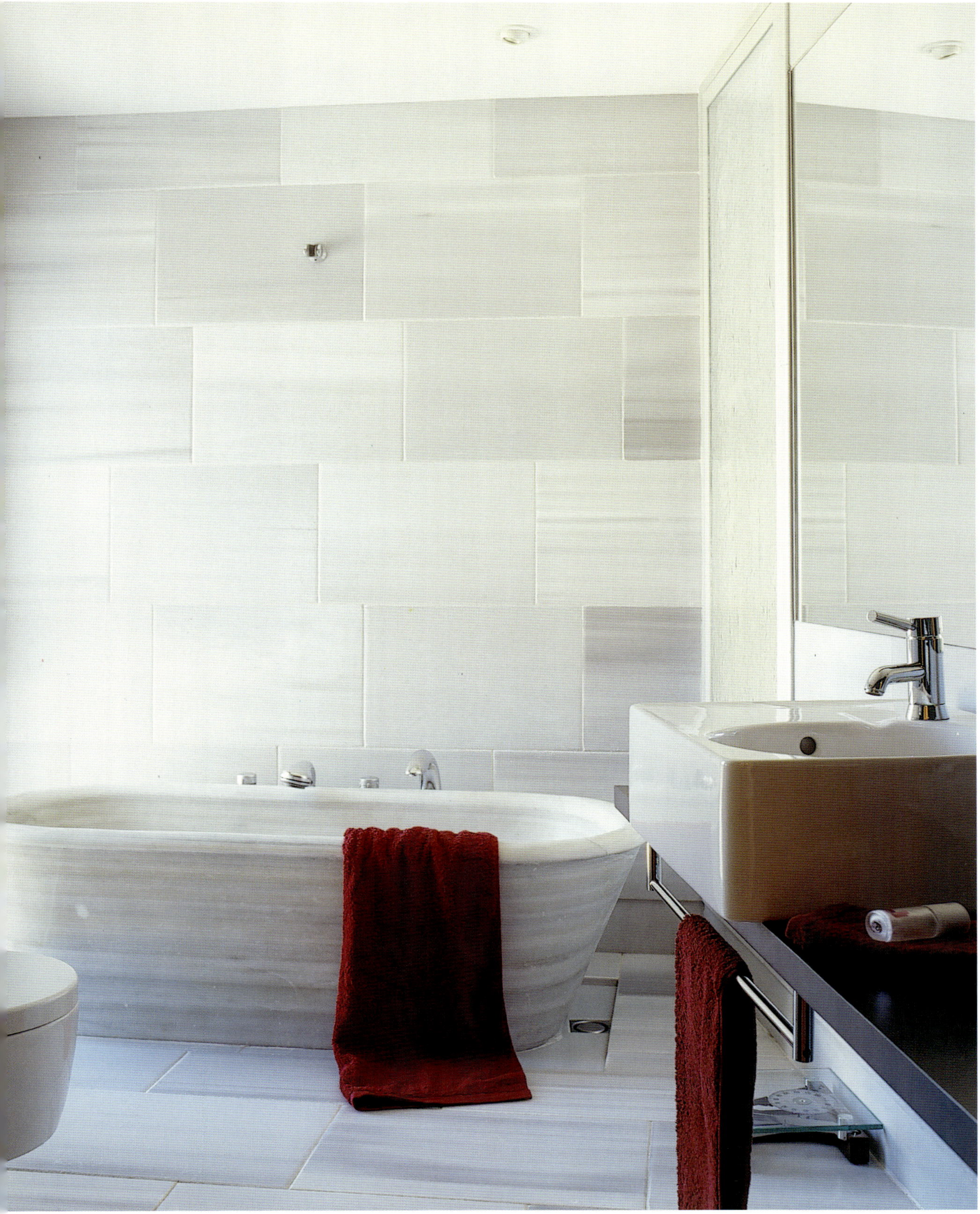

ソレダード邸

パブロ・サンチェス・エリア建築設計事務所
スタイリスト：
　　　レネー・アルマス ＆ レネー・サエンス
撮影：バージニア・デル・ジュディチェ

SOLEDAD HOME
PABLO SÁNCHEZ ELÍA (ARCHITECT)
RENÉE ARMAS AND RENÉE SÁENZ (STYLISTS)
PHOTO: © Virginia del Giudice

ジョイア・ヴェナートとカルカッタ・ドラダの2種類の大理石が、このブエノスアイレスの住宅のバスルームを貫く、重量感とフォルムの純粋さを生み出している。壁面と床の美しく磨かれた大理石タイルは、ただそれだけで色彩的統一感を生み出し、空間を絵画的に彩っている。バスタブとシンクの天板も同じ大理石で作られ、その豪華さは古代ローマの浴場を彷彿とさせる。大理石の縞模様にそって空気は優しく漂い、アール・ヌーボー様式の小物や調度品との対比がその優しさをさらに強調している。

The heavy and pure shapes prevailing throughout the bathroom of this Buenos Aires home were achieved thanks to the gioia venato and calacatta dorada marble used to make them. In this way, the polished and bare surfaces of the floors and walls create a chromatic unity which visually amplifies the space. The bathtub and the counter-top for the sink, made of the same material, recall antique bathrooms. This gives the area a gentle air, reinforced by its contrast with the small art nouveau style fixtures and furniture.

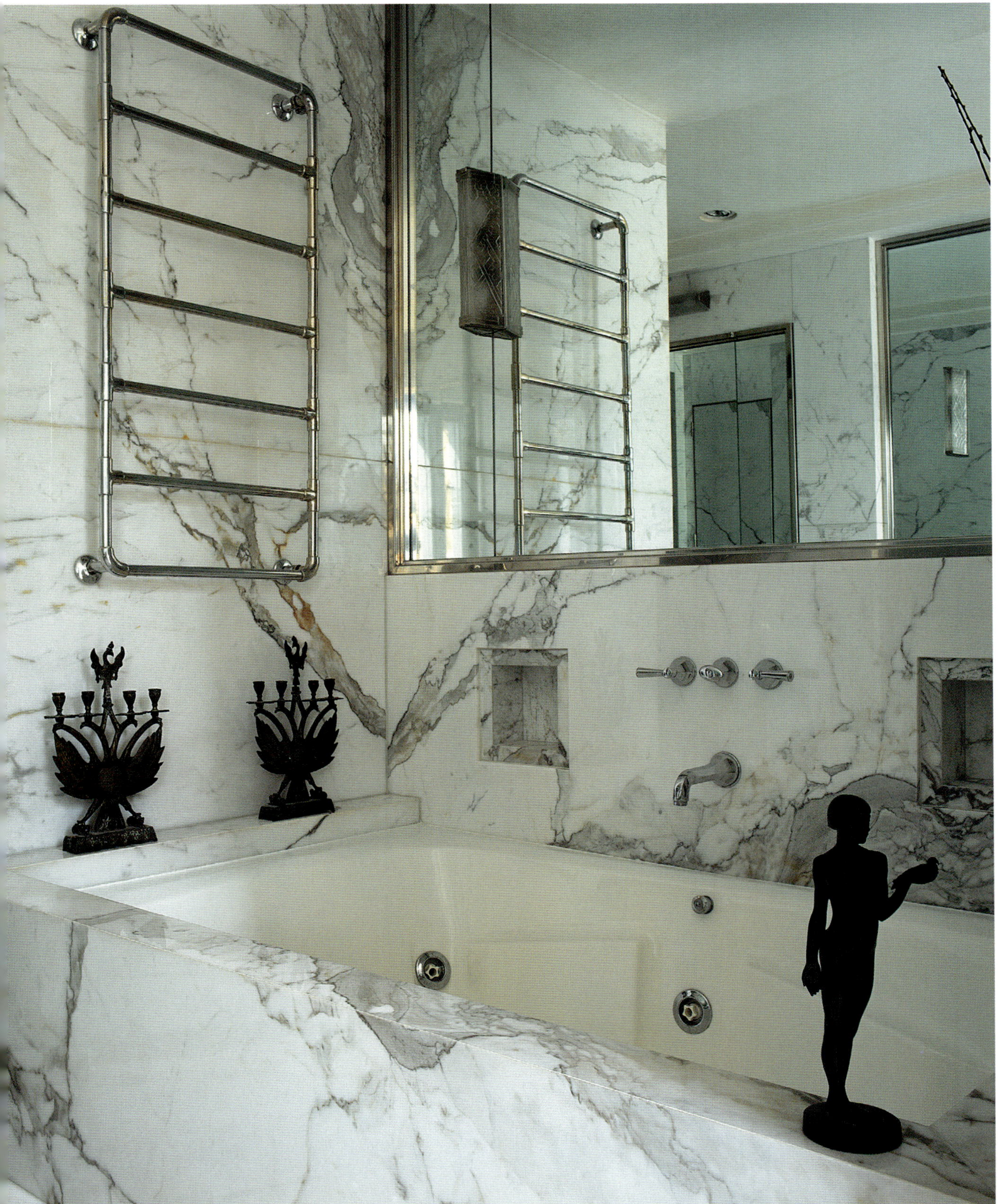

プロジェクト・ヨー

フィリップ・スタルク／ヨー
撮影：デュラビット

PROJECT YOO
PHILIPPE STARCK/YOO
PHOTO: © Duravit

　大理石という素材は、その独特の高貴さによってどんな装飾様式にも合う。しかしそれが最も似合うのは、やはり豪華で壮麗な空間だろう。フランスのデザイナー、フィリップ・スタルクはこれを現代的平面で実証しようとした。そのため彼は、華麗な形状と滑らかな表面の対話が特徴のネオ・バロック様式を選択した。大理石の白い輝きと墨流し模様が、鏡や蛇口などの備品の金属的光沢をさらに煌かせる理想的な背景となっている。

Because of its nobility, marble is a material capable of combining well with any decorative style, even though it has always been associated with opulence and luxury. French designer Philippe Starck returns this concept to a contemporary plane. For this he opted on a neo-baroque style, characterized by a dialogue between overdone shapes and clean surfaces. In this fashion, the luminosity of the white marble background, with splashes of black, becomes ideal for bringing out the shiny metal fixtures.

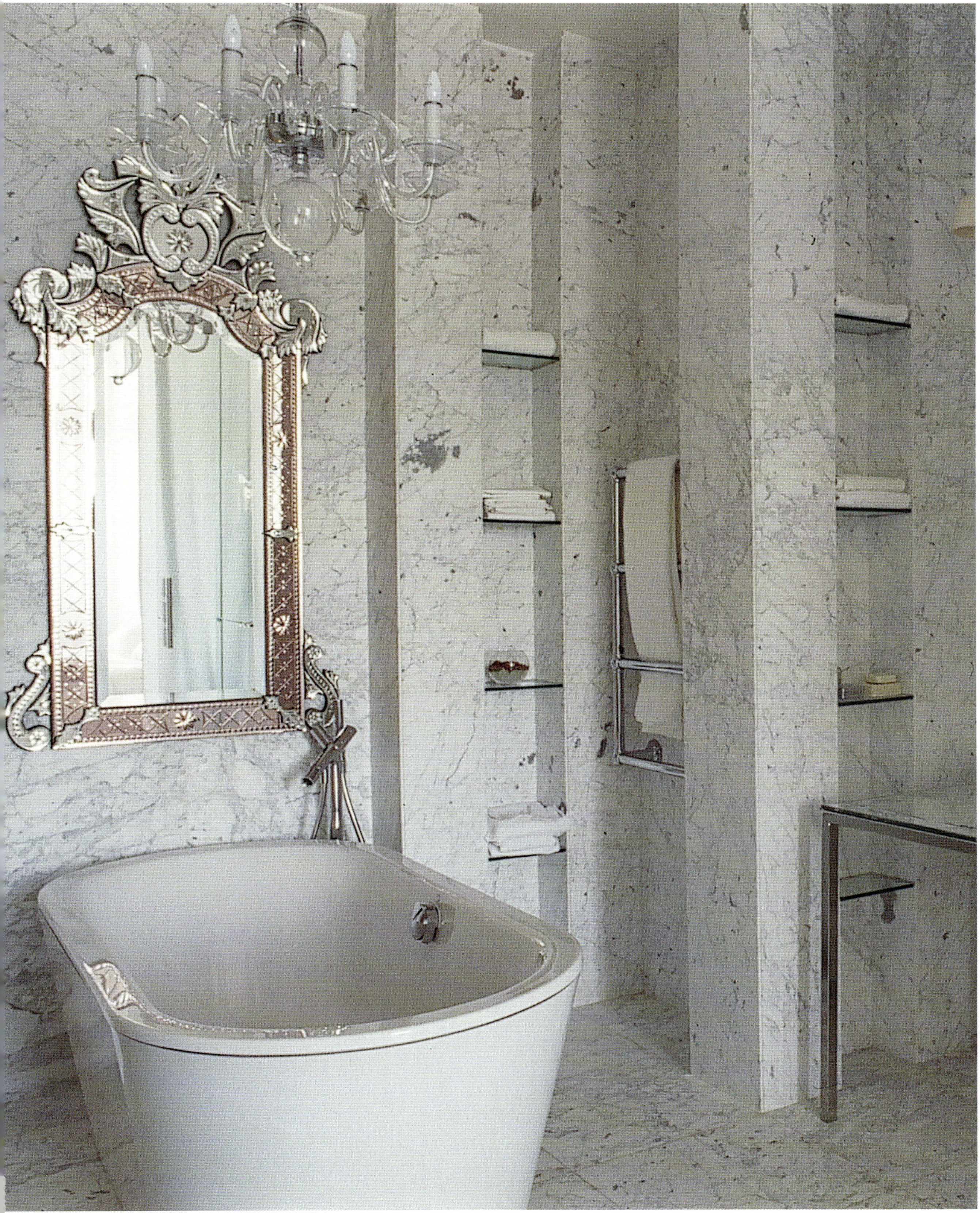

サン・ジュセッペの住宅

グイド・アントネッロ／
クリスティアナ・ヴァンニーニ
撮影：サンティ・カレカ

SAN GIUSEPPE HOME
GUIDO ANTONELLO/CRISTIANA VANNINI
PHOTO: © Santi Caleca

　床と壁の表面から反射されるさまざまな性質の光が、トスカーナ平原にあるこの住宅を折衷主義的(エクレクティック)なモダンな空気で満たしている。ブルー・アクエリアスとジャッロ・ドゥルストリアの2種類の御影石タイルが張られた滑らかな床面と、内壁の一部やカウンター前面を被っているほとんど手が加えられていない野石を積み上げた石積み壁の荒々しい質感の対比が、独特の演出効果を生み出している。それ以外にも、モザイクタイルで仕上げられた壁面、印象的なイグアナグリーンが華麗な縞模様を描く大理石の間仕切り壁、さらには漆喰仕上げの壁面など、さまざまなディテールを持った面と面の交錯が、奥行きの深い豊かな空間を創造している。

The shiny floor surface and bathroom walls lend an eclectic modern air to this Tuscany field home. The paved stone – blue aquarius in one case and giallo d'Istria in another – contrasts with the rugged texture of the almost untouched, pure-state rock that covers a part of the walls and counter-top. The rest of the walls are dressed with mosaics and marble plates boasting magnificent streaks of an intense iguana-green color.

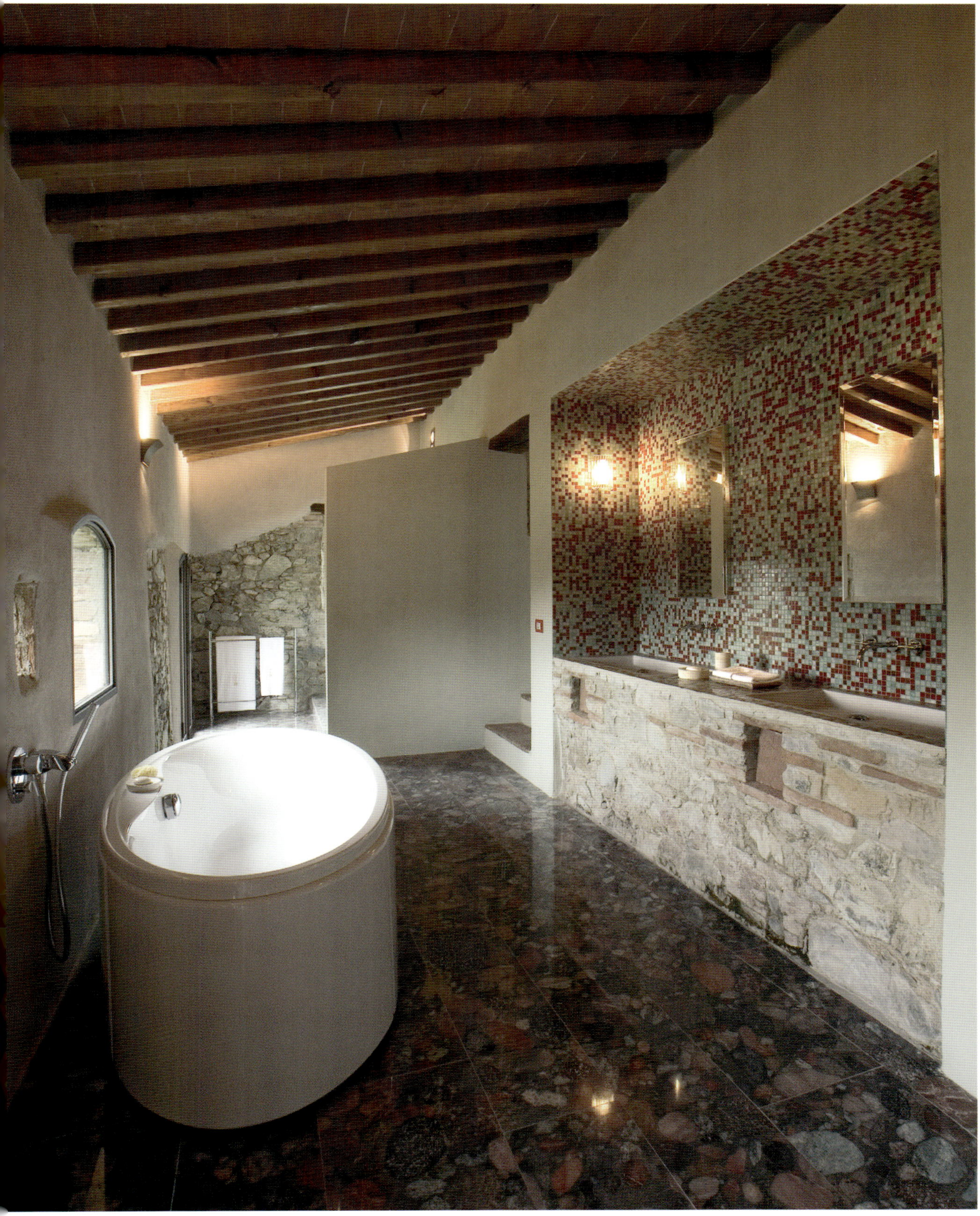

ヴェミグナーノの別荘

グイド・アントネッロ／
クリスティアナ・ヴァンニーニ
撮影：サンティ・カレカ

CASALE IN VEMIGNANO
GUIDO ANTONELLO/CRISTIANA VANNINI
PHOTO: © Santi Caleca

　この田園地帯の大きな古い民家を改築するにあたって、建物の構造はそのまま残すことにした。しかし元のバスルームを現代的な広いバスルームに改修することは不可能だったので、別の大きな空間をそれに充てることにした。その結果、厚い石積み壁には何も変更を加えないで済んだ。結果、間仕切り壁のモザイクタイルやセメントのカウンターの光沢のある表面と、石積み壁や本石タイルの床面の重厚な質感との間に、面白いコントラストが生まれた。シャワーや蛇口など、バスルーム備品の簡潔で現代的なフォルムが、自然石の存在感を強調し、それをより現代的な建築の地平に招き入れている。

The act of recovering an old rural home kept the edifice's original distribution intact. To make way for modern and comfortable bathrooms, large spaces in the home were chosen in order to make sure that the thick stone walls would not be affected by the change. This way, the mosaic formed by the dividing wall and the smooth cement of the counter-tops contrasts with the rugged texture of the walls and paved areas. The pure and modern form of the bathroom fittings, the shower and faucets highlight the stone and bring it to a more contemporary level.

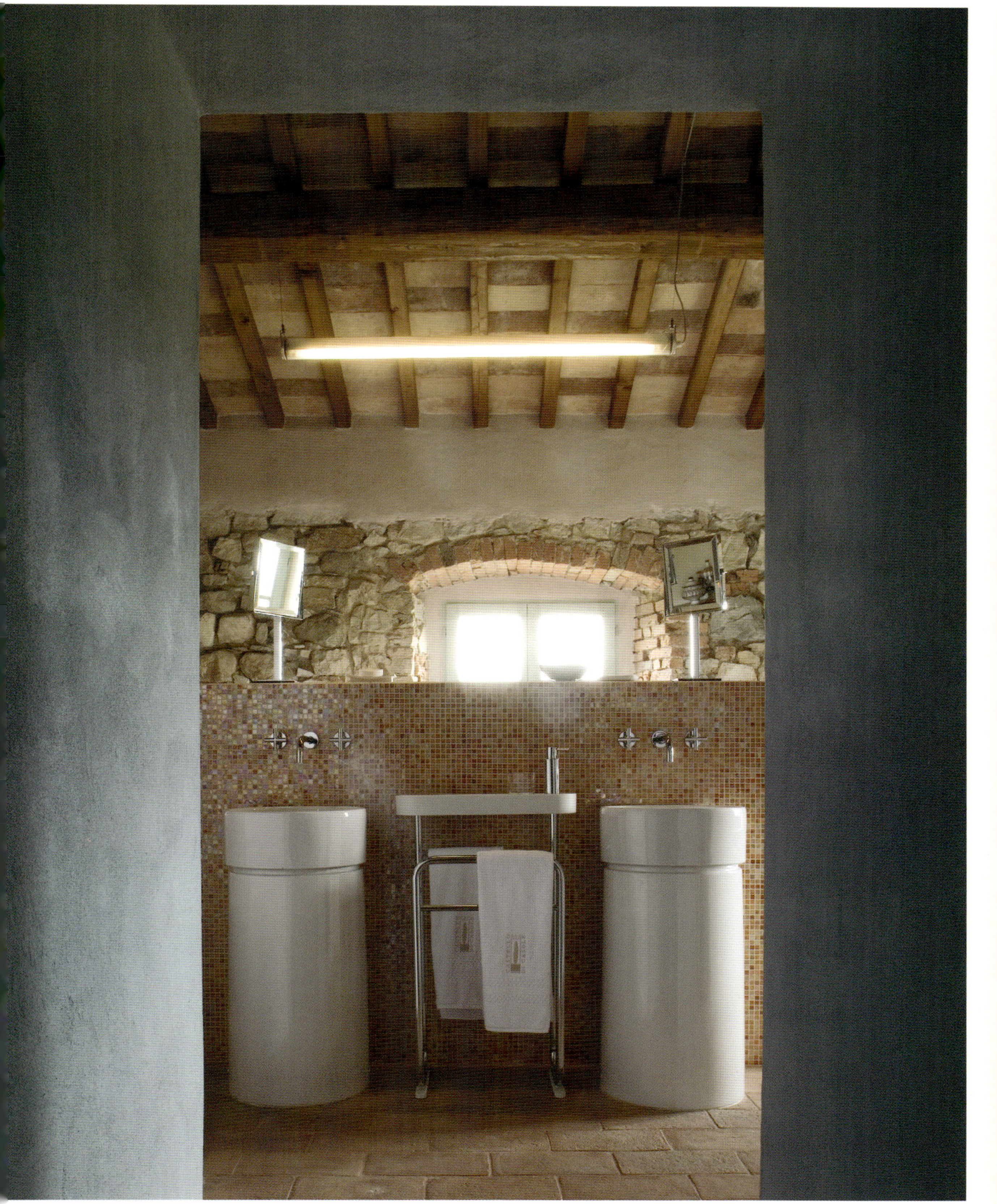

モンテ・タウロの住宅

レゴレッタ+レゴレッタ
撮影：ルルド・レゴレッタ

HOUSE IN MONTE TAURO
LEGORRETA Y LEGORRETA
PHOTO: © Lourdes Legorreta

　大都市の喧騒から離れた静かな別荘の一画に、幸福な生活の核となる強靭な肉体を創りだすためのジムと石造りのプールが設置されている。スライド式窓のついたガラス天井が、プールと自然を融合させ、天空からの光を導き入れている。その光は壁のピンク色をいっそう華やかなものにし、プールを囲む大きな花崗岩テーブルの柔らかな色調を強調している。

The stone pool located on the terrace comes together with the gym to form a nucleus of well-being, in a house designed to serve as a refuge from the big city.
A glass ceiling with a sliding window keeps it connected with the outdoors and allows for a zenithal light to come in.
This intensifies its pink walls and highlights the lighter tones of the large granite table surrounding the pool.

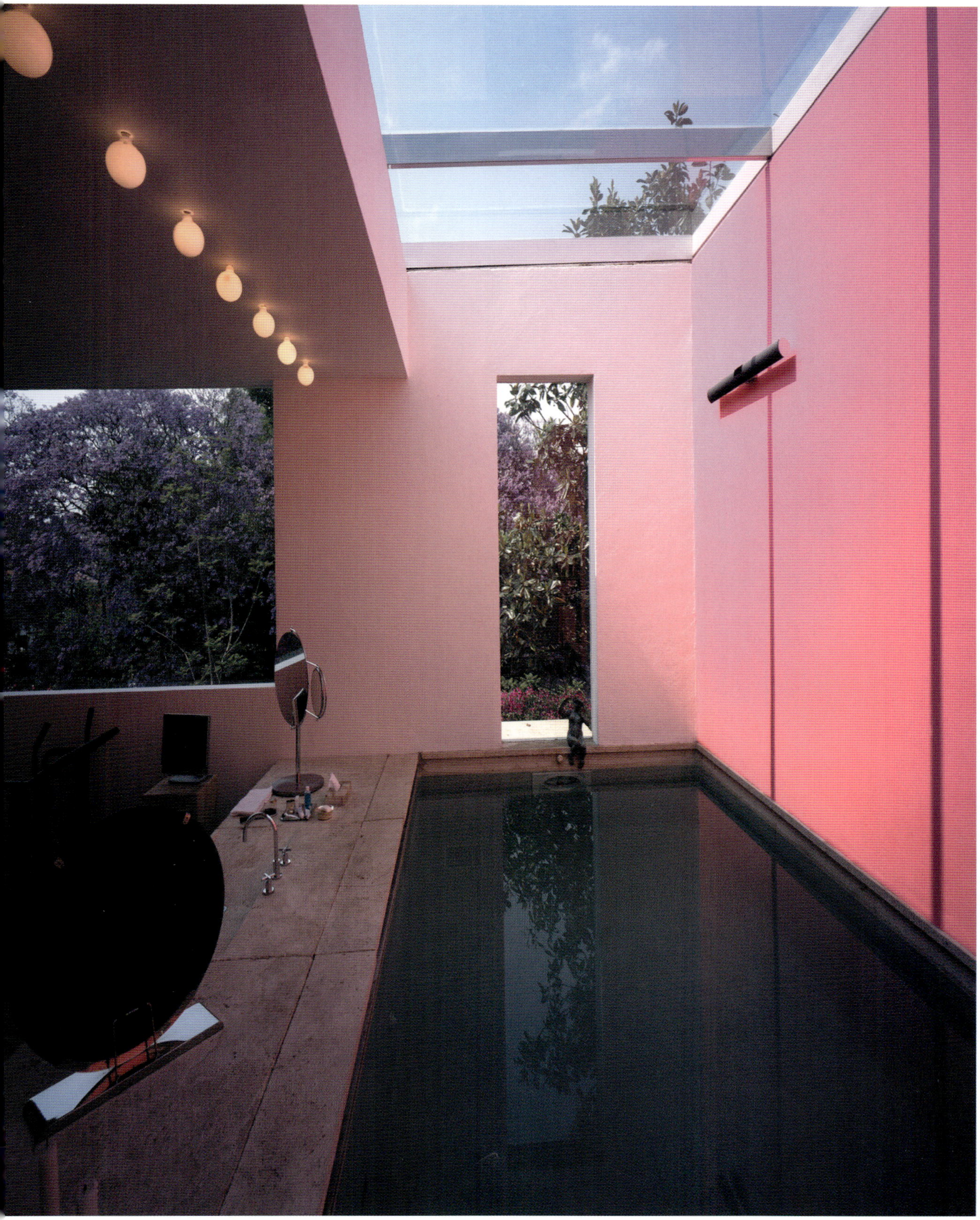

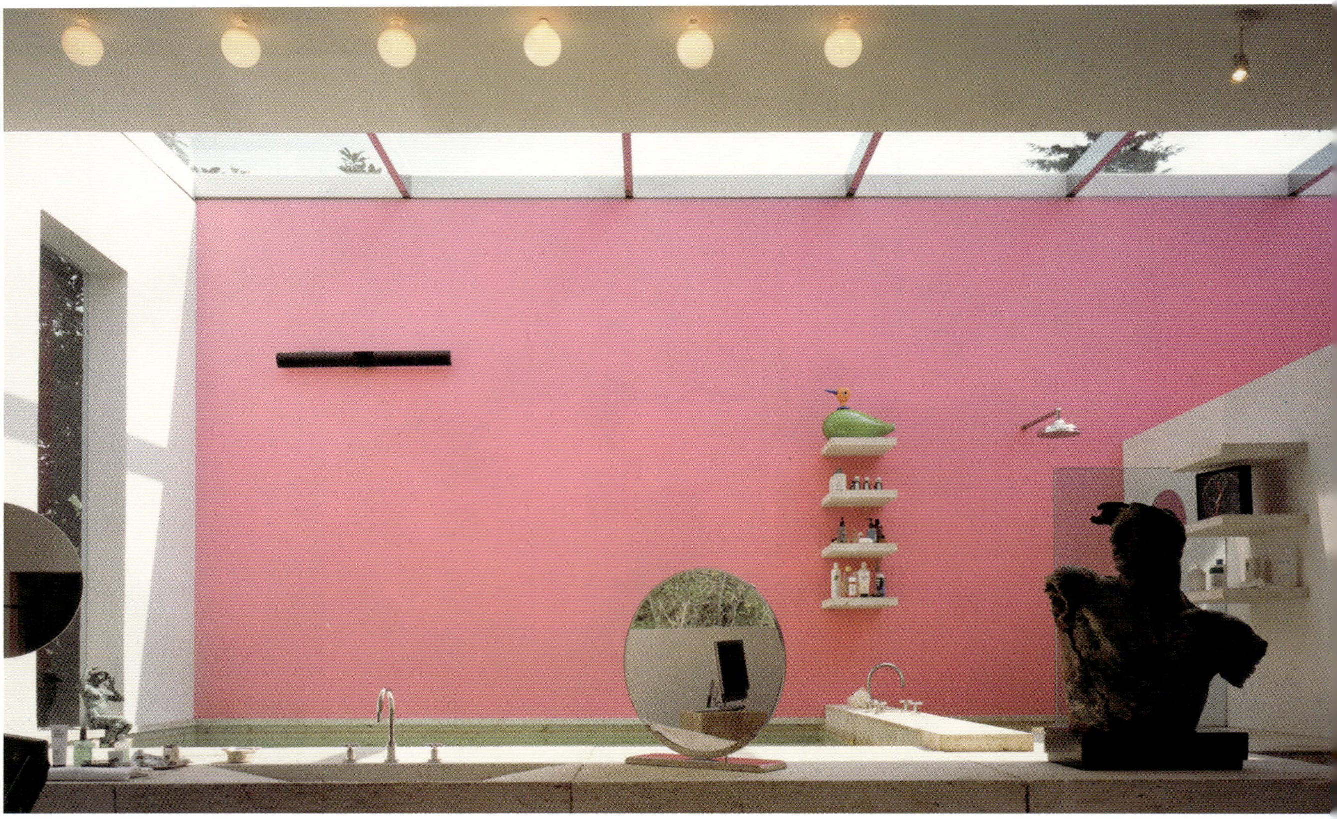

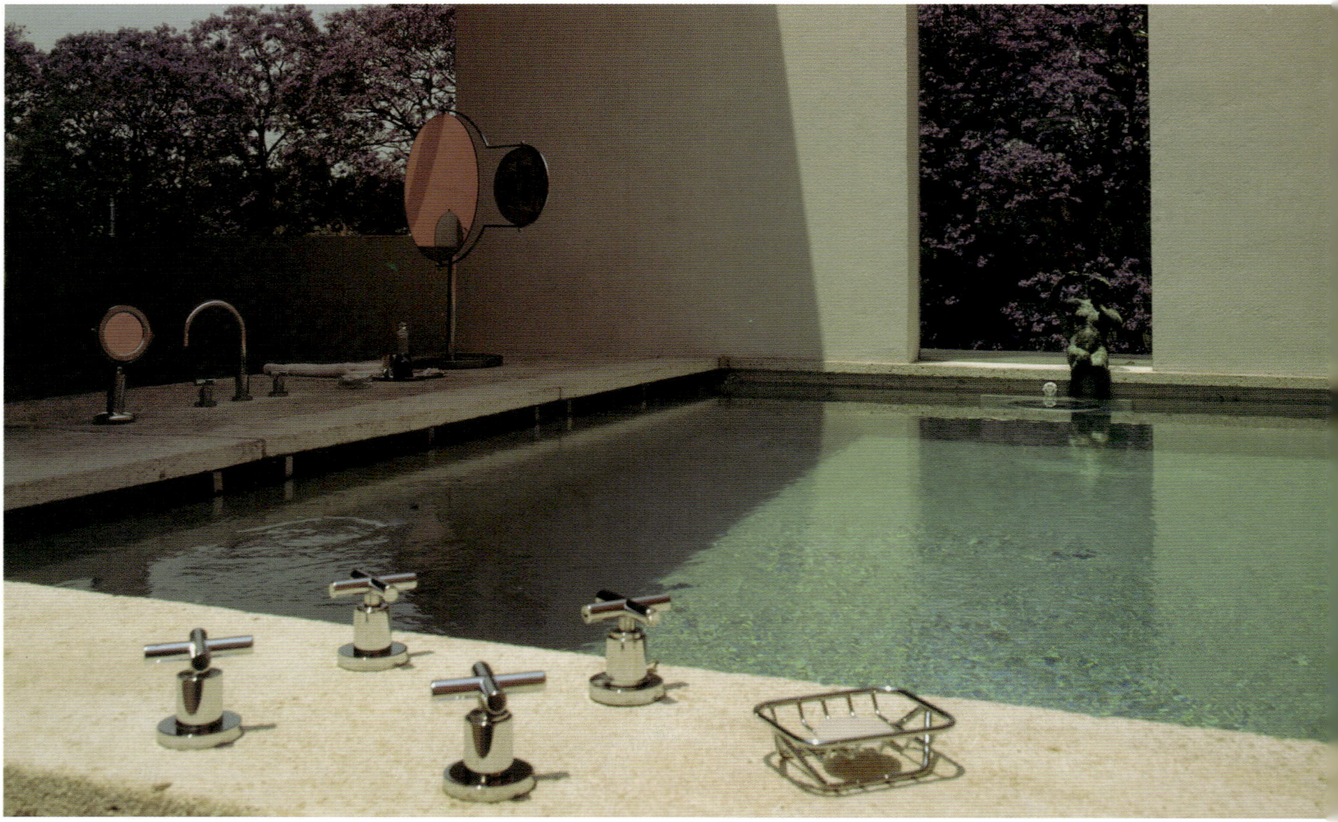

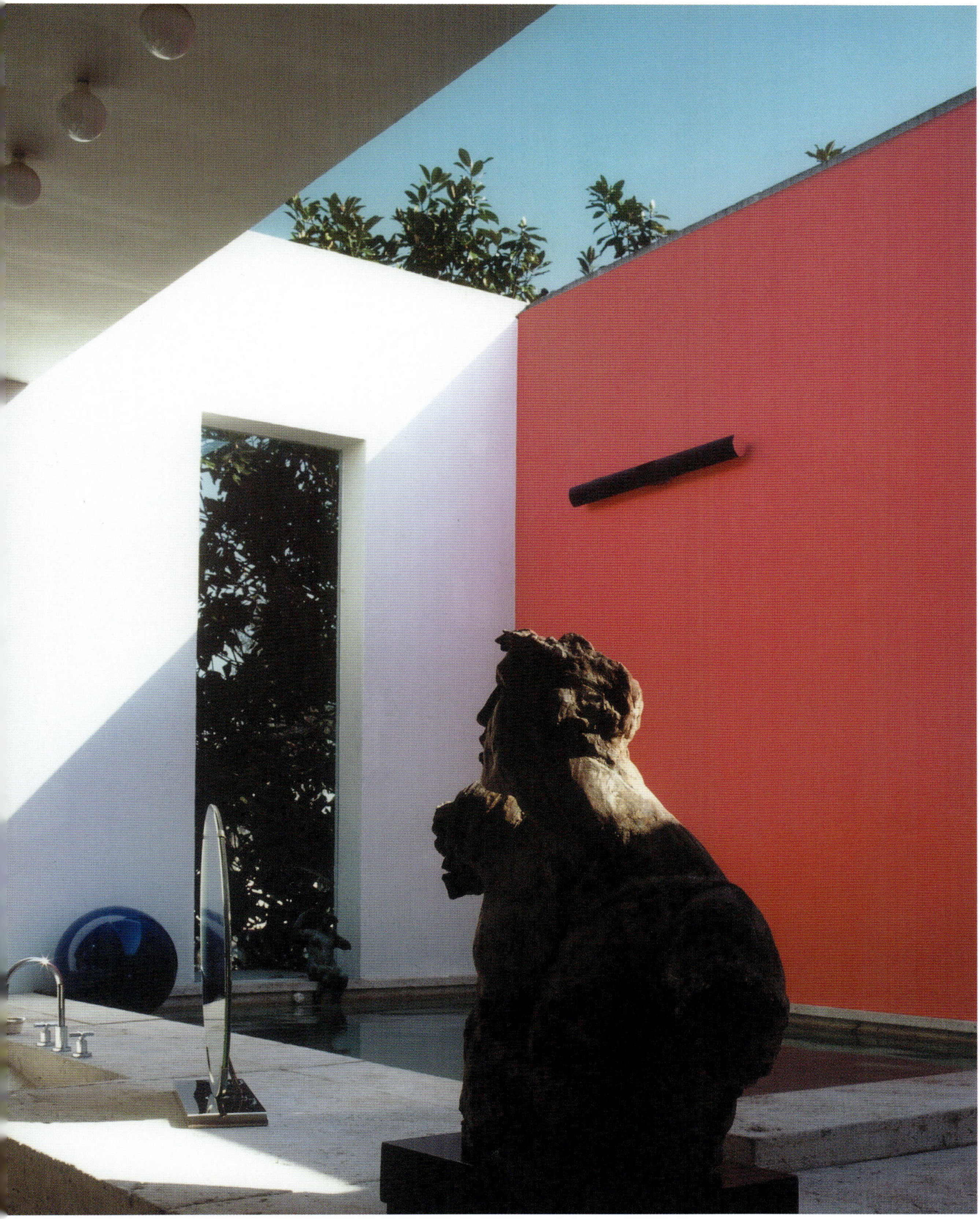

パルマの集合住宅

パガーニ‐ディ・マウロ建築設計事務所
撮影：マッテオ・ピアッツァ

APARTMENT in PARMA
PAGANI-DI MAURO ARCHITETTI
PHOTO: © Matteo Piazza

　この天井裏バスルームの主人公は、ブラジル産黒御影石と、その組積が創りだす玄妙な色調の変化である。この石が持つモノトーンの多彩な色調は、サウナで最もよく表現されており、そこだけは幾何学的雰囲気を出すため、わざと縦向きにタイルを張りつけている。この石は耐久性に優れているため、壁にも床にも使うことができたが、さらにはプールの底にも、防水加工を施さずに同様に使用することができた。

The protagonist in this loft's spa area is the black Brazilian stone and its rich array of nuances. The tonal variety is intensified in the sauna where, as opposed to the rest of the home, the slabs have been placed vertically to create a geometric texture. Thanks to the stone's resistance, it was possible to dress the walls and floor – including the bottom of the pool – in the same way, without needing water-proof materials.

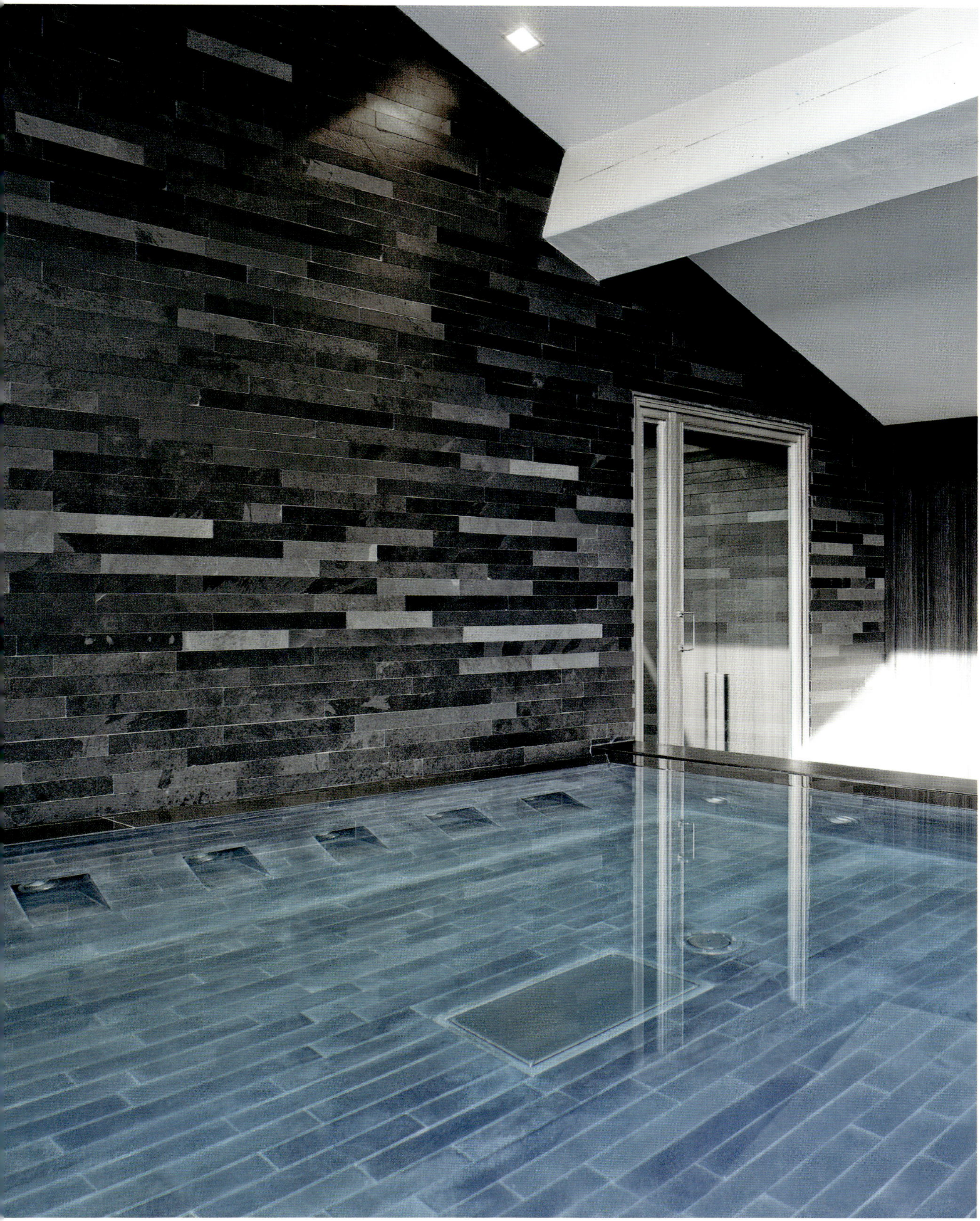

迷宮の家

オスカー・トゥスケッツ・ブランカ
撮影：ジェームズ・シルバーマン

LABYRINTH HOME
OSCAR TUSQUETS BLANCA
PHOTO: © James Silverman

　この地下のインドアプールのコンセプトは、地下水の溜まった石窟の探検。石がこの迷宮の家の地階全体を支配し、石と水だけの世界が出現している。水面に映った光が、1階へと導く石窟の出口をさし示しているが、その連絡階段はインゴ・マウラーがデザインしたピンク色の蛍光管で縁取られている。巨大な地下の水溜りとその周りに展開する水上庭園が、この迷宮の家の謎を完結させている。

The interior pool at the Labyrinth House was conceived as an excavation in stone in which only rock and water exist. This explains the predominance of this material throughout the lower level. The water reflects one of the entrances to the home, where the pink fluorescent lighting created by Ingo Maurer runs along the access stairway. Enormous dimensions and surrounding aquatic gardens give the home its finishing touch.

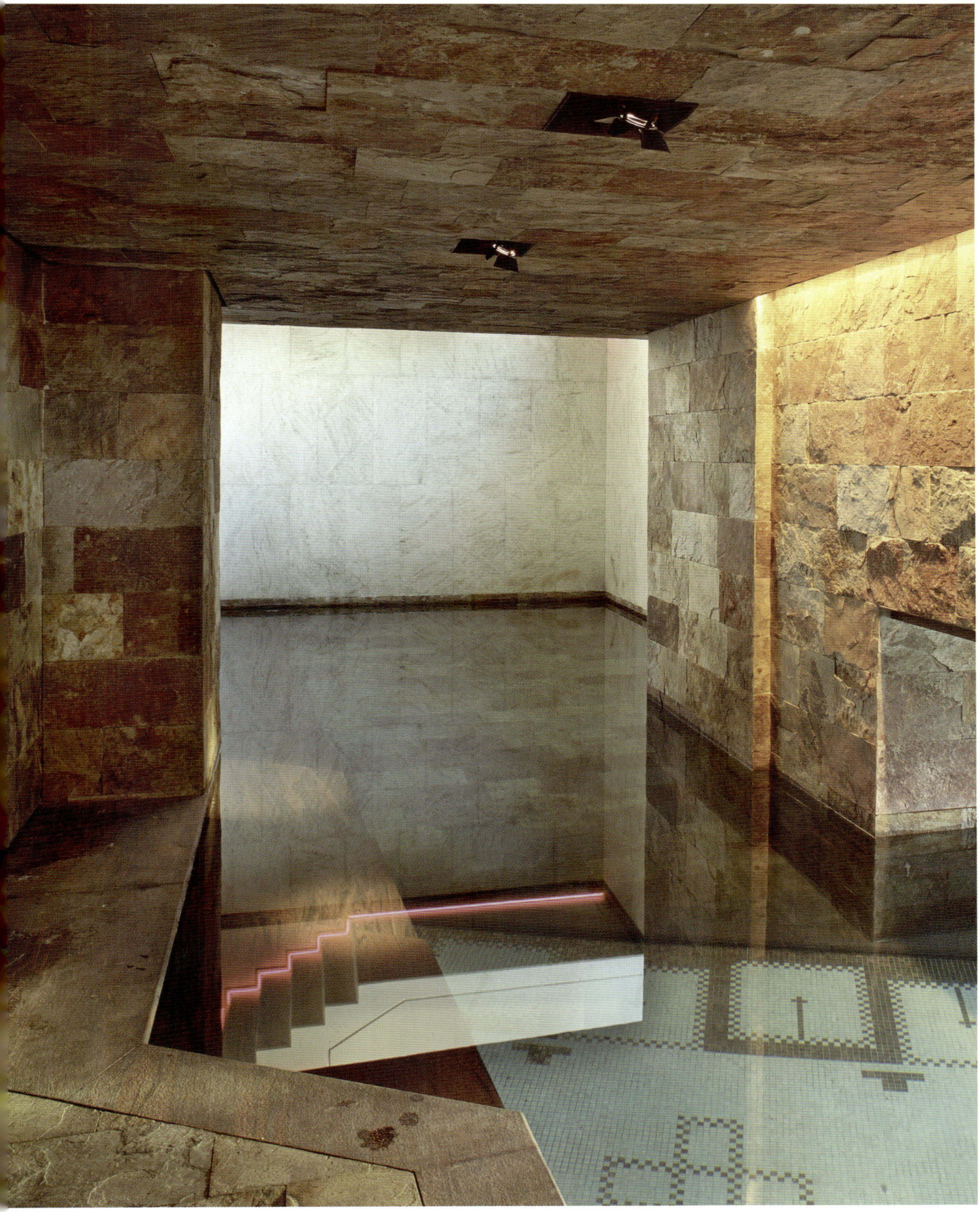

ロンドンの住宅

ウェルドン・ウォルシュ
撮影：ジョナサン・ムーア

LONDON RESIDENCE
WELDON WALSHE
PHOTO: © Jonathan Moore

　使用する材料を厳選し巧みに構成することによって、ロンドンの住宅の一画に、古代の温泉浴場を彷彿とさせるバスルームが創造された。プール周りの石灰岩タイルは、滑って転倒することがないように、シャワー室と通路を仕切る縁石よりもやや粗い仕上げにしている。アイボリークリーム色を基調とした柔らかな光が空間を満たし、古代へと誘っている。

Thanks to the materials used, the interior pool in this London residence evokes the hot-springs and bathrooms of ancient history. To avoid slippery surfaces, the paved stone, which is an ivory-crème color, is slightly more porous than the kind used to border entry-ways at bodies of water, though both run in the same chromatic range.

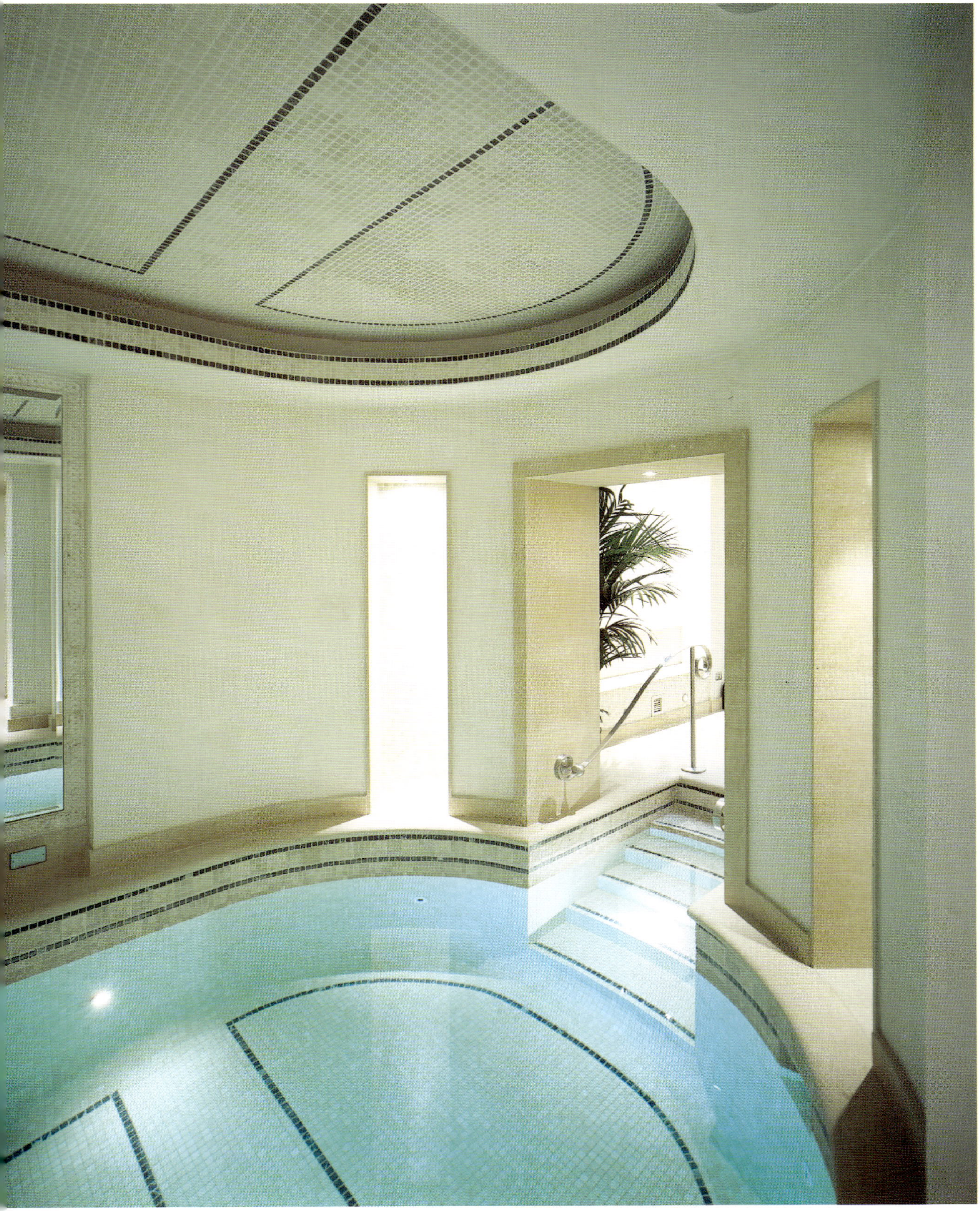

ゴルドの別荘

リラ・コンラッド／LKDコンセプト
撮影：レト・ガントゥリ／Zapaimages

VILLA GORDES
LILA KONRAD/LKD CONCEPTS
PHOTO: © Reto Guntli/Zapaimages

　アジア文化に霊感を与えられて、住宅のすべてのエレメントは風水の法則に則って配置された。なかでも、小さなインドアプールとバスルームの位置には特別の注意が払われ、その結果、かつて厩舎が建っていたところに、それを配置することとなった。石積みのアーチとカラーラ大理石が、リビングルームからも眺めることができるこの広々とした空間を定義している。全体を石で構成し、大理石が生み出す純粋な線を際立たせることによって、古代ローマの浴場を連想させる空間が創造された。

Inspired on Asian culture, all of the elements in the house have been arranged according to the laws of Feng Shui. With special attention being placed on the small pool and bath area, which are located where a stable once stood. The stone arch and the Carrara marble define an open area that communicates with the living room. Thanks to its pure lines and the predominance of stone, the space evokes Ancient Roman baths.

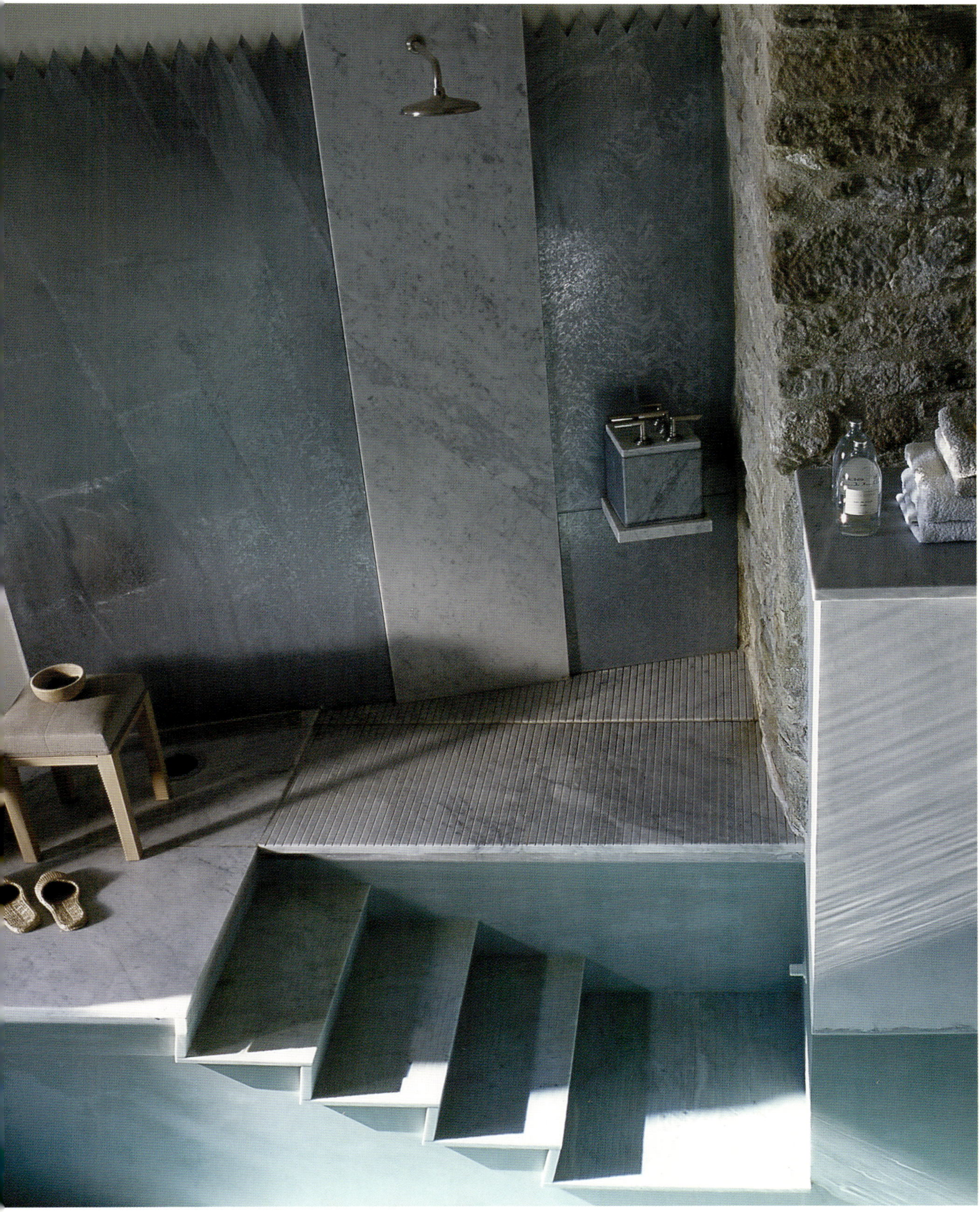

ラス・エンシーナスの住宅

A-Cero
撮影：ホアン・ロドリゲス、鈴木 久雄

LAS ENCINAS HOME

A-CERO
PHOTO: © Juan Rodríguez, Hisao Suziki

　この石造りの堂々とした住宅は、華美な装飾をすべて削ぎ落とし、質感と量感の狭間で遊んでいる。1階は内部の床もテラスの舗床もマカエル大理石で仕上げられ、他方、外壁その他の垂直平面は、トラヴァーチン大理石で仕上げられている。インドアプールの傍には、白砂の上に大きな岩が配置された日本庭園が造られている。それはこのプールで沐浴する人に生命力と平穏の気をもたらすようにと、建築家が考えたもの。

Stripped of all sumptuousness, this imposing home dominated by stone makes the play between textures and volume its principal attraction. Macael marble is used for the floors of the ground level, on the inside and outside of the home, while the walls and other vertical surfaces are dressed in Travertine marble. The large rocks placed beside the interior pool form a Japanese garden, conceived by the architects to inspire vitality and serenity.

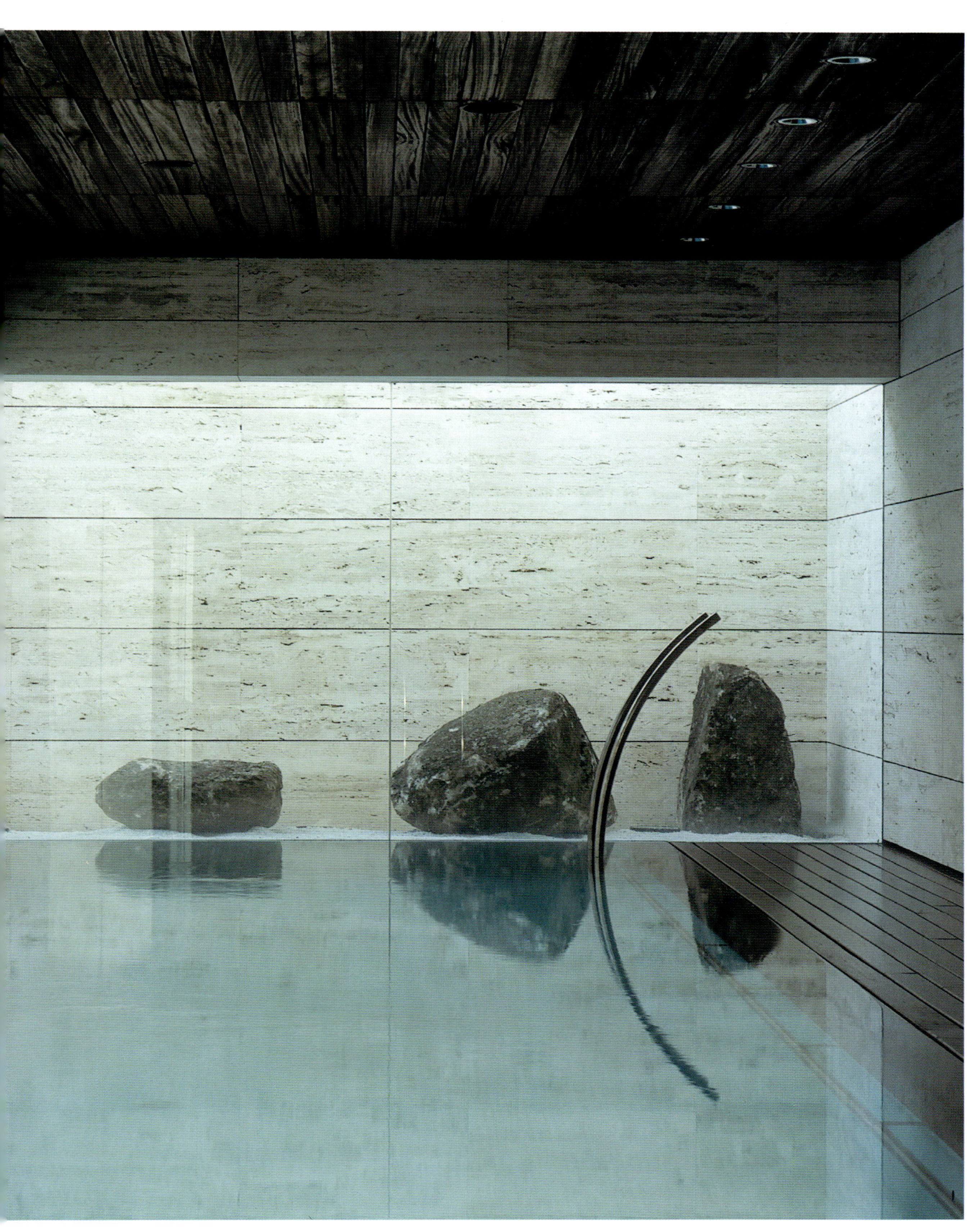

ソーラー・ボックス

ドリエンドル建築設計事務所
撮影：リュー・ロダン

SOLAR BOX
DRIENDL ARCHITECTS
PHOTO: © Lew Rodin

　環境負荷が低いことから、日干し煉瓦は、実用的で安価な材料として近年建築の世界で注目を集めている。それは簡単に製造でき、再使用も容易だ。また乾燥した地域では、湿度を保ち、暑熱をやわらげる働きがある。この広いテラスの舗床で実証されているように、日干し煉瓦はどんなスタイルの建物にも合う美しさを持っており、その適応能力は理想的である。日干し煉瓦に、木、ガラス、鉄が加わり、お互いの美しさを増幅させながら、きわめて現代的な空間が創造されている。

Thanks to its low environmental impact level, adobe has become a practical and economic solution in the world of construction: it is easy to create and recycle, maintaining humidity in dry areas while absorbing high temperatures. Its esthetic flexibility is ideal in accompanying all kinds of styles, as can be seen in the pavement of this large terrace. The space is the product of amplification along with the joining of wood, glass and steel in a completely contemporary style.

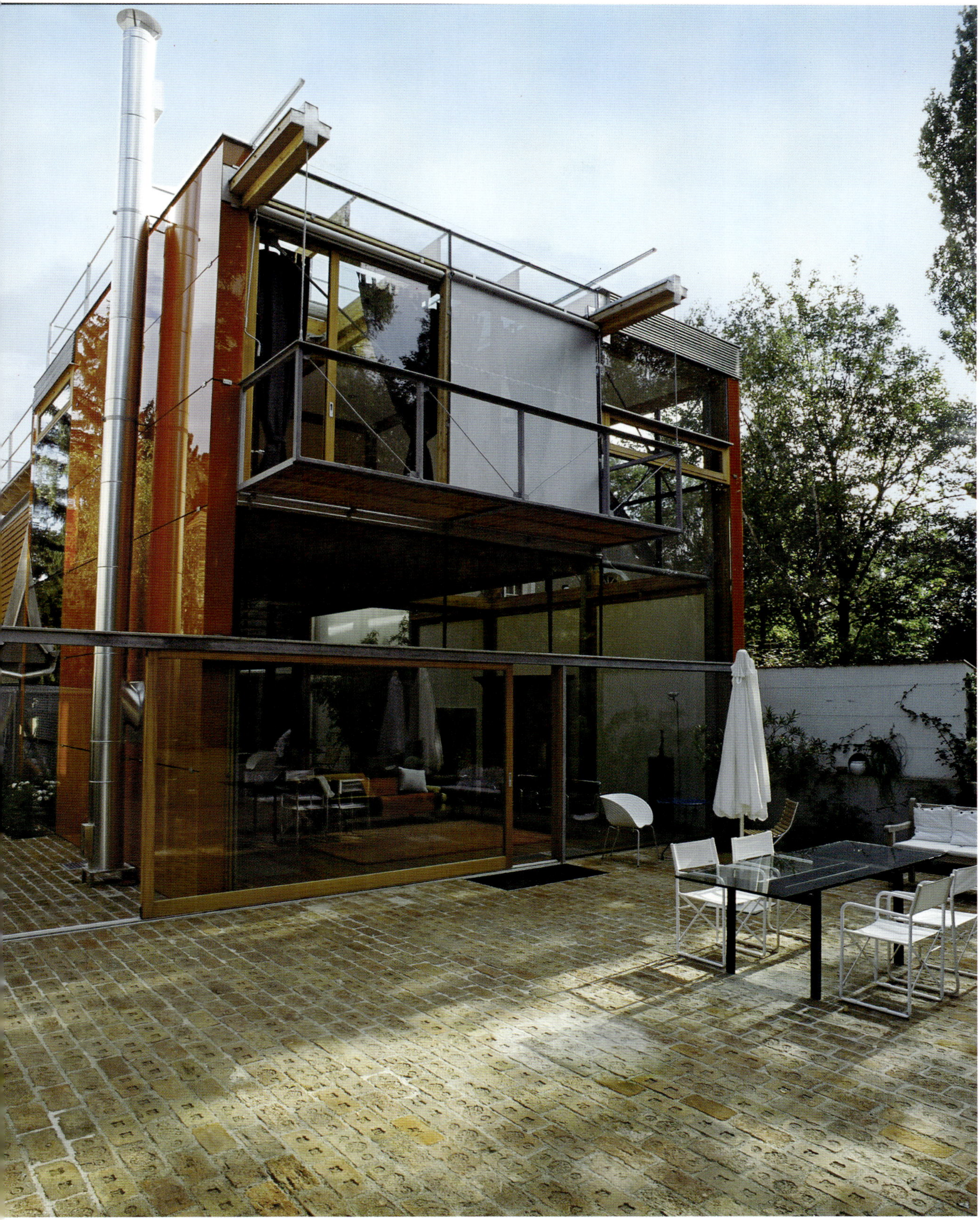

アンドリュー・テート邸

テート & ヒンドル建築設計事務所
撮影：カルロス・ドミンゲス

ANDREW TATE HOUSE
TATE & HINDLE ARCHITECTS
PHOTO: © Carlos Domínguez

古い貯水タンクが、建築家アンドリュー・テートの手によって、広々とした彼自身の住宅に変貌させられた。貯水という以前の機能は失われたが、その特殊な形状は最大限に生かされ、中央のタワーに造られた寝室からは、イギリスの牧歌的な田園風景を一望することができる。新しい建物が中庭を囲むように建てられているが、それは、用いている材料の面でも、フォルムの面でも、レンガのタワーとは対照的である。中庭の端に、漂礫を金属網の中に押し込んで造った石の壁が築かれているが、それがこの住宅を自然と統合している。

An old water tank was converted by architect Andrew Tate into a spacious home. With the idea of taking full advantage of this particular design which erases the building's previous function, the bedrooms were placed in the central tower, where one can enjoy a panoramic view of the bucolically rural English countryside. The new building shapes an exterior patio which contrasts in materials and shape with the brick tower. Its edges are marked by boulders which are bound within a metallic mesh and integrated into the surrounding nature.

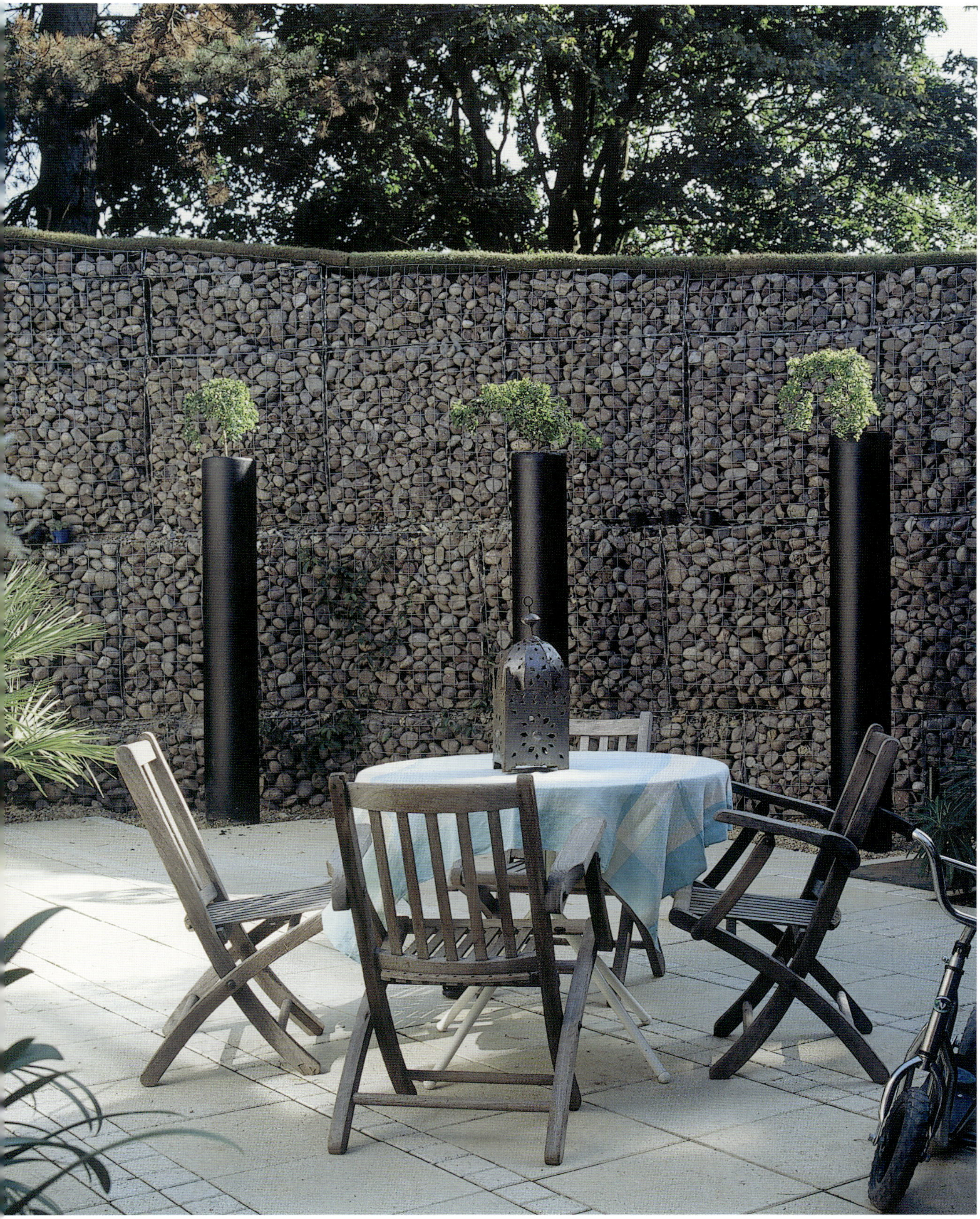

デュ・プレシ邸

マルシオ・コーガン建築設計事務所
撮影：アルナルド・パッパラルド

DU PLESSIS HOME
MARCIO KOGAN ARQUITETO
PHOTO: © Arnaldo Pappalardo

このL字型の住宅が、かくも現代的で、禁欲的に感じられるのは、すべて石のなせる業だ。外壁を被っているのは、地元の石切り場から切り出したペドラ・ミネイラで、それをストライプ状に張りつけることによって、建物の幾何学的形状が強調されている。庭の塀には大きな開口部があり、それが生命力に満ち溢れた景観の額縁となっている。庭の舗床は玉石のモルタル埋め込み洗い出しにして、ミニマリスト的下地を造り、そこに植木を等間隔に整然と配置することによって、背景となる熱帯の自然との対比を強調した。

This "L" shaped home owes its austere and contemporary appearance to stone. The exterior is made with *pedra mineira* extracted from local quarries and placed horizontally to highlight the building's geometry. The large openings in the patio walls frame the exuberant landscape. The paved cement and natural stone on the patio create a minimalist stage where the vegetation is kept in order, in contrast with the tropical background.

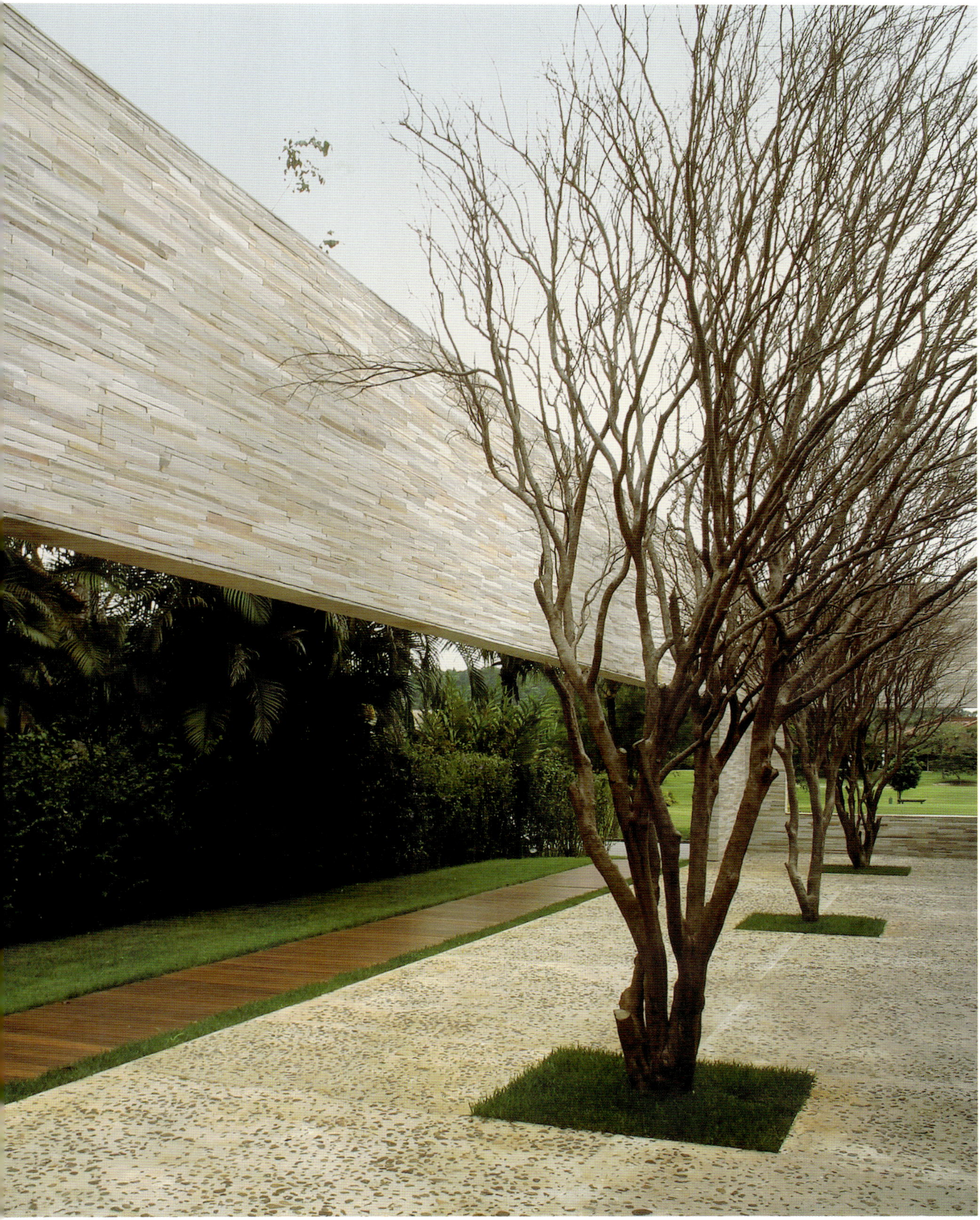

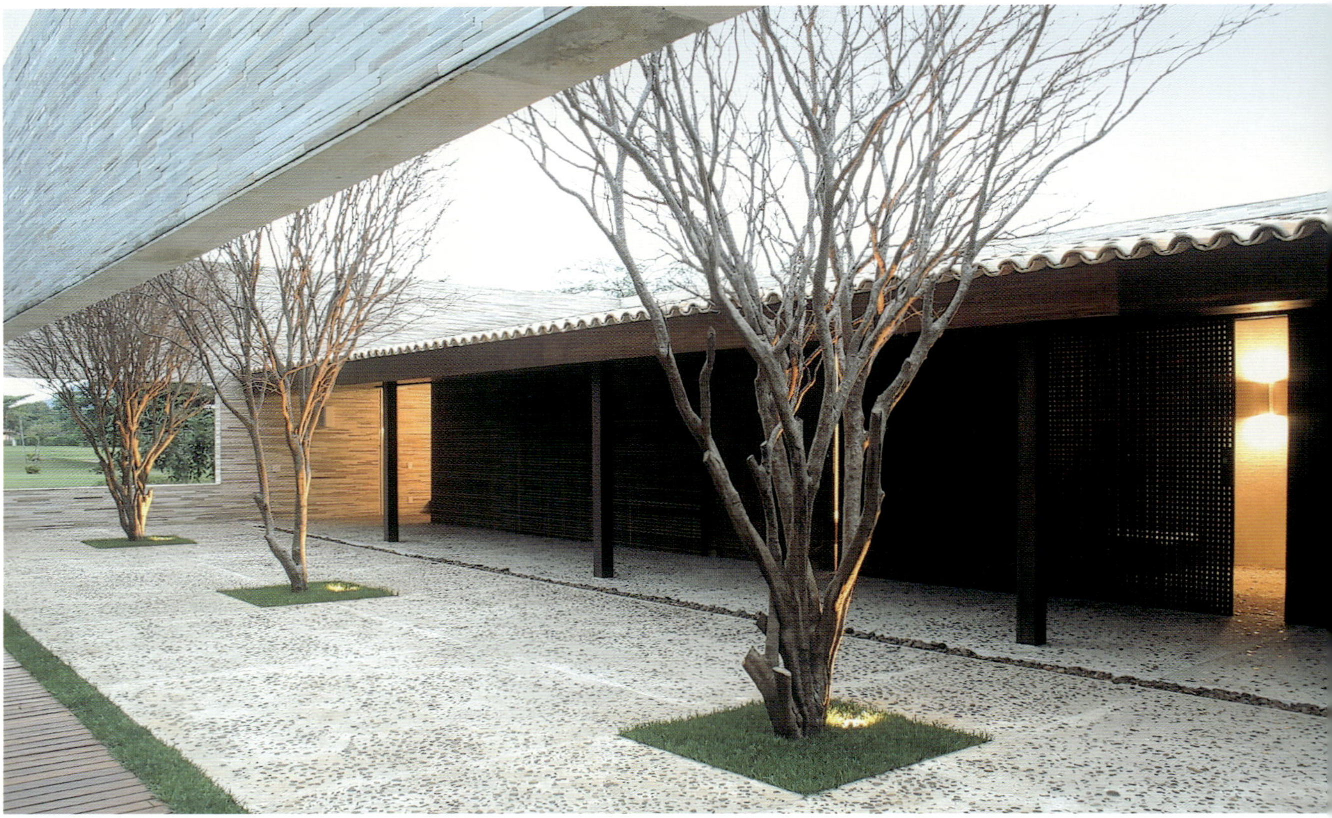

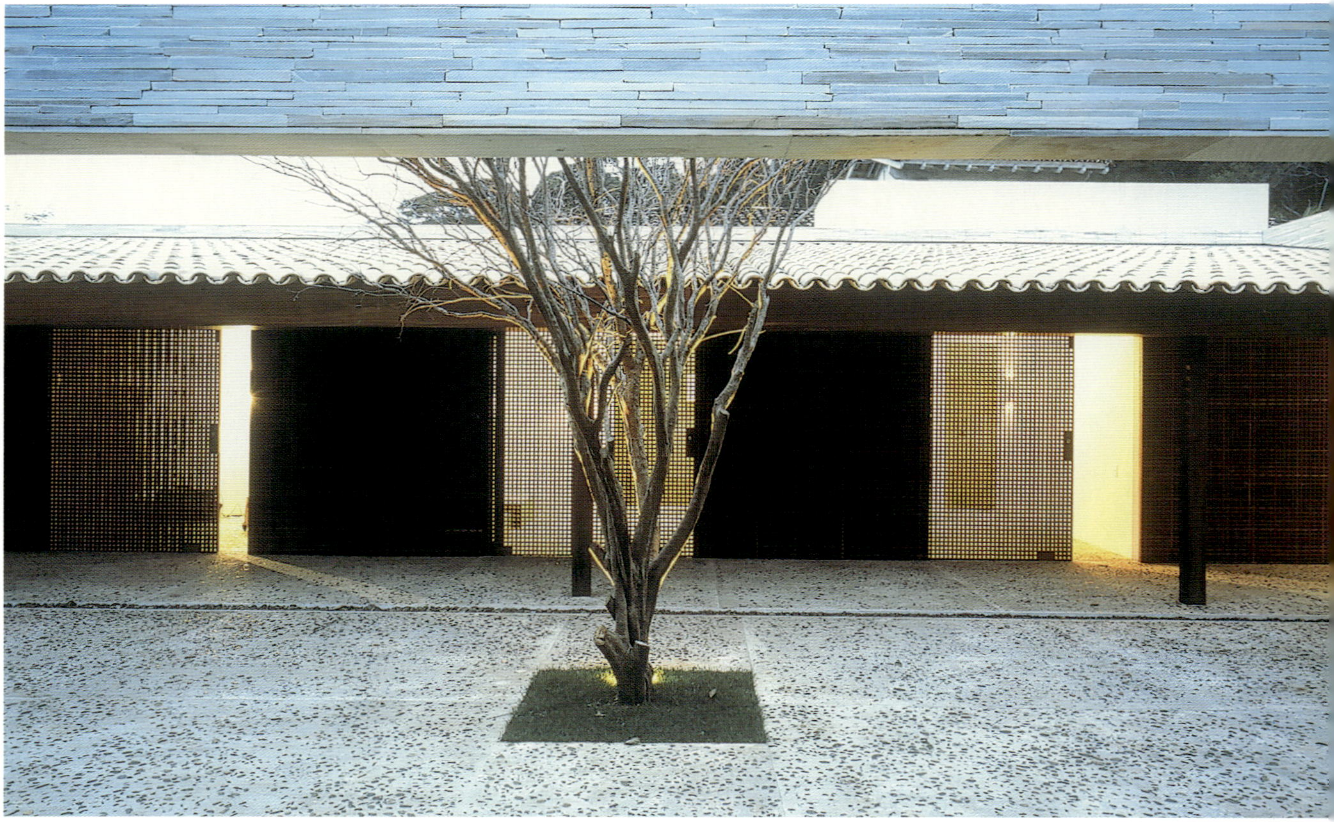

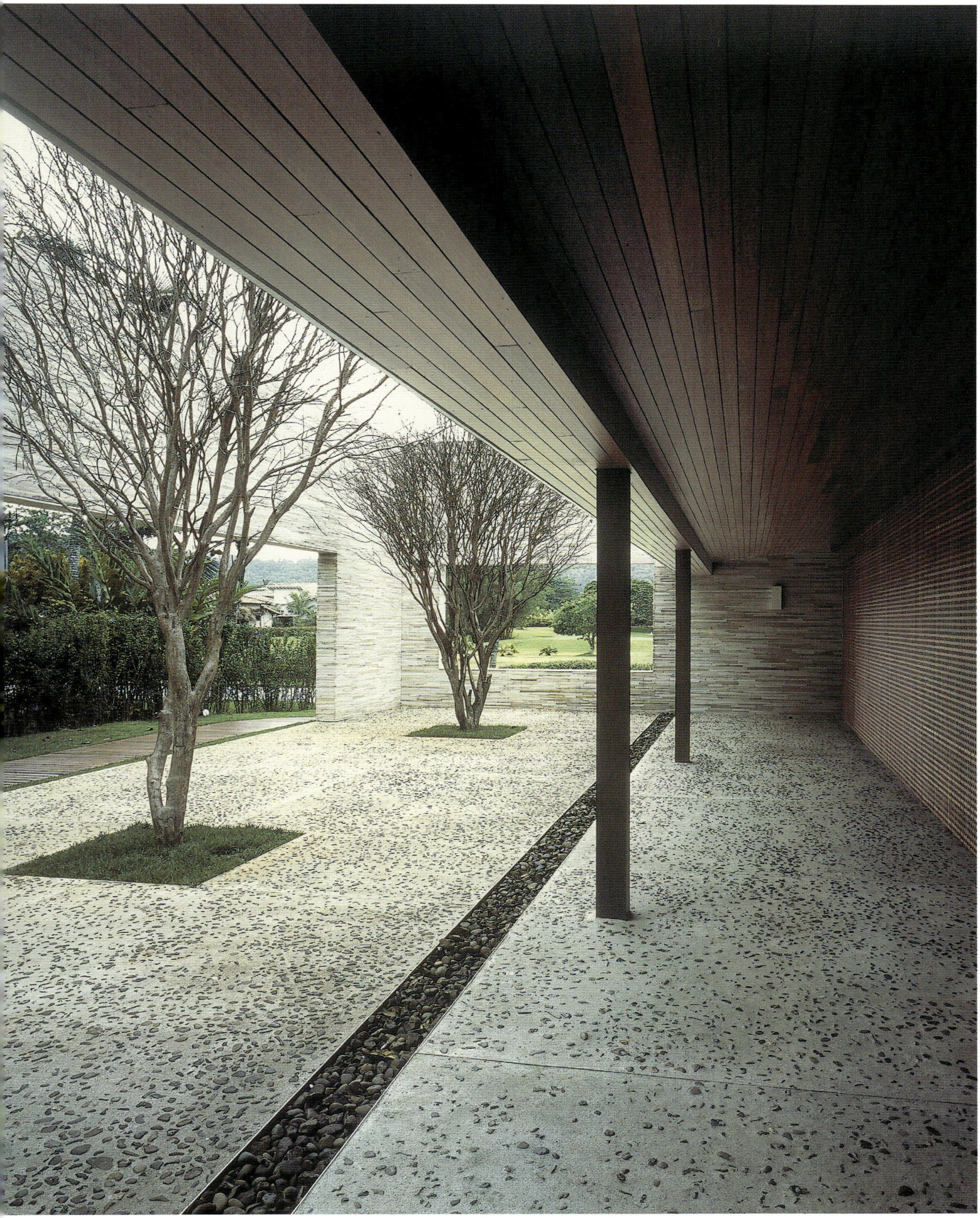

ブライトン・ガーデン

アン・ファーズ
撮影：ジョン・グローバー

BRIGHTON GARDEN
ANN FIRTH
PHOTO: © John Glover

　この独特の庭の製作者であるアン・ファーズは、自身が手がけた石を使った庭の設計に関して多くの著書を出版している。このブライトンの庭では、彼女は玉石を使って渦巻き紋様を描いたが、それはこの地に多く棲息する蛇に敬意を表したもの。玉石の微妙な色合いの相違、一見自由気ままに見える大小の玉石の配置、これらがこの住宅の、色彩に溢れた魅惑的な表札となっている。

The author of this particular garden has many publications to her credit which deal with the use of rocks in exterior design. In the Brighton garden, these polished stones have been placed in a spiral pattern in homage to the dense population of snails colonizing the property. The different tones in the rocks, placed with apparent randomness, lend an attractively colorful signature to the home.

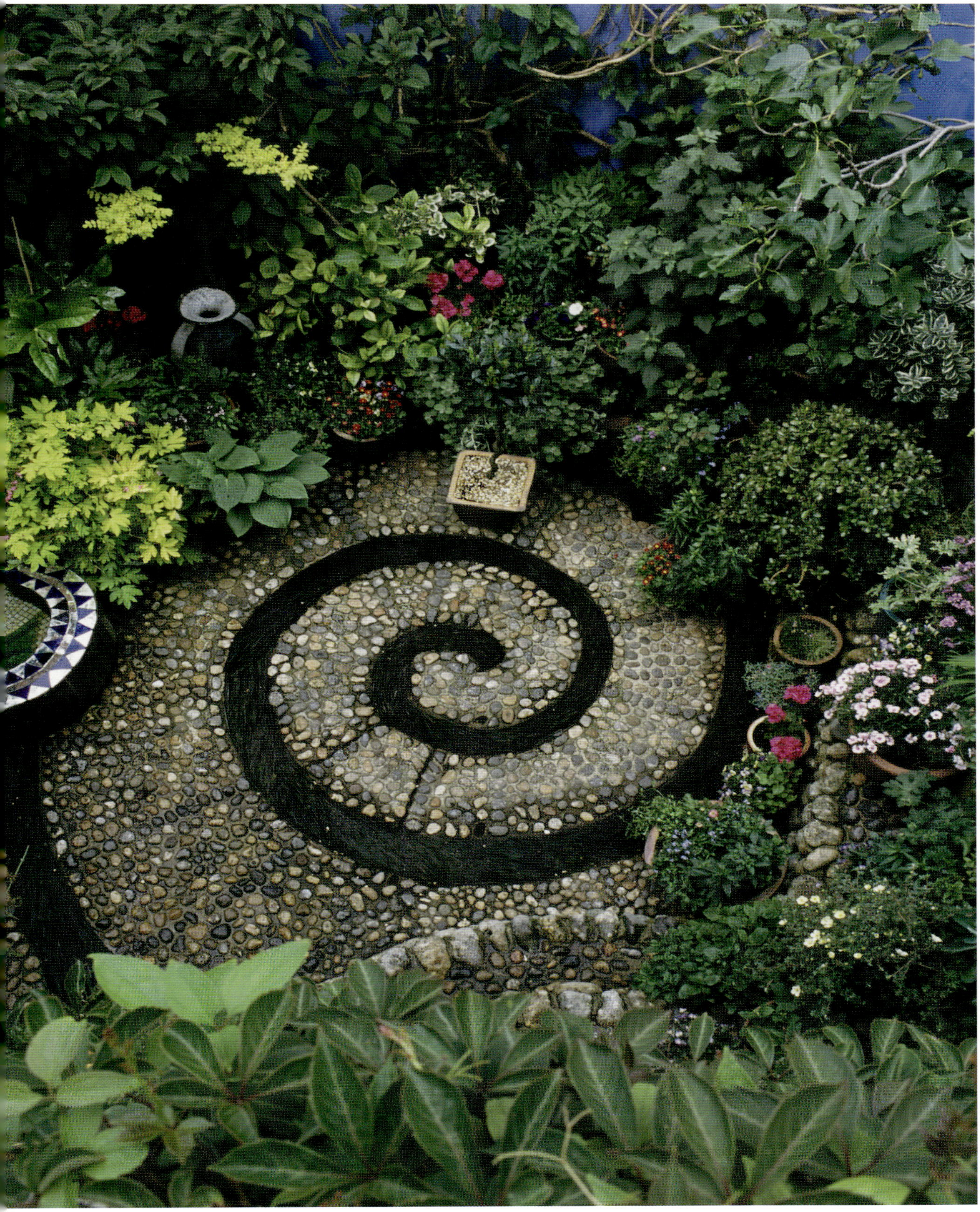

コルドヴァのパティオ祭り

所有者
撮影：ジョン・グローバー

CORDOBA PATIO GARDEN FESTIVAL
OWNER
PHOTO: © John Glover

　この私庭は、コルドヴァで毎年開かれるパティオ祭りで最も多く賞賛を浴びているものの1つ。種類や色を見ながらモルタルの上に玉石を巧妙に埋め込むことで、黒い石が背景となって、白い愛らしい花が咲き誇る様が庭一面に広がっている。コルドヴァでは、このような玉石による庭の装飾が1世紀前から行われ伝統となっているが、たいていアラベスク様式の石造りの泉が一緒に置かれている。

This private patio is on of the most acclaimed of those exhibited annually at the Patio Festival in the Spanish city of Cordoba. The large rocks on the floor have been arranged by type and color, so that the larger ones become the background and the lighter ones shape a floral design that extends throughout the property. This arrangement follows a centuries old tradition in this area, usually accompanied by a fountain of arabesque stones.

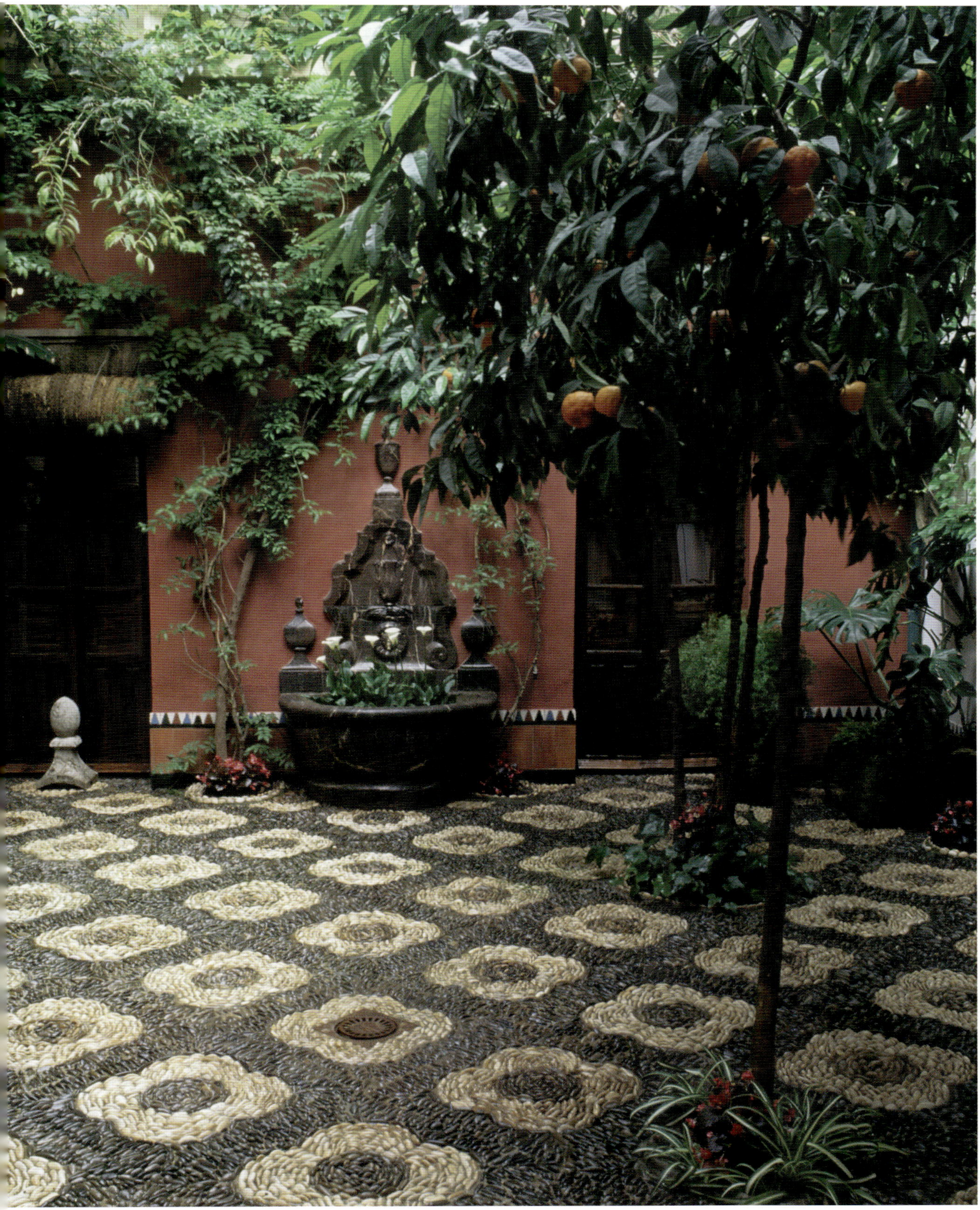

砂漠の庭

テイラー・カリティ・レスリーン
撮影：テイラー・カリティ・レスリーン

DESERT SPACE GARDEN
TAYLOR CULLITY LETHLEAN
PHOTO: © Taylor Cullity Lethlean

　円形の中庭にリズミカルに配置された同寸法の正方形のなかに、さまざまな種類の石や砂が敷き詰められ、色彩豊かな幾何学的構成が出来上がっている。オレンジ色の背景は、地元産出の砂に5％のモルタルを混ぜて造った混合舗床材。正方形のなかには、白や黒の漂礫、立方体や厚板にカットされた砂岩、自然に採取した地元の砂、そして岩を砕いた砂礫など、さまざまな種類、形状、色の石が敷かれ、その上に砂漠で見られる植生やオブジェがあしらわれている。まるでこの土地の地質標本のようだ。

The geometric composition and intense colors in this garden is the result of the different types of stone and sand used in each piece. Their shared orange background is a compacted mix of local sand and 5% cement. Each square's appearance varies in form and the stones selected. Mostly, these are white and black boulders, different styles of sandstone cut into cubes and local sand obtained through nature or from broken rocks.

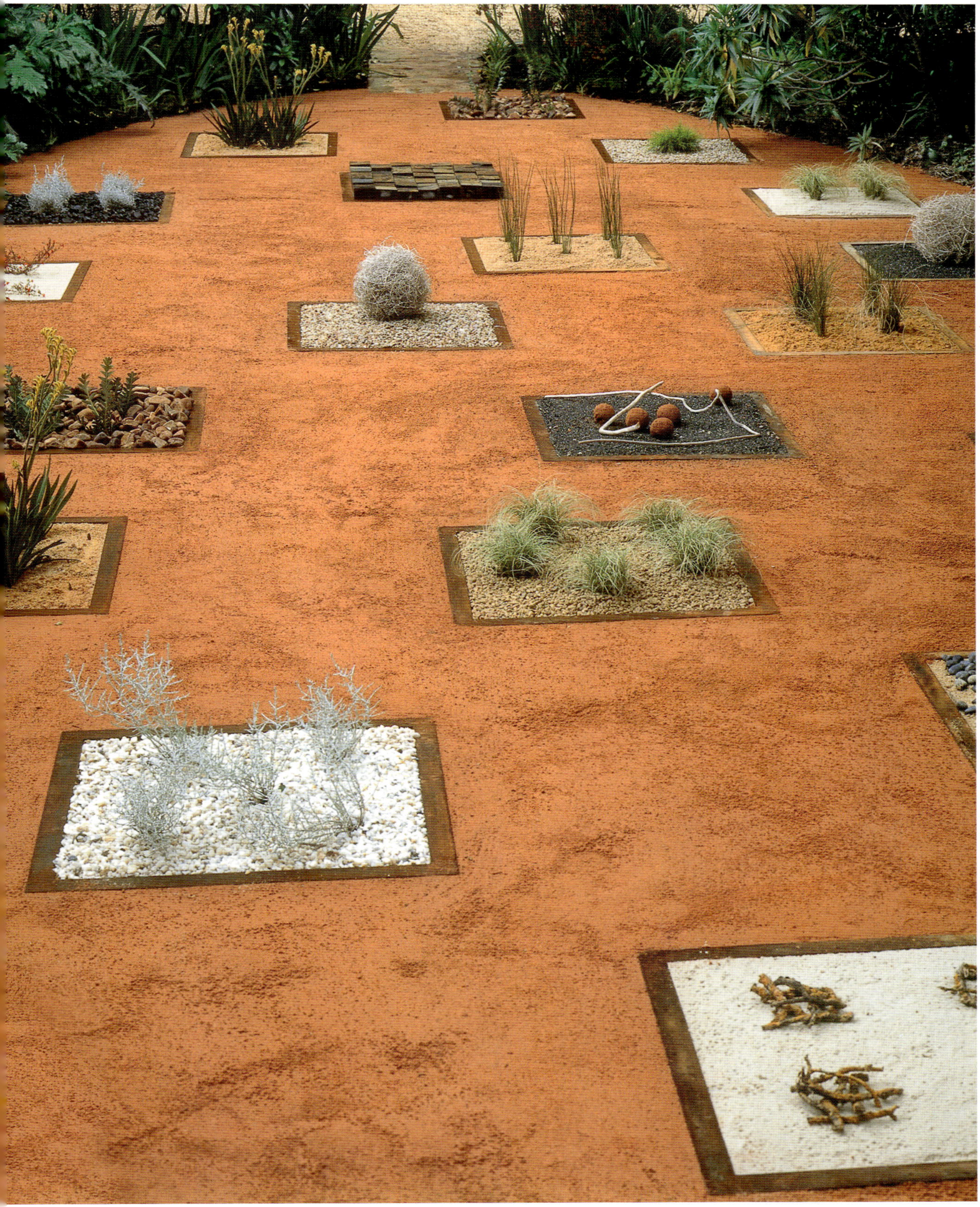

龍門庭

枡野　俊明
撮影：マイケル・フリーマン

RYUMONTEI
SHUNMYO MASUNO
PHOTO: © Michael Freeman

　枡野俊明は宇宙を寓意する空間をこの庭で創造した。伝統的に禅庭では、石は日本を形作る島々と山麓を表し、それを取り囲む、通常は火成岩の一種である玄武岩が風化されてできた白砂は、海を表す。しかしこの庭は、そうした大方の禅庭の構成とは異なり、大きな石は、禅の教えによって結ばれた人々を象徴している。

Shunmyo Masuno designed a space which constitutes an allegory of the universe. Traditionally, in Zen gardens the stone represents Japan's geography with its islands and mountains situated in the middle of the sea, represented by sand; the type most commonly used is of volcanic origin, usually Basalt. In this case, in contrast with the majority of these types of gardens, the large stones from Ryumontei represent people bound together by Shintoist teachings.

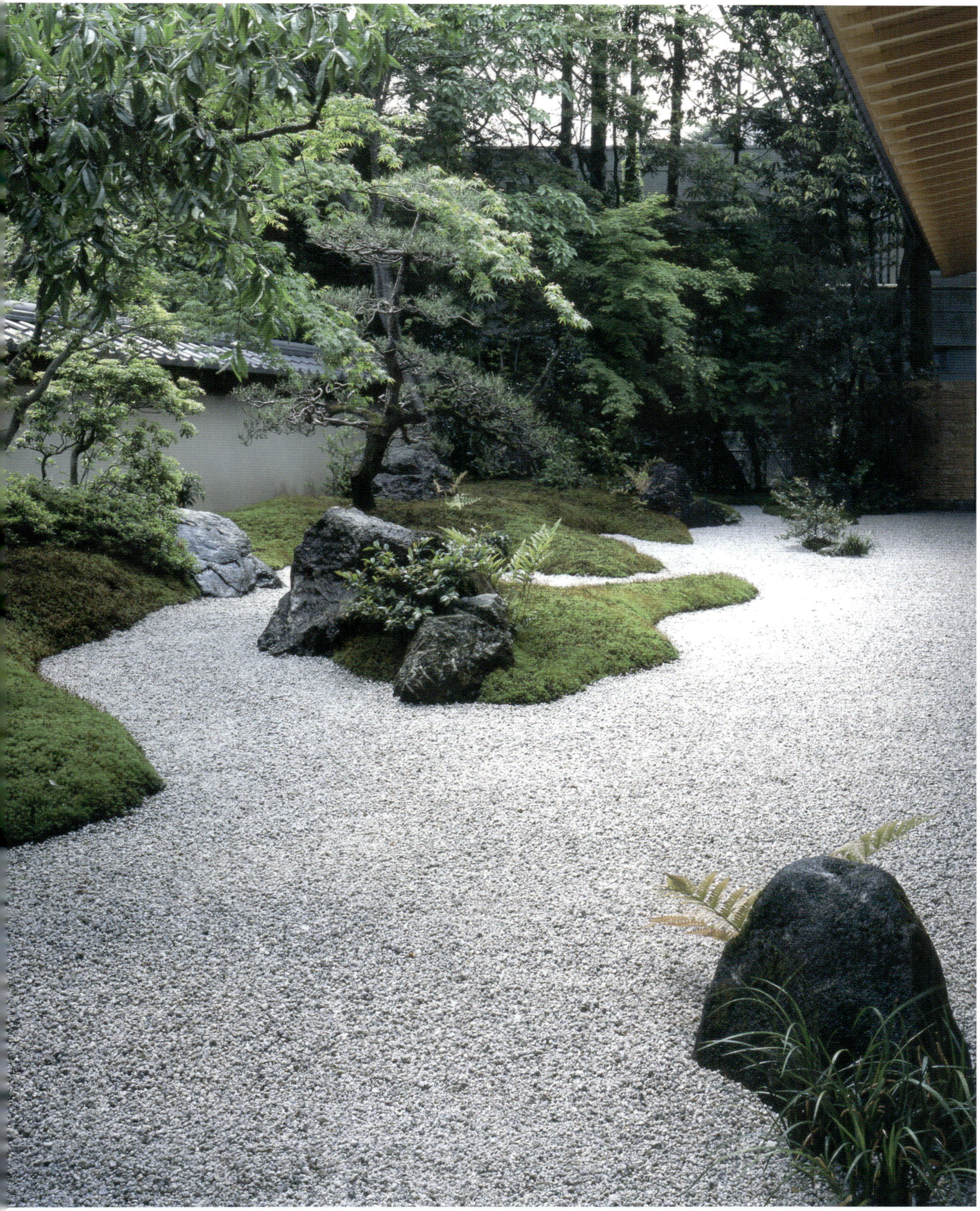

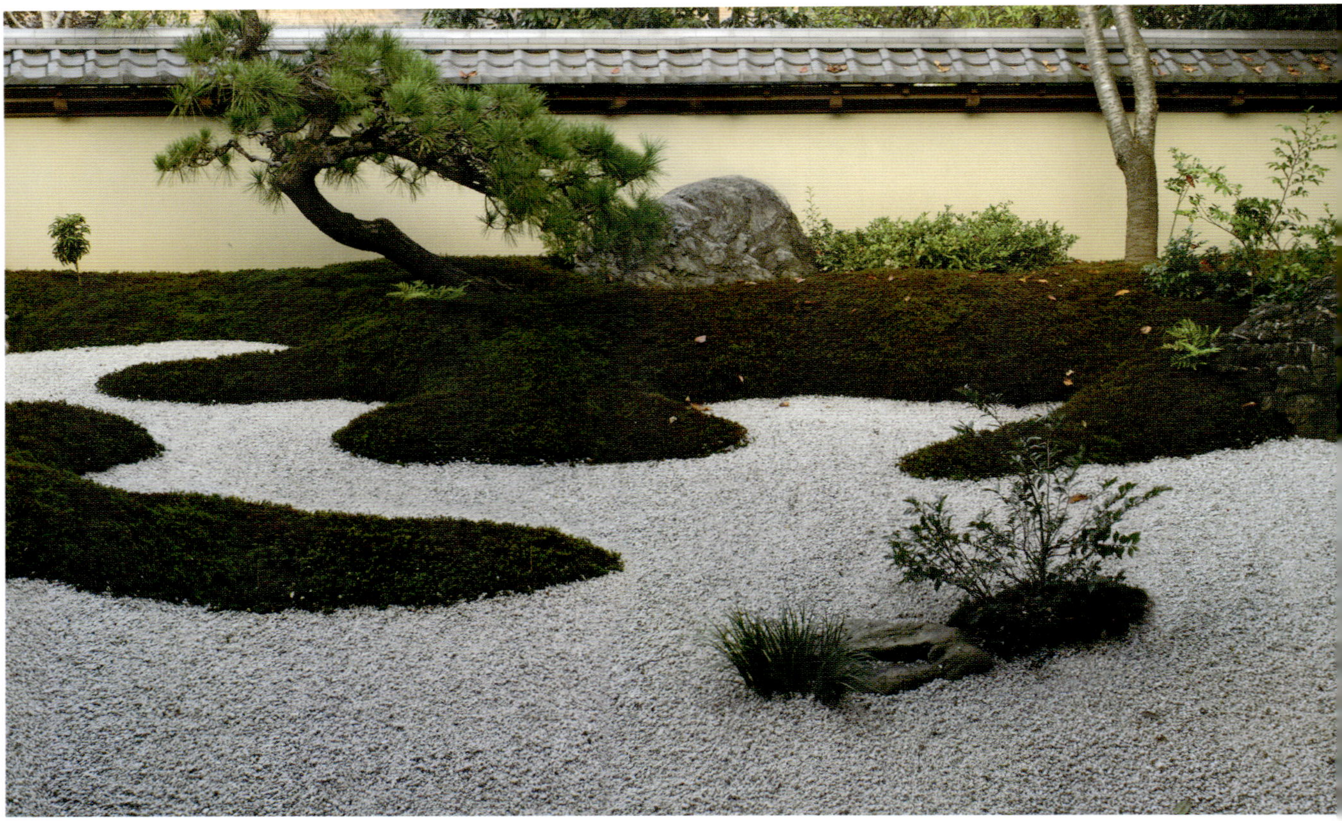
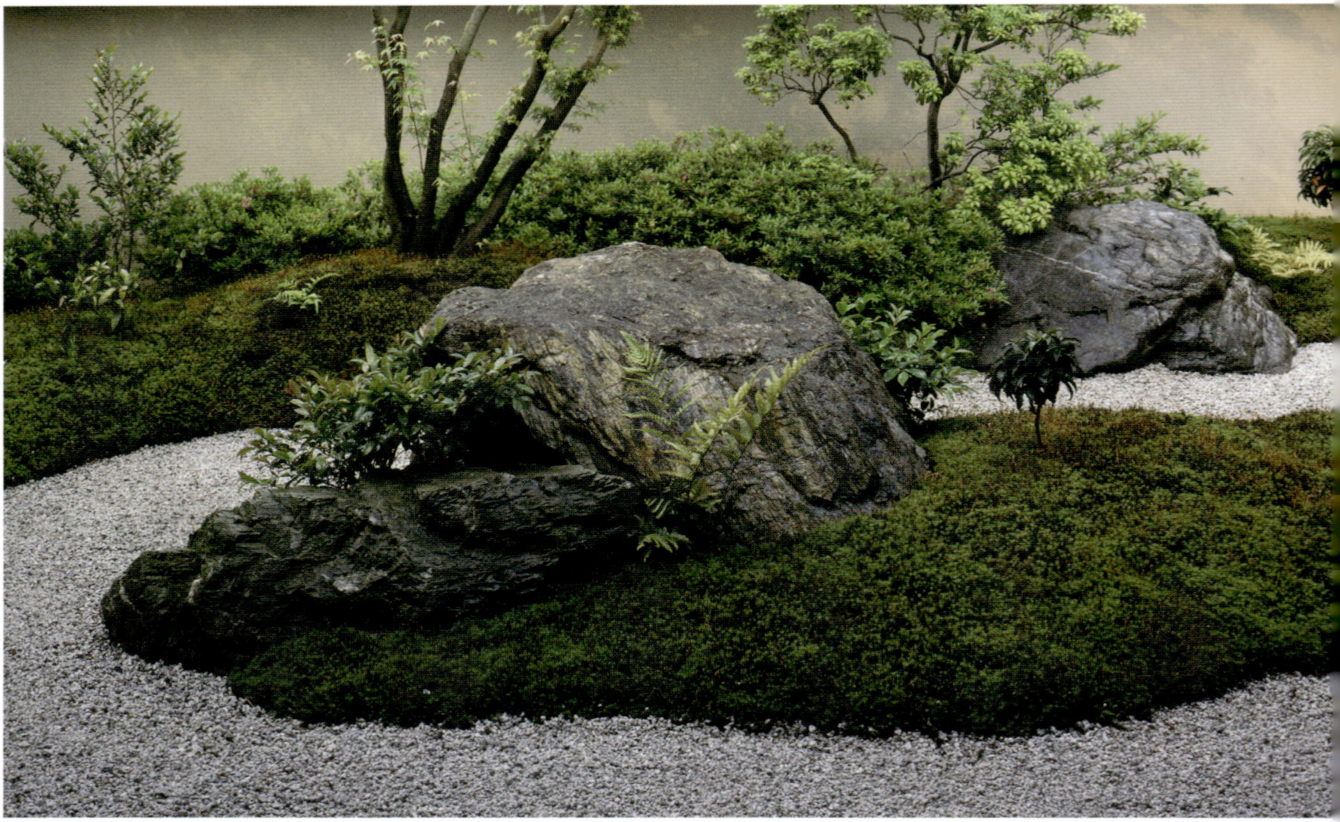

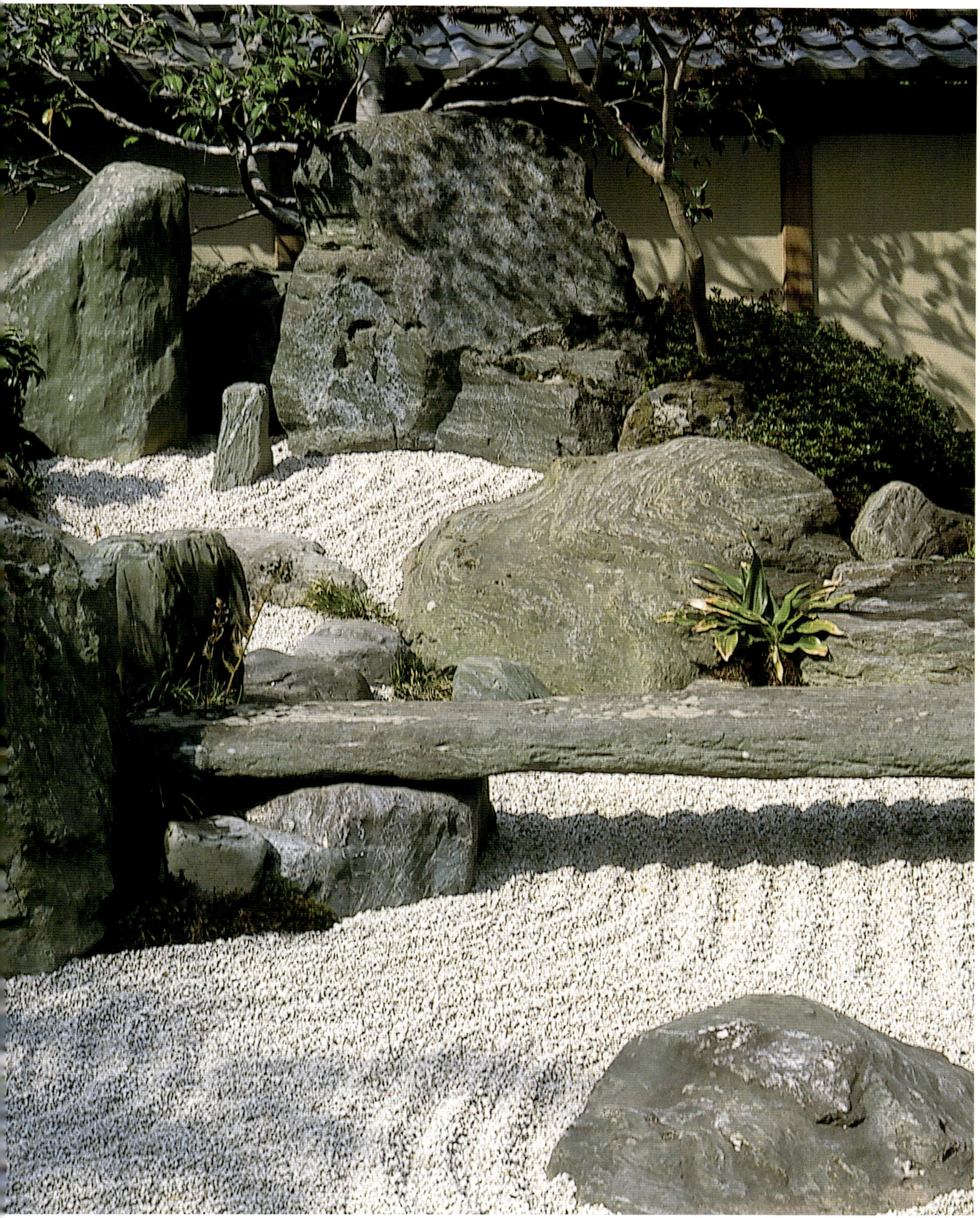

ポルトラ・ヴァレーの住宅

ピーターソン建築設計事務所
撮影：マリオン・ブレナー

PORTOLA VALLEY HOUSE
PETERSON ARCHITECTS
PHOTO: © Marion Brenner

　このカリフォルニアの住宅の中庭が東洋の庭園様式の影響を強く受けているのは、部屋の外から見ても明らかだ。それは池をめぐる踏み石や、全体の構図、造園に用いられている材料から観取される。目を室内に転ずると、バスルームとキッチンの床には大きな花崗岩スラブが敷かれているが、それは中国の街を抜ける往還に実際に敷かれていたもの。長い時間人や荷馬車によって磨かれた滑らかな質感のおかげで、そのやや不釣合いな大きさや重量感は気にならない。

The oriental influence in this California home is visible from the outside, in the design of its gardens, which run along stone paths, as well as in its structure and the materials used for its construction. In its interior, the large granite slabs which pave the bathroom and the kitchen come from the streets of China. Their irregular appearance and rich textures are compensated by a surface worn smooth over time.

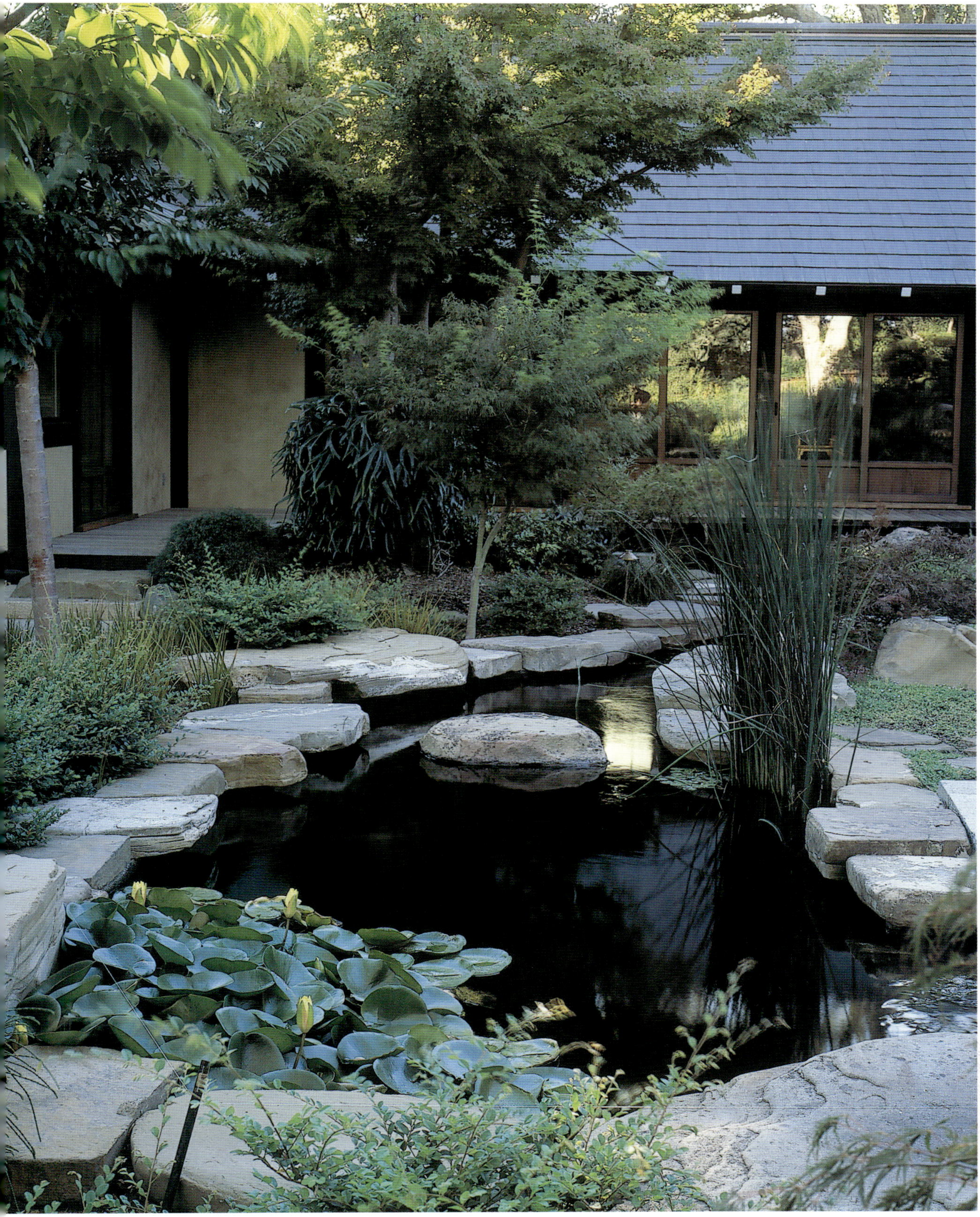

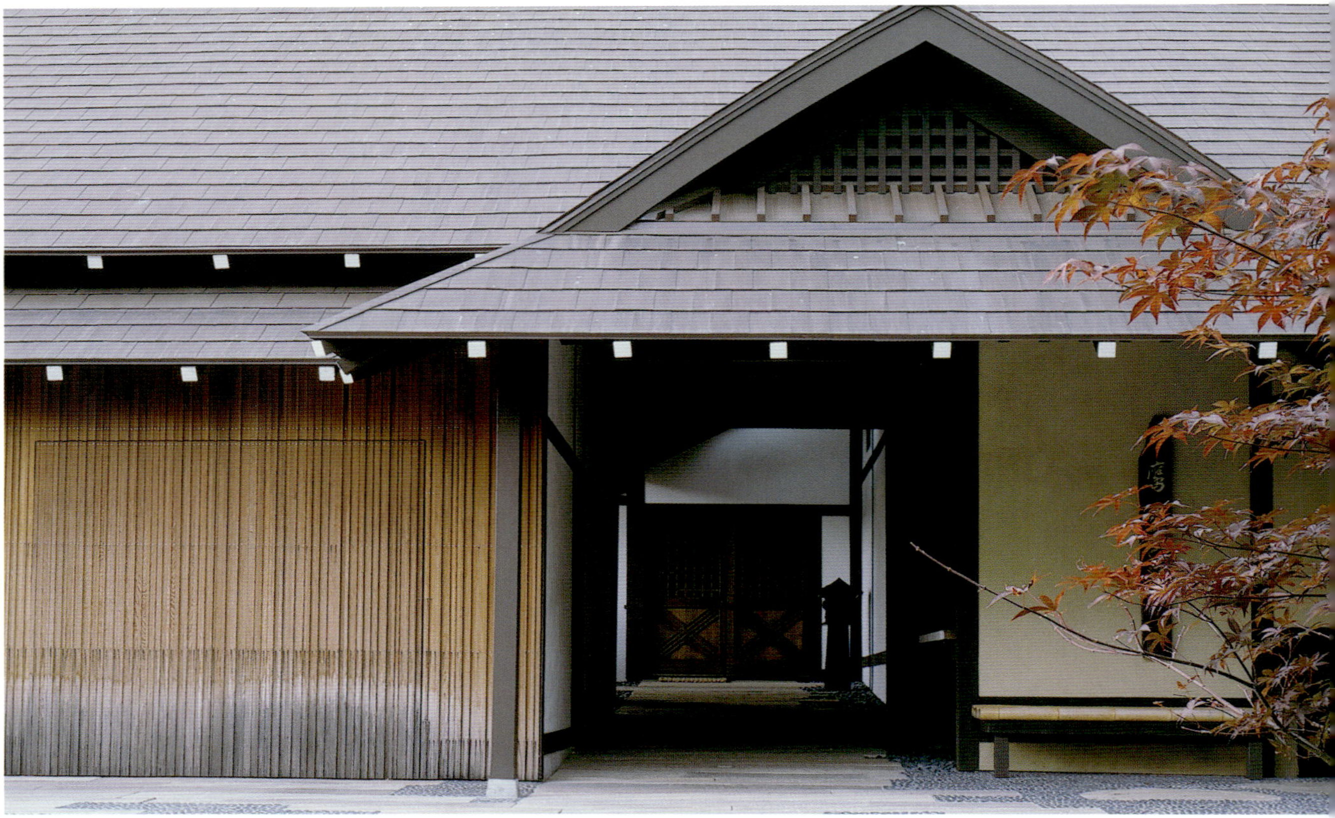

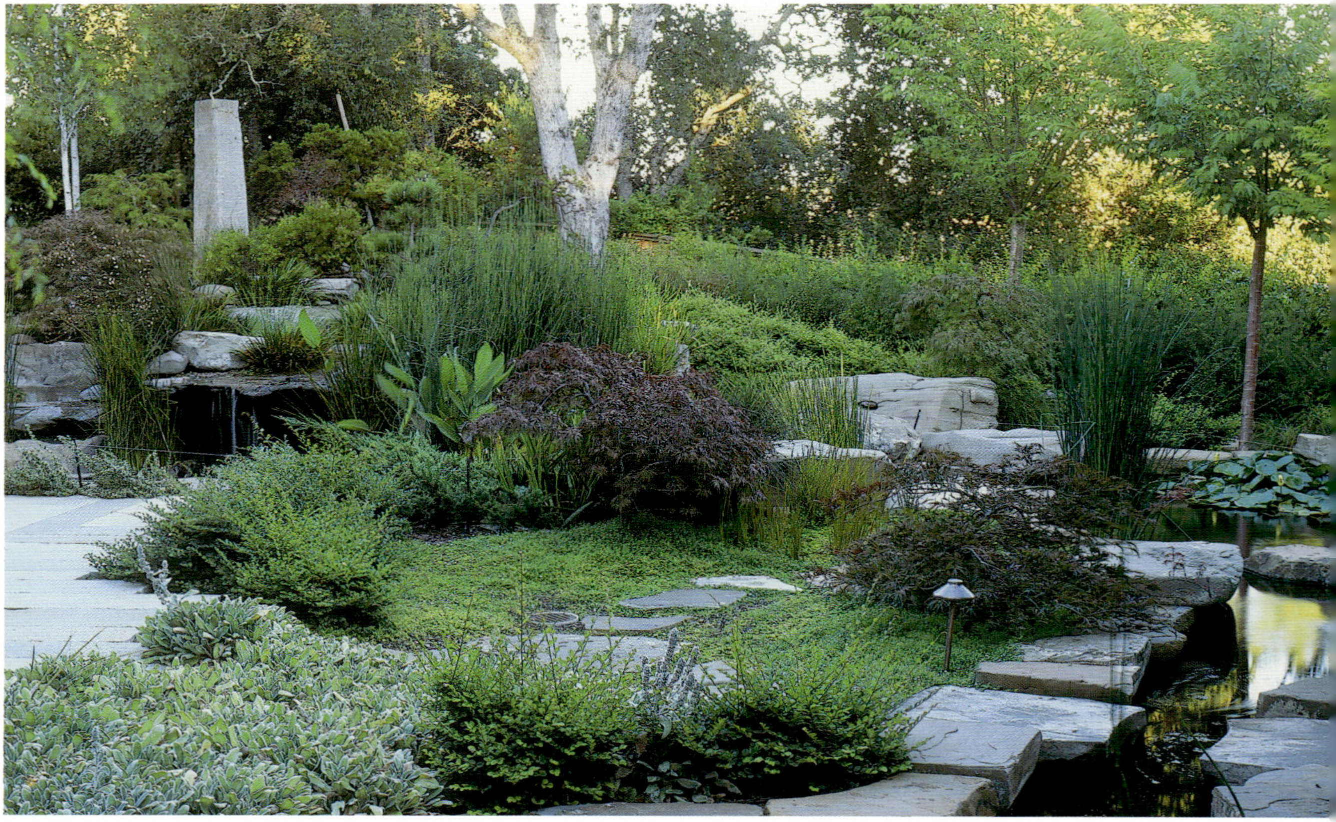

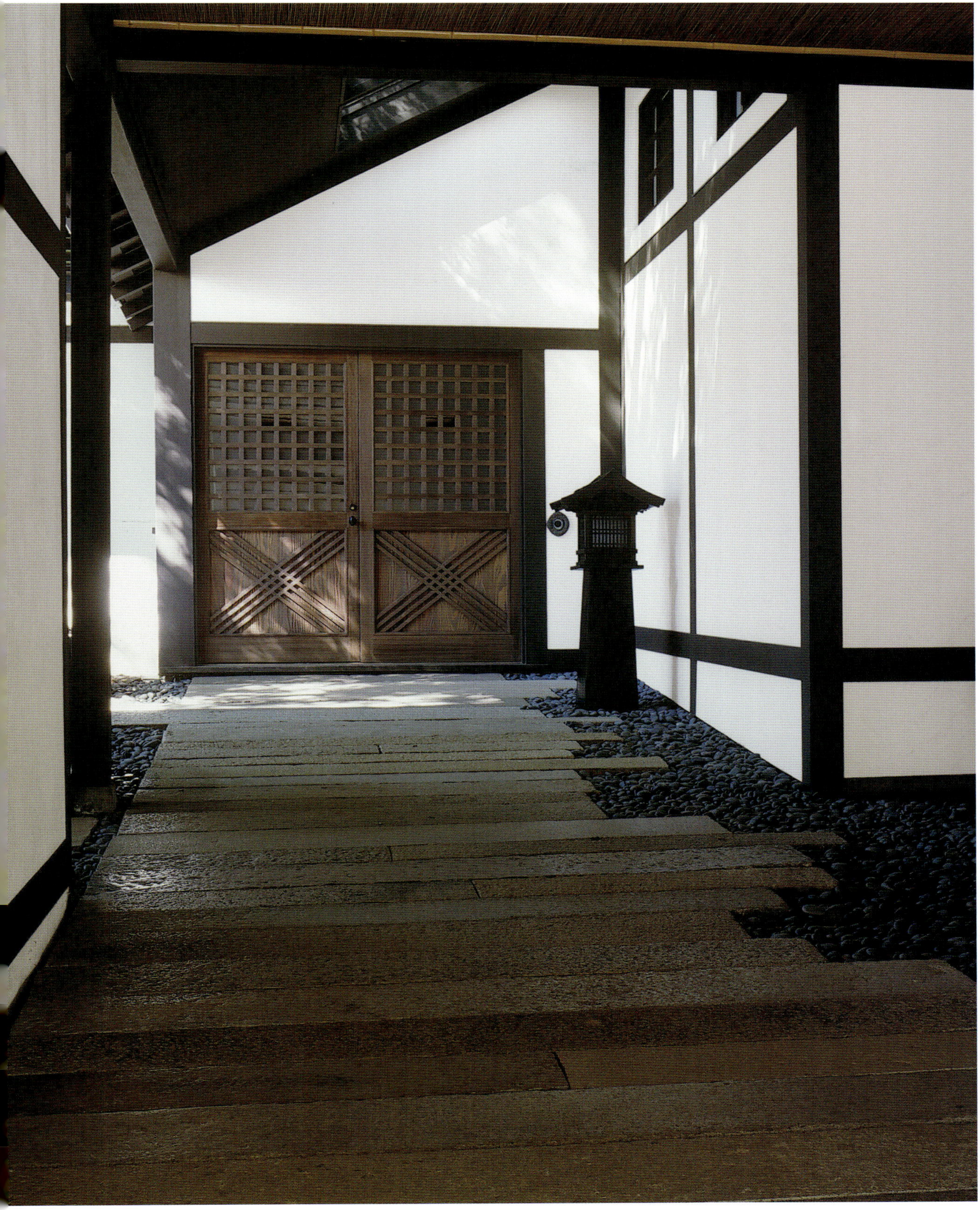

エリー・サーブ邸

ウラジミール・シュロヴィッチ・
ランドスケープ・アーキテクチュア
撮影：ジェラルディン・ブルネール

ELIE SAAB RESIDENCE
VLADIMIR DJUROVIC LANDSCAPE ARCHITECTURE
PHOTO: © Geraldine Bruneel

世界中から注目を集めるトップデザイナーとなったエリー・サーブの住宅は、彼の要望から、2つの前提条件を齟齬をきたすことなく満たすことのできるものとして設計された。1つは、彼自身が静かに瞑想できる空間であること。そしてもう1つは、そこに集う人々の印象に残るパーティーが演出できる舞台であること。住宅のその他の部分同様、プールサイドのこの広々とした庭も、その2つの条件を見事に満たしている。芝生の上に段差をつけて幾何学的に配置した石灰岩スラブは、この雄大な景色の中を逍遙する散歩道となり、またレバノンの砂漠で夜を過ごす遊牧民を追想するための焚き火の炉床となる。

The home of celebrated fashion designer Elie Saab was conceived as a stage capable of complying in an effective manner with the two pre-requisites given by the client: to serve as a private space for contemplation and as a setting for memorable reunions. Like the rest of the house, the ample garden beside the pool complies with both demands. In that environment, these stone slabs create geometric shapes on the lawn and help delineate various esplanades of differing heights for different uses.

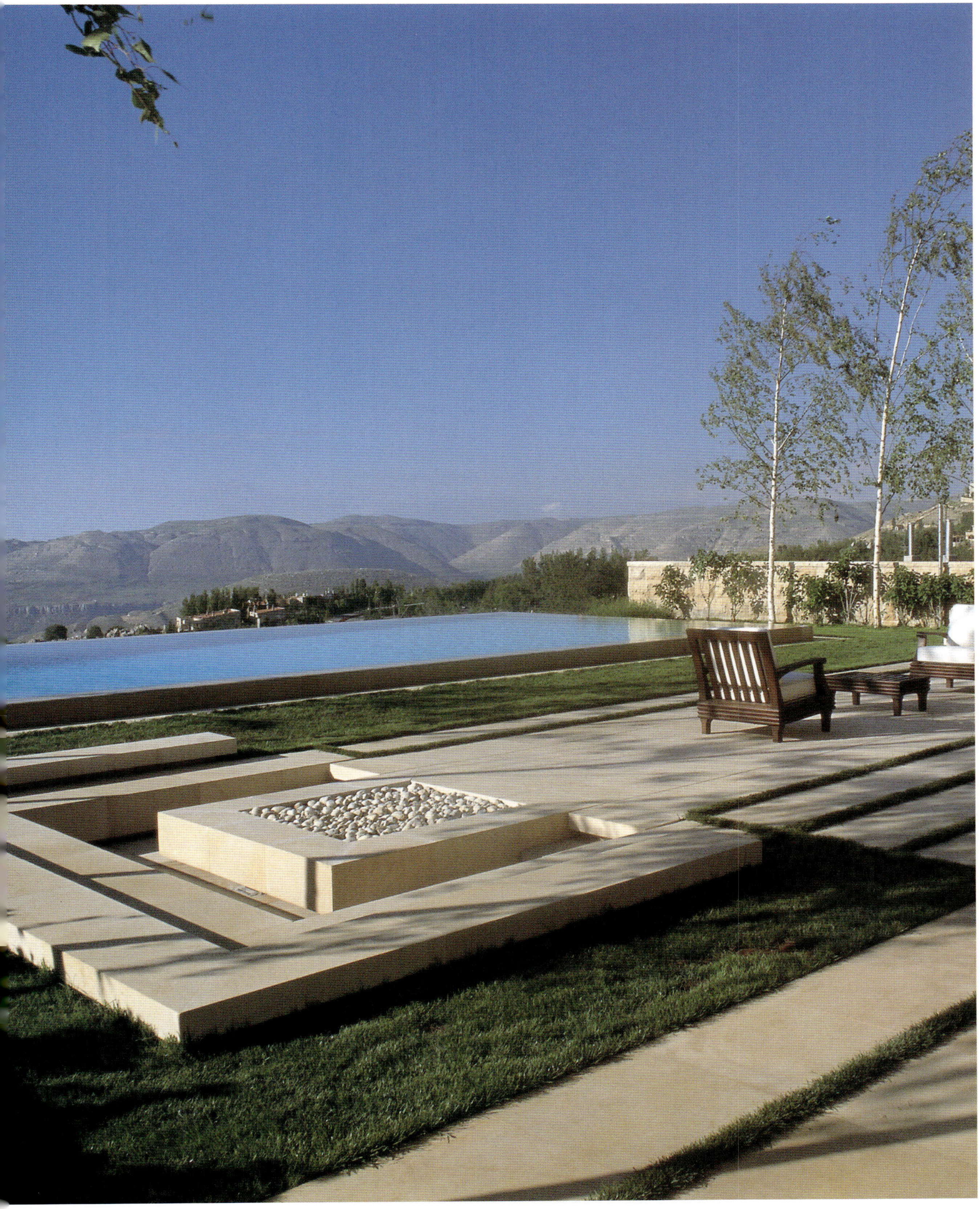

サンタクルーズのプール

ファン・ロカ・パジェホ
撮影：ジョルディ・ミラレス

SWIMMING POOL in santa cruz
JUAN ROCA VALLEJO
PHOTO: © Jordi Miralles

プールは自然のオアシスを模して、ゆるやかに入り組んだ円形に造られ、周囲の緑の中に完全に溶け込んでいる。オアシスの多くがそうであるように、庭は中心のプールに向ってゆるやかな下り勾配になっており、プールの中には椰子の木が伸びる岩の浮島がある。すべての材料が、自然のままのオアシスの色を再現するように選ばれている。夜には、照明が自動的に点灯し、漆黒の暗闇のなか、オアシスを幻想的に浮かび上がらせる。

Designed like a natural oasis, this pool has been constructed in an irregular, circular shape, perfectly integrated with the lush surrounding landscape. Much like on the coast, entry is gradual over an incline in the terrain that leads to the center of the pool, which has been splashed with rocks and palm trees.
The materials were chosen because they reflect the color of natural springs. At night, an automated system illuminates the pool to create a dramatic effect that contrasts with the pitch black surroundings.

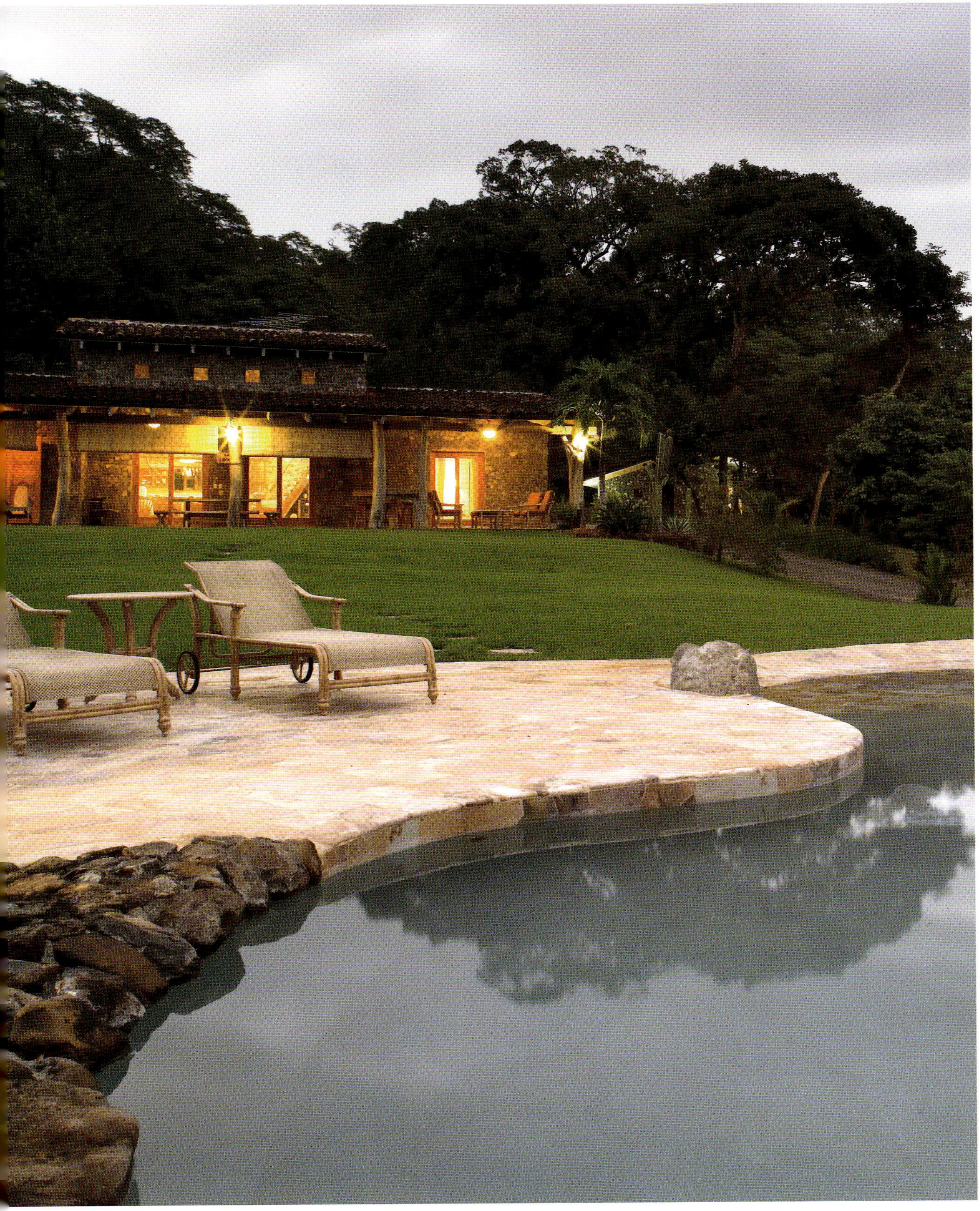

サン・ベルナールの住宅

ビオタイッヒ／J.Nジャルダン・ナチュレルス
撮影：エリック・サイエ

HOUSE IN ST. BERNARD
BIOTEICH/J.N. JARDINS NATURELS
PHOTO: © Erick Saillet

このプールは、中に入って水浴びしても、ただ眺めているだけでも楽しめる小さな池となっている。10m×3mの水面には、石を伝って流れ落ちる滝もあり、岸には水生植物が生い茂る沢がある。岩を積み重ねただけの低い石垣が自然の擁壁となり、そのまま池を囲む堰堤となっている。木の甲板と桟橋が人と自然の統合の象徴となり、色鮮やかな淡水魚と睡蓮が豊かな生態系を創造している。

This pool unites the pleasures of bathing with the advantages of an aquatic garden. The water surface occupies a total of 33 x 10 feet, including the stone waterfall and the aquatic plant area beside it. Made with rocks, a low wall becomes a natural protector, extending all the way to the edges of the water. The terrace and wooden footbridge integrate into the landscape while the colorful fish and water-lilies make for a rich ecosystem.

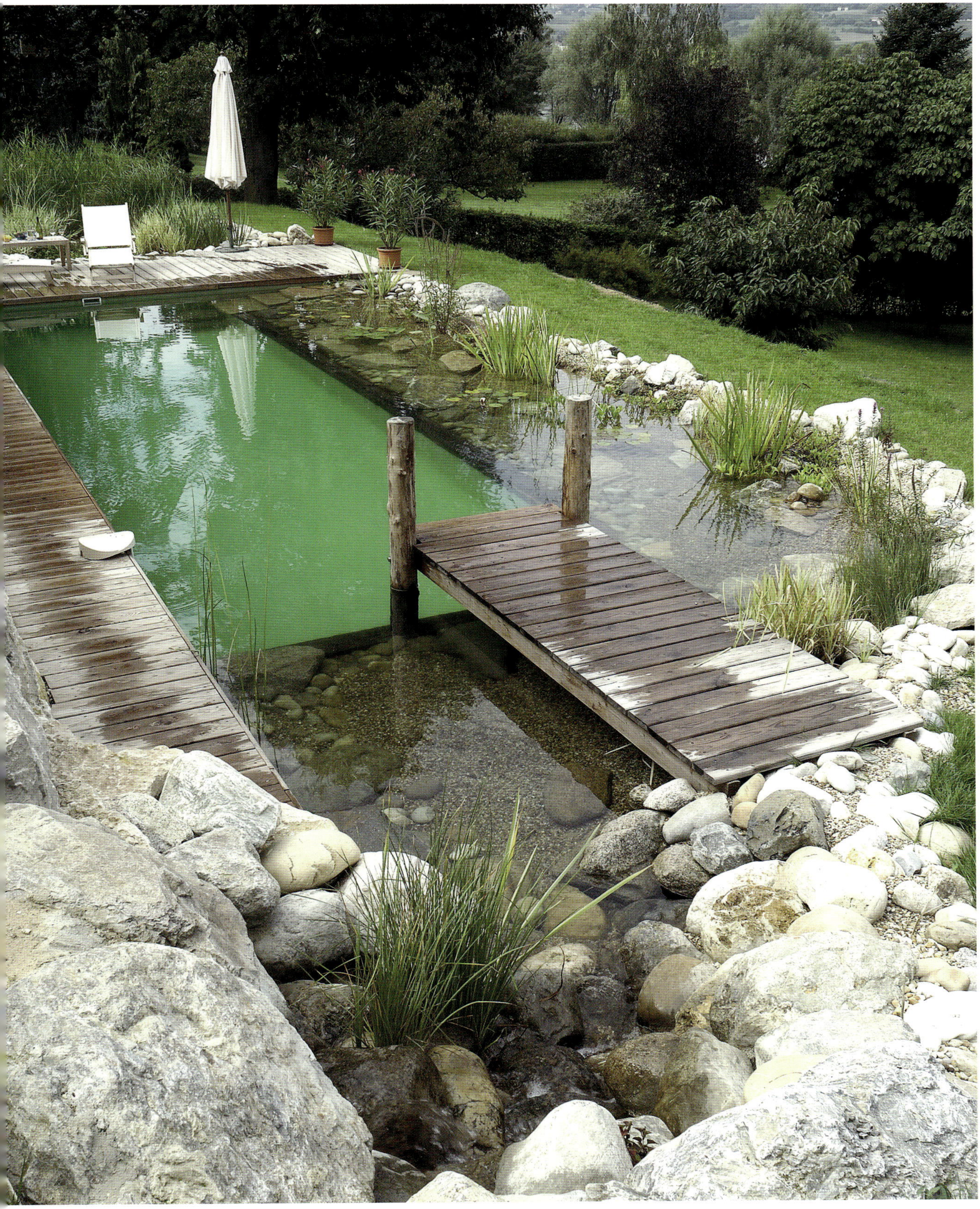

ゴリオンのプール

ビオタイッヒ／J.Nジャルダン・ナチュレルス
撮影：ビオタイッヒ

SWIMMING POOL IN GOLLION
BIOTEICH/J.N. JARDINS NATURELS
PHOTO: © Bioteich

60㎡のプールを囲むように石庭が造られているが、それは継ぎ目なしに周囲の地形に溶け込んでいる。どこまでが建築家の仕事であり、どこからが元の自然であるのかを見分けるのが難しいくらいだ。プールへは、木の甲板から足をつけても良いし、プールに水を注ぎ込んでいる泉のある巨石から淵へ飛び込んでも良い。

The sixty square meters of the pool are framed by a rock garden that seems to mix seamlessly with the surrounding terrain. At this point, it's hard to discern where the architectural work stops and where nature starts. Access to the pool is provided by a wooden deck on the other side or from the large rocks through which the water springs to fill the pool.

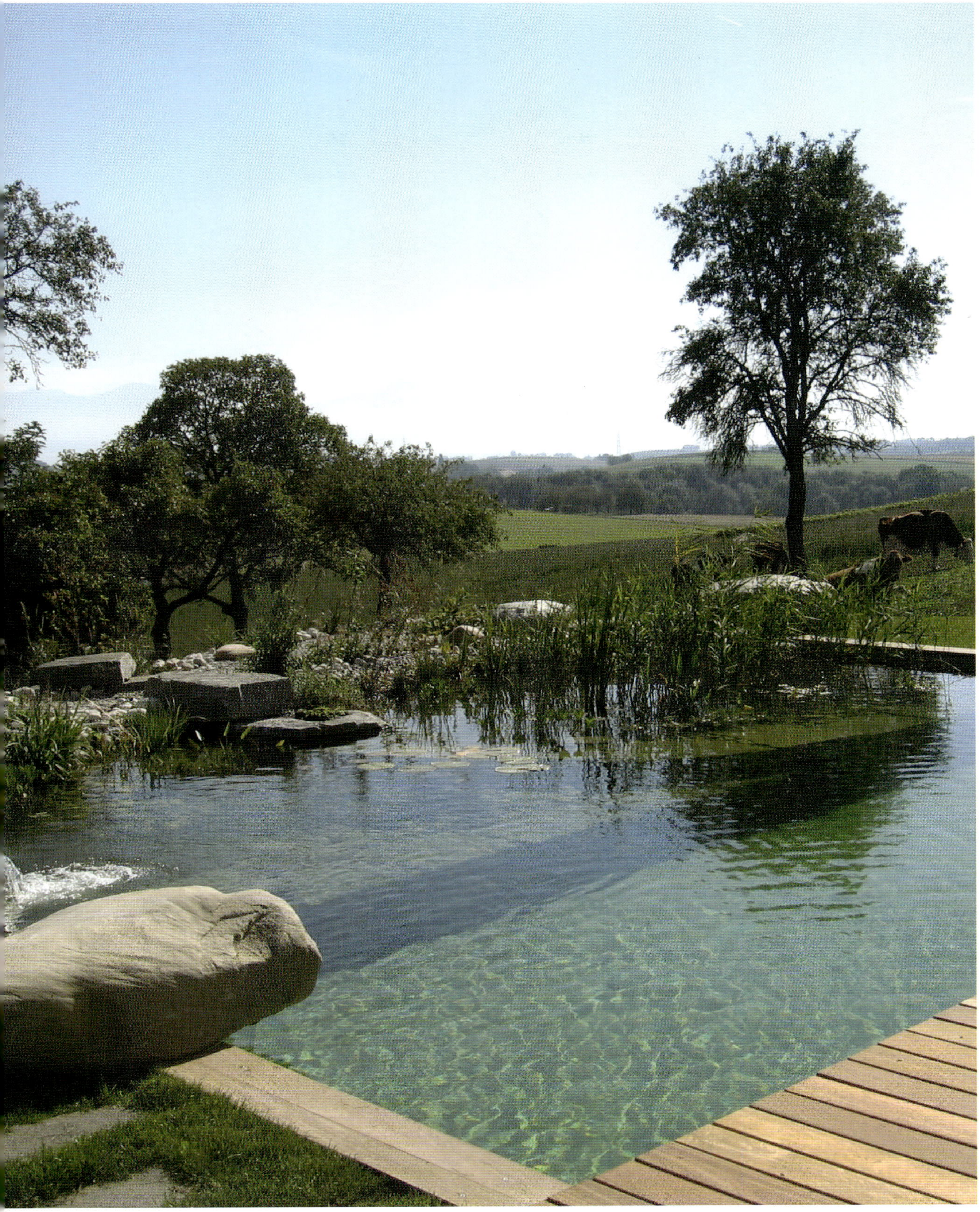

作品・建築家一覧
Directory

リヴォ・ハウス	12	ペソ・フォン・エルリッヒスハウゼン建築設計事務所 Lo Pequén 502 Concepción, Chile T +56 41 2210281 F +56 09 92776645 www.pezo.cl
輪の家	18	武井 誠&鍋島 千恵／TNA一級建築士事務所 5-10-19-3F Yakumo Meguro-ku Tokyo, Japan ZIP 152-0023 T +81 3 5701 1901 F +81 3 5701 1902 www.tna-arch.com
ラスティック・キャニオンの住宅	26	グリフィン・エンライト建築設計事務所 12468 Washington Blvd. LA, CA 90066, USA T +1 310 391 4484 F +1 310 391 4495 www.griffinenrightarchitects.com
ガンダリオの住宅	32	カルロス・クインタンス・エイラス Petunias 3-2º izquierda Coruña, Spain T +34 981 918 005
ラス・エンシーナスの住宅	38	ヴィセンス＋ラモス Barquillo 29, 2º izqda 28004 Madrid, Spain T +34 915 210 004 www.vicens-ramos.com
タマリュの住宅	42	ジョルディ・ガルセス Carrer d'en Quintana 4, 2n pis 08002 Barcelona, Spain T +34 93 317 31 88 F +34 93 317 22 65 www.jordigarces.com
ジェニングス邸	48	ワークルーム・デザイン 1A York Street Richmond VIC 3121, Australia T +61 3 9417 0044 F +61 3 9029 6490 www.workroom.com.au
プチュブレオの住宅	54	アルヴァロ・ラミレス&クラリサ・エルトン Nueva costanera 4076, Santiago de Chile, Chile T +562 9535248 F +562 2074805 www.ramirez-moletto.cl
マターヤ邸	60	ベルツバーグ建築設計事務所 1501 Colorado Ave., suite B Santa Monica, CA	90404, USA T +1 310 453 9611 F +1 310 453 9166 www.belzbergarchitects.com
OSハウス	66	ノラスター Francisco Silvela 77 6D 28028 Madrid, Spain T / F +1 34 912994354 www.nolaster.com
乱気流の家	72	スティーブン・ホール建築設計事務所 450 West 31st Street, 11th floor New York, NY 10001, USA T +1 21 2629 7262
		F +1 21 2629 7312 www.stevenholl.com
ブラウン・デュブイ邸	76	ヴェルナー・シュミット建築設計事務所 Fabrikareal 117 CH-7166 Trun, Austria T +41 81 9432528 F +41 81 9432639 www.atelierwernerschmidt.ch
リギ・シャイデックの住宅	82	アンドレアス・フェーリマン―ガブリエル・ヘフラー Architekten ETH / BSA Hardturmstrasse 66 CH - 8005 Zürich, Switzerland T +41 44 271 04 80 F +41 43 204 06 09 www.afgh.ch
ラ・レセルバの住宅	86	セバスチャン・イラリャズバル O' Brien 2458 Vitacura Santiago de Chile, Chile T +56 2 2456252 www.sebastianirarrazaval.com
レンガウのロッジ	92	ジョン・ジェニングス／ドライ・デザイン 5727 Venice Blvd. Los Angeles, CA 90019, USA T +1 323 954 9084 F +1 323 954 9085 www.drydesign.com
ストーン・ハウス	100	三分一 博志 建築設計事務所 8-3-302 Nakajima-cho Naka-ku Hiroshima 730-0811, Japan T +81 82 544-1417 F +81 82 544-1418
ヒュッテの家	106	スタジオNL-D Postbus 21749 3001 AS Rotterdam, The Netherlands T +1 31 10 2810791 F +1 31 10 2819399 www.studionl-d.com
トーレス邸	112	ルイス・デ・ガリード Blasco Ibañez 114, ptas 7 y 9 46022 Valencia, Spain T +34 96 356 70 70 F +34 96 356 81 81 www.luisdegarrido.com
カンタロプスの住宅	118	ニコラ・トレマコルディ／NM建築設計事務所 Travessera de Gràcia, 128 1er 08012 Barcelona, Spain T +34 93 217 9772
ハウス9×9	124	タイタス・ベルンハルト建築設計事務所 Gögginger Straße 105 a D - 86199 Augsburg, Germany T +49 821 599 605 -0 F +49 821 599 605 -10 www.titusbernhardarchitekten.com
ピクセル・ハウス	128	スレード・アーキテクチュア&マス・スタディーズ 150 Broadway # 807 NYC, 10038, USA T / F +1 212 677 6330 www.sladearch.com Mass Studies Fuji Bldg. 4F

		683-140 Hannam 2-dong Yongsan-gu Seoul 140-892, Korea T +82 2 790 6528/9 F +82 2 790 6438 www.massstudies.com
リアス・アルタスの住宅 ラス・エンシーナスの住宅	132 252	J・トーレス&R・リャマサーレス／A-Cero Arriaza 6, bajo/28008 Madrid, Spain T +34 915 489 656 F +34 915 489 657 www.a-cero.com
ワイルドキャット・リッジの住宅	136	ヴォーサンガー建築設計事務所 246 west 38th street, 14th floor New York, NY 10018, USA T +1 212 302 6464 F +1 212 840 0063 www.voorsanger.com
サルゾー近郊の住宅	140	エリック・グースナール
ミ・デリリオの住宅	144	ルイス・フローレス・アベジャン Pellegrini, 217 2900 San Nicolás, Argentina T / F +54 3461 424457 www.floresabellan.com.ar
フリンダース・ビーチの住宅	148	サイモン・スワニー建築設計事務所 Level 1, 243 Liverpool St East Sydney NSW 2010, Australia T +61 2 9380 7288 F +61 2 9380 7280
葡萄畑の住宅	152	ジョン・ウォードレ建築設計事務所 Level 10, 180 Russell Street Melbourne Victoria, 3000 Australia T +61 3 9654 8700 F +61 3 9654 8755 www.johnwardlearchitects.com
ボルケラ・デ・ロス・ インファンテスのロフト	156	ヘスス・カスティージョ・オリ Calle del Poxo, 20 1º izda 34800 Aguilar de Campoo, Spain T +34 979 125005
第2部　インテリア	164	
ポルタス・ノヴァスの住宅	166	ヴィクトール・カニャス Apartado 340 2050, San José, Costa Rica T +506 253 2112 F +506 224 0127 victor.canas.co.cr
サバデルの改築住居	168	M2建築設計事務所 Comte Borrell 209 entlo. D, 08029 Barcelona, Spain T / F +34 93 3630511 www.m2arquitectura.es
プッチェルダの住宅	172	カルレス・ジェルピ・アロヨ Avenida Vallvidrera 69, bajos 08017 Barcelona, Spain T +34 93 418 6447 carles_gelpi@coac.net
サン・ヴィチェンテの住宅	174	マルセール・デル・トルト Olazabal 1838 1C, Buenos Aires, Argentina T / F +54 11 47800247 marcelodeltorto@ciudad.com.ar
アストリッドの別荘	176	ウィンガーズ・アーキテクトコントロール Katarinavaggen 17, SE 11645, Stockholm, Sweden T +46 (0) 84474080 F +46 (0) 87444005 www.wingardhs.se
アル・マーレ ラ・アデュアナの住宅	178 224	マーティン・ゴメス建築設計事務所 Ruta 10, km 161,La Barra, Uruguay T / F +5982 (42) 772004 www.martingomezarquitectos.com
ベリマ通りの住宅	180	ウォーハ・デザイン 29 Hongkong Street, Singapore 059668, Singapoore T +65 6423 4555 F +65 6423 4666 www.wohadesigns.com
アベル邸	182	1100アーキテクト 475 Tenth Avenue, New York, NY 10018, USA T +1 212 645 1011 F +1 212 645 4670 www.1100architect.com
ブエノスアイレスの住宅 ソレダード邸	184 232	パブロ・サンチェス・エリア建築設計事務所 Ramsay 2414, Buenos Aires, Argentina T +54 11 4789 9630 int. 122/123 estudio@pablosanchezelia.com.ar Renée Armas and Renée Sáenz Avenida del Libertador, 1513, Piso 12 Apartamento 24, Montevideo, Uruguay T +5982 900 5643 rsaenz1954@gmail.com
オストゥーニの住宅	186	スタジオ・トランジット Via Emilio Morosoni, 17, 00153 Rome, Italy T +39 06 5898431 www.studiotransit.it
ヴィラドマの住宅	188	ベナサール・ノゲラ／アルバート・アウバッハ Aragón 224, 3-1 08011 Barcelona, Spain T +34 93 452 04 54 Albert Aubach Major de Sarria 216 planta baja 08017, Barcelona, Spain T +34 934 494 035 www.albertaubach.com
クーヴィオ・ヴァレーゼのロフト	192	シモーネ・ミケーリ建築設計事務所 Via Aretina 197r/199r/201r, S0136, Florence, Italy T +39 055 691216 F +39 055 65 044 98 www.simonemicheli.com
カルデスの住宅	196	ジョルジュ・スビータ Bruc 6, 08010, Barcelona, Spain T + 93 932 680 652 www.jorgesubietas.com
ミナス通りのロフト	198	ウンルガール Valentín Beato 11 3º D, 28037 Madrid, Spain T +34 91 440 09 28 F + 34 91.440.09.27 www.unlugar.es
アイオルフィ邸 カンビの集合住宅 パルマの集合住宅	200 216 244	パガーニ-ディ・マウロ建築設計事務所 Via Emilia 14, Ponte Enza di Gattatico, 42043 Reggio Emilia, Italy T +39 0522 902145 www.paganidimauro.com
ムジェーヴの住宅	202	カルロ・ランパッツィ CH - 6612, Ascona, Switzerland

		T +4191 785 19 19 www.crandsv.com
Pペントハウス	204	クラウディオ・シルヴェストリン建築設計事務所
イズリントンの住宅	222	Unit 412 Kingswharf, 301 Kingsland Road, London, E8 4DS, UK T +44 (0) 20 7923 8670 F +44 (0)20 7275 0762 www.claudiosilvestrin.com
ボダール邸	208	所有者
ポジターノの別荘	210	ラッツァリーニ・ピカリング建築設計事務所 Via Cola di Rienzo 28, 00192 Rome, Italy T +39 06 3210305 F +39 06 3216755 www.lazzarinipickering.com
ビアジョッティ邸	212	所有者
フロリダの住宅	214	プレストン・T・フィリップス建築設計事務所 Post Office box 3037 Bridgehampton, New York 11932, USA T +1 (631) 537 1237 F +1 (631) 537 5071 www.prestontphillips.com
アルゼンチンの海浜住宅	218	マネイロ・ヴァスケス建築設計事務所 Avestruz entre Laurel y Lambertiana, 7167 Cariló, Provincia de Buenos Aires, Argentina T +54 225447 0163 www.maneirovazquez.com.ar
ラック邸ロフト	220	ラック・ビンスト／クレパン・ビンスト建築設計事務所 Kerkstraat 53, 1851 Humbeek, Belgium T +032 477 75 2991 F +32 2 305 9130 www.lucbinst.be
マドリードからの天然スレート	226	ペドロ・ボニーラ Jorge Juan 141 6ºB Madrid, Spain T +34 657 94 73 83
カルデス・デ・モンブイの住宅	230	アントニー・グラウ・ギルバー／エウセビ・グティエレス Montserrat 6, 1-2, Caldes de Montbui, Spain T +34 938651076 agg@coac.net
プロジェクト・ヨー	234	フィリップ・スタルク／ヨー 2, Bentinck Street, London W12FA, UK T +44 (0) 207009 0100 F +44 (0) 207009 0200 www.yoo.com
サン・ジュセッペの住宅 ヴェミグナーノの別荘	236 238	グイド・アントネッロ／クリスティアナ・ヴァンニーニ Via Tognano 14, CH - 6877 Coldrerio, Italy T +41 91 6828126 F +41 91 6828129 Cristiana Vannini c.so XXII Marzo 42, 20135, Milan, Italy T +39 02 70121354 F +39 02 70121354 www.vc-a.it
モンテ・タウロの住宅	240	レゴレッタ＋レゴレッタ Palacio de Versalles 285-A, Mexico DF 11020, Mexico F +52 55 5596 6162 www.legorretalegorreta.com

迷宮の家	246	オスカー・トゥスケッツ・ブランカ Cavallers, 50 08034 Barcelona, Spain T +34 93 206 55 80 F +34 93 280 40 71 www.tusquets.com
ロンドンの住宅	248	ウェルドン・ウォルシュ 20 Grosvenor Place, London, SW1X 7HN, UK T +44 (0) 20 7235 4100 F +44 (0) 20 7235 6678 www.weldonwalshe.co.uk
ゴルドの別荘	250	リラ・コンラッド／LKDコンセプト Neuhausstrasse 3, 6318 Zug, Switzerland T / F +41 41 758 22 49
ソーラー・ボックス	254	ドリエンドル建築設計事務所 Mariahilferstrasse 9 A-1060, Vienna, Austria T +43/1/585 18 68 F +43 (0) 1 585 18 69 www.driendl.at
アンドリュー・テート邸	256	テート＆ヒンドル建築設計事務所 1 Lindsey Street, Smithfield, London ECA 9HP, UK T +44 (0) 20 7332 4850 F +44 (0) 20 7332 4888 www.tatehindle.co.uk
デュ・プレシ邸	258	マルシオ・コーガン建築設計事務所 Al. Tietê, 505, Sao Paulo CEP 04616-001, Brazil T +55 11 308 13522 www.marciokogan.com.br
ブライトン・ガーデン	262	アン・ファーズ 5, Chesham Street, Brighton, Sussex, UK T +44 (0) 1273 625365
砂漠の庭	266	テイラー・カリティ・レスリーン 7 Hutt Street, Adelaide SA 5000, Australia T +61 8 8223 7533 F +61 8 8223 3533 www.tcl.net.au
龍門庭	268	枡野 俊明
ポルトラ・ヴァレーの住宅	272	ピーターソン建築設計事務所 975 High Street, Palo Alto, California 94301, USA T +650 327 1161 www.petersonarchitects.com
エリー・サーブ邸	276	ウラジミール・シュロヴィッチ・ランドスケープ・アーキテクチュ Rizk Plaza, 1st floor, Broumana, Lebanon T +961 4 862 444 / 555 F +961 4 862 462 www.vladimirdjurovic.com
サンタクルーズのプール	278	ファン・ロカ・バジェホ Apartado 35, 5200 Nicoya, Costa Rica T / F +1 506675 0537 www.aquart.net
サン・ベルナールの住宅 ゴリオンのプール	280 282	ビオタイヒ／J.Nジャルダン・ナチュレルス Le Grand-Pâquier 1373 Chavornay, Switzerland T +41 (0) 24 442 8844 F +41 (0) 24 442 8845

Architecture Earth

Idea/Ideazione/Ideación
Mariarosaria Tagliaferri

Realization/Realizzazione/Realización
LOFT Publications

Architecture editor/Editor architettura/Editor arquitectura
Sergi Costa Duran

Interiors editor/Editor interni/Editora interiores
Daniela Santos Quartino

Editorial assistance/Assistenza editoriale/Asistencia editorial
Esther Moreno, Julio Fajardo, Macarena San Martín

Editorial coordinator/Coordinamento editoriale/Coordinadora editorial
Catherine Collin

Graphic design/Progetto grafico/Diseño gráfico
Mireia Casanovas Soley

Layout/Impaginazione/Maquetación
Ignasi Gracia Blanco

Translations/Traduzioni/Traducciones
LiberLab - Servizi Editoriali, Januaria Solari (Italian),
Antonio Moreno (English)

© Edizioni Gribaudo srl
Regione Domini, SS 30 km 40 - Terzo (AL)
tel. 0144 594374
e-mail : info@gribaudo.it

Editorial coordinator/Coordinamento editoriale/Coordinador editorial: Franco Busti, Paola Morelli
Editorial assistant/Segreteria di redazione/Secretaría de redacción: Anna Gribaudo
Editing/Redazione/Redacción: LiberLab - Servizi Editoriali, Savigliano (CN)

Japanese translation rights arranged with Edizioni Gribaudo srl, Savigliano Italy through Tuttle-Mori Agency, Inc., Tokyo

---

産調出版の本

Newナチュラルハウスブック
エコロジー、調和、
健康的な住環境の創造

デヴィット・ピアソン 著

住まいの設計を、健康と環境に結びつけて考える本書は、家を幸福を高める聖域に変える方法を示す、この道のバイブルと評価される。100枚以上のフルカラー写真とイラストで、毒物のない、優美で簡素な住まい。身体と精神を豊かにする生活を提案する。

本体価格3,800円

世界木材図鑑
世界中で最もよく使用されている
用途の広い木材150種を厳選

エイダン・ウォーカー：総編集
ニック・ギブス／ルシンダ・リーチ他：共著

序章では木の組織・生長過程や製材方法等、また森林保護について。木材一覧では、世界で最も使用されている樹種150種について豊富な情報を提供、精密な写真も掲載。木材の美しさを愛する全ての人々に捧ぐ総括的木材図鑑。

本体価格4,800円

Architecture Earth
現代建築家による〝地球〟建築

発　　　行　2008年11月15日
発　行　者　平野　陽三
発　行　元　**ガイアブックス**
　　　　　　〒169-0074 東京都新宿区北新宿3-14-8
　　　　　　TEL.03(3366)1411　FAX.03(3366)3503
　　　　　　http://www.gaiajapan.co.jp
発　売　元　産調出版株式会社

企　　画：マリアロザリア　タリアフェッリを
　　　　　主としたチーム

翻　訳　者：乙須　敏紀　（おとす としのり）
九州大学文学部哲学科卒業。訳書に『現代建築家による木造建築』『現代建築家による水建築』『屋根のデザイン』『世界木材図鑑』（いずれも産調出版）など。

Copyright SUNCHOH SHUPPAN INC. JAPAN2008
ISBN978-4-88282-676-7 C3052

落丁本・乱丁本はお取り替えいたします。
本書を許可なく複製することは、かたくお断わりします。
Printed and in China